The Colonial Empires

A Comparative Survey from the Eighteenth Century

D. K. Fieldhouse

Vere Harmsworth Professor of Imperial and Naval History
Cambridge University

MACMILLAN

First English edition © 1966 published by
Dell Publishing Co., Inc., New York
and George Weidenfeld and Nicolson Ltd, London

Second edition 1982
Reprinted 1986, 1987, 1991

Published by
MACMILLAN EDUCATION LTD
Houndmills, Basingstoke, Hampshire RG21 2XS
and London
Companies and representatives
throughout the world

Printed in Hong Kong

ISBN 0–333–33023–4

Contents

PART TWO

THE COLONIAL EMPIRES AFTER 1815

Maps

Maps by Design Practitioners

Preface

The character of the first edition of this book, published in German in 1965 and in English in 1966, was largely dictated by the fact that it was commissioned as one volume of an integrated series of histories, the Fischer *Weltgeschichte*. Other volumes were to deal with most countries which were at one time or another European colonies on a national or regional basis: for example, two volumes on Latin America, one each on the United States, India, South-east Asia, Africa, Modern Asia, and so on. My book had thus to fill a precise gap: to describe modern imperialism from the end of the seventeenth century, when the first colonial systems were well established, to 1945 when decolonization was about to begin; and to treat these empires as a specifically European phenomenon rather than as part of the history of particular non-European areas. I had, moreover, to do this very briefly.

I therefore decided to concentrate rather narrowly on three questions which seemed basic to all European colonial systems: why these were established; how they were run; and what advantages they provided. By the criteria of modern area studies this implied a one-sided approach because it largely ignored the indigenous history of the countries which became European colonies. Yet I believed, and still believe, that the process by which one country imposes and sustains control over another is a valid historical study and that the history of imperialism is distinct from that of particular imperial possessions. I also thought that European imperial history had a basic unity, so that to study one empire in isolation was likely to lead to distortion: hence the subtitle 'a comparative survey'.

The result was a highly condensed book in which I attempted to distil what seemed to me the essential features of modern European imperialism. Its value, as I thought, was that for the first time, so far as I know, it brought most of the imperial systems into a single focus, even though through a long-distance lens. Since 1965 imperial history has developed immensely and area studies have affected the way historians approach it. My original bibliography became badly out of date and my own ideas on some matters changed: for example, my interpretation of the 'new imperialism' of the period 1870–1914. Yet no other single book has yet covered quite the same subject-matter; and, since I am happy to stand by almost all that I wrote originally, it has been decided to issue a second edition, making only four significant changes. Some minor inaccuracies in the text have been corrected. The illustrations, interesting but very expensive to reproduce, have been omitted. I have extended the last chapter on decolonization to take account of events between 1965 and 1981, making some tentative generalizations concerning the early effects of the end of empire on its one-time dependencies. Finally, I have revised and considerably extended the bibliography, cutting out books which are no longer the best in their field and adding a selection from the vast number published since 1965. I hope that in its new form the book may provide a first foothold for students as they start work on any aspect of modern imperial history.

DAVID FIELDHOUSE
Jesus College,
Cambridge

PART ONE

The Colonial Empires before 1815

1

Introduction: The First Expansion of Europe

By 1700 the older colonial empires were some two centuries old, and Europe took their existence for granted. Yet the first European expansion into Africa, Asia and America was one of the most surprising and significant facts of modern history. Looking back from the 1770s Adam Smith could state confidently that

> The discovery of America, and that of a passage to the East Indies by the Cape of Good Hope, are the two greatest and most important events recorded in the history of mankind.[1]

Smith was, of course, taking a narrowly Eurocentric view. Europe had no monopoly of distant trading or overseas empire. Turkish power still stretched from the western Mediterranean to the Indian Ocean. Hindus from India had colonized South-East Asia in earlier centuries and still controlled much of its trade. Muslims from the Middle East had spread over southern Asia, and Islamic rulers governed India and most of South-East Asia in the eighteenth century. Further east the Chinese empire was greater in size than anything in the experience of Europe, and many states of South-East Asia still recognized the overlordship of Peking. Hence the importance of the first expansion of Europe lay in its effects on Europe rather than its uniqueness as a world phenomenon. Only in the nineteenth century did European empires affect the whole of the world.

But for Europe the discoveries were indeed one of the great events. Mediaeval Europe had not been uncivilized, but it had been parochial. It was influenced to some extent by the Islamic world and by Byzantium; but it was isolated by the Atlantic, by Muscovy, Islam and the unknown continent of Africa. The discovery of America and the direct oceanic route to the east liberated Europe from a geographic and mental cell. It stimulated her intellectually by enabling her to draw more easily on the superior civilizations of the east, and stirred her imagination by giving her experience of utterly different peoples in the west. Neither the later discoveries in the Pacific, nor even twentieth-century investigations of space, had as great an impact as this first widening of the mediaeval horizon.

Discoveries, and the trade and conquests which followed them, had practical consequences. Every colony or trading centre was a new economic stimulus. America provided an immense market for European manufactures and agricultural products. American bullion increased the supply of money circulating in Europe and intensified existing economic and social developments. Eastern manufactures were copied by European producers. Asian spices and American 'groceries' increased the volume and profitability of the intra-European trade, and carriage of these distant trades gave an immense stimulus to merchant marines and shipbuilding. The European commercial system had never been entirely closed, for it was linked with North Africa and, through the Levant, with Asia. But these were marginal trades. The cost and physical problems of the overland routes to the east acted as a bottleneck. The discoveries led to distant trades comparable in volume or value with those inside Europe. Trade with the east remained small in volume though high in value; but the Atlantic trade offered greater possibilities. America, unlike the east, depended on Europe for most of its manufactures and was near enough to make bulk cargoes profitable. By the eighteenth century transatlantic merchant fleets numbered thousands of ships, carrying goods as bulky as slaves, sugar and even timber. America could never replace the internal trade of Europe, but it provided an absolute addition to it.

Land in America was possibly as important for Europe as its trade. Europe was not overcrowded; but parts of it were densely populated in relation to known agricultural methods, and wars and religious conflicts created an artificial demand for more space. For four centuries America was a safety-valve for European land-hunger. Columbus had in effect extended Europe westwards for several thousand miles, giving her the same opportunities for expansion and colonization as Siberia offered Muscovy.

By the early eighteenth century the geographical distribution of European overseas possessions was well-established. Its obvious feature was that colonies and bases were very unevenly distributed in different parts of the world. America was gradually being covered by the territorial dominions of Spain, Portugal, England, France and Holland. But in Africa and the east, though there were many settlements, they had few European inhabitants; and there was little sign that coastal bases would develop into substantial colonies. The contrast between the American empires and these African and Asian bases was so great in the eighteenth century that they will be treated separately in this study. But the contrast also presents an historical problem which is fundamental to understanding the character of the first colonial empires. Why did Europe occupy America but remain on the periphery of Africa and Asia? The answer lies partly in European motives and partly in the resources which the founders of the first European empires possessed.

The motives of the discoverers and first settlers are difficult to know and impossible to generalize. In most cases one thing led to another, and initial intentions changed according to new circumstances. Thus the earliest Portuguese discoveries in north-west and western Africa were a by-product of their crusade against Islam which began with the attack on Ceuta in 1415 and led them gradually down the coast. The discovery that gold-dust, ivory and slaves could be acquired further south led them on, until Bartholomew Diaz discovered the Cape of Good Hope in 1487 and Portugal projected the oceanic route to the Indies. Thereafter Portuguese achievements closely conformed to deliberate intentions. They set out to acquire a direct trade in eastern spices and manufactures to break the Venetian monopoly of the old overland route, and so to establish trading bases rather than territorial colonies. Missionary zeal continued, stimulating the Portuguese to attack Islamic power in the Red Sea and Indian Ocean and to impose Christianity on Asians within the tiny fortresses they established throughout the east. To this extent the character of this first European enterprise in the east approximated closely to deliberate intentions; the absence of large colonies reflected Portuguese concentration on a trading system which did not require them.

The American colonies, however, did not fulfil the intentions of their discoverers. Columbus sailed west in 1492 confidently expecting to find a shorter route to China than that projected by the Portuguese. America was an immense disappointment, a heart-breaking obstacle on the hoped-for route to the east. It was occupied only because it offered unforeseen possibilities. Gold and silver in the Caribbean, Mexico and Peru stimulated investigation and conquest, and attracted immigrants. Thereafter the availability of ample land and a docile indigenous population to work it encouraged permanent colonization and the creation of large semi-feudal estates. The challenge of discovering millions of pagans induced the Catholic church to send missions. Between them bullion hunters, settlers and missions effectively occupied large areas of America.

This was private colonization: it had not been planned, and the Spanish Crown was not directly responsible for it. Brazil also, which was inadvertently discovered by Cabral in 1500 when on his way to India, was colonized by individual Portuguese subjects who were given grants of authority by the Crown, but used their own resources. Thus, whereas the original Portuguese empire in the east was largely planned and carried out as a royal enterprise, the American colonies of Spain and Portugal, and similarly those of later arrivals such as England and France, owed little to the rulers of these countries. By the eighteenth century the American settlements had been tidied up; patterns of government and commerce had been imposed by European governments: in retrospect they appeared to be the result of 'mercantile' planning. This was an illusion. Like most later colonies they were almost accidental, a natural reaction of European subjects to an unforeseen challenge and opportunity.

Yet, even if Portugal had not deliberately concentrated on trade rather than settlement in Africa and the east, this natural emigration to America could not have been repeated there: the east in particular was not open to colonization. The reasons for this demonstrate the contrasting relationship of Europe with America and Asia before the later eighteenth century.

The resources which enabled Europeans in the fifteenth and sixteenth centuries to establish bases in Asia and to colonize America were very limited. Their most important asset was the ability to sail to any part of the known or imagined world with some likelihood of arriving and returning. Oceanic travel out of sight of land was the new tool of European expansion, made possible by a number of European artifacts and skills. By the fifteenth century Europe had ships capable of long oceanic voyages; large carracks and smaller caravels, whose construction combined the experience of northern and Mediterranean Europe with the skills of the Islamic Middle East. Navigation out of sight of land was made possible by the use of magnetic compasses and by quadrants, astrolabes and cross-staffs for taking astral bearings and establishing latitude. Pilot books, *portolani* (directions for coastwise sailing from place to place) or 'rutters' helped navigators to steer from one known place to another, and they were further helped by navigational almanacs giving practical information on such essential matters as latitudes and declinations of the sun at different times of the year. But intercontinental navigation for long remained largely a matter of luck and faith, since most charts were defective, and pilots had no accurate means of calculating longitude before the invention of the chronometer in the eighteenth century. Primitive though these ships and navigational devices were, they were good enough to enable determined men to reach any part of America, Asia or Africa.

They did not, however, necessarily enable Europeans to dominate the places they reached. Ships alone could not create land empires. They could be useful in defending small coastal fortresses, such as the Portuguese built throughout the east; but even these needed substantial land forces as well. Once ashore Europeans depended on their military equipment and techniques: how successful they were and whether they could occupy large areas, was determined by their strength in relation to that of the indigenous peoples. In the first three centuries of colonization Europe had no significant technical or military advantage over much of Asia and countries governed by Islam. By the sixteenth century Europeans had cannons and primitive muskets; but they still used older weapons such as pikes, swords and cross-bows. Their fighting efficiency depended on discipline and experience in European wars rather than fire-power. Their ships were armed with cannon, and were secure against those of any other civilization: but until late in the sixteenth century they lacked the fire-power necessary for effective bombardment of enemy vessels or land fortifications.

With these resources Europeans found themselves in contrasting situations in different parts of the newly discovered world. In Islamic North Africa and the Middle East they had no advantage over Turks or Arabs. Throughout the Indian Ocean and farther east they not only possessed no technical superiority, but were handicapped by distance, very small numbers and lack of cavalry. Whatever their intentions Europeans could not have established territorial empires in any of these places.

By contrast, most parts of sub-Saharan Africa and all areas of America were weaker than Europe in military and industrial techniques. Asians had powerful political organizations, professional armies and guns. Africans and Amerindians had not. The Portuguese had little difficulty in establishing their power up the Congo and the Zambezi early in the sixteenth century, and could have created territorial empires here and elsewhere in Africa if they had chosen. In fact they did not. In most parts of Africa the climate was unattractive to Europeans. The eastern trade and the carriage of slaves to America proved more attractive, and Brazil offered Portugal a better field for settlement and plantations. In the seventeenth century a Dutch settlement was made at the Cape of Good Hope which, contrary to the intentions of the East India Company which founded it, soon became a sizeable settlement colony. But for the rest Europeans did not choose to exploit their power in Africa: they were content with slaves, gold dust and ivory, all of which could be obtained by barter from African middlemen, and required them to maintain only the most primitive coastal bases.

America was as defenceless as most of Africa: it was occupied because it was also eminently attractive to Europeans. The Aztecs of Mexico and the Incas of Peru were in many ways very civilized and highly organized military empires. But their weapons were those of stone-age Europe and they could not compete with European methods of fighting. In time they might have adopted both, but their political systems were destroyed very quickly by tiny bands of Spanish adventurers, like Cortez in Mexico and the Pizarros in Peru, whose main assets were mobility, determination, and skill in using native auxiliaries. Once these empires had been destroyed their component parts were powerless. Elsewhere in America there were no comparable civilizations. Europeans were confronted only by tribes whose capacity to resist was less than that of most Africans. They could be dangerous to weak European settlements on the frontier, but for the most part they were forced to retreat as the frontier of settlement advanced.

Thus the territorial empires of the eighteenth century were to be found in America rather than in Asia because only America was at once attractive to European settlers and technically possible for them to acquire. This fact is crucial for a comparison between the old colonial empires and those founded in the nineteenth and twentieth centuries. The first empires represented European ambition, determination and ingenuity in using limited resources rather than European predominance throughout the world. Expansion across the Atlantic and by the sea-route to the east was in a sense an escape from the harsh realities of Europe itself. The western maritime powers could not expand into North Africa or the Levant. Turkish power threatened the sea-board Mediterranean states until late in the sixteenth century, and the Turks could still invade Austria a century later. Christian Europe was still on the defensive against Islam. It escaped from this encirclement by going west to the weaker continent of America and east to trade with the powerful but generally tolerant east. The water-shed between the dominance of Islamic and other eastern civilizations and that of Christian Europe came late in the eighteenth century. The nineteenth century European empires at last represented the real predominance of Europe and not merely its ingenuity in crossing the oceans.

2

The Spanish and Portuguese Empires in America

At every stage of European overseas expansion there were one or more colonial powers which overshadowed the rest. In the modern period these were Britain and France; before 1815 Spain and Portugal. Their primacy lay not only in the fact that they were the discoverers, but that they worked out four of the five models for effective colonization which were typical of the first colonial empires and were copied by other colonizing powers.

Spain showed Europe how to establish a great territorial empire in the New World, making full use of its natural advantages. The Spanish colonies in Mexico and Peru were the first 'mixed' colonies in which a substantial minority of white settlers created societies as similar to that of Old Spain as alien conditions allowed, controlling and, as far as possible absorbing, the indigenous population. Conversely, in the less obviously profitable parts of America and in the Philippines, where geographic or demographic conditions made full settlement unattractive, Spain established colonies of 'occupation', in which there were few settlers and the indigenous peoples were loosely supervised on what may be called a 'frontier' system. A similar system of loose control was used by Portugal in Angola and Mozambique, but this was not the characteristic Portuguese method. Portugal had two chosen models. In Brazil she created the first 'plantation' colony, in which a small European minority settled permanently and tried to reproduce their metropolitan civilization, as the Spaniards did in 'mixed' colonies; but because Brazil lacked a docile indigenous labour force or known precious

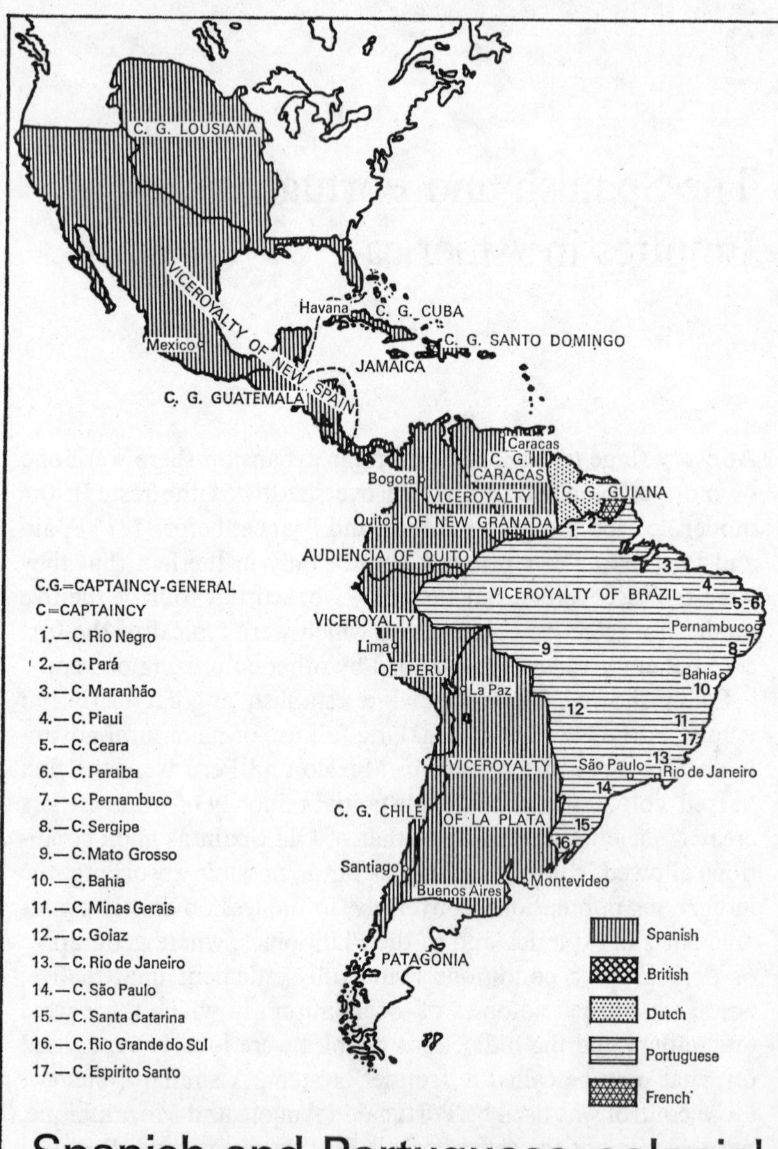

Spanish and Portuguese colonial territories in Southern America c.1790

metals, the Portuguese imported negro slaves from Africa and produced exotic 'groceries', such as sugar, for the European market. In the quite different conditions of the east, however, Portugal evolved another pattern. Her eastern empire consisted of small tide-water trading settlements and naval bases containing little territory and few permanent settlers, whose function was to organize a lucrative trade in local products or manufactures. It was a commercial, not a settlement empire.

In 1700 there was only one other important pattern of colonization – the 'pure' settlement colony of British and French North America, where, because Amerindians would not work for Europeans and conditions were unsuited to plantation production, emigrants created a still closer facsimile of European society than the Spanish 'mixed' colonies. Important though these colonies later became, in the early eighteenth century they were regarded by Europe as an inferior substitute for other and more profitable types of overseas possession. With the colonies of 'occupation' they were the Cinderellas of the first colonial empires.

By the later eighteenth century the great age of Spanish and Portuguese empire was over. Both were decadent powers, and Portugal had lost most of her colonies except Brazil. Yet a balanced interpretation of the character of the first European colonies must start with analysis of their aims and methods.

The Spanish Empire in America

'Colonial history is made at home; given a free hand, the mother-country will make the kind of empire it needs.'[1] Of no colonial empire was this more true than of the Spanish. By the eighteenth century it was some two centuries old, but still reflected the character of Old Spain and the interests which had led to Spanish colonization. The Spanish did not initially go to America as missionaries or explorers, but for private profit and national wealth. When Columbus and his successors did not find the hoped-for route to the spice trade of the east, they turned to exploit whatever advantages lay to hand. Initially this meant gold and silver: had no bullion been found it is doubtful whether Spanish occupation would have been consolidated. The Indies offered no indigenous trades, and for long the home government showed no enthusiasm for export staples of primary products. The silver mines of Peru epitomized the empire Old Spain wanted.

Yet precious metals were not the only reward. For the majority of settlers the aim was to establish landed estates like those of the Castilian nobility at home. In Mexico and other parts of central America conditions were ideal for reproducing this pattern. The land was suitable for stock-raising or agriculture; the towns offered markets; above all the indigenous population was sedentary and agricultural, excellent material for a subordinate peasantry. By the eighteenth century New Spain and parts of Peru repeated the social structure of Castile – an urbanized upper class, living on the profits of large landed estates worked by a dependent peasantry. In most parts of the Caribbean and in much of northern and southern America, however, neither climate nor the indigenous population was suited to this pattern. If they offered no bullion, these areas were ignored: in the eighteenth century much of Spanish America was either left to its native inhabitants, or occupied only by Catholic mission stations.

The Spanish were, in fact, selective, occupying only those places that satisfied their criteria of colonization; yet the social pattern which emerged was determined as much by the character of the Amerindian peoples as by Spanish policy. The special feature of Spanish colonies was that the more developed of them became 'mixed' societies, dominated by a minority of 'creoles' – local-born whites – and *mestizos* – half-castes – but based on a native working population. Because the peoples of Mexico and Peru filled the role of a European working class, there was no place in Spanish America for a white proletariat; and this distinguished Spanish colonies from others in North America which became 'pure' European settlements. The Spanish pattern was not, in fact, repeated until similar 'mixed' colonies developed in Algeria and other parts of Africa in the nineteenth century.

At the beginning of the eighteenth century the distribution of Spanish settlements accurately reflected both Spanish colonizing objectives and the facts of the American environment. By the Treaty of Tordesillas of 1494, Portugal had recognized Spain as

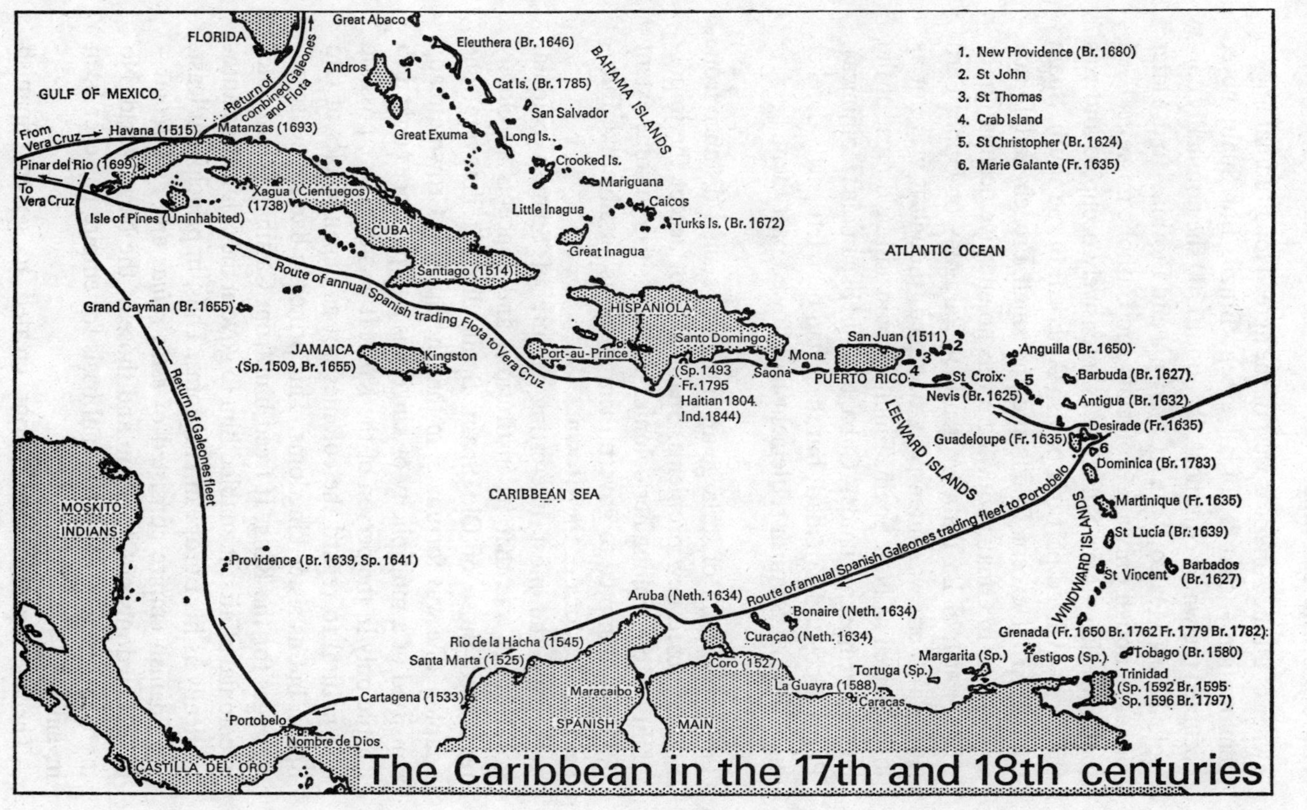

The Caribbean in the 17th and 18th centuries

owner of all the Americas west of the agreed longitudinal line of demarcation – that is, of all except Brazil. But Spain never occupied the whole continent. By about 1700 she nominally controlled New Mexico, Texas, California and Florida – to use later names – though only a few officials and Catholic missions lived there. Mexico – New Spain – was intensively occupied and was the most civilized part of Spanish America. In the south, Spain controlled all except Brazil and the small French and Dutch settlements in Guiana; but there was no effective occupation of Chile, much of La Plata (Argentine), Paraguay or Upper Peru (Bolivia). Peru was intensively occupied, though it was not as hispanicized as New Spain. Finally, Spain still held most of the larger Caribbean Islands – Cuba, half of Hispaniola (Dominica), Porto Rico, and Trinidad; but these had been left partly derelict once the first Spanish settlement had flowed past them.

The government of so large an empire at such a distance from Europe posed new problems. Spain did not accept the impossibility of controlling her colonies, as the British to some extent did, but attempted to govern them as far as possible like European possessions of the Crown.

Perhaps the most interesting feature of Spanish colonial government was that its institutions and concepts so closely resembled those of Old Spain. Spain did not innovate: she adapted. She was fortunate, in that the Spanish Crown already consisted of a multiplicity of kingdoms and provinces linked to Castile only in the person of the King. It was therefore possible and natural to regard the colonies not as dependencies of Old Spain, but as sister kingdoms. This principle had immense advantages for the King. It freed him from Castilian interference in colonial affairs; it enabled him to govern the colonies as autocratically as his European kingdoms. Thus, in principle at least, the Spanish empire consisted of *estos reinos* and *esos reinos* – these kingdoms of Old Spain and those of the New World. No more satisfactory constitutional basis for empire has ever been invented.

The metropolitan institutions created to govern Spanish America embodied this principle in that they alone dealt with colonial matters and were responsible only to the king. Chronologically the first was the *Casa de Contratación*, set up in 1503 on the model of the Portuguese *Casa da India*. Its functions were to license all trade with the colonies; to organize shipping and navigation; run a postal service; and exercise jurisdiction in cases arising out of American trade. Sitting until 1720 at Seville and then at Cadiz, the *Casa* united many functions which in England, France and Portugal were distributed inconveniently among a number of domestic institutions.

The chief advisory and administrative body in colonial affairs was, however, the *Real y Supremo Consejo de las Indias* – the Council of the Indies – which lasted from 1524 to 1834, and performed the same functions for the Indies as the Council of Castile for Castile. It advised the King on legislation, dealt with all colonial correspondence, and was the court of last resort both for appeals on important civil cases from the colonies and for civil and criminal cases from the *Casa de Contratación*. Staffed by nobles, lawyers and men with colonial experience, it was typical of the Spanish tradition of conciliar government – paternalistic, legalistic, authoritarian – the forerunner of colonial offices in the nineteenth and twentieth centuries. It built up a vast body of information on colonial matters and acted on the highest moral principles. Its defects were over-concern with minutiae and bureaucratic inflexibility. In the eighteenth century it lost its real powers; in 1714 to the new Secretary of Marine and Indies, then in 1790 to the five chief ministers of the Spanish peninsular government. These changes produced greater efficiency, but they broke the original theory that the colonies were distinct kingdoms, reflecting a policy of imperial centralization which was to have adverse effects on the loyalty of the colonists to the Crown.

But the main weakness of Spanish colonial government lay in the practical difficulty of controlling colonies across the Atlantic. The Council of the Indies never admitted that such control was impracticable; and throughout the centuries a vast stream of regulations were sent out dealing with matters of minute as well as of great importance. By about 1700 at least 400,000 such *cédulas* still had legal force. With difficulty these were reduced to some 11,000 laws and published in 1681 as the *Recopilación de leyes de las Indias*, the most impressive feat of its kind in colonial history. The difficulty was, of course, to ensure that colonial officials obeyed them. Recognizing the difficulty, Spain used two inquisitorial devices. The first was the *residencia*, a formal review by a judge, appointed by the Council, of the records of all senior administrative and judicial officers at the end of their period of office. The second was the *visita*, an inspection of anything from a whole province to the affairs of a single official, instituted at any time by the council, and held in secret. Both *residencia* and *visita* were potentially powerful weapons: their effects varied according to the personalities involved and the support colonial officials could obtain in Madrid. At best they produced temporary improvements and discouraged disobedience and dishonesty: at worst they were, as one Peruvian viceroy said of the *visitas*, no better than a gust of wind, which merely raised the dust, straw and refuse in the streets.

Fundamentally, effective metropolitan control was impossible with the poor communications available before the nineteenth century. Recognizing this the Spanish tried to limit the power of any one man or institution by checks and balances within the colonies. At each level, from the viceroy downward, absolute power was tempered by counter-balancing authority

The structure of government in the Indies nominally consisted of vice-royalties – each of which was a separate kingdom – sub-divided into provinces. In practice it was more complicated. Before the eighteenth century there had been the two vice-royalties of New Spain and Peru, each sub-divided into provinces known as *presidencia* under direct vice-regal control. But in addition there were three captaincies-general – Santo Domingo, Guatemala and New Granada – which were in fact independent governments corresponding directly with Madrid. In the eighteenth century, as the population and wealth of other areas increased, further devolution took place. New Granada became a vice-royalty in 1739 and Buenos Aires in 1778. Cuba, Venezuela and Chile also became captaincies-general between 1764 and 1778. Thus at the end of the century there were four vice-royalties, four captaincies-general, and thirteen presidencies.

At each level the power of the senior official was balanced by that of his *audiencia*, which was both court of law and advisory council. Like the viceroys and captains-general, members of the *audiencia* were normally peninsular Spaniards, directly appointed by the Council of the Indies to ensure their independence. Unlike the governors, who were normally appointed for from five to eight years only, members of the *audiencia* held office for long periods, and knew far more about local conditions. The governor could over-ride his *audiencia*, but only an unusually determined man was likely to do so. Madrid could maintain some degree of control by playing one against the other, but the capacity of an able viceroy to do good was as likely to be restricted as that of an incompetent or greedy one to do harm.

At the lower levels of government, however, there were no comparable checks on the power of royal administrators. As in Old Spain, the basic unit of local government was the municipality, and the royal official who controlled it was similarly the *corregidor*; although in America those in charge of larger areas were *gobernadores* and some municipalities had an *alcalde mayor*. By any title the *corregidor* was the foundation of colonial government. Unlike more senior officials he was often a creole, though always appointed by Madrid on the advice of the colonial government. Peninsular Spaniards held the office for five years, creoles for three, though either could be reappointed. Their functions were endless. They combined administrative and judicial authority; they controlled local government, including the municipal councils, and supervised Indian townships in the areas outside Spanish settlement. There was little effective check on them. Appeals could be taken from a *corregidor*'s legal decisions to the *audiencia*, and he was liable to be visited by agents of the central government: but for the most part he was left to himself; and most of the worst features of Spanish colonial government derived from his inefficiency or abuse of power.

In the second half of the eighteenth century Spain made major changes in local government, mainly to increase royal revenues. The French system of intendants had been introduced in Old Spain since 1700, and between 1764 and 1782 it was established also throughout Spanish America. In New Spain twelve *intendencias* replaced some 200 *corregidores* and similar officials, combining the previously distinct administrative authority of the governors and the fiscal powers of exchequer officials. Sub-delegates were appointed to supervise smaller districts. The new system derived from the increased efficiency of Madrid under Charles III and was part of an attempt to make the colonies more profitable, similar to that being made at the same time by the British in North America. The results also were comparable. The intendants increased the yield of taxation and improved local administration and defence. They gave Madrid and the central governments in America unprecedented control. Yet they may have had profound effects on the loyalty of the creole population. Intendants, who always came from Old Spain, often superseded creoles; administrative reform ended profitable abuses; bishops did not welcome the control exercised by the intendants over ecclesiastical patronage. Sub-delegates, being miserably underpaid, were often as corrupt as the *corregidores*. The new system may in fact have stimulated the independence movements of the early nineteenth century.

Spanish colonial government at its higher levels was characterized by autocracy and the predominance of peninsular Spaniards. This was natural. The representative principle was moribund in Castile, and no other colonial power permitted its colonists more liberal political institutions than existed at home. Some degree of autonomy in the administration of municipalities, the centre of creole life in the colonies, would however have been consistent with the Spanish tradition, even though most Castilian municipalities were in decay by 1700. Did the municipality offer the creole a compensation for his exclusion from government and politics?

To a large extent it did. Although municipal affairs were supervised by the *corregidores*, they were directly in the hands of municipal corporations – *cabildos* – who were responsible for services such as roads, hospitals and jails; organized a local police and militia; and raised taxes to pay for them. In addition the corporation elected two magistrates – *alcaldes* – annually, who had civil and criminal jurisdiction, subject to appeal to the *corregidor* and the *audiencia*. This was municipal self-government of a sort: but it had ceased to be elective in most parts of America long before 1700. *Regidores* – members of the corporations – were elected in the early sixteenth century, but later came to be nominated by local governors, and then appointed for life. By 1600 *regimientos* were being sold by the Crown for life. From 1606 they and all subordinate offices in America were made hereditary, provided certain dues were paid to the Crown on each transfer. Membership of the *cabildos* thus became the monopoly of the richer creoles, as symbols of status rather than sources of profit, and the corporations became closed oligarchies similar to those in Europe. The only surviving element of popular representation was the *cabildo abierto*, a special meeting of the corporation and local notables, held in times of crisis or to take some unusual step, such as making a voluntary gift of money to the Crown. These were exceptional; but in the revolutionary period after about 1790 they became increasingly important and often evolved into independent local *juntas*, taking over administration from the royal officials. For the rest, however, municipal government was largely moribund, since the local patriciates were too indolent to maintain elementary amenities, and in the smaller towns *cabildos* had often ceased to exist. At the end of the period the intendants and their agents remedied some of these defects; but their interference was resented by the creoles, and constituted another grievance against Spain.

To this point the structure of government in Spanish America has been described as if these were simple colonies of European settlement comparable to those of England and France in North America. In fact, they consisted primarily of non-Europeans. Spain was the first imperial power in modern times to be faced with the problem of native administration, and her attempts to solve it constitute the starting point for any comparative study of European methods of dealing with subject peoples.

The native problem in Spanish America was complex. The indigenous peoples varied immensely in civilization and character, from the sophisticated and partly urbanized Aztecs of Mexico and Incas of Peru, to the primitive Caribs of the Caribbean islands and littoral and the equally primitive peoples of central and southern America. As in Africa during the nineteenth century, no single native policy would meet all conditions. Moreover, the Spanish could not consider the native problem in isolation, for European settlement had produced mixed societies in many places in which the interests of the settler had to be made compatible with that of the Amerindian.

In all 'mixed' colonies there has been conflict between the principles of native policy thought desirable by the metropolitan power and the interests of European settlers: actual policy has usually been a compromise between them. In Spanish America the principles gradually built up by the Crown during the first half of the sixteenth century were in most respects a model for the future. Following Castilian practice towards the Moriscos, the Indians were declared to be full subjects of the Crown (though not of Castile), thus evading the problem of dual status which complicated some later colonial systems. As subjects they could not be enslaved. Their property was protected by Spanish law and their legal status was identical with that of Spaniards, except that indigenous customs could be used in cases involving only Indians. They were to be converted to Christianity, but not by force; and the unconverted suffered no major disabilities. In short, Spanish native policy assumed that natives were equal to settlers, and that the duty of the colonial power was to assimilate them to European religion and civilization. They were encouraged to live in towns or villages of a European type, which were governed by native chiefs and elected *alcaldes* under the supervision of the local *corregidor*; and this way, it was hoped, self-administration would be combined with gradual assimilation.

Admirable though these principles were, they had to be related to the facts of American life. The colonies had been conquered by Spaniards in search of wealth. Whether this took the form of mineral extraction or farming, it needed native land and labour. The instinct of the *conquistador* was to take what land he required and to enslave natives to work on it. The Crown recognized that compulsion was necessary if the Indian was to work for the settlers. Compulsory labour was consistent with Spanish principles, since feudal obligations survived in Castile. The problem in the Indies was to make it consistent with Christian principles and Spanish laws.

In the three centuries before 1800 three main devices were used to induce the native to work if the financial incentive was insufficient. The first was the *encomienda*, introduced soon after 1500 as an alternative to slavery. It resembled the manorial rights granted to Spaniards over Moriscos; and in America it meant that the Crown conferred on individual settlers or officials the responsibility for protecting and civilizing native communities, together with the right to demand their labour in place of tribute due to the Crown. The grant did not involve native land, and could be justified on many grounds. But the Crown always disliked the system because it led to abuse of the natives and smacked of feudal independence for the *encomiendero*; and it had almost died out by the eighteenth century.

It had to be replaced. From the middle of the sixteenth century the Crown, as it regained its claim to tribute from the Indians by withdrawing the *encomiendas*, commuted its right into forced labour. Indian villages, through their headmen, had to provide a proportion of their labour force to work in rotation throughout the year. This labour was allocated by local officials either to public works or to privately owned mines, factories or farms. Attempts were made to prescribe conditions and hours of work and to define wage rates; but in practice there was much abuse; and in the early seventeenth century the Crown again attempted to abolish forced labour. The attempt failed, for the protests of colonists could not be ignored. As the *mita* in Peru and *repartimiento* in New Spain, it lasted until the end of the Spanish American empire.

A third method used to force reluctant Indians to work was debt peonage. By getting Indians into their debt, factory owners and farmers reduced them to virtual slavery, and some of the worst labour conditions existed in textile mills and silver mines where Indians were held in this way.

But abuse of non-European labour by these and other devices was by no means universal in Spanish America. Exploitation was worst in Peru, where intensive European settlement and the mines, mills and sugar factories made the greatest demand for labour. Things were much better in New Spain where there was considerable marriage between the races and the Amerindians mostly became hispanicized. In most other parts of Spanish America the presence of Spaniards made little or no impact on indigenous ways of life. In the eighteenth century Chile, Yucatan Honduras, New Mexico, La Plata, Venezuela and Central South America were all frontier regions where Indians were ruled by their own chiefs under loose supervision, and where the paternalistic mission station was the only evidence of European penetration.

In view of such contrasts it is impossible to reach any verdict on Spanish native policy and its impact on Amerindian peoples. At its best it was enlightened and offered them the advantages of being members of a Europeanized Christian society. At its worst it reduced them to helots. In either case it shared with all colonial régimes the defect that it ended the natural evolution of native society. In the words of Salvador de Madariaga – the chief protagonist of the Spanish colonial achievement:

> the discovery and conquest of the New World dispossessed the Indian aborigines of the free and sovereign possession of their continent, brusquely deflected their historical evolution, mixing it inextricably with that of an utterly alien lineage of men, and in the process caused them a psychological shock of incalculable gravity.[2]

In government and native policy Spain had necessarily been a pioneer: the same was true of her commercial and financial policies. She showed Europe how to obtain concrete rewards from American colonization.

From the European point of view the disadvantage of settlement colonies of the American type, as contrasted with trading bases such as those of Portugal in the east, was that they might provide no advantages to the parent state, benefiting the settlers, not the Crown. Spain's achievement was to make the colonies serve her interests in three ways: by transferring colonial revenues to the Castilian treasury; by retaining a monopoly of colonial trade; and by regulating the colonial economies to suit

Spanish interests. Later empires had merely to adopt all or some of these principles. Spain did not, however, invent them: like American forms of government they were adapted from traditional European practices. Most European states, towns and provinces used monopolistic or protectionist regulations to exclude rivals from their trade or industries. Navigation acts excluding foreign ships, staple regulations excluding foreign merchants, protective tariffs and bullion controls were common by the fifteenth century. The nation states had originally adopted these monopolistic regulations from the larger towns, treating the state as a single economic interest: the colonial empires were similarly treated as extensions of the nation state, with an assumed identity of interest. In each case the ultimate objective was the political power of the sovereign, rather than the economic welfare of the individual subject.

The extent to which Old Spain extracted taxes from the colonies distinguished her empire from most others; and here the theory of multiple kingdoms served the Crown well, for no constitutional objection could be raised to the transfer of royal revenues from America to Madrid.

Spanish colonial taxes fell into three categories. First there were duties on trade. From 1720 these were collected entirely in Old Spain to prevent customs evasion in America. Second there was the royal *quinto*, a levy made at the royal assay offices in America on all bullion brought there for smelting into stamped bars. Until 1723 this was normally a fifth of the value of the silver, thereafter a tenth. Third, there was a miscellany of minor taxes levied in the colonies: customs on inter-colonial trade; native tribute; ecclesiastical tithes; the *cruzada* – a relic of mediaeval Spanish warfare exported to the colonies; the *alcabala*, a Castilian sales tax, imposed on the colonies at rates of about 2 per cent; proceeds from the sale of public offices; royal monopolies and other lesser taxes. Customs collected in Spain went immediately to the royal treasury. Taxes collected in the colonies were divided. One group, including royal monopolies and tithes, were transmitted direct to the Crown in Spain. The remainder formed a general fund available to the colonial governments; only after local expenses had been met, including subsidies paid by the richer to the poorer colonies, was any surplus transmitted to Old Spain. By the eighteenth century the colonies had long ceased to send home vast quantities of silver, and local government absorbed all the general revenues. For example, between 1785 and 1789 general revenues in New Spain averaged about nine million pesos (£3,000,000), of which three were distributed between the poorer provinces such as Havana, Florida, Porto Rico and the Philippines. On the other hand, the increasing prosperity of the vice-royalty in this period produced special funds averaging 4·3 million (£1,400,000), largely from the tobacco monopoly, of which about 3·5 million were sent annually to Old Spain.[3] This sum, equivalent to about £1,000,000 sterling, together with the yield of customs collected in Spain on the colonial trade, constituted the imperial 'tribute' to offset expenditure on central administration and naval defence. It was not a vast sum; but, by contrast, neither the British nor French obtained any significant fiscal yield from their colonies. Portugal was the only other imperial power to make a fiscal profit from the colonies in this period.

Commercial monopoly and regulation of the colonial economy were a still more important source of Spanish profit. The principles involved in these 'mercantilist' devices were simple. Spain alone was entitled to whatever economic advantages her colonies offered: the interests of the Crown – and in practice of Old Spain – took preference over those of the colonies. By 1700 the Spanish had embodied these principles in three sets of regulations.

The first excluded foreigners from the colonial trade. No foreign ship might enter a colonial port or sail from Spain to the Indies. No foreigner could send goods to the colonies in his own name, even in a Spanish ship, nor take bullion out of Spain in payment for goods he sold to a Spanish merchant without special licence. Thus the American colonies were insulated from the outside world, and Spaniards gained a middleman profit on all goods from Europe because they were channelled through Spain and Spanish merchants. This monopoly was strictly enforced. Until the mid-eighteenth century trade was restricted to an annual fleet, half of which, the *flota*, sailed to Vera Cruz; the other, the *galeones*, to Cartagena and Portobello. The fleets wintered in America and met at Havana for the return voyage in the following spring. These were the only colonial ports to which Spanish ships might sail direct.

A second set of regulations was designed to make the colonies economically complementary to Old Spain. Industries, and even primary products like wine, were forbidden in certain colonies to preserve the market for imports. Inter-colonial trade was restricted for the same reason. The importation of negro slaves, increasingly necessary as plantation production grew in the eighteenth century, was limited by the grant of *asientos* to monopolistic companies – usually foreign – and a tax was levied on each slave landed. Spain showed little concern for the economic welfare of her colonies, always putting their interests second to her own.

The third set of restrictions primarily affected Old Spain. For 250 years colonial trade was channelled through a single port – Seville until 1720, thereafter Cadiz: only after 1765 were other Spanish ports allowed a share. Even within Seville, the right to trade with America was restricted to members of the *consulado*, a closed merchant corporation comparable to the English Merchant Adventurers Company, the intention being partly to use them as a source of loans to the Crown, partly to ensure that foreigners could not intrude.

Spanish devices to ensure their monopoly of colonial trade were more extreme than those of other colonial powers and took 'mercantile' principles to the point of absurdity. By the early eighteenth century the need to modify the system was obvious and was pressed by leading Spanish economists. Illicit trading by the British and others, both through Old Spain and direct to the colonies, could not be checked since it was in the interests of too many Spaniards on both sides of the Atlantic. The Spanish therefore made considerable changes during the eighteenth century, not because they were converted to the principle of free trade, but because they saw that the fundamental advantages of a monopolistic system could best be preserved by sacrificing its inessentials. By 1789 the colonial trade was open to all Spanish ports, and licensed ships could sail direct to most ports of Spanish America. Restrictions on the inter-colonial trades were removed, and in 1790 the *Casa de Contratación* was abolished. By the end of the century slaves could be imported freely and the *asiento* system was abolished. Positive impetus was also given to economic development in the colonies by the formation of Spanish trading and plantation companies with monopolies in backward regions such as Venezuela, Central America, Havana, and other Caribbean territories, though only the Caracas Company was financially successful.

By the beginning of the nineteenth century the Spanish commercial system was as liberal as that of other colonial powers. All that remained was the basic 'mercantile' principle that colonial trade must be a monopoly of the parent state. It was not free trade, but what the French called *l'exclusif mitigé*. The results were in some ways spectacular. Hitherto backward places like La Plata, Venezuela and Cuba developed rapidly; in the decade 1778–88 Spanish colonial trade increased by 700 per cent,[4] and the new prosperity was reflected in increased Spanish revenues from the colonies. But by then liberalization was not enough to satisfy the colonists. Spain could not fill the central role required of her in an imperial trading system: and the desire of many colonists for freedom to trade with the rest of the world made for revolution and colonial independence.

It is easy to criticize the Spanish imperial system. Its administrative structure reflected the cumbrous bureaucracy of sixteenth-century Castile; the interests of the colonists were subordinated to those of the metropolis; colonists were excluded from their own government; Spain drew wealth from the colonies; the Amerindians were exploited by Spanish settlers. Yet Spanish colonial administration was no worse than that of Old Spain; no colonial commercial system was liberal in the eighteenth century; Spanish native policy was more enlightened than that of any other colonial power; the Spanish empire was still the most impressive of all in 1800. Her richer American colonies were mature and cultivated societies which made those of Britain and France, and even the now independent United States, seem mere frontier settlements. Spain's achievement had been to build in the new world societies which possessed many of the merits and also the defects of the *ancien régime* in Europe, and which were stamped with her own character as few other colonies have ever been. Above all she had been the pioneer in American colonization. Among the old colonial empires Spain played as pre-eminent a role as did Britain after 1815 in the new.

The Portuguese Empire in the Atlantic

By 1700 Portugal had possessed an overseas empire for two and a half centuries. During the sixteenth century her achievement had been the establishment of bases in Africa – in Guinea, the Congo, Angola and Mozambique – and the creation of a maritime empire stretching from India through the Archipelago to Macao. By 1700, however, Portugal was primarily an Atlantic power. Except for Goa and some trading forts in India, part of Timor Island and Macao, she had lost all her possessions in the east to the Dutch or British. In Africa her east coast territories had shrunk to some coastal forts and semi-independent inland fiefs, and in the west she kept only the ports from which the slave trade was run. But in the Atlantic she possessed the Madeiras and Azores, the stepping stones to America, and above all, Brazil. With the disintegration of the eastern empire Brazil became the hub of Portugal's overseas possessions, closely linked with West Africa which supplied the slaves on which the Brazilian economy depended.

Brazil was important in the general history of European colonization because it was the prototype of the plantation colony. Spain showed Europe a highly organized and urbanized colonial empire, based on the use of precious metals and a large advanced native population. But such a formula depended on uniquely favourable geographic and demographic conditions, which had been found mainly in Mexico and Peru. In Brazil no precious metals were discovered until the 1690s, and the indigenous population proved useless as a labour force. The Portuguese had therefore to improvise. They brought sugar canes from their Atlantic islands, which in turn derived from earlier sugar plantations in the Mediterranean, and negro slaves from Africa. With the addition of other crops, such as tobacco, coffee, cocoa and cotton, this formula proved widely adaptable: by 1700 it was used throughout the Caribbean and parts of North America by the French, British, Dutch and even the Spanish, as the best method of drawing wealth from otherwise unpromising tropical or sub-tropical territories. Everywhere its consequences were similar. Colonies consisted of large rural estates which were run by a small minority of white planters and mulattoes, and were worked by negro slaves. It was a much cruder colonial pattern than that of Spanish America, but it was no less profitable; and the contrast in style accurately reflected the differences between Spanish and Portuguese civilization.

During the early years of the eighteenth century, however, new forces were making Brazil a more complex and much richer society. The discovery of gold and diamonds in Minas Gerais after 1690 produced a large mining industry, and a shift of population to the south; and the constant search by the *bandeirantes* for more precious metals created a hollow inland frontier of settlement which led to new boundary demarcations with Spain in 1750 and 1777. In the third quarter of the century, also, Pombal, as first minister in Lisbon, did much to stimulate the development of Pará and Maranhão by granting monopolies and wide privileges to Portuguese companies in these areas. Cattle ranching was developing in the far south, and coffee production near Rio de Janeiro. By the end of the century the population had risen to about four millions. Brazil was becoming rich, but remained simple and rural. None of the towns was large and there were few industries. The sugar estate remained the basis of the economy and the centre of society. The richer planters, closely related by marriage with each other and with the merchants, professional men, shipowners, and ecclesiastics who dominated the towns, constituted a semi-feudal oligarchy. They had lost the political powers granted to their ancestors as *donatários* – proprietors, similar to those in some English colonies – but they were still given minor administrative and judicial posts; and, as officers in the militia, their influence was considerable. This ruling class remained predominantly white, though Brazil differed from the Spanish colonies in that there was no formal colour bar. Yet Portuguese claims to have been colour blind were exaggerated. They may have been so in matters of sex, for intermarriage was common, and miscegenation produced every possible racial permutation. But prejudice against African blood remained strong, and mulattoes had almost no hope of rising to high office in church or state. By contrast with most other colonizing countries the Portuguese showed a casual tolerance of other races: but their treatment of negro slaves was indistinguishable in its brutality from that of other planter societies in America.

Portuguese colonial government and constitutional theory reflected the political character of Portugal herself: by comparison with that of Old Spain it was crude but serviceable. Portugal made no constitutional distinction between her colonies and the metropolis. Until 1604 she had no colonial department; even then the older tradition survived and colonies were dealt with indiscriminately by any metropolitan department. In the eighteenth century they were open to interference by the Council of State, the Council of the Indies – renamed the Council for Overseas – which was primarily responsible for their government, the Council of Finance, the Treasury, and the Privy Council. It was not until 1815 that Brazil became a separate kingdom and was no longer treated as a mere province by the Lisbon departments.

The structure of government in Brazil and the other Atlantic colonies showed both lack of constitutional precision and the desire of the metropolis to retain full control. Royal government had gradually replaced that of the *donatários*, and by 1700 no colony was governed by a proprietor. Theoretically Brazil was then a single vice-royalty, sub-divided into provinces under captains-general and smaller areas under captains: lesser colonies in the Atlantic and Africa had mere captains. But the viceroy had little control over the provinces. He was ignored by the captains-general, who corresponded directly with Lisbon, and by the Portuguese government when dealing with individual provinces. Colonial dependence was further increased by the hearing of appeals from colonial courts in Lisbon, which continued even after two colonial courts of appeal were set up in 1751.

Within the colonies government was much less complex than

in Spanish America. There were no formal councils comparable with the *audiencias*: governors were advised and checked only by the judges – appointed by Lisbon – and by the *provedor da fazenda* – the Crown's financial representative. Government was autocratic. There were no representative bodies, but creoles could exercise some influence on government through the municipal councils – *senados da câmara* – in the provincial capitals, which were elective and carried weight. In contrast with Spanish practice, creoles were also able to hold most official positions other than those few reserved for appointment by Lisbon; but legal posts were in practice restricted to peninsular Portuguese, since there was no university in Brazil at which creoles could gain legal qualifications. In short, although Portuguese colonial government was theoretically autocratic, colonists played a considerable part in public affairs. There was never the resentment at rule by metropolitan expatriates such as existed in Spanish America; and in this Brazil more closely resembled English colonies in North America.

Portuguese commercial policy was very like that of Spain: indeed, the Spanish may originally have adopted practices begun by Portugal in the east. Colonial trade was restricted to Portuguese subjects. No foreign ships were allowed in Brazilian or other colonial ports. Only a direct trade to and from Lisbon was permitted, which was further restricted until 1765 by being carried in annual fleets. Between 1765 and 1777 Pombal gave monopolies of the trade of individual provinces to private companies; but after his fall the trade was thrown open to all Portuguese nationals and the convoys were not revived. In practice, however, much of the Brazilian trade was handled by British or Dutch merchants in Lisbon who, like those in Seville or Cadiz, supplied cargoes for Brazil and bought most colonial products. In the eighteenth century interest in the trade was increased by their being able to take gold and diamonds in part payment for their goods.

Portugal was too weak economically to profit much from her colonial trade, except as middleman. She obtained her share of increased Brazilian prosperity by transferring colonial revenues to the metropolitan treasury. Precise figures are unobtainable; but in 1711 it would seem that some 420,000 *cruzades* were sent home from Brazil and another 126,000 collected by the *Casa da India* in Lisbon. In 1750 the Crown received about 6,800,000 *cruzades* either from Brazil or from taxes levied on her trade in Portugal; the increase reflecting the growth of Brazilian primary production and the immensely larger sums produced by royal taxes on gold and diamonds. If these figures can be trusted they indicate that Portugal received the equivalent of £72,000 sterling in 1711 and £900,000 in the mid-century. Since Portugal's total domestic revenues did not rise above about £1,000,000 Brazil was providing about as much as the metropolitan tax-payer.[5] Even more clearly than Spain, she obtained profit from her colonies without performing any more useful economic function than to build and man the ships which carried the transatlantic trade and to maintain the supply of slaves from Angola. Even so, colonial tribute did not make her rich. It was exhausted in maintaining a lavish court, in pensions and salaries to courtiers and high officials, and in ambitious public works, such as the monastery at Mafra. When the court left Lisbon for Brazil in 1808, it also left a public debt of some £8,000,000.

By a paradox typical of Portuguese imperial history, the Brazilians did not appear to resent their subordination. By 1800 Brazil was more populous and far richer than Portugal. She had every incentive to break free from the weakest of the imperial states, and could not have been held by the puny Portuguese army or navy. Yet Brazil produced no nationalist movement. This may have been because neither political nor economic controls really pressed hard on her, or because she lacked an intelligentsia to which the nationalist concepts current in the British and Spanish colonies might have been attractive: the very crudity of Brazilian civilization may have made for contentment. Yet Brazil and the Atlantic islands demonstrated a perennial feature of Portuguese colonization – its extraordinary capacity to generate loyalty. The links between colonies and parent state were common language, law, religion, and culture. Brazil became independent in 1822 by an historical accident: she never deliberately rejected these fundamental links with the parent state.

3

The French and Dutch Empires in America

The French Empire

The French empire in America had certain features in common both with the Spanish and British colonial systems, forming a link between them. Like Spain and Portugal, France was an absolute monarchy: her colonies were therefore ruled as dependencies without constitutional rights or representative institutions. Like them also she was an intolerant Roman Catholic state, permitting no religious liberty in America and imposing religious tests on emigrants. But in most other ways French colonies resembled the British. Both empires were relatively late foundations, still brash and undeveloped in 1700. Both were relatively poor, for neither country had discovered precious metals and neither could use indigenous peoples as a labour force. Both possessed plantation colonies in the Caribbean on the Brazilian model and settlement colonies in continental North America. Both, finally, were rapidly expanding in the early nineteenth century.

The French empire was divided between the Caribbean and continental North America. In the north the French had a line of forts, towns and trading settlements stretching up the St Lawrence from Acadia to Montreal, whence fur traders, missionaries and explorers penetrated the Great Lakes region and went down the Mississippi to Louisiana. French Canada was lightly held, with some 15,000 colonists in 1700 and 70,000 by 1759, and was economically still very undeveloped. But it was strategically strong, cutting off the English settlements on the Atlantic coast from the rest of the continent, and offered great future possibilities. By far the most highly valued French colonies, however, were those in the Caribbean: St Christopher, Martinique, Guadeloupe, Tobago, Grenada, part of San Domingo, Louisiana and Cayenne, bordering Dutch Guiana. These were all plantation colonies, relying on slave labour, supplying France with sugar and tobacco for her own consumption and for re-export to Europe. Canada exported only beaver furs and cost France more than her trade was worth in government and defence. Voltaire later marvelled that Britain should spend so much on conquering *quelques arpents de neige vers le Canada.*

It has often been said that the French, unlike the English, were forced to colonize by the Crown; that the American empire was the expression of state enterprise. This was not so. Atlantic colonization was the work of individual Frenchmen acting on their own initiative. It is true that the Crown, from the days of Henry IV and Richelieu, supported and encouraged colonization for reasons of state. The government believed that colonies were necessary to make France self-sufficient in 'groceries' such as sugar and tobacco; even more to generate a merchant marine and so make France a great naval power, capable of matching Spain. From the beginning French colonization was thus expected to increase state power as much as private wealth. Yet colonization required more resources than the French monarchy could afford: it was vital to harness the wealth and energy of subjects acting for private advantage. As in England, the method used to correlate state interest and private investment was the chartered company.

The French empire was created by these chartered companies, which did the work of the state at minimum cost to the government. Seventy-five have been listed between 1599 and 1789, the majority in the seventeenth century. In the formative period of colonization, before 1660, they were given ownership of the land they occupied, a monopoly of trade, and varying degrees of administrative autonomy. The Crown reserved only ultimate sovereignty, the reversion of rights after a period of years, and the power to restrict colonial trade to France. The companies received royal support: for example, the nobility was allowed to belong to them without loss of status, and emigration was encouraged by a law obliging all ships going to the colonies to carry a proportion of *engagés* – men who had signed indentures to work in the colony for not less than three years: hence the nickname *les trente-six mois*. Yet most companies were short-lived; it is doubtful whether any produced a cash profit. They discovered, as did most chartered companies in colonial history, that the creation and government of a new colony were too heavy a burden on the profits of land sales and trade monopoly which were their main source of income.

By the 1660s private enterprise had done its work. The companies were mostly dead, but the colonies survived and quickly became full royal possessions – Canada in 1663, the rest of the existing American colonies in 1674 after the dissolution of Colbert's West Indian Company. Chartered companies were later created for colonies such as Louisiana and San Domingo; others were given merely the commercial monopoly of a colony or region, like Law's all-embracing Company of the Indies of 1719. But none was very successful, or survived for long.

Once they emerged from the chrysalis of company rule, the French colonies rapidly took on the markings of the parent state. France was an absolute monarchy: the colonies were now part of the royal domain. Government was put in the hands of royal agents, unlimited by local assemblies or chartered rights. Royal edicts and less formal regulations had full force of law. Taxes were imposed by royal order, though their allocation was sometimes left to quasi-representative assemblies. In principle French colonial government was as authoritarian as that of Spain.

But it was less rationally organized. There was no French equivalent of the Spanish Council of the Indies. Primary responsibility lay with the Ministry of Marine, which became a distinct department in 1699. From 1710 a sub-department of this ministry, the colonial bureau, specialized in colonial matters; and from 1750 colonial finances were for the first time separated from those of the navy. By the 1780s the bureau contained several sub-departments, divided variously on a geographical and subject-matter basis: and in 1783 it was renamed the *Intendance Générale*. Within the limitations of French bureaucracy in the eighteenth century it was reasonably efficient. What it lacked was political power. Colbert, as Minister of Marine, had centralized the empire in order to control and develop it: few of his successors at the ministry showed much interest in colonies or used their power constructively. Moreover, the colonies were open to interference by other departments of state. Defence was primarily the responsibility of the Ministry of Marine, but the Ministry of War also had interests in it. The Controller-General of Finances – the chief minister – managed customs and some colonial revenues, and interfered in patronage. The Council of Commerce, re-created in 1730, influenced commercial policy. Colonies were liable to be visited by royal intendants as agents of the *Conseil d'État*. The colonial empire suffered from too much interference with insufficient concentration of responsibility.

In this respect the colonies were treated as provinces of metropolitan France; and their internal administration appropriately followed the French provincial pattern. At its head was a governor-general, governor, or lieutenant-governor, according to the importance of the colony. He was almost invariably a noble and soldier, the personal representative of the King, solely responsible for the armed forces, the enforcement of commercial regulations, and reviewing death sentences passed in the courts. But every governor had his intendant, whose functions were as characteristic of French colonial government as the *audiencia* of the Spanish system. His office was a microcosm of French administrative history transferred from the provinces of the metropolis to the colonies. Provincial governors had always been *noblesse d'épée*, necessary but suspect because of their status and possible disobedience. Intendants were lawyers, appointed to supervise provincial governors because their loyalty and efficiency could be relied on. By the mid-seventeenth century few provincial governorships survived in France, and those that remained were largely honorific: the intendants ruled the provinces. In the colonies, however, the old dual system survived.

The intendants were appointed by Paris and were directly responsible to the minister for all financial matters. They controlled the police and the law courts, presided over the *Conseil Supérieur*, and made appointments to all minor posts in the civil administration. Effective government depended on their co-operation with the governors, since either could bring government to a standstill. The system was unique. It had the advantage of giving the French Crown effective power by dividing the men on the spot; but it was undesirable from a colonial point of view, and was jettisoned finally in 1816. Thereafter the governor had full control over colonial administration.

The only other institution in French colonies with real authority was the *Conseil Souverain*, or *Conseil Supérieur*, which derived from the *Parlements* of Paris and the main provincial capitals. All important colonies had a *conseil*; San Domingo had two. Their members included the intendant as president, civilian officials, senior army and navy officers and some colonists, all appointed by the Crown. The councils had two main functions, legal and administrative. They heard appeals from the courts of first instance and supervised the various special tribunals, such as courts martial. In their quasi-legislative capacity they had the right of registering edicts and other regulations sent from France and ordinances drawn up by the governor or intendant; and in this they came nearest to giving colonies some legislative autonomy. On the one hand they tended to limit the application of French metropolitan laws and regulations in the colonies by failing to register those they disliked or thought inapplicable; with the result that colonial law became increasingly out of step with that in France. Conversely, by registering and therefore debating minor regulations made by the governor or intendant, they acted as quasi-legislatures, and tended during the first half of the eighteenth century to build up powers analogous to those of assemblies in English colonies. This was contrary to French constitutional theory; and in 1763 Choiseul, then chief minister in France, cut back their powers and insisted that they be called *Conseils Supérieurs* to indicate that, like the *Parlement* of Paris, they were merely courts of law, without proper legislative functions. The councils thereafter had limited power, but great local prestige. Loyal service for twenty years entitled a *conseiller* to a much coveted patent of nobility of the second class.

Under normal conditions there were no elected assemblies in the French empire and in this also the metropolitan model was followed. The Estates General of France had not met since 1614 and had become an antiquarian possibility rather than an actual institution. The Crown regarded such bodies as dangerous: when Frontenac as governor of Canada wanted to summon an elected assembly in 1672, he was reminded by Colbert that it was royal policy not to summon the Estates General in France, and that colonies should follow the same principle. Thereafter there were no elective bodies in the French colonies until local assemblies were set up in France in 1787, and were duplicated in Martinique and Guadeloupe. But from 1759 Chambers of Agriculture and Commerce were instituted in these colonies and in San Domingo. Their members were nominated by the local councils, and the chambers had the right to keep a deputy in Paris to represent their interests and negotiate with the minister.

French colonial government was therefore centralized and autocratic: but it was not arbitrary. It was conducted within a framework of law and administrative convention which tempered royal power and protected the rights of the subject. This was particularly evident in finance and taxation, in which the French came nearest to accepting the principle that colonies had rights and the concept of 'no taxation without representation'.

The basic principle of public finance in metropolitan France was that the Crown had a right to certain revenues as part of its *regalia*; all other taxes were a voluntary gift by the subject. By the eighteenth century this distinction was obscured by the fact that the main voluntary tax – the *taille*, levied on the third estate only – had not been voted since the fifteenth century and was collected at rates fixed annually by the Crown, though the parallel tax on clerical income – the *don gratuit* – was still voted periodically by the assembly of the church. In the colonies this distinction was more evident. The Crown collected its normal *regalia*, including customs duties, which formed collectively a fund known as the *Domaine d'Occident*, and other taxes which were accounted for separately. But there was no equivalent of the *taille* as a tax on personal income or landed property (the alternative forms in France); and the principle was accepted that this or any other form of additional taxation would constitute a voluntary gift by the colonists and should in some way be granted by them.

The difficulty of obtaining such extra revenues was that the Crown did not want to allow representative assemblies. In Canada, which was poor, the problem was evaded altogether by not attempting to raise them. But the Caribbean sugar islands were rich; and the increasing costs of naval defence after 1690 made the Crown anxious to tap their wealth. In the process, a clear distinction was made between the original islands, centred on Martinique and Guadeloupe, and the French colony in San Domingo, which was only ceded formally by Spain in 1697.

In Martinique and Guadeloupe the Crown conceded that it was desirable for colonists to be consulted in some informal assembly when any additional form of tax was imposed, but maintained its right to act on its own authority if agreement was not reached. In 1715 representative assemblies were summoned in Martinique and Guadeloupe to agree to the continuation in peacetime of a wartime export tax – the *octroi*. The Martinique assembly gave conditional assent; but since that in Guadeloupe did not, the government evaded the issue by increasing the existing import and export duties in all the Leeward Islands. After 1763, however, the need for stronger defences led to another attempt to get agreement on new taxes. Assemblies met in Martinique in 1763 and 1777 to discuss their form; and from 1763 annual accounts of receipts and expenditure were presented to the *Conseil Supérieur* of Martinique. The way was thus prepared for the assemblies created in 1787.

San Domingo was treated differently: it was the only French colony recognized before 1789 as having constitutional rights in the same sense as English colonies. The reasons put forward in the 1703 Royal Instructions to the governor for making this distinction were that

cette Colonie s'est établie d'elle-même; elle a souffert des pertes pendant la dernière guerre; et pour n'en point empêcher l'accroissement, Sa Majesté a bien voulu laisser les Habitans dans un entier affranchissement de Droits:...[1]

On this basis the Crown consulted the two regional *Conseils Supérieurs*, separately in 1713 and jointly in 1715, before instituting an *octroi*; and, although this tax was continued until 1738 without summoning further special meetings – despite the fact that it had been voted for one year only – other conditions attached to the grant were faithfully observed. Further joint meetings of the councils were held in 1738 and 1751, each of which renewed the *octroi* for a further five years, though again the tax was continued: and in 1761 the Minister of Marine strongly criticized the governor and intendant for having imposed an additional three per cent export duty on goods carried in foreign ships on the grounds that

> *la constitution de Saint-Domingue est différente des autres Isles, en ce que, dans la première, il n'a jamais été établi que des droits d'Octroi, et que ... il ne doit en être perçu a Saint-Domingue qu'après qu'ils auront été proposé par les Habitans representés par les Conseils Supérieurs, et confirmés par Sa Majesté.*[2]

Thereafter the constitutional and political development of San Domingo became even more unusual. In 1764–5 three separate assemblies, one of which included colonists other than members of the two councils, were summoned to vote additional taxes. The colonists attempted to gain control of almost all taxation and to change other aspects of government. The Crown took fright. In 1766 an *ordonnance* defined the future membership of such assemblies, including in them senior officers in the militia as well as members of the councils. It admitted their right to vote all additional taxes; but denounced their claim to appropriate revenues other than the *octroi*, or to interfere in colonial administration. On this restricted basis further assemblies were summoned in 1770 and 1776 to renew and increase the *octroi*, and created no trouble.

In the field of taxation, therefore, the French colonial system was less than absolute. The Crown had to choose between a strictly limited income or making concessions to representative bodies which might weaken its political power. It preferred to forgo revenue; with the result that the colonies were lightly taxed. On the eve of 1789 receipts from taxes in all the colonies were about seven million livres (£275,000), while expenditure was about seventeen millions (£668,000).[3] The French colonial system, despite its authoritarianism, was more expensive than that of Britain: unlike Spain and Portugal, France made no fiscal profit from her colonies.

Local administration, the courts, law, land tenures and ecclesiastical organization in the colonies were modelled as closely as possible on those of France. There was no municipal autonomy, since Louis XIV had revoked all French municipal charters. Towns and rural areas in the colonies were administered by the intendant and his subordinates as in France, but without the honorific office holders who survived there. Colonists, particularly holders of commissions in the militia, were used for many administrative functions; but the Crown never sold offices in the colonial administration.

The judicial system in the colonies was simple. Courts of first instance run by magistrates enforced French customary law, modified by such royal edicts and other orders as the local council chose to register, and used standard French procedures. Appeals lay to the local councils. There were also special tribunals to deal with land tenures, admiralty and prize cases, as well as councils of war to enforce military discipline. Land law was based on the principle that all land belonged to the Crown and was granted in fief to individuals or companies on conditions which normally involved occupation and development. Tenures in freehold existed but were rare. Royal policy was to reproduce the feudal system of tenures and social relationships as it still existed in France as a support for royal authority. Feudal authority was strong in Canada, but never took root in the Caribbean. Nowhere was there such social stratification as existed in France.

In ecclesiastical matters the Crown, after an initial period of uncertainty, decided to establish the Roman Catholic religion as it existed in France and not to permit heresy. Jews and Huguenots were denied freedom of worship from 1683, and religious toleration did not return until 1763. The Crown was slow to create secular bishoprics in the colonies, though these were an essential feature of a 'Gallican' church. For more than a century religious orders – Jesuits, Jacobins, Recollets – provided most of the clergy, acquiring large estates and considerable political influence: Canada, in fact, verged on a theocracy. But after the expulsion of the Jesuits from France in 1763 the Crown set up bishoprics and parishes throughout the colonies which remained in its hands.

The year 1763 also marked a turning point in colonial defence. Hitherto France had relied mainly on local militias in which all males between 16 and 60 were liable to serve. They were commanded by French regular officers, but subordinate commissions were highly prized by colonists as symbols of status. In Canada the militia was a formidable force, expert in Indian warfare and able to put up a good showing against British regulars; but in the Caribbean it was mainly a safeguard against slave risings. The Seven Years War, which included the loss of Canada and British occupation of Guadeloupe, showed that these militias were an inadequate defence force if France could not command the sea; and after 1763 France kept an increasing number of regulars in the Caribbean, and formed special regiments for colonial service. Their cost was a major inducement for France to bargain with colonists for higher taxes, even at the cost of making constitutional concessions.

The French commercial system was similar to that of the older empires on which it was modelled. It was based on assumptions which the *Encyclopédie* (published between 1751 and 1768) defined as follows:

> *Les colonies n'étant établies que pour l'utilité de la métropole, il s'ensuit:*
>
> 1. *Qu'elles doivent être sous sa dépendance immédiate et par conséquent sous sa protection;*
> 2. *Que le commerce doit en être exclusif aux fondateurs.*[4]

L'exclusif, was not, however, applied to the colonies from their foundation. The colonizing companies had a monopoly of trade, but were free to trade with other countries, and foreign ships could enter French colonial ports. The French mercantile system began in the 1660s, when Colbert used the West Indian

Company to exclude foreign ships, mostly Dutch, from the colonial trade. Thereafter a series of royal regulations of 1670, 1695, and 1717 excluded foreigners from French colonial ports and forbade any direct contacts between colonies and foreign states. Colonial trade in both directions had to go through French metropolitan ports, whatever its source or destination. This system, the *pacte colonial*, was less rigorous than that of Spain, since colonial trade was open to all French subjects (except in colonies included in a commercial monopoly), and was not restricted to a single annual fleet or any one French harbour. But it was more restrictive than the English system, since no French colonial goods were left 'unenumerated' and so free to be sent direct to a foreign country in Europe.

The concept of the *pacte* implied that the system was two-sided, offering advantages to the colonists as well as to the metropolis. To some extent this was true. France gave tariff preference on colonial goods, paid bounties on ships, slaves and other things needed by colonists, and created the *engagé* system to provide white settlers. The government also took a paternalistic interest in colonial welfare, supplying technical advice on agriculture, and encouraging colonies to diversify their economy by growing foodstuffs and exporting a wider range of goods than tobacco and sugar. Yet on balance the advantage clearly lay with France. In the later seventeenth century she had been unable to supply sufficient shipping for the colonial trade; throughout the eighteenth century French freights were higher than those of England or Holland. French merchants, with a monopoly of supplying the colonies, took little trouble to supply what they needed, and charged excessive prices. In order to protect French brandy producers the colonies were forbidden to export molasses or rum to France: until 1763, they could not even be exported to foreign markets. Again, though sugar refining was permitted in the French islands – whereas it was forbidden in those of England – no new refineries were allowed to be built after 1684 and refined sugar paid heavier duties on entering France than crude or clayed sugar. Even the argument that France earned her advantages by giving protection was unconvincing since the colonies were cut off by English blockade in every war from 1689 to 1763 and many were occupied and devastated.

To meet complaints the French modified the restrictions on colonial trade after 1763: like the Spanish and British they chose to strengthen the fundamentals of the system by concessions in detail. Under the so-called *l'exclusif mitigé* the colonies were allowed to import foreign livestock and other necessities from foreign colonies in America provided that they were paid for in molasses and rum and not in cash or in commodities wanted by France. In 1767 and 1784 a number of 'free ports' were opened in the islands at which foreign vessels could trade: this was similar to the free port system inaugurated by the British in the same area in 1766. In each case the aim was to placate the planters without reducing the advantages gained by the metropolis – a monopoly market for European exports, a monopoly of valuable colonial products, and employment for the metropolitan merchant marine as a nursery of seamen and a foundation for naval power.

Mitigation of monopoly did not satisfy the colonists; but the system was most advantageous for France. Had the colonial trade been open, French merchants and shipowners could not have competed with the British: as it was, they had a monopoly on their own terms. In the eighteenth century the West Indies were a major source of commercial prosperity for France. The immediate beneficiaries were shipowners, merchants and sugar refiners in the French ports – Bordeaux, Nantes, Le Havre, La Rochelle and Marseilles; but the benefits were more widely dispersed. Colonial products were sold in many parts of Europe and helped the French balance of trade: in 1788 more than two-fifths of French exports consisted of colonial goods, and these more than accounted for France's favourable international trade balance. The needs of the colonial markets were also a stimulus to all types of French industry. Unlike Portugal or Spain, France was not merely levying tribute on trade artificially canalized through her ports, for she was a great industrial power in her own right. Yet there was no doubt that the colonies would benefit from the ending or modification of the *pacte colonial.*

The Revolution of 1789 was the most important turning point

in French colonial history since Colbert's reorganization between 1664 and 1683. Colbert had ended the system of chartered rule in the Caribbean colonies, made the colonies full dependencies of the Crown, and established an economic system which subordinated the interests of the colonies to those of France. Such extreme subordination of the colonies was not compatible with the principles of the Revolution, and had been under attack by liberals in France long before 1789. Turgot had defined the true colonial policy as one which gave the colonies '*une entière liberté de commerce, en les chargeant des frais de leur défense et de leur administration*', and which treated them politically '*non comme des provinces asservies, mais comme des Etats amis, protégés si l'on veut, mais étrangers et séparés*'.[5] The colonists themselves demanded commercial freedom, or at least equality with the metropolis within the closed imperial system, and greater control over their domestic government. But they would have been content to be treated, in the words of Dubuc, a colonist who was also chief clerk in the colonial bureau, as '*des provinces du royaume de France, aussi Françaises de sentiment que les autres, égales aux autres*'.[6] This implied integration with France, not distinction as separate states. The colonists wanted equality with the metropolis, not separation from it.

The Revolution gave the colonists this equality: by 1794 they were completely assimilated with the metropolis. By the constitution of the Year III (1794), they were declared to be '*parties intégrantes de la République et sont soumises à la même loi constitutionelle*'. All laws in force in France were also to operate in the colonies. They were to be divided into departments, like those in France, which were to be governed by commissioners and elected assemblies on the new French pattern. Colonists were represented in the metropolitan legislature, and had the same fiscal system as the metropolis. On the same principles, colonial trade with France was made duty free to put the colonies on the same footing as other departments of the Republic; but foreign trade had to be carried in French ships or those of the country from which the goods originally came.

These principles were welcomed by the colonies. But the obverse of assimilation was the application to the colonies of the new metropolitan disapproval of slavery. In 1791–2 full citizenship and electoral rights were given to free mulattoes and ex-slaves: in 1794 all slaves were declared free; though in 1798 the Directory tried to meet complaints that the end of slavery meant ruin to the plantations by restricting full political rights to those with professions or crafts, members of the armed forces and workers on the land, and by making vagabonds who refused to work liable for punishment.

The legislation of this decade provided the theoretical basis of the French republican approach to empire throughout the nineteenth century; but, for the time being, many of the new laws could not be made effective in the colonies. Since 1789 these had taken advantage of confusion in the metropolis to run their own affairs through the new assemblies and recognized only such French laws and orders as pleased them. Moreover, the outbreak of war with Britain in 1793 led to British occupation of most French colonies until the Peace of Amiens in 1802; and by that time the republican theory of empire had been superseded by that of the Consulate and Empire. The republican principle of *assimilation* to the metropolis was replaced by that of subordination and separate legislation, as before 1789. The French executive regained the power to legislate for the colonies by decree; colonial representatives ceased to sit in the French legislature; and colonial government reverted to pre-1789 forms under different titles – a *capitaine-général* replacing the governor, a *préfet colonial* the intendant, a *commissaire de justice* undertaking the intendant's judicial functions. In commercial matters the full *exclusif* system was reimposed on trade between the colonies and France. Slavery and the slave trade were once again made legal.

The new colonial system, however, still existed largely on paper. San Domingo rose in 1802 against the return to slavery, and became independent in 1803. Louisiana was given back by Spain in 1800 after being ceded to her in 1763, but was sold to the United States in 1803 before it was taken over by the French. The remaining colonies were reoccupied by the British after the war began again in 1803. Thus the Napoleonic system of empire was as theoretical as that of the Republic. Its importance lay in the future, for it supplied the French with an alternative imperial concept which had considerable influence during the nineteenth and twentieth centuries. Against the republican doctrine of full *assimilation* of colonies to the metropolis in law, institutions and commerce, the empire set the principle that '*le régime des colonies françaises est déterminé par des lois spéciales*'. This was the nucleus of a principle which was eventually to replace *assimilation* as the basis of French imperial organization.

At the end of the eighteenth century, even ignoring the ignominious consequences of the wars that began in 1793, France's achievement as a colonial power was unimpressive. In 1660 she had been as well placed as England to build an empire overseas: by 1789 she had lost all her North-American possessions except the islands of Saint-Pierre-et-Miquelon off Newfoundland. She retained her Caribbean islands and had regained her West-African possessions in 1783; but she had failed to become the dominant European power in India, and kept only five small trading bases there. Why was this? Did these failures indicate that France lacked the interest or ability to become a major colonizing power?

France's relative failure was due not to any one national characteristic, but to a number of factors which differed from one part of the world to another. In Canada failure was due in the last resort to inability to match British naval power during the Seven Years War: but the weakness of Canada resulted also from the lack of immigration from France which made her vulnerable to attack by the far more populous English colonies. This lack of immigration certainly reflected French reluctance to emigrate in the eighteenth century, for the growth of Canada's population to its peak of about 70,000 in 1759 was largely the result of natural increase. But the disparity was the result of geography rather than of superior English enthusiasm or colonial policy. The English had acquired those parts of North America which, because of their climate, accessibility and ample hinterlands were the natural target for working-class emigrants from Europe. Changed political conditions after 1763 made little difference. Canada was marginal land for settlements: only land shortage in the south or political influences on the direction of emigration could lead to intensive occupation. The fact that the French had done little to populate it by 1759 did not indicate that they lacked enthusiasm or ability as a colonizing power.

By contrast, the French were quite as successful as the British in other American fields. As explorers in the Missouri-Mississippi region and as fur traders they were more energetic than the English. Their relations with the Indians, on whom the fur trade depended, were generally better. French Catholic missions had a virtual monopoly in North America. In the Caribbean French planters were probably more successful than those of English islands. In West Africa the two countries were in much the same position. The striking French failure was in India, where the French company of the Indies never really matched the resources of the English East India Company, and where the French finally lost their chance to become the dominant European power in 1763. To some extent this failure reflected the reluctance of French investors to put money in speculative ventures of this kind – a reluctance which may also have had adverse consequences in Louisiana and Cayenne. Yet the loss of India, like that of Canada and other French possessions, was due in the last resort to lack of naval power. Colbert had seen that colonies would stimulate a large merchant and fighting navy, but that conversely they would survive only if an adequate navy defended them. In the next century France's preoccupation with continental wars condemned her to perpetual naval inferiority. Throughout this period, the British were dominant at sea: French colonies were always liable to be conquered and French trade to be cut off. Conversely, during the American revolutionary war of 1776–83, France for the first time met England on her own terms at sea without facing also a European war. The temporary command French admirals achieved in the Caribbean and Indian Ocean, and the fact that France lost no colonies but regained Tobago and Senegal, showed how close was the connexion between sea power and empire in the eighteenth century. France had given place to England mainly because in a century of Anglo-French conflict the British concentrated on the sea and the colonies, France necessarily on Europe.

The Dutch Colonies in America

The eighteenth-century Dutch colonies in America and the Atlantic were merely the rump of an empire. Their importance in colonial history derives from two characteristics. They remained until 1791 under the control of the chartered West India Company, and so illustrate the consequence of company rule in contrast with direct metropolitan government. The fact that most Dutch colonies had representative political institutions by the end of the eighteenth century, underlines the tendency of the old empires to reproduce the traditions of the parent state.

Dutch traders and slavers were active in West Africa and America from the 1590s, but colonization began only with the creation of the West India Company in 1621. The date was significant. The company had been projected earlier; it had been held up until the truce of 1609 with Spain and Portugal expired, for its main function was to attack enemy possessions overseas and divert resources from the war in Europe. There were admittedly other hopes. Some supporters wanted to establish settlement colonies in America for Calvinist refugees from Flanders, others to acquire bases in the Caribbean for illicit trading with foreign colonies. In the long run political and colonizing motives proved incompatible; but during the quarter century after 1621 the temporary alliance between different groups in the United Provinces gave the company sufficient capital and political backing to establish a substantial empire.

By 1648 the company had three groups of colonies. In North America it possessed New Amsterdam, on the Hudson river, and Long Island, which traded in furs with the Indians and was developing into an agricultural settlement; and also Delaware, founded in 1623 and extended in 1655 by the conquest of the neighbouring Swedish colony of New Sweden. A second group consisted of trading bases on both sides of the Atlantic. Arguin, Portendic, Goree, Elmina, São Tomé and Loanda in West Africa were conquered from Portugal as slaving centres; Curaçao, St Eustacius, Tobago and other Caribbean islands from Spain for contraband trade with Spanish colonies. Finally the company occupied much of Brazil and the previously unsettled region of Guiana.

In 1648 the future of this empire seemed bright; but it dissolved as quickly as it had been acquired. The Portuguese retook Loanda and São Tomé in 1648, and Portuguese colonists finally ejected the Dutch from Brazil by 1654. The British captured New Amsterdam and Delaware and kept them at the peace of 1667. The French captured Arguin, Goree and Tobago. By 1700 the Dutch retained only the trading bases of Curaçao, St Eustacius and parts of St Martin, together with the Guiana plantations and Elmina as a base for the slave trade. The reasons for this decline were complex. The company lacked good leadership. The death of the Stadtholder William II in 1650 deprived it of its chief political ally, and the subsequent republican government was hostile to it. Portugal, now independent again, was determined to regain her colonies; the English, once the civil war was over by 1646, were eager rivals. There were too few Dutch colonists to secure the larger colonies against attack. But fundamentally the Dutch lost their empire because the majority preferred trading illicitly with foreign colonies to maintaining their own colonies. Once the Spanish war ended in 1648 the company had served its purpose and was left without further state help. The effort to protect its possessions was too much for it, and by 1674 it was bankrupt and dissolved. The remaining colonies reverted to the States General: but rather than administer them, it vested them in another chartered company.

Like its predecessor, the new West India Company reflected the decentralization of the United Provinces. It was a federal body consisting of largely autonomous Chambers in the provinces and main towns, each operating on its own account. The company as such had little power over the members and had few distinct functions. It was run by a Council of Ten, nominated jointly by the Chambers and deputies of the shareholders, and, after 1750, by the Stadtholder as *ex officio* Director-General. Its main collective activity was the slave trade between Africa and the Caribbean, of which it held the monopoly: beyond that it was a holding company for enterprises run by the Chambers or their deputies, making its profits from a levy on their trade. Each American colony was under separate management. Curaçao belonged to the Amsterdam Chamber, St Eustacius to that of Zeeland. Surinam was run by the Surinam Society, founded jointly by the Amsterdam Chamber and by Cornelius Van Aerssen, whose interest was transferred to the company in 1770. Berbice belonged to the Society of Berbice from 1720; Essequibo and its daughter colony, Demerara, to the Zeeland Chamber.

The financial record of the company and its subordinates in the period 1674–1791 showed how difficult it was for a chartered company to make profits from colonies which it had also to govern and defend. Between 1674 and 1720 its dividend averaged 2·5 per cent; between 1720 and 1772 it was 1 per cent; thereafter no dividend was paid. The company was again bankrupt by 1791 and was then dissolved.[7] Of the private companies, Surinam paid modest dividends and Berbice none at all. But company rule was bad also for the economic development of the colonies. They were held back by limited investment; by restrictions on the establishment of private plantations in competition with those of the companies; by the artificially high prices charged for slaves and other imports; and by the duties levied on trade. Surinam was fortunate in that its trade was from the start open to all citizens of the United Provinces, whereas that of the others was for long restricted to the company's ships or forced to go to the controlling province at home. Apart from Curaçao and St Eustacius, none of the colonies really prospered until late in the eighteenth century, when the end of company rule in 1791, followed by British occupation in 1796, widened their commercial opportunities, brought in foreign settlers and capital, and reduced the price of slaves. The great age of Guiana as a plantation economy came after the end of Dutch company rule.

The fact that the Dutch initially thought of colonization in terms of war or commerce rather than of emigration and settlement resulted in the West India Company being empowered to govern its American colonies as if they were mere factories or estates. Its charter, like that of the Dutch East India Company, did not specify constitutional rights for Dutch settlers. The interesting fact was that the liberal traditions of the metropolis won out in Guiana because there was substantial free settlement and the claims of settlers to political and legal rights had to be conceded.

In the eighteenth century the main constitutional development took place in Essequibo and Demerara. The other Guiana colonies already had liberal constitutions which gave settlers a share in government and control over taxation; and the Caribbean islands had too few settlers to be given similar institutions. Essequibo and Demerara were controlled by the Zeeland Chamber which, unlike the private companies in the other Guiana settlements, took the narrowest view of their purpose. The colonies were administered by officials of the Chamber as if they were exclusively sugar estates, and private planters were not officially allowed to settle there until 1716. Thereafter concessions had to be made, because settler co-operation was necessary to form a militia, and taxes beyond those few originally authorized by the States General could not be imposed on settlers without their consent. During the half century after 1739, when the first planter was admitted to the company's council in Essequibo, a complex constitutional system gradually evolved which gave settlers an ever-increasing role in government and the administration of justice. In 1789 the constitution was given formal and nearly final shape in the Plan of Redress, drawn up by a committee representing the company and the States General, after colonists had petitioned against projected restrictions of their rights. After further changes had been made in 1796, just after the British had occupied Guiana, the system of government contained four bodies on which colonists were represented. The chief administrative body was the Council of Policy, responsible for both colonies, consisting of the Director-General (governor-general), three officials and four colonists. The governor's casting vote gave the official side a majority, but it was difficult to ignore the settler's point of view. The second institution was the College of Kiezers, one in each colony, who were elected for life by planters owning twenty-five or more slaves, and whose sole function was to select the unofficial members of the Council of Policy. Next were the Councils of Justice, one in each province. These were the senior courts of law, and consisted of two officials and six colonists. Finally there was the Combined Council set up in 1796. It consisted of the Council of Policy together with six Financial Representatives, elected by the planters for two-year periods. It met annually to examine the state of the 'colony chest' – the revenues raised from taxes voted by the settlers for the general purposes of the colony, as distinct from the revenues accruing to the 'company chest' – and voted and appropriated taxes for the next year.

Complex and curious though it was, this constitutional machinery gave the settlers effective control over the company's policy and expenditure; it imposed similar restraints on the British, who promised to preserve the constitution in 1796, and did not finally abolish it until 1928. Its evolution showed that even company rule could not prevent Dutch settlers from obtaining the political and legal rights they were accustomed to at home. Like England, the United Provinces believed in representative government: Dutch settlers expected to carry their rights with them, and forced concessions from a reluctant Zeeland Chamber. Guiana thus became the only colony in America, apart from those of England, which had representative institutions, and thus, in its contrast with other colonies, reflected the differences between the United Provinces and the absolute monarchies of France, Spain and Portugal.

4

The British Empire, 1700–1815

The Spanish, Portuguese, French, and Dutch colonial empires have been described as if they remained constant throughout the century before 1815. In fact, of course, this was not so. Change was constant, and was still accelerating on the eve of their disintegration. Yet the distortion is only partial: there was an essential continuity of type in all these empires. None changed its basic approach to colonial government or economics, or added a radically new type of colony to its possessions. In 1815 all still bore the stamp of their parentage and were clearly products of the first phase of European expansion.

This cannot be said of the British empire in 1815. Until 1763 it was an American empire, reflecting the traditions of the parent state. By 1815 it had changed fundamentally, and included both previously foreign colonies which did not fit the British pattern and territories in the east which were of such size and complexity that they were entirely new in European colonial history. The British empire did not merely evolve: it underwent reconstruction. There is, of course, a danger in over-emphasizing this discontinuity, or talking of the 'first' and 'second' British empires as if they were distinct. There was in fact no clear break in time or tradition. The 'first' survived into the twentieth century in the Caribbean islands and other small American possessions; the 'second', consisting in 1815 of old colonies captured from foreign states and parts of India, existed before the continental American colonies became independent. Hence the real contrast was between the relatively small and largely homogeneous American empire as it was before 1783 and the complex world-wide empire

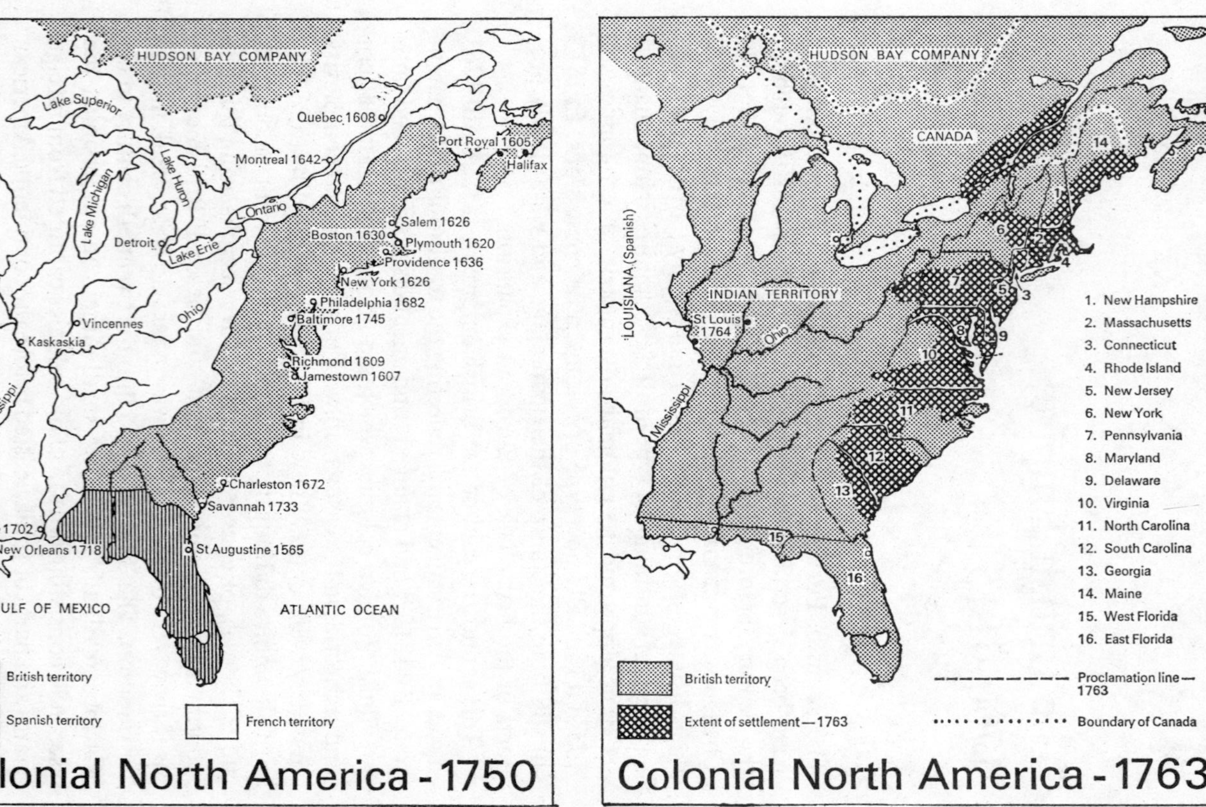

HUDSON BAY COMPANY
Lake Superior
Lake Michigan
Lake Huron
Quebec 1608
Montreal 1642
Port Royal 1605
Halifax
L. Ontario
Lake Erie
Detroit
Salem 1626
Boston 1630
Plymouth 1620
Providence 1636
New York 1626
Philadelphia 1682
Baltimore 1745
Vincennes
Ohio
Kaskaskia
Richmond 1609
Jamestown 1607
Mississippi
Charleston 1672
Savannah 1733
Mobile 1702
New Orleans 1718
St Augustine 1565
GULF OF MEXICO
ATLANTIC OCEAN
British territory
Spanish territory
French territory
Colonial North America - 1750
HUDSON BAY COMPANY
CANADA
LOUISIANA (Spanish)
INDIAN TERRITORY
St Louis 1764
Ohio
Mississippi
1. New Hampshire
2. Massachusetts
3. Connecticut
4. Rhode Island
5. New Jersey
6. New York
7. Pennsylvania
8. Maryland
9. Delaware
10. Virginia
11. North Carolina
12. South Carolina
13. Georgia
14. Maine
15. West Florida
16. East Florida
British territory
Extent of settlement—1763
Proclamation line—1763
Boundary of Canada
Colonial North America - 1763

of 1815. To divide them in 1763 is to create an artificial distinction. It is nonetheless useful to do so in order to isolate the basic British colonizing tradition, as expressed in the original colonies, from the contrasting traditions which were evolved later to meet the different problems of the colonies acquired for the first time in and after 1763.

The British Colonies in America Before 1763

Because the British colonies and ex-colonies in America eventually became the richest and most populous of all European overseas settlements, and because the nineteenth-century British empire was the greatest of its time, it is tempting to antedate Britain's primacy as an imperial power. Yet before 1763 the British colonies in North America and the Caribbean could not compare in size, wealth, population or civilization with such Spanish possessions as New Spain or Peru. The British colonies were young; the oldest had existed for barely a century; and in 1715 they did not cover the eastern seaboard of North America let alone their hinterlands. For the most part they were poor, lacking the endowments of the richer Spanish colonies – precious metals and a large sedentary indigenous labour force. Population growth depended on immigration, free or slave, and its natural increase. In 1715 the total population of the mainland colonies was only about 400,000. Their economic development was held back by shortage of capital. Their exports averaged about a quarter of a million pounds annually in the early eighteenth century.[1] There were only four significant towns – Boston, Philadelphia, New York and Charleston. Settlement was restricted to the coastal strip east of the Appalachians. Some of the Caribbean islands were relatively more advanced, producing sugar, tobacco and other tropical crops; and their exports to England averaged £609,000 in 1701–5.[2] But these were primitive societies in comparison with the main Spanish provinces. The immense potentialities of British America were largely embryonic at the beginning of the eighteenth century.

British colonies fell into three categories. The first were plantation colonies in the Caribbean and on the southern seaboard of

North America, all of which reproduced the pattern of Portuguese Brazil – large estates growing tropical crops for the European market; inhabited by relatively few Europeans and a great majority of imported African slaves. In the Caribbean Britain possessed Jamaica, Barbados, and a number of smaller islands; on the mainland Virginia, the Carolinas, and Georgia. These plantation colonies were, in British eyes, the most valuable part of the American empire. They provided the tropical 'groceries' that made Britain independent of foreign supplies and gave a surplus for re-export to Europe. Of the two other groups of settlements on the mainland, the 'middle' colonies – Maryland, Delaware, New Jersey, Pennsylvania and New York – were also valued in Britain because they produced a wide variety of primary products, especially tobacco, grain and timber, the last mostly for consumption in the Caribbean or in southern Europe. By contrast, the New England colonies – Connecticut, Massachusetts, Rhode Island and New Hampshire – were regarded with suspicion. They produced little that was wanted in Britain: in 1763 total exports were £74,815, and none of them were essential to the British economy.[3] They competed with British ships in the Newfoundland fisheries, built their own ships in rivalry with metropolitan shipyards, and made up their trade balance by trading illicitly with foreign colonies in the Caribbean. In short, the British had the highest opinion of those colonies which most closely resembled Brazil, and the lowest of those which were most like herself.

But it was the northern and middle continental colonies which made the British empire different from all others before 1763, excepting only French Canada. They were 'pure' settlement colonies, whose indigenous Amerindian inhabitants had retreated to the margin of English settlement. Because the climate was not suited to a plantation economy they did not import African slaves as a labour force. Emigration and natural increase had to supply the whole colonial population: because there was no indigenous working class it was possible for a European proletariat to develop. Hence the social and economic structure of New England and most of the middle colonies, with their villages, market towns, temperate agriculture, shipbuilding and commerce, was far closer to that of the metropolis than to the southern and Caribbean colonies. This similarity made them unpopular in Britain, which expected colonies to be economically complementary, not competitive with her. But it attracted emigrants not only from England but from Ireland, Scotland and Europe, who could expect to re-create in the settlement colonies the pattern of life they knew at home. By 1763 immigration had raised the total population of British North America to about two and a half millions,[4] and the frontier of settlement was beginning to move over the Appalachians into the Ohio valley. By the end of the century the now independent British settlements in North America were the most advanced and potentially wealthy European societies in the New World.

The social and economic patterns of the settlement colonies in British North America were the result of geography rather than of British policy: they differed as much from the British plantation colonies as they did from foreign colonies. But the constitutional autonomy which they shared with all British colonies was the consequence of their English parentage.

Like all colonial powers England transmitted to America her own political concepts and institutions. There was no attempt to construct new forms: statesmen and lawyers used whatever lay to hand.

The relationship between the colonies and England derived from the pattern of English possessions within the British Isles. There a basic distinction existed between the 'realm' of England and Wales (and Scotland after the union of 1707) and the 'dominions', which included Ireland, the Channel Islands and the Isle of Man. These dominions were not sister kingdoms on the Spanish pattern, but dependencies of the Crown. They had their own political institutions – assemblies, legal systems, and finances – and the Crown could not tax them or make laws for them on its own authority any more than it could within the realm. On the other hand the parliament at Westminster could legislate for them, even though they were not represented in it. Illogical though this was, it was an essential means of preserving unity and authority within the British Isles. The Irish Declaratory

Act of 1719 stated the accepted doctrine of parliamentary supremacy half a century before the same doctrine was expressly stated for the American colonies.

These dominions supplied a ready-made constitutional pattern into which the new American colonies were fitted without difficulty: and most of their fundamental rights sprang from the assumption that colonists had the same rights as subjects in places like Ireland. But within this framework the English also adopted two other devices. The first was the mediaeval system of the palatinate – the delegation of quasi-sovereign powers by the Crown to a subject to rule a territory on its behalf. In the seventeenth century palatinates survived in Durham, the Channel Islands, and the Isle of Man. Although anachronistic, they offered a convenient legal form by which the Crown could encourage colonization without losing ultimate authority. A large proportion of the American colonies were based on these proprietary patents: for example, Maryland was granted by Charles I to Lord Baltimore in fief. Such grants were similar to the Portuguese *donatária*; the difference was that the English never succeeded in revoking all of them. Maryland and Pennsylvania remained in the hands of feudal proprietors until the American revolution.

The palatinate was archaic; but the chartered joint-stock company was a sixteenth-century device to finance hazardous commercial or piratical ventures by spreading the risk among a body of subscribers. Its use by the English, in common with the French and Dutch, indicated that little distinction was at first made between trading and colonizing: both were financial ventures. A number of English colonies were founded by such companies, which were given full control over the area they occupied, subject to the authority of the Crown. All were short-lived: like their foreign contemporaries they found it impossible to establish a new colony and distribute a dividend. They withered away by the second half of the seventeenth century, leaving the colonies to be directly administered by the Crown, as 'royal' colonies. But they left behind also the concept of 'chartered government'. By the eighteenth century only three colonies – Rhode Island, Connecticut and Massachusetts – still possessed valid charters which made them privileged corporate bodies like chartered boroughs in England. But other colonies like Virginia, which had once been under a chartered company, claimed the rights which had belonged to their company; and even colonies which had never had a company or a charter assumed that they were entitled to the same rights as those which had. Thus the use of chartered companies reinforced the assumption that the colonies had rights against the Crown and the mother country.

These seventeenth-century origins gave the eighteenth-century American empire its two distinctive features. First it retained a multiplicity of political forms and constitutional relationships. Attempts to eradicate differences and to rationalize government on the pattern of 'royal' colonies like Virginia and Jamaica were unsuccessful. The three chartered New England colonies had lost their charters and were combined into the Dominion of New England under an autocratic governor-general between 1685 and 1688, but regained their rights after the Revolution of 1688 on the principle that property rights must be preserved. Similarly an attempt of the newly created Board of Trade between 1696 and 1714 to abrogate all colonial charters and patents was defeated by the refusal of the British Parliament to tamper with rights of individual proprietors and corporate bodies. Hence the American empire remained a museum of mediaeval and near contemporary institutions. The Caribbean colonies, surviving the war of independence, retained these peculiarities, some until the later nineteenth century, others into the second half of the twentieth century.

But if the English empire was a ramshackle building, liberty grew in its crevices. Its second distinctive feature was the freedom the colonists retained in the eighteenth century. In no colonial empire then or since had the metropolitan state less direct power. Colonial autonomy was at its extreme in two of the New England chartered colonies, in which even the governor – the nominal representative of the Crown – was elected, together with the executive council. Here the Crown had no authority at all. In the proprietory colonies also it could do little; and even in the 'royal' colonies, where governor and council were royal appointments, and where no charter or patent stood between the King and his subjects, the English government had little power. Like the British dominions the 'royal' colonies were constitutional organisms, not mere municipalities dependent on the British government. Each had its legislative body, consisting of a representative assembly and a nominated (or sometimes elective) upper house, which was also the executive council. These legislatures had plenary powers to make laws for their colony, provided they were not contrary to imperial statutes and were assented to by the sovereign in London. No foreign colony had comparable legislative powers in the eighteenth century.

In other aspects of government also the colonists were as free as their fellow subjects in Britain. They had English common law and replicas of the English courts. Juries and habeas corpus (though not in the terms of the English Habeas Corpus Act of 1679) were regarded as their birthright. Local government was in the hands of colonists as justices of the peace or, in a few towns, as members of municipalities with powers similar to English chartered boroughs. In short, the English had given their colonies the institutions they took for granted at home. English colonists were more free than those of other nationalities precisely because Britain was one of the most liberal countries in Europe.

But in fact the colonists were considerably more self-governing than the English intended them to be. The theory in England was that the colonies had modified versions of the seventeenth-century English constitution. Executive government was the sole responsibility of the governor and council as agents of the Crown, as the King in council was the executive authority at home. On seventeenth-century theory there could be no institutional link between the executive and the legislature, since the 'balance of the constitution' required that each should be independent of the other. In England a *de facto* link between the Crown and an irresponsible legislature evolved in the seventeenth century through the system of ministerial responsibility, whereby individual ministers took full legal responsibility for their actions as ministers of the Crown, and were liable to answer for them before parliament. In this way the legislature gained some control over the membership of a ministry and the policies it adopted. By the end of the eighteenth century government by a 'cabinet' collectively responsible both to parliament and the King was within sight, though it did not reach maturity until the 1830s.

In the eighteenth century, however, the colonies were supposed to possess the constitution in its original form. A ministerial system was not applicable since the governor was personally responsible to the Crown for all acts of his government. The assemblies were assumed to have the functions the early Stuarts had allotted to the English parliament – to pass laws, vote taxes and put forward petitions; the colonial executive to be independent of the legislature and an obedient servant of the English government. By the mid-eighteenth century practice in the colonies had ceased to fit this theory. There was no formal ministerial system: heads of departments remained servants of the governor. There was no link between executive and legislature, and these frequently came into collision: but the problem of reconciling such conflicts, which had produced the ministerial system in England, generated a substitute in almost all American colonies, whether they were proprietory, chartered or 'royal'. Assemblies used the power of the purse to gain effective control over government in their own way. Policy was controlled by appropriation of supply to objects of which the assembly approved. The independence of the executive was checked by threats to refuse to appropriate official salaries: in four colonies even the governor's salary had to be voted annually. Supervision was maintained even when the assemblies were not sitting by their delegates – a treasurer and commissioners, or a standing committee – to whom all taxes were paid and whose warrant was necessary for making payments. This was not ministerial government, but was as effective in controlling the governor. The result was that the colonies were really governed by their assemblies.

Like these colonial systems of government, the metropolitan institutions through which England attempted to control the American colonies reflected the lack of any positive theory of empire. Their confusion and inefficiency made it impossible for Britain to check colonial autonomy.

Because the American colonies were dependencies of the Crown, analogous to the nearby dominions, every British agency of government or legislation had the right to interfere in them.

Because they also had constitutional rights, there was no certainty about how far this interference should go. Theory and practice varied so greatly at different times that in the debate over colonial rights that preceded the American revolution it was possible to take diametrically opposed views by appealing to conflicting precedents.

The Crown was, of course, responsible for colonial administration; but the King of England, unlike the King of Spain, had no single minister or office which was solely concerned with the colonies. Before 1768 the Secretary of State for the Southern Department handled colonial correspondence, linking the colonial governors and the Privy Council; but he did not possess even a specialized sub-department like the French bureau for colonial business. The Colonial Department of 1768–82 with its colonial secretary had the makings of a true colonial office, but was abolished after the American war as an economy measure. The Home Secretary (newly named) again took over colonial correspondence until 1801, when it was transferred to the new Department of War and Colonies, from which the Colonial Office of the nineteenth century developed. Thus for most of the eighteenth century there was no British minister to supervise the empire and make colonial policy.

These functions were theoretically the responsibility of the Privy Council. But by the early eighteenth century this had become a largely honorific body, and colonial business sent to it was handled by *ad hoc* committees of privy councillors. Since these lacked specialized knowledge and continuity, the council relied on the Board of Trade, created in 1696, to give it advice. The board demonstrated the peculiarities of the English system. It was not an executive body and could take no action on its own authority. Its president was not a member of the cabinet until 1757, though normally a minister. Yet it was the nearest thing in England to a colonial office before 1768, acting as a repository of information, and from time to time generating 'policies' on demand from other authorities.

The colonies, then, were nobody's business and everybody's business: each part of the British administration dealt directly with them according to its interest. Treasury, Commissioners of

Customs and Post Office acted independently, and each claimed a share in colonial patronage. The Admiralty and War Office, though responsible for colonial defence, seldom consulted each other or the Board of Trade. Even the Bishop of London had a hand in the colonies, for there were no colonial bishoprics before Nova Scotia was given one in 1787, and the colonial churches were part of his own diocese. Such wide dispersal of power produced confusion and inefficiency. It made a calculated 'colonial policy' virtually impossible. In conjunction with the constitutional principles on which the empire was based, it ensured that the colonies could not be governed from London. Distant supervision and occasional interference were the most they expected or feared before 1763. Attempts made in the following twenty years to improve administrative efficiency seemed a revolution to the colonists, suggesting that the British might treat the colonies as if they were indeed part of an empire.

Given the weakness of metropolitan executive authority, the only body in Britain which could have exerted effective authority was the parliament at Westminster. Although it represented only the lords and commons of the realm of England and Wales, and of Scotland after 1707, it had always claimed and exercised power to bind all dominions of the Crown. This doctrine of parliamentary supremacy was inconsistent with the principle of colonial – or dominion – autonomy; yet, after the Civil War, it was not seriously challenged until the 1770s. It could have been the means of creating an integrated empire, for whereas the Crown was restricted by the powers of colonial assemblies and by the legal rights of colonists as subjects, no such rights could stand up against the authority of parliament. Yet this great hammer was seldom used before 1763; almost never to enforce administrative obedience. No colonial constitution was created by act of parliament before 1765 – all were granted by the King in council. Few acts were passed concerning the internal affairs of colonies. Since no British act applied to the colonies unless it necessarily or expressly did so, most British legislation did not affect them. None of the penal laws against Roman Catholics or dissenters applied in the colonies, which from the start were the only European colonies with full religious freedom.

Yet when parliament chose to act it was able to make the dominions look like a true empire: significantly the one field in which it did so was colonial trade and economics. There was no legal or logical basis for making a distinction between economic and other fields, though finely spun arguments were produced in the period after 1763 to do so. Yet the conventional limits of parliamentary action were clear. Parliament did not interfere in the domestic affairs of the colonies nor impose taxes on them: the one British authority which might have given the colonial empire some degree of unity did not attempt to do so. This was why the use of parliament's latent authority after 1763 to tax and control the colonies was so great a shock to them.

It was, therefore, only in the economic sphere that the British before 1763 treated their colonies as if they were an integrated empire. Government was largely free, but trade, and to some extent industry, were rigidly controlled in the interests of the metropolis. This ambivalence distinguished British practice from that of all contemporaries.

The British commercial system followed the normal pattern of *l'exclusif*. Like other colonizing powers the English applied traditional controls to colonial trade in the early seventeenth century, adapting them from metropolitan precedents such as the fourteenth-century wool staple at Calais and acts which attempted to restrict carriage of English exports to English ships. In their mature form the navigation laws began in 1651, and were expanded in a series of acts between 1660 and 1696. They embodied three principles. All trade to or from the colonies had to be carried in English (after 1707 British) owned and manned ships, so that no foreigner might enter a colonial harbour. All goods going to the colonies, whatever their place of origin, had to go through an English port and be trans-shipped there. Colonial exports which were 'enumerated' must be exported direct to an English port, even if their eventual market was elsewhere. These were the foundations of the 'old colonial system' until the 1820s.

The enforcement of these regulations was naturally made more difficult by the weakness of British executive government in the colonies. The British therefore evolved ingenious devices to ensure obedience. To ensure that 'enumerated' goods went to the right destination, captains of ships engaged in the colonial trade had to deposit substantial bonds, which were forfeit if they took their cargoes anywhere but to Britain. Ships leaving colonial ports had to pay a 'plantation duty' which was equivalent to the duty paid on entry to a British or colonial port, and these made it less profitable to take their cargoes illicitly to a foreign harbour. From 1696, a 'Naval Officer' was appointed in all colonies to enforce the navigation laws. The British Commissioners for Customs had agents in the colonies, in addition to customs officials appointed by local assemblies, to search for contraband. Vice-Admiralty courts were set up there to try cases arising out of breaches of the laws of trade. Thus control of commerce was the one sphere in which British imperial organization was really efficient and centralized.

The British also adopted the principle that colonies should not compete with the metropolis in industry: like the Spanish they banned or restricted certain colonial products. In 1699 an act forbade the loading of wool, wool yarn or cloth produced in a colony in any ship, thus limiting colonial textile production to local needs. In 1732, the Hat Act banned the export of hats from one colony to another and imposed English regulations on apprenticeship and labour. In 1750 the Iron Act banned the establishment of new slitting or rolling mills, plating forges or steel furnaces in the colonies, while encouraging the production of pig and bar iron for export to England. Although in principle harmful, these acts had little practical effect, since high labour costs and limited local markets made industrial growth very unlikely in eighteenth-century America. Conversely, shipbuilding in New England and Bermuda was encouraged because it added to the maritime strength of the empire: and an attempt by the Thames shipbuilders in 1724 to ban the industry was rejected by Parliament.

In principle, the British commercial system resembled that of Spain and other colonial powers; but its effects were much less damaging to colonial prosperity. The British never restricted colonial trade to one or more specified British ports, organized ships into annual fleets, or imposed restrictions on inter-colonial trade, other than those mentioned. From 1766 they began to liberalize the system still further by permitting foreign ships to enter specified 'free ports' in the Caribbean colonies. Moreover, the British colonies never suffered from shortage of shipping or goods, for in the eighteenth century the British merchant marine and commercial organization were the most advanced in Europe, and were illicitly supplying foreign colonies as well as those of Britain.

There were, of course, inherent disadvantages in so artificial a system of imperial trade, though, as Adam Smith pointed out in 1776, these were not all on one side. American tobacco and rice producers suffered from having to sell their products in the British market rather than in Europe: conversely, producers of timber, indigo, sugar and other goods benefited, at the price of the British taxpayer, from bounties or preferential duties on their exports. Consumers at both ends suffered from increased prices; but merchants in the colonies profited from monopoly as well as those in Britain. On balance, however, the colonies must have come off worse. One estimate puts the cost of commercial monopoly and the small duties levied in Britain on the transit trade to America at between $2·5 (£500,000) and $7 millions (£1,500,000) a year in the early 1770s.[5] Against this had to be placed the cost to Britain of colonial defence, the colonial wars of the mid-century and administration. This was recognized in the colonies. There were few complaints against the navigation laws; and as late as 1774 the American Declaration of Rights issued by the First Continental Congress stated that

> we cheerfully consent to the operation of such Acts of the British Parliament, as are *bona fide*, restrained to the regulation of our external commerce, for the purpose of securing the commercial advantages of the whole empire to the mother country, and the commercial benefits of its respective members.[6]

It is inconceivable that the subjects of any contemporary empire would have made such a declaration.

The British imperial system of the century before 1763 was aptly summed up by Edmund Burke in 1774 as a 'state of commercial servitude and civil liberty'.[7] No particular merit attached to Britain for achieving this 'happy and liberal condition', for it resulted from historical fact rather than imperial planning. Unfortunately for the British it proved impossible to preserve it, for the transitory conditions which had made it possible disappeared. The two salient features of the colonies in North America – their autonomy and their refusal to co-operate with each other – were possible only while the colonies remained small tide-water settlements insulated from each other and from the French by distance and bad communications. During the first half of the eighteenth century immigration and population growth created land hunger and a moving frontier of settlement. Within the British sphere this produced conflicts between established colonial interests and the settlers on the frontier and between different colonies for ownership of the land outside their ill-defined territorial limits. Expansion over the Appalachians led to difficulties with the Indian tribes and with the French, which were intensified by a parallel expansion of French influence. By the 1740s they had completed a line of forts from New Orleans up the Mississippi to the Great Lakes – thus putting off the British from future westward expansion – and French traders were clashing with the British vanguard in the Ohio region. Further north British expansion towards Lake Champlain brought the two nations into proximity in an area of strategic importance to both. Only the continued strength of the Iroquois Indian federation until the 1740s held the balance between these two weak European forces.

Once they had ceased to be isolated the British colonies could no longer indulge in disunity: this was shown by the Anglo-French wars of 1741–63, when the difficulty of obtaining co-operation between different colonies and between colonial militias and British regular troops suggested that centralized imperial control of colonial defence was essential. Similarly the problem of controlling the western lands, available for British settlement after 1763, could not be solved by each colony acting independently, in its own interests. The only alternatives were colonial federation or imperial regulation. The colonies refused to federate in 1754 after the Albany Congress, so there was no alternative to closer British supervision of colonial affairs. Defence and

Indian policy inevitably raised the question of finance. In the past budgetary autonomy had been feasible, since Britain undertook few imperial functions for which she had to pay. After 1763 the prospective burden of paying for a regular defence force in America in place of the colonial militias and for a system of native administration for the Indian tribes beyond the Appalachians, coming on top of a British national debt swollen by the cost of conquering Canada, forced the British to reconsider the financial question. Since the wars had also shown that the navigation laws themselves needed more effective enforcement, because many colonists evaded the wartime ban on trade with the enemy, it was clear that the 'happy and liberal condition' of the past could no longer be preserved.

The decade after 1763 was therefore a moment of truth for the British empire. 1763 did not mark the beginning of the problem; nor were the policies then put into operation suddenly arrived at, for they grew naturally from the experience of the previous twenty years. Yet to the Americans it seemed that all the old landmarks were disappearing. The British tried to impose a common defence and western lands policy; to raise taxes to pay part of its cost; to tighten up the commercial system; to regulate colonial currencies; to make an integrated empire out of a string of balkanized settlements. The ultimate, though not the immediate or necessary, result was the American revolution and the independence of the United States. The new experiment had failed. But the British did not conclude that they had been wrong in their assessment of the situation. They determined that the same problem must not be allowed to recur in their remaining colonies in the Caribbean, and in those acquired from the French and Spanish in 1763 and during the next half-century of war. The British empire in the later eighteenth and early nineteenth centuries inherited not only the inherent liberalism of the first phase of British colonization, but also the principle that colonies must be under effective imperial control. In the first British colonies the principle of liberty had been predominant: in the modern empire it was coupled with authority.

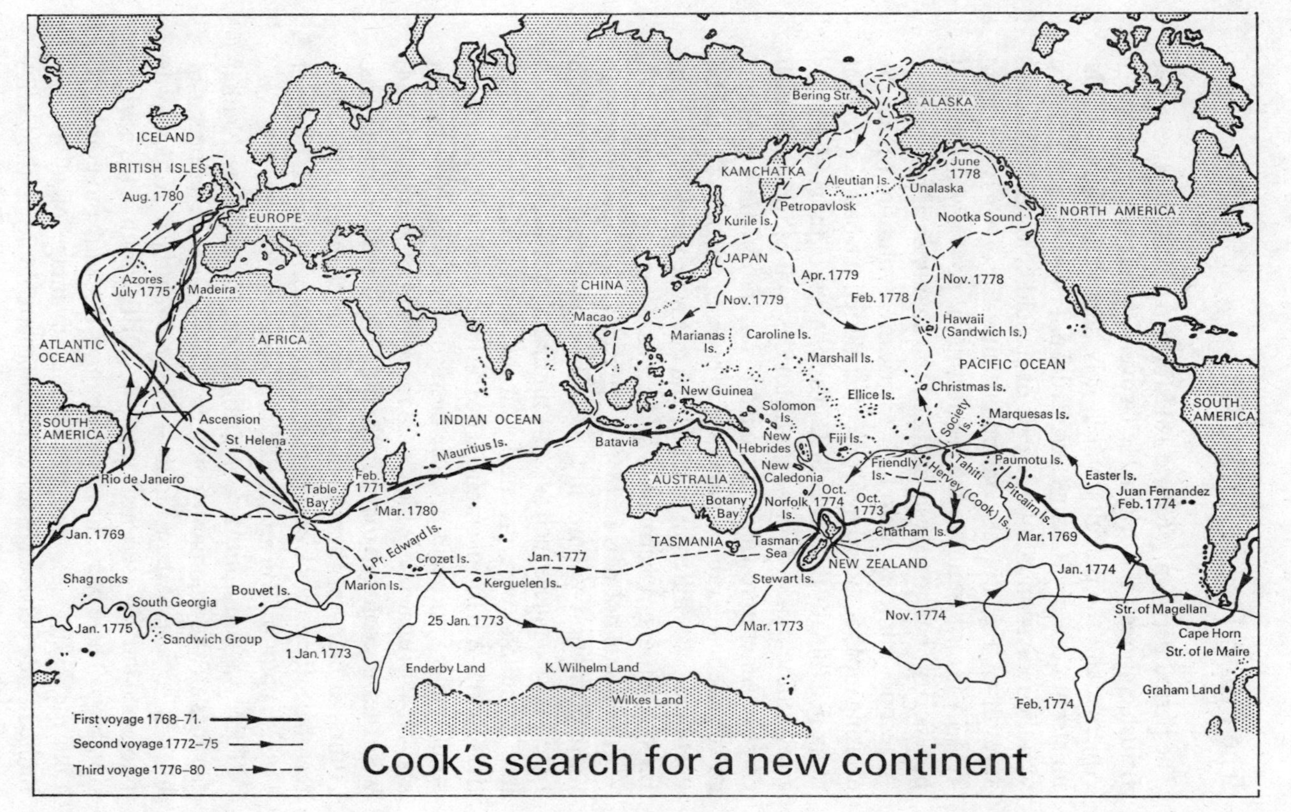

Cook's search for a new continent

The British Empire, 1763–1815

The period between 1763 and 1815 formed a bridge between two British empires – the original self-governing settlement empire in America and the polyglot and largely dependent empire of the nineteenth century. Change resulted from three events. The first was the redivision of a large part of the old colonial empires as a result of the almost continuous inter-European wars from 1756 to 1815. Britain, as the greatest naval power, was the chief beneficiary: her conquests changed the character of her empire. A second influence was the American revolution which, by excising most of the original colonies, altered the balance of what remained. Finally there was Britain's conquest of India which was a revolutionary event in world history as well as for the British empire. An empire which included two hundred million Asians as well as considerable numbers of French, Spaniards, Dutch and Portuguese was different in kind from one which had consisted of English settlers, Amerindians and negro slaves.

Yet all was not new in 1815. Continuity was most obvious in those plantation colonies in the Caribbean which (together with barely settled places such as Newfoundland, Acadia, Hudson Bay and Honduras) were practically all that remained after 1783 of the original American empire. The Caribbean colonies were constitutionally important because they, together with Nova Scotia and New Brunswick (which were carved out of Acadia in 1784) were the only colonies to retain the old representative institutions. Although many of them underwent major changes in the nineteenth century, they were the main link between the first phase of English colonization and the empire after 1815.

There was continuity also in British commercial policy. Neither the loss of the mainland colonies in 1783 nor the criticism of liberals such as Adam Smith – whose *Wealth of Nations* was published in 1776 – seriously weakened British faith in the navigation laws. There were, however, changes in detail and emphasis. Like the French the British saw the advantage of allowing a limited trade between their own and other colonies in the Caribbean for the first time since the 1660s. By opening a few 'free ports' they could infiltrate into the commercial preserves of others and draw Spanish bullion and certain non-competitive raw materials into their closed commercial systems. Provided the direct trade with Europe was still barred to foreigners, such modifications of the 'mercantile' system merely strengthened it.

Nevertheless, the loss of the mainland colonies produced a different interpretation of the purposes the navigation acts were supposed to serve. The remaining colonies were of limited value as monopolistic markets; even Caribbean sugar became less esteemed as a glut developed on the international sugar market. Conversely, the British went back to the function the first navigation acts were intended to serve – to provide the British merchant marine with guaranteed routes and so strengthen the foundations of British naval power. Hitherto economic advantage and the shipping monopoly had conveniently coincided: after the loss of North America they did not. The problem was the carrying trade of the Caribbean colonies, and whether United States ships, as now 'foreign', should be allowed to take part in it. The case for doing so was that the islands depended for their prosperity on American food and timber, on the American market for molasses, and on cheap American shipping freights. On the other hand, United States ships might well monopolize the Caribbean trade, including the supply of African slaves and the carriage of West Indian products to Europe. This in turn would deprive the British merchant marine of the 'long-haul' route to America, much valued as a 'nursery of seamen' for the royal navy. Hence the choice in 1783 was between the economic needs of the sugar islands (and the profits of British plantation owners), and the assumed needs of British naval security. The British chose security and excluded American ships, even from the free ports. The navigation acts survived the crisis and lasted intact into the 1820s. They were not finally repealed until 1849.

Yet commercial monopoly was not applied universally. In their full form the navigation laws affected only the Atlantic. In West Africa, India and other places east of the Cape they applied only to the extent that foreign ships might not trade directly between such places and Britain or British colonies. Far from being excluded, foreign ships were positively encouraged to enter ports controlled by the British. As with the free ports, their motives were realistic rather than liberal. Eastern trade operated on different principles from that in the Atlantic. India, for example, did not provide much that was wanted in Britain, apart from calicoes, which were legally excluded in order to protect the Lancashire cotton industry. Most European markets were closed to the British East India Company in favour of local companies. It was therefore profitable for the British company to sell goods in India to foreigners for sale in their own European states, and to be paid in cash in Europe. This was a convenient means of transferring home the profits made out of government in India: the chief alternative being to exchange Indian products for tea at Canton and transmit that to London. In short, a degree of multilateralism was inevitable in the eastern trade, and the British navigation acts never fully operated east of the Cape of Good Hope.

A third element of continuity between the old empire and the period after 1783 was the continued lack of effective central control. Although many new colonies lacked self-government, the tradition that London would not interfere continued almost unchanged. Improved administrative agencies were not fully used. After 1801 the colonial department within the Department of War and Colonies, though still unable to exclude other departments from interfering, was free to specialize in colonial administration; but it was not prepared to drop the older tradition. Similarly Indian affairs had been brought under the control of the British government for the first time in 1773, and Pitt's India Act of 1784 gave the new official Board of Control the right to dictate to the company in most matters other than patronage. Yet it did so only on major matters such as waging war. Domestic administration in India was left to the governors of the three Indian presidencies, Calcutta, Madras and Bombay. In 1815 the British empire was still almost as decentralized as it had been in 1763.

The British were as conservative as circumstances allowed; but it was quite impossible to treat most of their new dependencies as if they were colonies settled by Englishmen, since most were inhabited by French, Spanish, Dutch, Indians, or other races. Diversity of character and of function was the dominant feature of the enlarged British empire of 1815; and diversity of imperial policy followed inevitably.

The reasons for which a particular dependency is acquired normally determine its character and functions as a colony. The old empire had consisted almost entirely of territories which were occupied by European settlers because they wanted to live there and make use of local resources. They were governed as far as possible as if they were part of the sovereign's European dominions, on the assumption that colonists were full subjects with the same rights and interests as those in the metropolis. This was seldom true of the dependencies taken by Britain in and after 1763. Before 1815 no new possession resulted from voluntary emigration or, with the sole exception of Sierra Leone, from the enterprise of colonizing companies or individual proprietors. For the first time government rather than the subject was responsible for extending the empire, and its motives were different. Yet annexation still owed less to imperialist planning than to transient circumstances; and two main situations tended to lead to imperial expansion.

The first was a by-product of war and strategy. The recurrent large-scale wars of the period 1741–1815 pulled the colonial empires more closely into the framework of European strategy and diplomacy. Because Britain was a major participant in all these wars, and because she was a naval power, she attacked such continental enemies as France, Spain, and (after 1793) Holland at the periphery where they were weak and she was strong. In each war, except that of American independence, the British occupied many enemy colonies. For the most part they did not want to keep them: they were occupied in order to attack and distract the enemy and to acquire bills of exchange which could be cashed at the peace negotiations. But it was possible that a particular foreign colony might be retained at the peace, either because no adequate compensation was forthcoming, or because it had some special significance. This did not usually lie in its intrinsic economic value or suitability for white settlement but in its relevance to British 'strategic' interests. As early as 1713 Acadia had been kept because it dominated the sea approaches to Newfoundland and the St Lawrence and was a threat to the security of New England. Canada was retained in 1763 partly because too much money and emotion had been invested in its capture by Wolfe for the government to return it; but still more because possession would end the French threat to the mainland colonies.

Slightly different motives dictated the peace settlement of 1763 in the Caribbean. Guadeloupe was returned to France, despite its value as a sugar island, because planters in British islands feared its competition within the imperial system. Grenada was retained as a plantation colony, but Dominica only as a naval base and centre for illicit trade with foreign colonies. Florida was taken from Spain to complete British occupation of North America east of the Mississippi rather than for settlement. Elsewhere the 'strategic' motive was equally dominant in 1763. The French trading bases in Senegal were taken to end conflicts with British traders in the Gambia. The French were allowed to keep their five trading bases in India on condition that they did not fortify them or keep more troops than were necessary for internal security. As in North America the aim was to ensure that France would not endanger British predominance.

At the peace treaties of 1802 and 1815 this pattern was repeated. For some twenty years Britain possessed naval predominance and had occupied virtually all French and Dutch colonies, and some belonging to Spain. She could have retained all she wanted: she kept relatively little. Again the criterion was often strategic. Trinidad was kept in 1802 as a base for illicit trade with the Spanish Main, but it was soon occupied by British sugar planters and resembled the earlier sugar colonies, though with a polyglot population. In 1815, further islands were retained: the Dutch colonies in Guiana, because there had been immigration and investment by British planters even before 1793; Tobago and St Lucia, both French, because of their importance to the naval strategy of the Antilles. In Africa the British kept the Cape of Good Hope because it was essential to British communications with the east, and because it was now impossible to leave it in Dutch hands with the certainty that Holland would be a friendly power.

This concern to safeguard the links with India and the Far East explains most other British annexations in 1815. Mauritius was kept to deprive the French of the best harbour in the southern India ocean; the Seychelles and Maldives to prevent their being used as hostile naval bases near India. Ceylon was taken from the Dutch not for its cinnamon but for the harbour at Trincomalee, the only safe port in the Bay of Bengal during the monsoon. Penang, off the Malay coast, had been acquired by treaty with the local sultan in 1786 to safeguard the route to China and to act as a commercial entrepôt. By contrast, the Dutch were given back their entire empire in Indonesia in 1815, despite its commercial value. In 1819, the British took Singapore and in 1824 acquired Malacca by treaty with Holland. These were naval and trading bases: their occupation did not indicate regret at having returned the bulk of the Dutch colonies. Strategy also dictated what was kept in the Mediterranean: Malta and the Ionian Islands strengthened naval power east of Gibraltar and secured the tenuous route to India via Alexandria and the Red Sea.

Merely to list the acquisitions made by Britain in this period of imperial redivision shows how much her new empire differed in purpose and character from colonies occupied in the first phase of colonization. Almost all new possessions related to British naval power or commerce, or were strategically important for the safety of existing British colonies. Most had little intrinsic value for trade, production or settlement. In many the advantages hoped for proved illusory or short-lived, as the situation which gave them relevance disappeared. Penang, for example, was already seen to be valueless for the navy or for trade by 1815; others became unnecessary as a result of changes in trade routes or naval strategy, or of new international relationships. It was at this point that the special character of such colonies became evident: they became useless to the metropolis. They were the first of a type of dependency which became increasingly common in the nineteenth century: colonies of occupation rather than of settlement, which outlived the temporary situation which had once made them seem important, or failed to fill the role for which they had been cast. Unlike real settlement colonies they then became white elephants, exhibited in an imperial museum as relics of past British history.

Not all new British dependencies of the period 1763 to 1815 were the product of European wars. Apart from India there were two special cases – Sierra Leone and New South Wales – neither of which had previously been European possessions.

Sierra Leone was established in 1787 as a refuge for negro slaves freed in England as a result of Lord Mansfield's judgement in Sommersett's case in 1772. At first it was run by a group of humanitarian philanthropists who became a chartered company in 1791. By 1808 the company could no longer afford to subsidize the colony, and it was handed over to the Crown. It had little commercial value and was not suited to English immigration. It became relatively important later as a base for naval action against the slave trade and a nucleus for expansion into the interior. Its government also posed the question of how to rule a colony which was technically acquired by 'settlement' by British subjects – and so was legally entitled to the traditional constitution and laws, and yet was clearly unsuited to have them.

New South Wales was established as a penal settlement in 1788 to fill the gap created by the loss of the American colonies as a destination for transported criminals. There was no intention of creating another settlement colony: free immigration was allowed only because it was found necessary to keep the penal settlement alive. Yet from Sydney much of the later colonization of Australia and the south Pacific sprang, and hence a new generation of British settlement colonies which reproduced the character of the old American colonies.

Despite differences between them, the new British dependencies had two features in common which distinguished them from earlier British colonies. They were not inhabited by voluntary settlers of British stock; and many possessed their own distinctive laws, social customs and political institutions. It is true that in the long run some of them, notably North America, South Africa and New South Wales, received British immigrants and came to resemble the earlier American colonies. But in 1815 this was predictable only of Canada.

The special character of these dependencies forced the British to consider how they should be governed. Colonists of European extraction and inhabitants of other races became British subjects when a colony was annexed: but, unlike British emigrants to a colony 'settled' by the British in the first instance, they had no legal right to British representative institutions or laws, and for the most part did not understand or want them. Contrasting circumstances produced differing results. By 1815 the constitutional uniformity of the old empire had been destroyed. In its place were four distinct streams: the old colonial system, surviving in the Caribbean, Nova Scotia and New Brunswick; a modified version of it in Canada; autocratic government derived from previous European régimes in a number of conquered colonies; and a special form of autocracy in India and Ceylon.

The first of these systems has already been described and did not change during the period after 1763. The second was the outcome of the special circumstances of Canada after its conquest. Like all the new forms it resulted from experiment rather than planning. In 1763, the British proposed to give Quebec the old British colonial system of government, ignoring the fact that the inhabitants were French, because they expected an influx of immigrants from the older colonies and wanted to divert them to the St Lawrence rather than to the western lands where settlement would cause complications with the Indian tribes. By 1770 this immigration had not taken place, and it therefore became obvious that an English constitution and English laws were unsuited to a colony of Frenchmen. In 1774, Parliament passed the Quebec Act in the hope of buying the loyalty of the French Canadians. Quebec was given autocratic government by a governor and nominated legislative council, together with French civil law and land tenures, and political and religious equality for Roman Catholics. Quebec thus became the first British colony with a deliberately autocratic system of government, based on preserving the institutions of a foreign colony after conquest. After 1793 these concepts were generally applied to other conquered colonies.

But in Canada itself the system was short-lived. The influx of English-speaking loyalists from the south after the American war belatedly fulfilled the expectations of 1763. The French type of government and French laws were unacceptable to the new settlers: they demanded the old colonial system. Yet quite apart from its unpopularity with the French-Canadian majority, there were now objections in England to a full return to the old system. The tendency after 1783 was to blame the American revolution partly on the weakness of government and on the excessive power of the assemblies in the old colonies. An attempt was therefore made by the Constitutional Act of 1791 to give Canada constitutional freedom without destroying the power of government. Quebec was divided into the provinces of Upper and Lower Canada to separate French and English and enable the French in Lower Canada to retain their own civil law. Each colony was given an elective assembly on the old pattern, but also a large nominated legislative council as an upper house which, it was hoped, would support the Crown against the democratic tendencies of the lower. A colonial peerage was projected with the right of sitting in the council. The Church of England was established and endowed to propagate correct political and social attitudes and to act as a bulwark to the executive. The Crown retained substantial sources of revenue to reduce its financial dependence on annual votes by the assembly.

The act of 1791 created a new hybrid constitutional pattern for colonial government. Except that there would be no colonial 'ministry', since the governor would be solely responsible for administration, it was an attempt to export the essentials of the constitution of Britain as it was in the later eighteenth century, as contrasted with the seventeenth-century constitutions possessed by the older colonies. Executive government was strengthened by alliance with the legislative council, by partial financial freedom, and by its increased ability to influence the assembly through patronage. The result should have been a 'balanced' constitution as it was believed to exist at home. In fact the experiment largely failed. Minor risings in 1837 in both provinces led to further changes which eventually produced the most important British colonial 'invention' of the nineteenth century – cabinet government in a dependency.

In 1815, however, Canada was the exception to the general trend of British policy. All the other newly conquered European colonies had some form of autocratic administration which reflected their foreign origins. With the exception of British Guiana, which retained its complex Dutch institutions, the system normally consisted of a governor with power to issue ordinances; a small nominated council whose advice he could ignore; and simple administrative and legal agencies based on pre-British practice. Such usages were a complete break with the older British tradition. These colonies were not dominions of the Crown in the old sense, but dependencies alien to the British tradition.

There were precedents for such autocratic government in earlier British history; in New England between 1685 and 1688, in Acadia from 1713 to 1763 and in Senegambia from 1765 to 1783. Yet in 1763 Grenada, Dominica and Florida, like Canada, had been promised representative government and English law. Thereafter two factors led the British to think again. Experience of working the old system in colonies consisting of Frenchmen or Spaniards, complicated by a minority of English immigrants, suggested that although all colonies should ultimately be given English institutions, there were advantages in not doing so immediately. Again the probability that many of the foreign colonies occupied between 1793 and 1815 would be given back when war ended made it pointless to change their forms of government under temporary military occupation.

The crucial period came after 1815 when a solution had to be found for permanent acquisitions; by then, time and usage provided the answer. Temporary military governments based on pre-existing systems had been in operation for periods of up to twenty years. There was every convenience in preserving them rather than making new departures; in addition, the positive advantages of not having to deal with fractious local assemblies was now recognized. Two principles supported expediency. In some colonies the terms of capitulation had specified the retention of pre-British institutions or laws. The humanitarians in Britain saw the convenience of not giving plantation colonies assemblies since these could obstruct the British policy of 'ameliorating' the condition of slaves; and they further argued that it was unjust for a colony with a majority of free non-Europeans to be ruled by a small minority of propertied whites.

As a result of these varied interests and principles the wartime expedients for governing conquered colonies were transmuted into a permanent system, which later became known generically as 'Crown Colony Government'. In course of time its institutions were refined and the principles on which it was defended came to be regarded as the reason for its establishment. But 'Crown Colony Government' was, in fact, the product of historical accident.

Autocratic government inconsistent with the old British tradition had evolved for rather different reasons in India and Ceylon. India is considered elsewhere. Ceylon, which was transferred to the colonial office in 1801 after conquest from India, was the first non-European dependency with which the British colonial administration had to deal. Because it was inhabited by Asians over whom the Dutch had exercised superficial control, neither the old British system of government, nor the alternative of preserving foreign European institutions, was applicable. The British adopted the model recently created in India. They governed Ceylon 'directly' and autocratically, with a professional civil service recruited in Britain, but preserved local law and custom and used indigenous agents at the lower levels of government. Another novelty was the idealism which infected the British administration, and was expressed by an early governor as being 'to ensure the prosperity of the island solely through the medium of generally increasing the prosperity and happiness of the natives'. In 1815 Ceylon was a singular anomaly. Acquired simply for the use of Trincomalee, governed allegedly in the interests of its indigenous inhabitants, unable for some time even to pay for its own administration, it was unlike anything in previous British colonial history. Yet it was the prototype of many other colonies acquired later in Africa and the east for similarly limited reasons and then administered in the same way with similar motives.

By 1815, then, the British empire had lost its unity. More significant, it no longer consisted primarily of true colonies. The old empire had expressed the character of Britain, the new reflected her power. Its history during the next century and a half turned on this contrast between the traditions of colonization and domination. The old liberal tradition was carried on by those colonies of British settlement, old and new, which achieved self-government, and eventually became known as 'Dominions'. The rest were mere dependencies.

5

Myths and Realities of the American Empires

Colonial history is as confused by myths as that of Europe itself. Metropolitan nationalists twist facts to highlight the achievements of their own country; counter myths are fostered in one-time colonies to provide an ideological basis for nationhood. Political and economic prejudices are supported by misleading examples from the imperial record. To dispel the more obvious of these myths and draw together those features common to the colonial empires, it is proposed to examine a number of related questions. Were the colonies established by European governments to serve interests of state? How much effect had 'mercantile' regulations on their character? How profitable were colonies to their owners? Did colonies differ substantially in civilization, forms of government and the rights possessed by colonists, from the European states to which they belonged?

The root of much misunderstanding of the character of the American empires is belief that these colonies were artifacts, first brought into existence by the governments of Europe to serve their calculated interests, then moulded along 'mercantilist' lines: hence the use of the term 'mercantilist empire' to distinguish colonization before 1815 from that during the next 150 years. Study of the process of colonization and the way in which the colonies developed before 1815 suggests that this is a misleading over-simplification.

The way that colonies were originally set up in America shows how little they owed to governments or economic theories. The work was done by individuals or groups whose aim was to establish not empires but private settlements which would provide them with bullion, landed estates or refuge from persecution. Patriotism usually played a secondary role; the missionary impulse was even less important. Colonial entrepreneurs normally gained royal approval – though not always from their own sovereigns – and expected to remain loyal subjects: but they were seldom royal agents. Governments, for their part, encouraged exploration and settlement, but could do little more for lack of money. Their turn came when the colonies had been established; for, by asserting that subjects could not throw off allegiance and that all land occupied by them belonged to the Crown, they eventually made dependencies out of what might have become independent republics.

'Mercantile' regulations were part of this secondary phase, designed to give their European owners the monopoly of colonial trade and wealth. Regulations themselves were derived from long-standing European practice rather than new economic theories: the economic parochialism of the Old World was simply imposed on the New. Common traditions produced a remarkable similarity between the practices of different states. All excluded foreign ships from colonial ports; insisted that colonial trade pass through metropolitan ports in both directions; and forbade colonial products or manufactures to compete with those of the metropolis. In course of time theorists rationalized these practices into a logical system: the eighteenth century called it 'mercantilism', and assumed that colonies had been founded to serve the powers of Europe by bringing them wealth. Thus cause and effect were reversed.

There is no doubt that control of colonial trade and production had some effect on colonial economic development: the question is how much. Did colonies concentrate on primary export staples rather than on industry and indulge in monoculture instead of creating self-sufficient economies because they were made to, or because it was natural and in their best interest? Was compulsory routeing of colonial trade through metropolitan ports a real hardship to the colonies? If so, how much did this vary from one empire to another? Were 'mercantile' regulations so deeply resented that they generated the desire for total independence?

European controls had least effect on the social and economic character of the colonies which, for the most part, evolved along predictable lines. Natural endowment dictated forms of settlement and production: no theorizing could make all colonies equal, or fit them into a 'mercantilist' pattern. Areas with cold climates, poor soils and no bullion were often attractive to settlers and developed viable economic patterns based on self-sufficient agriculture, fishing, shipbuilding and trade within America; but these were unpopular in Europe for they were competitive rather than complementary with her own economy. Conversely colonies which had bullion or could grow exotic crops delighted the theorists at home; but colonists exploited these advantages irrespective of metropolitan attitudes. Fundamentally the American economy was self-determining.

The question, then, is whether these natural trends were artificially exaggerated and healthy economic development was stunted by European controls. There is no denying the existence of a 'colonial economy' in many parts of America in which the forms of production and the balance between different types of economic activity were influenced by demand in Europe; or that colonies were heavily dependent on Europe for many things. Most relied on Europe for manufactures and some even for food. Monoculture made plantation colonies vulnerable to market fluctuations, and reflected European needs. Yet neither specialization nor lack of self-sufficiency were artificial. Extreme specialization on a few export staples was common in the independent states of the Baltic and eastern Europe in the eighteenth century, and was equally typical of nineteenth-century British settlement colonies under conditions of free trade and economic freedom. In America it preceded metropolitan controls, for the Caribbean planters specialized in tobacco and sugar from the start as the only way in which they could pay for imports of necessaries or luxuries. The alternative of self-sufficiency was unattractive; and if the European market had not existed, many tropical colonies would not have been established. In short, 'mercantile' controls did not create the specialized 'colonial economy' and it survived their final abolition.

It is easy also to exaggerate the extent to which metropolitan prohibitions prevented the growth of manufactures in America. Certainly all European powers feared the growth of colonial industry because it might reduce the market for their own products. All, therefore, forbade manufactures or products which seemed inconsistent with their own interests. The question, however, is what effect such restrictions actually had on the evolution of the colonial economy.

Restrictions fell into two categories. On the one hand they prohibited or limited manufactures, such as textiles or hardware, to preserve a market for European exports; on the other they prevented the processing of primary colonial products before export to Europe. The second category was far more important. The natural line of development for primary producers was to undertake the more advanced processing of their commodities before export. But the English entirely forbade sugar refining in their colonies. The French banned new refineries after 1684, and imposed heavier duties on refined sugar on its arrival in France. The British encouraged the production of bar and pig iron, but forbade the erection of steel slitting mills. Such regulations had an adverse effect on colonial wealth and slowed down development towards a more complex economic structure. But, as regards colonial manufactures for local consumption, the case is different. Industrial development required conditions which were rare in eighteenth-century America: capital, industrial skills, good communications, a substantial local market, an ample labour force. The majority of American colonies lacked some or all of these conditions. None of the mainland British colonies had a large labour force or much capital. Plantation colonies throughout the Americas lacked all the right conditions. Only Mexico and Peru were suitable: significantly these possessed some important industries in the eighteenth century. Precisely because they closely resembled European countries in their social structure and possessed the necessary capital, they were the most industrialized. For the rest of America industrial production of more than the simplest kind was uneconomic. Only prolonged shortages of imports from Europe, the growth of an urban proletariat, or political action to foster industry by such artificial measures as high tariffs could have made industry profitable in the favoured areas; and in most parts of America no artificial stimuli could have done so. European restrictions would have had a seriously retarding effect only if they had been retained throughout the nineteenth century: but by the 1830s most surviving colonies enjoyed almost complete economic freedom.

Specialization in primary production was not, therefore, imposed on colonies striving to become industrial giants: conversely, as natural producers of cash crops, they were considerably helped by their parent states. The profitability of 'colonial groceries' such as sugar depended on European price levels. Not all colonies were equally favoured by climate or soil, and under later free trade conditions the less efficient producers were squeezed out of the market. Probably the most important effect of the 'mercantile system' was to protect the high cost producer. Bounties on the sale of favoured products in Europe and preferences against foreign competitors were the mainstay of many planters in British and French islands: the end of these stimuli in the mid-nineteenth century largely ruined the Caribbean economy. Other primary industries owed their existence to metropolitan encouragement: for example, the Carolina indigo and silk industries and the large-scale export of North American timber. Such devices tended to produce unhealthy dependence on a protected metropolitan market; but the danger became apparent only in the nineteenth century, when international free trade altered the basis of colonial economics. During the previous three centuries imperial preferences and bounties enabled colonists to develop many parts of America which would have seemed unprofitable under free trade conditions.

The really artificial aspect of the 'mercantile system' was its effect on the pattern of colonial trade rather than on forms of production: the canalization of trade constituted the main grievance of most colonists. All colonial powers insisted that exports go direct to a metropolitan port, though the British permitted a few 'non-enumerated' goods which they did not think valuable to be taken direct to their eventual markets in Europe or South America. Conversely, all colonial imports had to come from the metropolis, even if produced elsewhere. Only nationally owned and manned ships were allowed to take part in these trades. Such restrictions were the main source of imperial advantage from the colonies. They were intended to make each metropolis self-sufficient in exotic goods; to give it valuable re-exports; to provide a middleman profit for its merchants; to employ a large merchant marine; to provide work for manufacturers and producers at home; to produce a healthy trade balance and prevent the export of bullion.

The result was that trade routes generally ran direct from each colony or group to its metropolis: virtually none ran legally between colonies of different nationalities – except as allowed by the free port system of the later eighteenth century – or between a colony and a foreign European state. Today this centripetal pattern of trade, running directly from the colonial perimeter to several European centres, appears extraordinary; but again its artificiality must not be exaggerated. All countries with dependent economies tend to be linked more closely with Europe, with which they are economically complementary, than with similar countries with which they compete. Even the exclusive trade between colonies and their own metropolis was not altogether unnatural, since national links were strong and colonial production was normally dependent on the commercial facilities offered by the parent state. It was the exaggeration of this Eurocentric trading pattern that was artificial. By the later eighteenth century the economic systems of America had reached the point at which far more inter-colonial trade was desirable; and the growth of this trade, part illicit, part legal, through the free ports, indicated that the older regulations were becoming a nuisance. Yet it was less the concentration of trade with Europe than its enforced canalization to particular European states that was then unnatural: this constituted the main grievance of the American colonies in the eighteenth century.

The economic interest of colonists was to sell in the dearest market and to buy in the cheapest; to trade freely with other colonies where their needs were complementary; and to use ships of whichever nationality offered the cheapest freights and the best service. In short, the colonists wanted a multilateral rather than the unilateral system imposed by 'mercantile' regulations.

But the hardship which imperial monopoly imposed on the colonies varied greatly from one to another and at different times. The test was whether the metropolitan power offered its colonies the best and cheapest commercial services. In the earlier seventeenth century the Dutch offered what all colonies needed: hence the adoption of 'mercantile' regulations by other powers to defeat Dutch enterprise. But in the eighteenth century Britain offered the lowest shipping freights, the best commercial facilities, the longest credits, the widest range of imports and the best international market for colonial produce. She was invading the monopolies of other powers, and this suggested that she would in any circumstances have dominated her own colonial trade. Moreover, British regulations were less strict than many others. British colonies could send some commodities direct to foreign markets. Colonial-built ships qualified as 'British' and shared the shipping monopoly. Inter-colonial trade was generally unrestricted. British colonies paid more for their imports and received less for some exports than they might have done under free trade: but the hardship was not seriously felt; nor was the British trade monopoly a likely cause of colonial independence.

The remaining colonies can be scaled according to the degree of hardship they suffered from imperial trade monopoly. The Dutch settlements suffered from the monopoly of the West India Company rather than from bad commercial facilities: their interest lay in being under the direct control of the States General. The French colonies suffered rather more. France had an adequate merchant marine, especially constructed for the West Indian trade, and an advanced commercial system. She produced most of the manufactures needed by her colonies and took their exports at reasonable prices. But French colonies could have done better in all these spheres if they had been British. They suffered also from the absence of French possessions in continental America which could have provided them with additional markets, food and raw materials. They also resented the ban on the export of molasses or rum to France, and relied on illicit trade with British North-American colonies instead.

It was, therefore, the Spanish and Portuguese colonies which suffered most from imperial monopoly. Neither country had the industrial strength to supply its colonies with manufactures, and neither consumed a large proportion of its colonial exports. Much of the trade of Spanish America and Brazil would not have passed through Cadiz or Lisbon had it not been forced to do so: it was artificially routed away from its natural destination. Transit through Iberian ports was very expensive. Colonists had to pay higher freights, insurances, commissions and customs than other Americans, and received an indifferent commercial service. Until the later eighteenth century the system of annual fleets and the use of a single Iberian port made trade irregular and more liable to disruption in time of war. For Spanish and Portuguese colonists, therefore, 'mercantile' economics were more burdensome than for others in America because they were least consistent with the natural patterns of international trade. Conversely, these two powers obtained the greatest advantage from a monopolistic system and their colonies had the greatest economic incentive to demand independence.

It is easier to say that 'mercantile' regulation of colonial trade benefited the parent states and harmed colonists than to measure how much it did so. Imperial profit and colonial loss are difficult to assess. Precise measurement is impossible for lack of reliable statistics; but even if sufficient information were available, it would still be conceptually difficult to draw up a satisfactory imperial balance sheet.

A 'profit' from empire implies economic or fiscal advantages to the parent state which it would not obtain if its possessions were independent. It could be acquired in two ways: from the transfer of colonial revenues to the metropolis or from monopolistic profit on colonial trade. It is relatively easy to discover how much revenue an imperial state drew from its dependencies, though evidence is intermittent. But commercial profit is bound to be hypothetical, since it is based on the hypothesis of a free trade norm by which to measure 'mercantile' prices. Yet, even if a total sum representing gross fiscal and commercial 'profit' could be estimated, the concomitant costs of empire would have to be deducted before a 'net profit' could be arrived at. Such costs are almost impossible to estimate. What proportion of a European state's total defence expenditure should be set to the colonial account, in addition to sums directly spent on troops and ships in the colonies? How much extra did the metropolitan consumer pay for protected colonial products? It is, in fact, impossible to measure with any accuracy how much 'net profit' any European state derived from possessing an empire. It is possible only to describe the methods used to maximize advantages, and to estimate very roughly in what fields they were successful. It is also possible to calibrate the empires according to the advantages each received and the proportionate inconvenience suffered by their colonists.

The American empires fall into two categories, according to whether the metropolis expected to make a profit out of its trade monopoly alone, or out of colonial taxation as well. The French and British were in the first category, the Spanish and Portuguese in the second. The Dutch colonies, being under private company rule, were in neither. These distinctions are not absolute, since the British Crown possessed certain sources of income in the colonies which were excluded from the general colonial budget: but essentially the difference was between states which regarded colonial revenues as transferable to the metropolis, and those which accepted budgetary autonomy in the colonies.

There was no constitutional reason why the French Crown should not transfer colonial revenues to France, since colonies were not distinct kingdoms and had limited control over local taxes. In practice, however, colonial revenues always fell short of local expenditure, and France had to subsidize their defence and administration. Her only fiscal profit came from customs levied on colonial trade in the metropolitan ports, which was not strictly a colonial tax. The same was true of Britain. There was no constitutional obstacle to parliament imposing taxes on colonies for 'imperial' purposes, though the Crown could not tax a colony which had a representative assembly without parliamentary sanction. Until 1764, however, the colonies were allowed fiscal autonomy similar to that enjoyed by dominions within the British Isles. During the next decade, Britain attempted to impose revenue-producing taxes on the colonies: even so this was not to extract profit, but to force the colonists to contribute to the cost of colonial defence and the administration of the western lands. Even if taxes had been successfully imposed, they would only have reduced an existing deficit. As it was, American resistance induced the British Parliament to pass an act in 1778 renouncing their intention – though not their right – to transfer taxes raised in a colony to Britain; and this promise was never broken.

Spain and Portugal were therefore the only countries which normally transferred revenues raised in the colonies to their own treasuries, and occasional evidence suggests that the growing prosperity of several Spanish provinces and Brazil resulted in increasing transmissions as the eighteenth century went on. It has been seen that Madrid was drawing about 3·5 million pesos from New Spain in 1785, and six millions during the middle 1790s: the first worth about a million pounds sterling, the second two millions.[1] These sums came from the taxes earmarked for transmission: the rest were absorbed by local expenditure. Peru was the only other Spanish colony capable of producing a revenue surplus, but statistics are not available. Most other provinces depended on subsidies from these two and never sent money to Old Spain. Portugal too benefited from the transmission of increasing sums from Brazil in the eighteenth century. Both metropolitan powers also collected customs on colonial trade passing through their ports: since only a fraction of this trade would have touched Spain or Portugal under conditions of free trade this was more clearly a profit from commercial monopoly than the customs collected by Britain or France.

Fiscal profits were made only by the Iberian states, but commercial profits were expected by all imperial powers. Since these were, by definition, the result of artificial monopoly, they must have been greater in proportion as any one country lacked the efficiency to compete on an open market. It is, nonetheless, easier to define than to measure them. The best available evidence is on the British continental colonies; and British profit is defined as 'how much less the colonists received for their products and how much more they had to pay for their purchases because of the navigation acts than ... if their commerce had been unfettered'. For the single year 1773 this has been estimated to lie between $2,884,000 (£590,000) and $7,362,000 (£1,500,000), from which about $324,000 (£66,000) must be deducted on account of the bounties paid in Britain on colonial indigo, naval stores and lumber.[2] This profit only represented a tax of one to three dollars per head in the colonies: its worst feature was that this implied a transfer of currency to Britain from colonies which were chronically short of capital and metallic currency.

No comparable figures have been worked out for other European colonies: but if they could be estimated, and if they showed comparable profits on commercial account, this would still not prove that Europe made an overall profit on her empires; working expenses would have to be deducted to arrive at net profit. How much did it cost Europe to administer and defend her colonies? Administration itself was seldom expensive: all colonies had to cover internal expenditure, and grants in aid by the metropolis were regarded as exceptional. Defence was a different matter, since it was the main service provided by a metropolis in return for the economic subordination of its colonies. The cost of maintaining regular land or naval forces in the colonies and of fighting other European powers to defend them could easily obliterate the profits laboriously squeezed out of colonial revenues and commercial monopoly. How expensive was colonial defence before 1815?

The history of colonial defence falls into two patterns, dividing in the 1750s. In the earlier period European governments spent little on defending their possessions. Very few regular troops or naval vessels were kept in America by any power. Colonies relied for their security, even in time of European wars, on local militias paid for out of local revenues. Distance from each other and from Europe was their main defence: major efforts made by Britain under Cromwell and again in the 1740s to capture Spanish possessions failed because an effective attack could not be mounted at so great a distance. The Anglo-French struggle between 1713 and 1756 in North America was fought mainly by colonial militias, with naval support as the main metropolitan contribution. Under such conditions, colonial defence was not a major imperial change.

Changes began in the 1750s. During the Seven Years War the British made America a major sphere of operations, and so forced other powers to take colonial defence seriously. After the conquest of Canada the British decided to keep an army of 10,000 regulars in North America at an estimated annual cost of £350,000. Naval costs were additional. It was recognized that such expenses would reduce or annihilate commercial profits: even the Stamp Duty imposed in 1765 to offset military expense would have produced only an estimated £60,000 a year. The conclusion seemed obvious to contemporaries: colonies became a fiscal liability if they had to be defended by regular armies as well as by expensive fleets. Adam Smith, writing in 1776, concluded that, if one took into account the cost to Britain of administering and defending her colonies, and the interest due on debts she had incurred for their defence in the past, 'Great Britain derives nothing but loss from the dominion which she assumes over her colonies'.[3] Two years earlier Dean Josiah Tucker had written that by giving the colonies independence 'we shall then save between 3 and 400,000*l.* a Year by being discharged from the Payment of any civil or military Establishment belonging to the Colonies...'.[4]

Other countries had the same experience. The French, frightened by the loss of Canada and British occupation of several of their Caribbean islands, stationed regular troops in their colonies, and founded permanent regiments for colonial service. They found the cost prohibitive, and had to make constitutional concessions to the colonists in return for new taxes. The Spanish and Portuguese followed suit. For them, however, colonial defence meant a reduction of the sums available for transmission home rather than subsidies from the metropolitan treasury. New Spain, for example, spent more than two million pesos (£650,000) on defence out of a total of 5·8 million pesos (£1,750,000) available for all local purposes in the years 1785–9.[5] In short, the recurrent wars of the later eighteenth century altered many assumptions on which the imperial balance sheet had previously been assessed, and posed a question of great importance to the modern empires: how much was it worth spending on colonies before they became economically unprofitable?

A tentative conclusion would, however, be that American colonies were a source of economic profit to all metropolitan powers in the eighteenth century: monopoly weighted the balance against the colonists. Yet 'mercantilism' had one further effect: it redistributed the advantages of American trade. American colonies were bound to increase the wealth of Europe, even under free trade conditions, simply by increasing the volume of trade and stimulating production. Without 'mercantile' restrictions, these advantages would have gone to whichever countries had the greatest industrial and commercial capacity. The main effect of economic nationalism was therefore to enable economically weak countries like Portugal and Spain to receive an unrequited share of the advantages of New World trade. Conversely, although the British obtained higher profits from their own colonies by their monopoly, they stood to gain far more by freedom to trade with other colonial areas. In short, 'mercantilism' was as much a way of defending the trade of non-competitive European powers as of mulcting the colonists. Free trade in the nineteenth century merely redistributed the colonial trade according to the economic capacity of European states, depriving the weak of their previous share.

The influence of 'mercantile' controls on the foundation and economic growth of the American colonies was therefore less than proponents and critics generally supposed. In government also the peculiarity and artificiality of colonial systems have been much exaggerated and the constitutional relationship of colony with metropolis misunderstood.

Modern attitudes to colonial government assume that colonists have ultimately the right to be independent; colonial constitutions are assessed according to the autonomy they provide and their propensity to prepare colonists to rule themselves. A conflict of interest between colony and metropolis is taken for granted and metropolitan authority is presumed to rest on force rather than consent. Colonial nationalism rather than acceptance of common imperial nationality and loyalty to the metropolis is taken to be inevitable.

These assumptions were incorrect for most American colonies before 1815. Imperial authority was not endured as an imposition but accepted as a permanent state. Colonies were not separate organisms but provinces or dominions of the Crown. This is not, in fact, surprising. The original settlers, even though they acted primarily in their own interests, believed that they were serving also those of their country. They did not cease to think of themselves as Spaniards or Frenchmen: if anything, patriotism was stimulated by isolation and by reliance on the metropolis for protection and trade. As late as 1776, many British subjects in the future United States found it difficult to conceive of a separate nationality and feared sovereign independence. Colonists, in short, were inherently loyal. Had they not been so, the colonial empires could not have survived as they did for periods of up to three hundred years. Certainly no European state possessed sufficient military or police powers to impose allegiance on a colony which wanted independence.

The assumption that metropolitan authority was imposed on colonists anxious to found independent states across the Atlantic generated the myth that forms of colonial government were deliberately concocted by metropolitan states to impose arbitrary rule on the colonies. This is quite untrue and leads to fundamental misunderstanding of the character of American colonization. Colonial government was no more arbitrary than that of the parent states, and no special forms of constitution were contrived for American colonies. Each colonizing power automatically exported a simplified form of its own system of government and law. Colonists had approximately the same political rights as they would have possessed at home. Spanish, French and Portuguese creoles had no representative assemblies and did not vote their own taxes: but parliamentary systems were practically defunct in Spain, France and Portugal. Government by bureaucrats was equally an export from continental Europe. Municipal government in France or Spain was as tightly controlled by officials as in America. Conversely countries with a strong parliamentary tradition expected colonists to share in legislation and taxation. England gave her colonies replicas of her own constitution, and colonists were more likely to be represented in their local assemblies than most Englishmen in the parliament at Westminster. Even the Dutch companies conceded representation of the planters in the government of the Guiana colonies. In short, subjects of each power in America were about as free politically as they would have been at home.

Colonists did not, therefore, have any basic constitutional grievance. What they disliked was not the form of colonial government but the practice of running it by European expatriates. This practice varied in extent from one empire to another. In Spanish colonies all senior posts, such as viceroy, governor, judge or senior officer in the militia, were held by peninsular Spaniards. In the British colonies expatriates were few; though colonists suffered from the practice by which the patent of an office was granted to a non-resident at home, and his duties performed by a deputy. The use of expatriates was justified on the grounds that they would give disinterested government and could be relied on to enforce imperial rules, especially the laws of trade. For the most part the practice was accepted; though in the more developed Spanish colonies it was becoming a significant grievance by the early nineteenth century.

Yet government by expatriates did not mean arbitrary government. Colonists were full subjects: they took their legal rights with them, and the Spanish extended these to all Amerindians within the limits of effective occupation. The basis of all New World society was the rule of law, which restricted the powers of government and made the courts the safeguard of the settler. A colonist was probably more secure against royal power in a French colony than in France, for the Crown did not use extra-legal agencies in the colonies. The full importance of these facts can be fully seen only by comparison with modern European possessions in Africa and the east, for there few non-European 'nationals' were full subjects, and arbitrary justice by unqualified officials became the norm.

Hence a correct interpretation of the political character of the old colonial empires begins with the fact that these were not mere dependencies but dominions of their sovereigns, differing little from other possessions of the Crown. Each country interpreted this relationship in different terms: the Spanish thought of parallel kingdoms like Aragon; the British of new dominions like Ireland; the French as provinces comparable to Lorraine. Similarity of status did not imply identity of function or practice. Colonies had special fiscal relations with the metropolis and their trade was treated differently. But contrasts were less important than similarities. The Atlantic was broader than the Irish Channel; but the English did not think Massachusetts different in kind from Ireland.

In the last resort, it was not 'mercantilism' nor political subordination that produced the special character of the American colonies, but the fact that they were colonies of European settlement. There were similar colonies in the modern period in Canada, Australasia, South Africa, and, with some differences, in Central Africa and Algeria. But apart from these, the modern empires were alien, consisting of colonies which lacked any organic connexion with their metropolitan states. Europe reproduced herself in America as she seldom did again. American colonies were not commercial artifacts but extensions of Europe herself, differing little from the inner ring of European colonies which had been occupied first and had acted as stepping stones to the west – Ireland, the Azores, Canaries, Madeiras and Iceland. All were organic European societies, created by settlers who took with them as much of their own environment as could be transported. American conditions favoured them. In some places climate was comparable to that of their homelands. Nowhere was a native civilization strong enough to give a decided twist to their way of life. Relative proximity to Europe enabled close links to be preserved, and continued emigration from parent states strengthened national similarities. American societies were necessarily different from those of Europe simply because they were new, and because many Old World institutions failed to take root there. But enough survived to stamp colonial society so indelibly with the character of its parent stock that a century and a half of independence had not eradicated it by the second half of the twentieth century.

6

The Disintegration of the American Empires

Imperial Redivision and Colonial Nationalism

The history of the European colonial empires falls into two overlapping cycles. The first began in the fifteenth century and ended soon after 1800; the second in the later eighteenth century, lasting into the twentieth. During the first cycle European power centred on America; in the second on Africa and Asia. There was no chronological break between them, and no reason why Europe should not continue to control America while she occupied other continents. But the disintegration of most of the original American empires in the period 1763–1830 constituted a water-shed between two epochs and changed the character of European imperialism. This alone justifies using the terms 'old' and 'modern' empires.

Why did the American empires break up after three centuries and at a time when they seemed more prosperous and more valuable than ever? Two processes were at work. The first was the redivision of existing empires between the imperial powers; the second the total rejection of European authority by American colonists.

Redivision of one colonial empire among others was cannibalistic. It was common before about 1660, for late colonizers such as France, England and Holland were formally barred from overseas expansion by the allocation of all non-Christian areas of the world to Spain and Portugal by papal bulls. This was unrealistic and could not be sustained. Yet most French and English colonies in America consisted of places which Spain had not bothered to occupy: her rights rather than her empire were re-divided. The Dutch were more obviously predators, creating their empire in Brazil, West Africa and the east from established Portuguese possessions. Between 1600 and 1756, however, remarkably few colonies changed hands. The Dutch made no new acquisitions. France took only San Domingo and Louisiana from Spain and some Caribbean islands and West African bases from the Dutch. The British seized only French Acadia, St Kitts and areas France claimed in Hudson Bay and Newfoundland.

The main period of imperial redivision was from 1756 to 1815 By then the extension of effective occupation throughout most of America made it difficult for any power to expand without ejecting a previous occupant. Outward pressures by existing colonies, commercial rivalries and the strategic problems of war provided the incentives. The British were the beneficiaries and the French the losers. By 1815 France had been deprived of all colonies in continental North America, retaining only her Caribbean islands; Cayenne; and St Pierre-et-Miquelon as fishing bases in the mouth of the St Lawrence. The Dutch lost Guiana, the Cape of Good Hope, Ceylon and other smaller possessions, also to Britain, and almost ceased to be an American power. Spain, rather surprisingly, lost only Trinidad to Britain, and regained Florida in compensation. Portugal lost nothing.

Changes, therefore, were relatively few: it was particularly surprising that Spain and Portugal, the weakest colonial powers, lost so little. Portugal escaped because she was a faithful ally of Britain. Spain was a British enemy in all wars from 1739 to 1783, and for periods after 1793. She escaped further loss for two reasons. British wartime strategy concentrated on defeating France in North America and the Caribbean rather than on occupying colonies for their own sake. Again, the British did not really want the larger Spanish colonies. They now recognized, as Cromwell had not when he attacked Spanish America in 1655, that it was difficult to conquer and unprofitable to hold down large foreign territories. Spanish colonies were important to Britain as markets and as sources of bullion and raw materials.

Britain was happy to leave Spain to administer them while British merchants infiltrated their markets. Hence the Iberian empires survived until 1815 largely because it was now anachronistic to conquer foreign colonies simply to possess them. The eventual independence of Latin America served British interests quite as well as incorporation into the British empire would have done.

Far more significant than the transfer of colonies from one master to another was the process by which colonies threw off European authority and became sovereign states. By 1830 continental America consisted of a number of independent states and a small minority of surviving colonies. The thirteen original British colonies formed the United States, leaving Britain only with Canada and other small settlements such as Nova Scotia, New Brunswick and Newfoundland. In central and southern America the only remaining colonies were those of France, Britain and Holland in Guiana. In the Caribbean the empires remained virtually intact, though French San Domingo had become the sovereign republic of Haiti. Europe had virtually lost control of America.

It is important not to assume that American independence was inevitable and always predictable: it was, rather, one of the most astonishing events in the history of European expansion. Analogies with the end of European rule in Africa and Asia during the twentieth century are false. In India, for example, the British were an alien race. Their authority depended on power and Indian nationalism was bound eventually to resent alien domination. All that has already been said about American colonization indicates that there European authority rested on firmer foundations. American colonies were the natural offspring of their parent states, sharing their institutions, culture and religion. Spanish colonies remained loyal for some three hundred years, British colonies for up to a century and a half. They had never been held by military power: before 1756 there were very few European troops in America, and even later these were too few to hold down empires covering half continents. Authority was very precariously supported by force; rebellions could be put down only if imperial action was adequately supported by loyal colonists.

It is essential, therefore, to approach the question of colonial independence with the assumption that loyalty was the norm and rebellion a break with long-established tradition. From this starting point two questions arise. Why did normally loyal colonies throw off their allegiance? Why were they successful in doing so? Such complex issues require detailed chronological treatment. In a short account it is possible only to isolate those circumstances which might make colonists of any nationality waver in their loyalty and to analyse the situations which led to the independence of the United States, the Spanish colonies, Haiti and Brazil.

The basis of imperial authority was the mental attitude of the colonist. His acceptance of subordination – whether through a positive sense of common interest with the parent state, or through inability to conceive of any alternative – made empire durable. Conversely the solvent of loyalty was colonial awareness that their interests were different from those of the metropolis: this was the root of colonial nationalism. How far did Americans accept their position as subjects of European sovereigns during the eighteenth century? Which aspects of empire were most important in eroding their loyalty?

There was a fundamental ambivalence in the attitude of all Americans to their parent states in the eighteenth century resulting from a conflict between loyalty to their sovereigns and awareness of their separate identity as Americans. They accepted their status as subjects because, as settlers or descendants of emigrants, it was natural to do so. Loyalty sprang from common race, language, religion and institutions. It was immensely strengthened by the lack of any alternative to subjection. Until the United States demonstrated that rebellious colonies could remain free, it was assumed that colonies were too weak to stand alone; so that rebellion from one master must lead to subordination to another. Since colonists valued their own laws, institutions and religion, transfer to a foreign power was regarded as a disaster. The British thought they were conferring benefits on the French Canadians after 1763 by offering them British laws and liberal political institutions: the Canadians thought otherwise. Thus habit underpinned natural colonial loyalty. Such loyalty was not, however, unconditional; it certainly did not imply blind obedience to the metropolis. Perhaps the best definition of American attitudes is that while they were fundamentally loyal, they were also habitually disobedient. Disobedience grew inevitably from the inconvenience of many imperial regulations and the relative ease with which they could be evaded. Evasion was the safety valve of American allegiance: if it became impossible, empire would be in jeopardy. The American empires rested on a nice and quite accidental balance between imperial restrictions and the capacity of colonists to evade them.

Against this basic colonial loyalty must be set the growth of colonial nationality. In all white settlements still under the rule of their original metropolitan states, the nature and extent of nationalism is difficult to define. The American colonist was conscious of his local interest and had strong local loyalties which increased in course of time. He resented the arrogance of metropolitan officials and measures which subordinated local interests to those of the parent state. He was likely to think himself a Peruvian, Brazilian, French Canadian or Virginian as well as a Spaniard, etc. The balance varied according to situation and social class. For all colonists local advantage preponderated over imperial interests, but awareness of distinct colonial nationality often varied in inverse ratio to social status. The successful and wealthy colonist was normally the most European in outlook. He tended to educate his children in Europe, to visit his parent state, even to take governmental service there as a compensation for exclusion from senior offices in America. Conversely, the less-wealthy colonists – the *mestizo* of Spanish America, the frontier farmer, European immigrant or urban worker of British North America – was less conscious of Europe, received fewer advantages from the imperial connexion, and was narrowly concerned with local affairs. For such men European nationality and loyalties meant little: they were true Americans in their parochialism and often in their conscious rejection of the Old World. It was no accident that much of the support for independence movements eventually came from men of relatively low social status, and from the frontiers rather than from the centres of trade, government and civilization.

There was always a possibility that this balance between American nationalism and loyalty to the parent state would be disturbed: but colonies were not perennially poised on the verge of rebellion because of their economic, fiscal or political subordination. For all their material progress and apparent capacity to stand on their own feet, American colonies were firmly established within a conventional pattern of imperial relationships. The danger to imperial authority arose not from conservatism but from innovation or a sudden crisis. Colonies were likely to remain loyal so long as they did not lose any of their existing rights or advantages: changes, even leading to greater efficiency, were a probable source of distrust. New taxes, new commercial monopolies, increased demands for military service, new administrative or legal institutions, were the solvent of colonial contentment. So were new ideas, such as those of the European Enlightenment, the revolution in British North America or the French Revolution. Most dangerous of all was a break in the continuity of metropolitan rule. The imperial balance depended on continuity. If colonies were left without European control even for relatively short periods and had to fend for themselves, the mental habits of centuries might be dissipated. Once suspended, the regulations and institutions which had always been accepted would seem intolerable. The American empires were the product of history: they were old bottles which could not contain new wine.

Change was the direct cause of rebellion and independence throughout America: but in each case it was war between the imperial powers that directly or indirectly disturbed the *status quo*. Inter-imperial wars had different effects on each imperial system at different times. Revolution in the British continental colonies resulted indirectly from the aftermath of the Seven Years War. For the other empires the Napoleonic wars were equally decisive, though for different reasons. To this extent the disintegration of the American empires was the penalty Europe paid for her domestic feuds.

The Revolt of the British Colonies, 1763–83

The revolt of the thirteen British continental colonies was the most important event in the history of European expansion since the discovery of America by Columbus. For the first time European settlers deliberately rejected European authority and succeeded not only in defying their own metropolis but also in remaining free of other predatory powers. The British colonists thus created a revolutionary ideology, based on the hypothesis that Americans had interests distinct from those of Europe, which was bound to have repercussions throughout the Americas.

Given the delicate balance between colonial self-consciousness and loyalty to Europe it was, of course, always likely that the scales might some day tilt towards independence. The surprising thing was that this should happen first in the British colonies, which had fewer grounds for resenting metropolitan authority than any others. Had Spanish or Portuguese colonists rebelled in the mid-eighteenth century, their action might be taken to prove that the old imperial systems were intolerable. The British colonists did not rebel against their traditional status within the British empire but against the changes made in this system after about 1763. Innovation, not conservatism, was the solvent of the first British empire.

The wars between Britain and France in the period 1741–63 and the territorial alterations they produced in North America, changed the assumptions on which the British colonial system had been based. The wars made co-ordination essential both between British forces and colonial militias, and between the governments and troops of the different colonies. It was no longer possible for each of the thirteen settlements to act as if it had no neighbours. Yet the colonies refused in 1754 to accept any federal authority to co-ordinate their military activities. They left Britain the task of running the war and of imposing some degree of unity. Once victory was won and the French out of Canada, colonists assumed the need for co-operation and British supervision was ended.

The British did not share this view. Victory merely brought new problems. The French were no longer in Canada: but it remained possible that France would invade it when she was next at war with Britain, and that the French Canadians would rise in welcome. Moreover the removal of French forts to the west of the British colonies opened the way for a vast movement from the tidewater settlements into the middle west as land became short in the old colonies and the flood of immigration from Europe passed through. This in turn created new difficulties almost as great as those created by the French, for the western lands were inhabited by Amerindians. The moving frontier of settlement created a racial problem which was similar to that in Spanish America and was to become common in parts of Africa in the next century.

The French threat and the Amerindian problem together convinced the British that it would be necessary to maintain a substantial army in North America. Experience of organizing colonial militias during the wars indicated that this must be a regular force supplied and controlled by Britain: the general rising of Indian tribes under Pontiac in May 1763, which threatened all the forts taken over from the French from the Great Lakes to Florida, seemed to prove this a right decision, for the colonies were most reluctant to call out their militias. Yet, necessary though the policy seemed to the British, it was the main root of the American revolution. The British maintained that the army and a system of military posts to control the western lands were necessary for the security of the colonists. As colonies were not prepared to supply forces themselves, the British would have to do so; and it was reasonable that the colonists should defray part of the costs. This in turn meant that the colonial assemblies must be persuaded to vote money to reduce British expenses; and that if they refused, the British parliament must break new ground by imposing taxes on them. As the colonists made it clear that they would not vote money of their own accord, the British Parliament duly imposed additional customs duties on colonial trade in 1764, with the stated aim of raising revenue rather than controlling the pattern of trade; and followed this by the Stamp Act of 1765, which made it obligatory for colonists to pay a duty on a wide range of legal documents and publications. Three years later further import duties were imposed, again with the stated aim of raising revenue.

This use of parliamentary authority to tax the British colonies was a natural outcome of their new strategic and demographic situation: it did not indicate that Britain had suddenly adopted Spanish or Portuguese ideas and hoped to obtain a fiscal profit from her dependencies. Yet American taxation had a catastrophic effect on the British colonial system. The taxes were not particularly heavy: the colonists would have remained the lightest taxed in America. They resented these British impositions as unnecessary because they did not accept the need for a regular army in North America; as unjust because they believed they already made a substantial contribution to British wealth through the imperial trade monopoly; as novel, because they believed that dominions of the Crown had always been allowed to control their own taxation. The dominions within the British Isles did so through their own assemblies, and those in America had never been taxed by an act of the imperial parliament. Between views so radically opposed, both on the practical needs of the situation and on the constitutional principles at stake, there could be no compromise.

American taxation was the most important, but not the only cause of discontent. A more general consequence of the war period was a new British determination to enforce existing commercial and other imperial regulations more effectively than before. Colonial evasion of the ban on trading with enemy islands during the wars had irritated British opinion, and the navy was now accustomed to a more effective supervision of American waters to catch smugglers than ever before. Hence, steps were taken throughout the decade after 1763 to tighten the customs service and make the vice-admiralty courts more effective in condemning smugglers. Unlike taxation, these measures raised no point of principle; but they gave the impression that imperial authority was now pressing more hardly on the colonies than ever before. This impression was strengthened by a number of isolated acts, such as the 1764 Currency Act, extending the existing New England ban on the use of paper money as legal tender, and the 1765 Quartering Act, which applied in the colonies the English common law obligation to supply billets and certain provisions to regular troops. In isolation all these measures could be justified by precedent: in conjunction with taxation they seemed to constitute a new colonial policy, a calculated attack on the liberties hitherto enjoyed by the colonists. Burke stated the point accurately in 1774:

> Any of these innumerable regulations, perhaps, would not have alarmed alone; some might be thought reasonable; the multitude struck them with terror.[1]

Here lay the roots of the American revolution.

In a general sense, therefore, the British colonies rebelled in 1776 because they valued the conditions which had existed before 1763 and resented attempts made thereafter to change them. Yet this is over-simplification. If the revolutionary war had begun in 1765 or 1766 it could be explained as a direct reaction to innovation. In fact, it did not begin until 1775–6: and long before then many of the substantive grievances had been remedied. Most taxes had been withdrawn, and those that remained had ceased to be talked about. The attempt to enforce commercial and monetary regulations continued, and British troops were still stationed in North America: but these were not inconsistent with the previous relationship between colonies and metropolis. Even the vast paper debate that raged in the 1760s over taxation and associated issues had almost burnt itself out by 1770. In fact, 1763 and 1776 did not stand as simple cause and effect.

The revolution itself was the outcome of an historical process too complex to be fully described here. The controversy over taxation and other specific colonial grievances had by-products which were more important than the issue themselves. The result of the taxation question was that Americans had to think about their constitutional rights and their relationship with Britain: they had to think of themselves as Americans rather than as British subjects and to define the limits of their obligations. It would be too much to say that they argued themselves into demanding independence because they could not accept the British interpretation of their status: but it is undeniable that by the early 1770s most Americans were so conscious of their legal and customary 'rights' that they were not prepared to give Britain the benefit of the doubt and assume she possessed the powers she claimed. The debate over colonial rights made the Americans ungovernable from Westminster, and incapable of being fitted into an imperial framework. By 1774 the only possible relationship with Britain was one in which colonial autonomy was virtually complete: and the American reaction to the so-called 'Intolerable Acts' of 1774, by which the British Parliament tried to punish Boston for the outrage of the Boston Tea Party, showed that they had lost the colonial mentality in the course of arguing about their rights.

The other product of the controversies of the 1760s and early 1770s was even more important. In all colonies metropolitan rule was based on the active co-operation of the colonial upper class of landowners, merchants and professional men – of those who had the greatest stake in the imperial connexion and could control the lower classes both in their own interests and in those of the metropolis. In 1763, the upper classes were loyal and firmly in control of colonial government. By 1775 they were partially disaffected and had largely lost control of government and society. Their influence had passed to different groups, led to some extent by radicals of the upper class, such as Samuel Adams of Boston, but more by men of lesser status and greater radicalism: lawyers, small farmers, artisans in the bigger towns. These radicals saw the outcry against British innovations as their chance to obtain political predominance at home. By being the most uncompromisingly American they gained the initiative in local assemblies and urban politics. By using the town mobs against British tax-collectors, customs officers and soldiers they showed how colonial resistance could be organized and where real power lay. Some of them wanted independence from the start as a matter of belief; the majority were probably less interested in principles than in the political importance they could obtain by being in the van of the nationalist movement. By 1774 radicals were in control of most of New England, and had powerful cells in most of the other colonies. It was not yet certain that they would gain universal control; and if they failed there was still the chance that a compromise settlement with Britain could be reached. The events of 1774–6 ensured that the radicals would win and that they would carry the thirteen colonies into a war for independence.

The colonial Congress which met at Philadelphia in September 1774 was critical for the future of British power in North America. Its nominal purpose was to make some response to the four 'Intolerable Acts' recently passed by the British government – the closure of Boston harbour until compensation was paid for the loss of East India Company tea; the remodelling of the Massachusetts constitution; and two other acts relating to trial of British officials and the quartering of troops. But it was still more important as the first real trial of strength on an intercolonial level between loyalists, moderates and radicals. If the radicals won, a colonial rebellion was almost certain, whatever measures were agreed on to influence the British government. By clever political tactics the radicals did win. Although the Declaration of Colonial Rights drawn up by the Congress was moderate in tone and involved the use of the now traditional embargo on British trade as a means of inducing Britain to make concessions, the concessions demanded were clearly unacceptable. The radicals calculated the British would refuse to withdraw the objectionable acts because to do so would mean abdicating all authority in America; and that this refusal would swing the majority of waverers in the colonies to the radical side and prepare them for full independence. By 1776 these expectations were proved correct. British concessions fell short of colonial demands; sporadic fighting began in 1775 in Massachusetts; only war could decide the issue. In May 1775, Congress voted to raise a colonial army. On 4 July 1776, it issued the Declaration of Independence. It remained only to see whether so brave a claim could be made good against the power of the metropolis.

It is unnecessary to describe the American revolutionary war. The relevant question is why the colonists were able to acquire total independence. They did so for two reasons.

Victory for the British had to be political as well as military. They were fighting to make the colonists accept imperial authority for the future; and this could be achieved only if the loyalists gained predominance within America itself and could then offer satisfactory conditions for future Anglo-American relations. This did not happen. The loyalists lost the moral and political initiative to their more dynamic radical opponents in 1774–6. They received little help from British military strategy, which never aimed to build up areas in which loyalists were dominant, and merely used them as military recruits. British military failures, particularly the key defeat of General Burgoyne's army at Saratoga in October 1777, encouraged the radicals and made the loyalist cause seem hopeless. By 1778 Britain had lost the battle for American loyalty; independence had become a national rather than a party cause.

Militarily the war was not finally lost by 1778: so long as opinion in Britain supported the King and Lord North in believing that it must be won, British naval and land forces might eventually have worn down colonial resistance to the point at which Congress had to ask for peace on terms short of full independence. If the war had remained a purely colonial one this might well have happened. The United States was saved by France, whose alliance with the rebels in February 1778 turned the rebellion into an international struggle. Spain joined the alliance in April 1779; Holland began hostilities in 1780 as a protest against British seizure of neutral ships carrying contraband. Thereafter the future of America depended on external factors. Washington's unstable army was strengthened by French troops; French naval forces broke the British blockade of colonial ports and prevented Britain from supporting her land forces by sea. The decisive victory of Washington at Yorktown in October 1781 was the consequence of Britain's temporary loss of naval predominance. Thereafter, despite British naval successes in 1782, American independence was certain. The resignation of Lord North in February 1782 led directly to negotiations with Congress; and the peace preliminaries signed in November 1782 recognized the sovereign independence of the United States.

The End of the Spanish-American Empire

The revolutionary movements which led to the independence of Spanish America differed from the revolt of the British colonies;

yet they had one feature in common. Neither in Latin nor in British America was revolution a reaction against the subordinate position traditionally assigned to the colonies. In each case it grew indirectly from disturbances in the traditional relationship between colonies and metropolis which led to fundamental changes in the structure of colonial society itself.

If colonial rebellion is assumed to reflect the defects of imperial rule it must be surprising that the Spanish colonists did not rise long before 1808. Spanish colonial administration left little opportunity for creoles to hold the highest offices; it was tightly controlled from Madrid, and therefore slow and inefficient. Changes late in the eighteenth century tended to make subordination less acceptable. The *intendencia* system led to tighter enforcement of regulations and deprived many creoles of valuable posts. Greater defence costs and metropolitan poverty led to heavier taxation and larger transmissions of revenues to Old Spain. Governmental monopolies of tobacco and spirits, dating from 1752, caused hardship to producers and consumers. Moreover Spanish America was now feeling the impact of radical ideas generated in North America and Europe.

On the economic side, admittedly, Old Spain did much to liberalize the system of commercial monopoly in the eighteenth century. The *flota* system was abolished; all peninsular ports were opened to colonial trade; colonies could trade freely among themselves; the slave *asiento* was replaced by competition between suppliers. Yet concessions did not keep pace with the economic growth of Spanish America. Rich provinces like New Spain and Peru were booming; hitherto undeveloped areas such as Venezuela, Cuba and the Argentine were expanding their exports of primary products. Even under the liberalized commercial system Old Spain could not supply the markets or the European goods the colonies needed. Colonial necessities were increasingly met by contraband trade with British possessions in the Caribbean and with the United States, which became easier under wartime conditions after 1793. Yet the contraband trade was no answer to Spanish colonial needs: it was expensive and risky. On the assumption that colonists were prone to rebel against economic inconvenience, movements for independence might have been expected on economic grounds in the late-eighteenth or early-nineteenth centuries.

The fact that they did not demonstrated the stability of the Spanish colonial system. Apart from a local rising of the *comuneros* of New Granada in 1780 against the tobacco monopoly and increased taxation, there is no evidence that any Spanish possession was on the verge of revolution before 1808. Indeed, when a Spanish officer born in Caracas, Francisco Miranda, who had adopted the republican ideals of the American and French revolutions and had made the liberation of the Spanish colonies his life work since 1790, arrived in Venezuela with a small British force in 1806 he could not induce his fellow creoles to rise against the powerless Spanish authorities. In the same year creoles in Buenos Aires rallied against the British naval force under Sir Home Popham which occupied the town. Thus, even during a war in which Old Spain had lost the power to enforce obedience, the dominant classes in the colonies remained essentially loyal.

The event which led to the independence of Spanish America was the occupation of Old Spain by Napoleon in 1808 and the abdication of Charles IV in favour of Joseph Bonaparte. Allegiance to the rightful ruler was the link between the colonies and Spain: for the first time in three hundred years it was broken. The creoles felt no obligation to an alien monarch. They had therefore the alternatives of recognizing Ferdinand VII as the legitimate heir to Charles and waiting for his restoration; or declaring their independence as republics. In a spectacular demonstration of loyalty every American province recognized Ferdinand, often against the inclination of their governors to obey Joseph. On his effective accession to the Spanish throne in 1814 Ferdinand was nominally still king of all his Spanish dominions.

Yet the intervening six years had momentous results. The decision to recognize Ferdinand was taken in most places by specially convened *juntas* of officials and leading creoles, often based on the traditional *cabildo abierto*, the enlarged municipal council. So momentous a popular decision was itself revolutionary in an absolute monarchy: it meant that in America Ferdinand was king by voluntary adoption rather than prescriptive right. Moreover, the fact that, unlike the exiled Portuguese royal family, he remained in Europe, meant that the American provinces were in effect republics for six years. Royal officials had to depend on creole support. If they proved difficult, they were simply replaced by others. Even a full royal restoration could not erase this experience of self-government by self-co-opted committees.

More important still, rule by local *juntas* meant the beginning of politics and split the colonial class structure. For three hundred years colonists had lacked institutions which could express the needs and aspirations of the people as a whole. Royal government had largely served the interests of the creole upper class who were its main supporters. The dependence of the *juntas*, consisting of notables, on popular support opened the political arena to other segments of society. Every provincial or municipal council became a political forcing house, and the split in the upper class over loyalty to Ferdinand cracked the framework of colonial society. Parties seldom followed class lines. In Venezuela, for example, the republicans were led by Miranda and then by another member of a rich creole family, Simon Bolivar. They were defeated by royalist forces led by a one-time Spanish sergeant, Boves, at the head of an army consisting of *mestizo* herdsmen and Indians from the back-country. Party struggles thus broke the upper class unity on which Spanish authority had ultimately depended.

Another product of the interregnum was the growth of social radicalism. Self-government by *juntas* inevitably brought to the surface many latent conflicts of interest which Spanish authority had so far concealed: between great landowners and frontiersmen; between wealthy merchants, with their vested interest in the monopolistic trading system, and the smaller traders, shopkeepers and consumers who stood to gain from free trade; between urban oligarchs and aspiring *mestizo* politicians; between creoles and Indians. Such conflicts cut across the royalist-republican division and transcended it. They implied the beginning of a social revolution. By 1814 many parts of Spanish America were seething with new ambitions and domestic rivalries which could not be stopped by a restoration of royal power.

But perhaps the most important product of the interregnum was the growth of colonial and provincial nationalism. This intensified awareness of the distinct interests of colonies and metropolis was partly the result of imported ideology – as in the case of educated creoles such as Bolivar: but also of the isolation of the colonies and their experience of fending for themselves. Post-war Spanish government would have to take more account of American interests and treat the colonies more as sister states under the same Crown than as mere dependencies. Wartime attitudes in Old Spain were, however, unpromising. The regency government and *cortes* in Cadiz, which upheld the cause of Ferdinand VII, was politically liberal. It legalized representative provincial and municipal councils in America, and appointed colonial representatives to sit in the metropolitan *cortes*. Yet it emulated the French republicans of the previous decade in hoping to tie the colonies more closely to Old Spain: in particular they refused to legalize colonial trade with foreigners, even though the colonies were virtually incapable of trading with Old Spain, and in fact traded freely with British colonies and the United States. Thus even the more liberal peninsular Spaniards failed to appreciate the changed conditions of the American colonies: the far less liberal restoration monarchy expected to return to the state of affairs that had existed before 1808.

In 1814, when Ferdinand VII was restored and colonial loyalty could become a reality, the omens for the Spanish colonial empire looked favourable. Royalist parties had won out everywhere, though the ruling *junta* in the Argentine had declared its independence of Old Spain and retained only allegiance to the person of the King. In Peru there was no republican party of importance; and in Mexico republican risings had been suppressed.

Within ten years all the continental colonies were independent republics: Spain had lost her empire except for the Caribbean islands and small territories in Africa and the Pacific. Why was this? Independence was certainly not inevitable anywhere except perhaps the Argentine. It came because it proved impossible to re-establish the old balance between American nationalism and colonial loyalty. The task was made much more difficult by the inability of the restored monarchy to understand the problem. Colonial royalism was to some extent conditional: it would lose its force if the restored monarchy did not show awareness of the interests of its American subjects; and without royalist support the Crown could not reimpose or sustain its authority in America. The Spanish monarchy showed that it had learned nothing. It attempted to restore royal government in its old form, to use military force rather than persuasion, and to reimpose commercial monopoly. Such reactionary measures did not automatically produce rebellion and colonial independence, but they were intensely unpopular, and weakened royalist parties by providing arguments for use by republicans. Wartime royalism had assumed reasonable reforms by the restored monarchy: its blank conservatism virtually wrecked the conservative and royalist cause in America.

The decline in colonial loyalty after 1814 was decisive because Old Spain lacked the military or naval capacity to conquer or hold down provinces as vast as those of Spanish America. Between 1811 and 1819 about 42,000 peninsular troops were sent to America; only about 23,000 survived disease, war and desertion in 1820. The royalist cause depended on colonial troops, and there were never enough regulars to deal with widespread rebel movements or guerillas. Moreover, Spanish naval power was insufficient to move large numbers of troops to America, to blockade rebel ports or defend royal ones. The conquest of Chile and the attack on Peru in 1818–20 by republican forces from the Argentine was made possible by the inability of Spanish naval forces to defeat the small rebel squadron under the ex-British naval officer, Cochrane. Never was it more obvious that naval power was essential to maintain a colonial empire.

In the last resort independence was the outcome of a struggle within the American colonies fought out between republicans and loyalists in which Old Spain played a relatively unimportant part. But such self-determination depended on the powers of Europe keeping the ring: the danger to the republican parties was that the restored Bourbons in France, with the support of other absolute rulers in Austria and Russia, would give military support to Old Spain. Such interference was prevented by

Britain. Her government remained officially neutral throughout, and banned British subjects from serving under foreign flags. Yet Britain had a major interest in the success of the revolutionary parties, since independence would legally open Spanish American ports to British trade. The government therefore refused to join an international alliance proposed in 1817 to reconquer the rebellious colonies. In 1822 Britain announced at the Congress of Verona that she had given *de facto* recognition to several ex-colonies, and refused to support the French invasion of Old Spain to restore the absolute monarchy. Meantime Spanish republicans obtained war supplies and money from unofficial sources in Britain, and a number of British subjects served in their armies and navies. In 1823 Canning made it clear to France that Britain regarded the independence of the Spanish colonies already achieved, although formal recognition would take time; and warned her off intervention. In the last resort, therefore, the independence of Spanish America was due as much to British naval power as to the efforts of the rebel forces. The Monroe Doctrine of 1823 was a corollary of the British declaration of the same year and was made possible by it, for the United States could not have prevented European intervention on her own account.

The domestic struggles within Spanish America which arose out of dissatisfaction with the restored régime after 1814 were too many and complex to be described. The main strength of the rebel movements in South America lay in the Argentine which, as the only colony which did not accept royal officials after 1814 – though protesting its loyalty until 1816 – felt obliged to liberate others and thus protect her own position. Between 1817 and 1818 San Martin, an Argentinian creole, took an army to Chile, and conquered it with the help of local republicans and Cochrane's naval force. In 1821 he occupied Lima, declared Peru an independent state, and retired. His satisfaction was premature, for royalist forces reoccupied Lima in 1822, and Peru was not 'liberated' again until 1824, Callao holding out in the royalist cause until 1826. This reconquest was the work not of Peruvians but of Simon Bolivar coming from the north. As a man pledged to make Venezuela and New Granada independent, he had begun an apparently impossible compaign there in 1816, relying on armies of guerillas recruited from the *mestizos* and Indians of the frontier regions. In the course of several heroic and also extremely barbarous campaigns he was in effective control of Venezuela and New Granada by 1821. Thereafter he turned to the conquest of Peru, which he had achieved by 1824. His aim was to weld all these territories into a single state, Colombia. But by his death in 1830, Colombia had split into its component parts, coinciding roughly with the old Spanish provinces or sub-provinces: Colombia (New Granada); Venezuela; Bolivia (Upper Peru); Ecuador (Guayaquil and Quito) and Peru.

This fragmentation and the political chaos which accompanied it symbolized the impact of Bolivar's campaigns on South American society and government. Obsessed with the justice of his cause, he used the resources of the uncivilized frontier against the towns, and stirred up resentments against constituted authority. Victory did not necessarily imply that the majority supported him: merely that irregular troops could not be suppressed by small regular forces and that loyalists had lost the initiative. Bolivar destroyed more than he created. Since the Spanish left no tradition of representative government, the vacuum created by the removal of royal authority was not filled. Power depended on armed force: the tradition of rule by military *juntas* had come to stay.

By 1824 the northern colonies also were free, but had escaped these horrors. Mexico seemed stable in 1814. Loyalists had put down several republican risings, and conservatives felt a strong interest in the Spanish connexion as a means of suppressing social radicalism. But in 1820–21 the royalist party split. General Iturbide declared New Spain to be independent of Old Spain, though recognizing Ferdinand as Emperor of the new Mexican Empire. This nominal allegiance was denounced by Spain. Iturbide became emperor in his own right; was forced to abdicate in 1823; and Mexico began her long period of political instability. Her independence entailed that of the Central American provinces which had been under Mexican control. Honduras, Nicaragua, San Salvador and Costa Rica all became separate states, rejecting union with Mexico or each other, and thus reproduced the political weakness of much of the southern continent.

By 1824, Spain had no empire in continental America. She had lost her colonies not because they had found her rule intolerable after three hundred years, but because her authority could not be reimposed after an accidental break of six years. Loyalty remained strong in principle, but it could no longer stand up successfully against the attacks of republicans. The balance between loyalty and nationalism had been destroyed.

The Independence of Haiti

The only French colony to become independent before 1815 was Haiti, formerly the French half of San Domingo. Although small and less important than the continental colonies, Haiti was the only Caribbean island to throw off European authority in this period, and the only plantation colony in which the slave and mulatto population ever seized control of government and economic life from the planter class.

Haitian independence was the product of an extraordinary combination of circumstances. Slave rebellions, always likely in plantation colonies, were normally put down by local militias or metropolitan troops. In Haiti slave rebellion was stimulated by the French Revolution, and suppression was made impossible first by political chaos resulting from the Revolution and then by war with Britain.

In 1789, French San Domingo was the most prosperous of all the Caribbean plantation colonies. It had a population of about 32,000 whites, 24,000 mulattoes and some 450,000 slaves. Its trade was considerable. Of the 562 ships that reached France from her American colonies in 1774, 353 came from San Domingo, and much additional trade was done with the United States and foreign islands through the colony's three free ports.[2] Politically, as has been seen, San Domingo was freer than any other French possession. Yet the planters were extremely dissatisfied. Unlike the other islands San Domingo was capable of doing without the French preferential market for its sugar, and resented French monopoly. On the eve of the Revolution it was thought possible that the planters would eventually try to throw off French authority.

The Revolution gave them autonomy. They did not wait for the French legislature to provide a more liberal constitution, but set up a virtually republican system on their own initiative. Yet the Revolution was potentially dangerous for planters in any colony which relied on slave labour and in which even free mulattoes had no political rights. The impact of revolutionary ideas and the rights of man on San Domingo was dynamic. The mulattoes were the first unprivileged community to react. They demanded political rights for all free coloureds, and rebelled when they were refused them. The rising was suppressed; but already rumours were circulating that the Revolution would free all slaves. France did not formally abolish slavery until February 1794; but slave risings broke out in most parts of the island in 1793 and the planters had to take refuge in the towns. The situation was made worse by the outbreak of war. British and Spanish forces invaded the island and were welcomed by many of the slaves.

Paradoxically, the revolutionary idea temporarily saved San Domingo for France. To meet the crisis the French commissioner in the island announced in August 1793 that all slaves were free. This immediately won the slaves to the French side. Their able leader, Toussaint L'Ouverture, who had been supporting the Spanish, now rallied to France. The foreign forces were ejected, and in 1795 Spain ceded her part of the island to France. San Domingo was now nominally loyal, but cut off by the British naval blockade. It therefore remained a republic governed by Toussaint L'Ouverture as dictator. France could only wait until peace enabled her to bring the colony under effective control again.

This opportunity came in 1802 with the Peace of Amiens; the difficult question was how a republic governed by ex-slaves could be converted into a dependency. Napoleon made certain the attempt would fail by announcing that slavery would be retained wherever it still existed, and giving secret orders that it was to be reintroduced elsewhere. Slavery was reimposed in

Guadeloupe in April 1802. In San Domingo the French governor, Leclerc, had managed to win the support of senior negro officers by playing on their jealousy of Toussaint L'Ouverture and had sent him prisoner to France. The prospects for reimposing French authority were therefore good. The news that slavery was to be reintroduced destroyed Haitian goodwill. The negro army revolted. Leclerc's French troops could probably have defeated them, but they were struck down with yellow fever, and the survivors were glad to be taken off by a British ship. The renewal of war and the British blockade in 1803 prevented another French attack until 1815; and in 1809 the Spanish half of the island threw off its short-lived allegiance to France. The result was an independent negro republic. Peace after 1815 gave France another opportunity to impose her authority; but after ten years of indecision in the face of pressures from exiled planters, the Restoration government decided the task was too expensive. In 1825, Charles X formally recognized the independence of Haiti on condition of an indemnity to planters for loss of their estates.

The Separation of Portugal and Brazil

The separation of Brazil from Portugal was even more directly an accidental result of the Napoleonic wars. The Brazilians had as much reason as Spanish colonists to resent metropolitan authority: they suffered from expatriate officials, centralized control, commercial monopoly and the transfer of colonial revenue to the metropolis. Yet there was no sign of separatist movements before 1807. There were small groups of republicans and Freemasons; but Brazil was far less sophisticated and open to new ideas than the more advanced regions of Spanish America. The creole upper class was generally loyal and conservative. Only a major disruption of the imperial system could produce a serious demand for Brazilian independence.

The disruption began when the regent of Portugal, Dom John, together with the mad Queen Maria I and the court, had to leave Lisbon in 1807 before the French occupied it. Alone among the emigré royal families of Europe they fled to the New World. Rio de Janeiro suddenly became the capital of the Portuguese empire, and in 1815 Brazil was declared a full sister kingdom of Portugal. Such elevation brought with it the advantages and some of the inconveniences normally possessed by a sovereign state. Brazil was now free to trade with all friendly countries and to develop her own industries. She acquired supreme courts of law, a national bank, a printing press, an official gazette, a military academy and a medical school. Economic freedom brought increased wealth; but the court and many of the trappings of sovereignty were expensive, and peninsular Portuguese monopolized most of the higher posts. Brazilian reactions were therefore mixed. Most were proud of their new status as the centre of the empire. The socially ambitious were able to buy titles and honours. But the republican movement was strengthened by the conspicuous expenditure of the court, and nationalism was stimulated by the pre-eminence of Europeans. The lesser provinces resented the unprecedented predominance of Rio, and a major rising occurred in Pernambuco in 1817.

The critical period for Brazil came after the liberation of Portugal by Wellington in 1811. The royal family were free to return to Lisbon; if they did so Brazil would revert to being a Portuguese dependency. The question was whether she would accept relegation. In fact the crisis was postponed until after 1820 by the court's preference for Rio where the regent – who became John VI of Portugal on the death of Maria in 1816 – chose to stay. The issue was ultimately forced when Portugal revolted against being merely a province of Brazil. Portugal was seething with discontent. Nationalists disliked continuing British influence; commercial interests wanted the revival of the old monopolistic system of colonial trade on which their wealth depended; the treasury was empty for lack of Brazilian subsidies; democratic forces demanded a liberal constitution. A liberal revolution broke out in 1820, and the regency summoned the *cortes* after a lapse of a hundred years. John reluctantly returned to Lisbon in 1821, leaving his son and heir, Dom Pedro, as regent.

The question thereafter was whether Portugal and Brazil could coexist as sister kingdoms; and this depended on the attitude taken by the liberal *cortes* in Lisbon. Like the Spanish *cortes*, however, this body was illiberal on imperial matters. Its aim was to reduce Brazil to its pre-war position. Portuguese acts dissolved the central Brazilian government at Rio and placed the provinces under metropolitan departments again. New legal, financial and other institutions were abolished to increase dependence on Portugal. The navigation laws were reimposed. This was short-sighted: Brazil was not prepared to return to subordination. The republican movement revived in São Paulo and Minas Gerais and demanded independence. The royalists were equally resentful; but they could combine nationalism and royalism only if a member of the royal family stayed in Rio as king or regent. Their dilemma was resolved by Pedro agreeing to be legitimate ruler of the kingdom of Brazil, and republicans and radicals were mollified by the promise of a liberal constitution. Thus united round the heir to the throne, Brazil formally renounced the authority of Portugal in September 1822 and crowned Pedro Emperor. Portuguese regular troops who refused to accept the new situation were expelled from strongholds such as Bahia with the help of naval forces under Admiral Cochrane, who had now left Chilean service. By the end of 1823 Portugal had lost all power in Brazil.

Formal separation was completed by British diplomacy. In 1825 George Canning negotiated a treaty by which Portugal recognized Brazilian independence in return for Brazil undertaking a debt of £1,400,000 due by Portugal to Britain, and paying £600,000 to John VI for his properties in Brazil. Brazil gained British recognition as a sovereign state, but had to renew the economic privileges Britain had enjoyed under treaty with Portugal and sign a convention against the slave trade. Even so Pedro did not formally renounce his claim to the Portuguese throne, though it was certain that he would not try to occupy it. Instead he abdicated in 1826, on the death of his father, but attempted to impose a constitutional charter on Portugal and bequeath the throne to his daughter Dona Maria. His brother, Dom Miguel, was to be regent on condition of marrying Maria. This tenuous connexion between the royal families in Brazil and Portugal was ended in 1828 when Miguel became King of Portugal in his own right as the result of a popular revolution.

Thus the independence of Brazil, like that of Spanish America, was the direct outcome of a temporary suspension of the traditional imperial relationship which led to a new national self-awareness in Brazil. The refusal of the Portuguese *cortes* to accept the new position after 1820 ended three hundred years of close association. In one aspect, however, Brazil was unique: she succeeded in combining nationalism with loyalty to the Crown. For sixty years Brazil remained a monarchy under the Braganza family until the creation of a republic in 1889.

7

Europeans in Africa before 1815

During the eighteenth century European empires in America reached their peak, and the foundations of European power were laid in the east. But in Africa there was little evidence of European activity. This is at first sight surprising, for the earliest European overseas expansion took place in North-West and West Africa. During the fifteenth century the Portuguese established bases on the west coast at Arguin, Elmina, São Tomé, and San Salvador; their discovery of the Cape of Good Hope in 1487 led to occupation of the main existing ports of East Africa – Sofala, Mozambique and others, extending as far as the Red Sea and Ormuz. During the sixteenth century it seemed possible that Portugal might establish territorial colonies in the Congo region, Angola and up the Zambezi, where adventurers and missionaries were following the same paths as *conquistadores* and religious orders in Spanish America. But gradually these enterprises withered. The Portuguese Crown lost interest in exploration and conversion; India and the east monopolized its energies; Africa was seen either as an obstacle on the route to the Indies or as a source of gold dust and ivory and of slaves for the American plantations. Portugal showed no desire or capacity to develop its coastal bases into colonies.

In due course other European countries adopted Portuguese attitudes and practices. The Dutch, English and French saw Africa in relation to America or the east. Their governments authorized private companies to acquire whatever bases they needed for trade. From the west coast these drew slaves for sale in America and whatever gold and ivory they could get. They by-passed western Africa south of the Niger altogether, and made no contacts in East Africa because the Portuguese or Arabs controlled all the ports. The Dutch established a port of call at the Cape of Good Hope, but thought of it merely as a revictualling depot for their ships. The French, failing to establish a secure foothold in Madagascar as an entrepôt for India, used Bourbon and Ile de France. The British, possessing only St Helena, relied on Dutch friendship after 1688 and used the Cape.

Before 1815, then, Europeans remained on the periphery of Africa, ignorant of its interior and uninterested in colonization. Yet even this marginal involvement was historically significant, for it supplied the nuclei from which expansion throughout Africa eventually grew.

The Portuguese position differed from that of other Europeans in that they had bases on the east as well as the west coast, and these were full colonies with royal administrations. In addition, theirs was an empire in decline rather than one yet to be made. But there was little to distinguish Portuguese from other bases. Angola, with its two ports of Kabinda and Massamedes, had a formal colonial government, with a military governor, judicial and financial officials and a garrison which exercised some authority inland, up the valley of the Kwango. The Congo area had been abandoned; even the Angolan bases were maintained only for slave trading, and were dependencies of Brazil whose market they supplied. The trade was run by Portuguese firms which bought a monopoly of rights for defined periods and paid a duty on slaves exported. The eighteenth-century demand for slaves brought some wealth to Angolan ports, but slaving was incompatible with territorial empire, and created an economic wilderness between the coast and the inland limits of Portuguese influence.

The other area in West Africa still claimed by the Portuguese, now that foreigners had taken their Gold Coast forts, was Portuguese Guinea. This was supervised, rather than governed, from the Cape Verde Islands. The Portuguese traded there, and missions were still active; but there was no slaving and no permanent settlement.

On the east coast the once promising Portuguese empire had

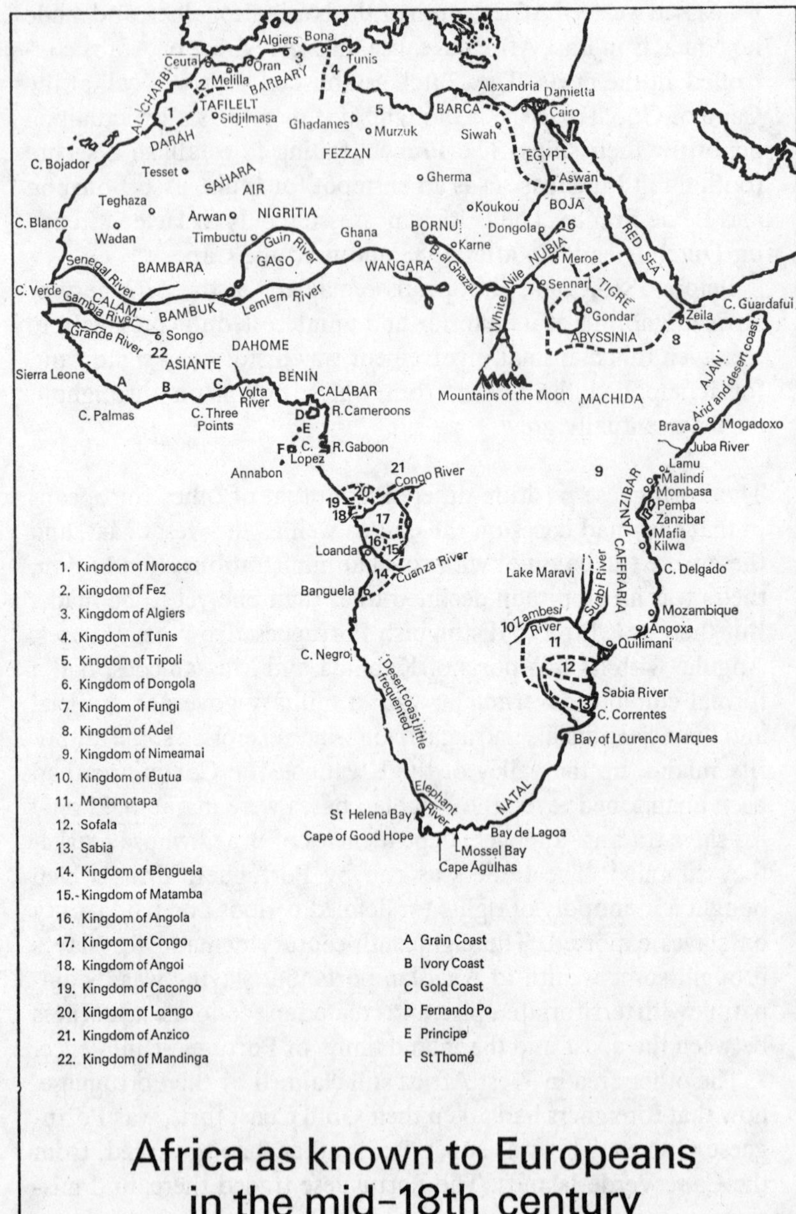

Africa as known to Europeans in the mid-18th century

shrunk to almost nothing by 1700. Portugal's power along the coast had succumbed to three different pressures during the seventeenth century. The Dutch attacked shipping and seized the Indian and eastern bases whose trade had previously brought wealth to Portuguese East Africa. Arabs were expanding from the north, and captured all ports north of Zanzibar. Inland the Changamires empire had broken the power of the Monomatapas, the allies of Portugal, and weakened her influence south of the Zambezi. Mozambique remained the Portuguese capital and became independent of Goa in 1752. But its only wealth came from the small export of slaves to Angola and its services to ships *en route* for India. It retained shadowy claims to allegiance and tribute from Africans inland, and from the *prazeros*, descendants of Portuguese adventurers who had created semi-feudal estates up the Zambezi similar to those of the *donatários* of Brazil or the early *conquistadores* of Spanish America. But the fact that the Crown had been unable to recall these grants of political authority and replace them by effective royal government, as it had done in Brazil, showed how weak Portugal was in East Africa. In the eighteenth century these *prazos* were left isolated like the feudal estates of the Anglo-Normans in mediaeval Ireland; and like these Anglo-Irish, the *prazeros* had gone native. They became important only during the period of partition late in the nineteenth century, when they provided Portugal with evidence of effective occupation of parts of central Africa.

Portuguese power in Africa was waning during the eighteenth century: that of Britain was surprisingly increasing. From the start the British thought of Africa as a source of slaves for America and an obstacle on the route to India. They established no proper colonies, and left private companies to run the slave trade. From the early seventeenth century privileges or monopolies of the West African trade were granted to private companies, culminating in the charter given to the Royal African Company in 1672, a joint-stock body, resembling the East India Company. It lasted until 1750; but its difficulties demonstrated the problems which faced all Europeans in Africa, and the reason why territorial empires were so slow to develop.

The basic problem was that it was not commercially profitable to maintain permanent bases simply for the slave trade. The company's forts – Fort James on the Gambia, Cape Coast Castle and subordinate factories on the Gold Coast – were thought necessary for security against Africans and European rivals. But administration ate into profits. Rent had to be paid to local African rulers. The supply of slaves was irregular, and African middlemen, who had a monopoly of supplying a fixed market, used it to force up the price. Service in the forts was dangerous to health; company servants were unreliable and corrupt as well as short-lived. Private merchants could usually make better profits by operating from ships or off-shore hulks, buying in any of the markets run by independent African rulers.

The British forts were retained for fear that Britain might lose her foothold on the Gold Coast, but the Royal African Company gradually decayed. Interlopers before 1698, and then private merchants who were legally entitled to use the company's facilities on payment of duties, destroyed its monopoly of supplying the British plantations in America. Wars with France increased defence costs and led to loss of ships. Decreased trade made administrative expenses more burdensome. The company received parliamentary subsidies from 1730, but was glad to give up its charter and responsibilities in 1750. Even then the bases and factories were retained. From 1750 to 1821 they were administered by the Company of Merchants Trading to Africa – a regulated, not joint-stock, corporation, to which any merchant could belong on payment of a small fee. Administration on the coast was kept to a minimum, with only a governor, a small council and a few soldiers at Cape Coast Castle and a chief and a small military force at the other bases. Even so the company was always in financial difficulties. It was dissolved and its possessions vested in the Crown in 1821; but in 1828 a new committee of London merchants was set up to administer the Gold Coast bases under supervision of the governor of Sierra Leone.

Nearly two centuries of British activity on the Gold Coast had produced no significant expansion of territory or influence. The reason was that under West African conditions trade alone was not likely to lead to colonization of any sort, and the slave trade inhibited economic activities which might have generated inland contacts. Hence the end of the British slave trade in 1807, which removed the chief commercial functions of these bases without immediately providing any substitute, made it probable that they would eventually be given up. But by 1815 Britain had other possessions in West Africa, Sierra Leone and the Gambia, and also the Cape of Good Hope, which were not slaving centres, but genuine colonies. The Cape was the most important of these; but, since it was acquired only in 1795, its problems can best be considered in relation to the previous Dutch rule.

Fort James on the Gambia was quite as unimportant as the Gold Coast bases. Its history was different because the French had nearby bases, and its trade consisted of spirit gum and other honest commodities rather than slaves. The French had a Gambian trading fort at Albreda, but their main sphere of interest was at St Louis and on the River Senegal. Competition between the two companies resulted from their desire to monopolize the supply of spirit gum which was used in processing printed silks in Europe. In addition there was gold and ivory to be bought. Yet war between Britain and France rather than commercial rivalry between two weak companies led to territorial consolidation. In 1758 a strong British naval expedition captured all French bases in West Africa. This was part of Pitt's general war strategy rather than a bid for empire: but all French possessions except Goree were retained at the Peace of Paris, and were incorporated into the new royal colony of Senegambia.

Senegambia was the first real British colony in Africa, and a classic example of the colonial hybrids wars could produce. It was given a constitution by act of parliament in 1765 – the first act ever to constitute a new British colony – which provided for a governor, executive and legislative councils (though with no representative element), a military establishment and an impressive array of English courts of law and administrative agencies. Trade was free to all British subjects and religious freedom guaranteed. Constitutionally this system was interesting as the first autocratic colonial government deliberately constructed to meet the needs of a non-settlement colony by the British, a forerunner of the 1774 Quebec Act system in Canada and ultimately of Crown Colony government in the nineteenth century. But like many of its successors it was expensive to run, and over-complex for a very primitive colony. Since it relied on grants-in-aid it might well have been modified or given up altogether in course of time: in fact Senegambia was destroyed abruptly in 1783 when Senegal and other pre-1763 French possessions were given back. Britain retained only the Gambia. It was still a royal colony, but was handed back for economical administration by the Company of Merchants as a mere trading factory.

Despite this, and although Lord Shelburne defended the loss of Senegal in 1783 with the classic argument that territorial empire in West Africa was undesirable and a monopoly of the gum trade impossible to achieve, these events and their residue were historically important. The Gambia remained a formal British colony and was far more difficult to give up than a base which was merely rented from Africans. The fact that all inhabitants were full British subjects coupled with commercial interests of resident merchants always defeated moves to evacuate it or give it to the French. Like every firm foreign base in Africa it eventually became a nucleus for commercial and territorial growth.

Sierra Leone was the other full British possession in West Africa in 1815, and its birth symbolized new forces which were to dictate later European attitudes to Africa. On eighteenth-century principles it should never have been acquired. An earlier base had been given up as unprofitable and it was not wanted for slaving, trade or British occupation. A settlement was made there in 1787 simply to provide a refuge for West Indian slaves liberated in England as a result of Lord Mansfield's 1772 judgement that slavery had no force there. This first settlement was destroyed by local Africans. Another was made at Freetown in 1791, this time by a chartered company which, like some of the early seventeenth-century American colonizing companies, hoped to combine modest profit with philanthropy. Financially it was disappointed. Sierra Leone did not pay its way, and in 1808 the company asked the Crown to take over its responsibilities. The significant fact was that it agreed to do so. The colony was saved by two novel considerations. There would have been a politically dangerous outcry from influential humanitarians if it had been given up; the abolition of the slave trade the previous year forced the Admiralty to look for a suitable naval base from which their ships could police the approaches to the slave markets. Freetown answered this purpose. It was retained, and became the centre of British authority in West Africa, in place of Cape Coast Castle. Sierra Leone was given a system of government like that of Senegambia after 1765, and had a court of Vice-Admiralty to deal with slavers caught by the navy.

In 1815, therefore, the British had two royal colonies as well as several trading forts in West Africa. Despite the end of the British slave trade it was certain that the British would remain there; but their reasons for doing so were now different. Suppression of slaving was primary; the development of a legitimate commerce came second. Together these provided the roots from which most British activities in West Africa grew during the next sixty years.

French attitudes to Africa before 1815 resembled those of Britain. France had no bases outside West Africa, and was interested only in slaves and other minor forms of trade. The French Crown showed no interest in colonies and left the slave trade to monopolistic trading companies. By 1718 a series of such chartered companies had come and gone, always financially ruined by wars and the costs of administration, leaving behind them French forts at Arguin, Goree and St Louis and factories on the River Senegal, in Gambia and on the Guinea coast. From 1729 to 1763 the West African monopoly was held by the Company of the Indies which was rather more energetic than its predecessors, and undertook some exploration up the Senegal. But it kept only the simplest administration at St Louis and the slave trade was largely run by private merchants under company licence.

War in Europe and its effects on the African trade routes wrecked this company as it did the British. In 1763 it gave up its monopoly and the surviving French base at Goree and the factories at Joal and Portendic were run by the Crown. The return of Senegal in 1783 enlarged French territories which continued to be under direct royal administration, but did not lead to further expansion. After 1793 wars practically destroyed French trade to Africa. In 1815 France was in a similar position to Britain. She was pledged to stop her slave trade (although this was not finally done until 1830), and to suppress that of others. Her legitimate trade was still small, but an expensive administration had to be kept in St Louis. Yet in the following century these relics of slaving and a small legitimate trade grew into the French empire in West Africa.

A number of other European states had slaving bases at various times in West Africa. The Brandenburg Company did so from 1682 to 1717, when it sold out to the Dutch. The Danes also had bases from which they took slaves to their West Indian entrepôt at St Thomas. Even the Spanish, who had kept out of Africa since 1494 in fulfilment of their treaty with Portugal, acquired Fernando Po and Annobon from Portugal in 1778 in response to the demand of their America colonies for slaves. Yet none of these enterprises was the starting point of a later territorial empire in Africa. In the eighteenth century only the Dutch were as important as the British or French, and they too later ceased to be an African power.

West Africa fell within the monopoly of the Dutch West India Company and was complementary to the empire it planned to build in America. The company rapidly acquired a string of Portuguese bases from Arguin to Angola, but lost most of them again to the Portuguese, French or British. In the eighteenth century its main base was Elmina, on the Gold Coast, and it had a few lesser factories from which it supplied the Dutch Guiana plantations and foreign possessions in America. It lost its monopoly, except for the supply of slaves to Guiana, in the 1730s, but maintained its forts and factories for the use of Dutch traders on payment of duties. On the dissolution of the company in 1791 these bases passed to the States General, but they showed no desire to extend them. By 1815 only Elmina was of any significance.

In West Africa the Dutch did nothing distinctive. Their special achievement was to create the first true European settlement colony in Africa, though by accident rather than design. The Portuguese left the Cape of Good Hope alone: the Dutch East India Company, whose trading monopoly began there, decided to use it as a port of call for ships on the eastern run. They encouraged limited immigration from Holland not because they wanted to create a colony but to grow provisions for their ships. The company controlled the settlers autocratically, imposed strict regulations on their trade, and tried to prevent them from moving away from the vicinity of the Cape, since dispersal increased the difficulty and cost of administration.

This policy was defeated by the facts of southern Africa. The coastal area east of the Cape and also the high lands to the north were the only easily accessible areas of Africa outside the Mediterranean coast (still barred to Europeans by the strength of Islamic states) which also offered climatic and demographic conditions comparable to those in America. The coastal climate was temperate, the high lands well suited to European pastoralists. No African state or powerful tribes barred white settlement, as they did in most parts of Africa. From the Cape to the Great Fish River in the east there was a political vacuum, inhabited only by Bushmen and Hottentots who could not resist European encroachment; indeed, the Hottentots became a docile labour force performing many of the same functions as Amerindians in New Spain or Peru. Farther east, there were powerful Bantu tribes; but they did not affect European settlement until late in the eighteenth century, when the frontier of settlement reached the Fish River.

By that time the Cape had become a settlement colony populated by Netherlanders and French Huguenot refugees. Restrictions on trade and movement slowed the rate of growth but could never stop expansion eastwards. When the British conquered the Cape in 1795 there were about 15,000 whites and 17,000 slaves there. Already the 'trek-boers' had reached the River Kei and were in dangerous contact with the Xhosa tribes. The trekkers could not be held back because their pastoral system required some 6,000 acres or more of land on the veld for each family. The Bantus in the east, who were also pastoralists, were equally in search of new land. Geography provided no possible frontier between them: the explosion of Zulu power in Natal forced the Bantu south and west as land-hunger led Europeans east and north. In South Africa the British found a frontier problem resembling the one they had tried to solve in North America after 1763. It remained intractable throughout the next century.

By 1815, however, European penetration of southern Africa was still in its early stages. There, as throughout the continent, the European impact was still marginal. If a catastrophe had then removed all Europeans from Africa few traces of their presence would have remained. Outside the Cape and Mozambique there were virtually no white settlers. Mediterranean Africa and much of the east coast were controlled by Muslims; Arabs were building an impressive slave-trading empire in East Africa. European trade was restricted to coastal ports, and depended almost exclusively on African middlemen. Even the slave trade, the most important European interest in Africa, which may have removed some 100,000 Africans a year in the eighteenth century, made a surprisingly small impact. It had significant effects in Angola and Mozambique, where slaving was concentrated and population in any case thin. Elsewhere, apart from the individual misery it caused, its main effect was to provide a good economic foundation for powerful African states, such as those in Guinea, the Gold Coast, Angola and Mozambique. The most important results of European activity, apart from the slave trade were, in fact, the introduction of new foodstuffs, notably cassava, maize and sweet potatoes from America, which greatly improved African diets; and of firearms, which strengthened the emergent African states and tended to redress the balance between Europeans and Africans.

In retrospect, however, it can be seen that the roots of effective European intervention already existed. Most important was the campaign against slavery. By 1815, it was illegal for citizens of Denmark, Great Britain, the United States or Holland to buy or sell slaves: all other colonial powers followed suit by 1842. Countries which had abjured slaving had a natural interest in preventing others from continuing it, both on moral grounds and because American sugar plantations denied new slaves would be handicapped if others could still obtain them. These considerations led to a crusade by Britain (and later also by France) to stamp out the West African slave trade: interest in East Africa came later. The crusade required bases and influence in West Africa, and nothing did more to ensure that old possessions were not given up, or to involve Europeans in African affairs.

Legitimate trade also existed in 1815; but it was so small that it did not yet constitute a major incentive for European expansion into Africa. For the moment the Christian missions, the allies of the anti-slavery movement, were far more important. By the early nineteenth century there were Protestant missions from several European and American countries in Africa: Roman Catholic missions did not revive until the second quarter of the century, and Portuguese missions were almost defunct. But even missionaries could have little impact on the interior of the continent until its geography was known to Europeans. In 1815 very little of Africa had yet been explored, except for short stretches of the Nile, the Senegal, the Congo and the Zambezi. But the thirst for information was strong. In 1795–7 and 1805–6 Mungo Park made two major expeditions on the Niger. No other important work was done until the 1820s, but it was already predictable that European curiosity, coupled with the Christian missions, would open up the 'dark continent'.

Whether explorers or missionaries would be followed by effective occupation by Europeans was another matter. Apart from the southern zone of settlement, Africa offered little to attract emigrants, traders or investors. The eighteenth century was the age of American empires; the nineteenth was foreseeably that of empires in Asia. Only at the very end of the century did Africa rival either in its appeal to Europe. Africa was left until last because it offered least.

8

Europeans in the East before 1815

Portugal and Spain

Five European countries had possessions in the east during the eighteenth century, but until late in the period there were no substantial territorial empires there. Portugal and Spain stood apart from Holland, Britain and France. These two pioneered European contacts with Asia by sea during the sixteenth century, and created the alternative patterns of activity which greatly influenced all later European arrivals. The Portuguese showed Europe how to trade profitably in areas with advanced civilizations and strong indigenous governments. They avoided large territorial possessions and built a system of forts and naval bases stretching from Lisbon to China and Japan. In the Philippines, where political and social conditions differed from those found in most parts of Asia, the Spanish used the colonizing techniques they had worked out in America and created the first, and for long the only, true European colony in the east. By contrast with their North European successors, both Iberian states vested their eastern possessions in the Crown.

The Portuguese were the first to discover and develop oceanic contacts with the east as an alternative to the overland routes via Persia or the Red Sea. In an effort sustained throughout the first half of the sixteenth century, astonishing for so small a country, they built bases round Africa and thence to Ormuz, Diu, Goa, Calicut, Colombo, Malacca, Java, the Moluccas and Macao. To these goods were brought from other parts of India, the Archipelago, China and Japan. Alliances were made with indigenous powers and minor states accepted Portuguese suzerainty. But the principle laid down by Albuquerque, the first viceroy of the Indies, was always adhered to. Portugal must hold only key fortresses and trading factories. She must rely on naval power to defend them. Territorial empire was beyond her powers and would be unprofitable. In fact, complete control of the ocean was never achieved. Turkish naval power proved too strong in the Red Sea, and the inter-Asian trades remained out of her control. Nor did she obtain a monopoly of importing Asian goods to Europe; for the traditional overland routes to the Mediterranean survived her attacks, and even grew in importance. Her real success was to exclude all other Europeans from direct oceanic contact with the east until the end of the sixteenth century.

Portugal's reward was in the supply of eastern goods she brought back and sold at immense profit in Europe. Her policy was to keep prices up by excluding rivals and restricting her own imports. To prevent evasion of her quasi-monopoly, and because the volume of trade was small, only one fleet was sent to the east each year. To protect the interests of the Crown, no foreigners were allowed a part in the trade, and even Portuguese merchants were not allowed to deal in the more valuable spices until after 1640. Monopoly was further strengthened by the canalization of all trade through Goa, the capital of the eastern empire.

Portuguese principles were repeated by their rivals and successors in the seventeenth century: so also was the corruption endemic among Portugal's administrative and military servants in the east. Civilians and soldiers were mostly recruited in Portugal: royal patronage provided the higher ranks, poverty and the desire to make a fortune the rest. All officials were badly paid and correspondingly corrupt. Service in the east gave unlimited opportunities for making fortunes through illicit trading, peculation, bribes from natives and so on. Attempts by the Crown to investigate abuses were thwarted by the mutual support of guilty parties; Goa could never control the lesser bases. Yet monopoly ensured such large profits that the Crown could largely ignore the inefficiency of its eastern establishments.

Three features of the Portuguese eastern empire were, however, not shared by its successors. The Crown never delegated control of bases to private companies, though in the later seventeenth century, and again after 1750 under Pombal, monopoly of the trade in a particular area was sometimes sold to Portuguese merchants. The Crown directly administered all its possessions. The viceroy and council at Goa had authority over all eastern bases (including Mozambique until 1752) and heard appeals in criminal and civil cases. Goa possessed a full Portuguese colonial administration resembling that in Brazil. Subordinate possessions had a simpler government consisting of a captain, aided by a few civilian and military officials, and a royal judge. Lisbon attempted to exercise control, but its authority was inefficient because dispersed among different metropolitan authorities. The Council of State appointed viceroys and governors and interfered in any field at will. The Council of the Indies – later renamed the Council of Overseas – was responsible for most colonial business; but the Council of Finances organized the annual fleets and royal monopolies; and the Privy Council advised the King on judicial appointments. There was thus no unity of control: but Portugal was the only state whose sovereign had direct control over Asiatic dependencies before 1800.

Two other features of Portuguese policy in the east were intolerance in religion and lack of racial bias. Throughout their possessions the Portuguese destroyed non-Christian temples and used force to convert Asians. Only converts, who were closely watched by the Inquisition, were covered by the laws or could serve under the Crown. Bishoprics and parishes were set up everywhere and the clergy received compulsory tithes. This policy caused much resentment among Asians, and in some places may have made the more tolerant Dutch welcome. Had Portugal possessed large dominions it could not have been sustained; but within her small bases it enabled her to create a body of Christian Asians who were Portuguese subjects and often deeply loyal to her. Such loyalty to an alien race was rare in eastern and African colonies. It was strengthened by the lack of Portuguese racial feeling. Inter-marriage and concubinage were common, since very few Portuguese women went to the east, and because there were few settlers other than those officials who stayed after their terms expired. Their half-caste offspring played an important role in government and defence, and constituted a solid basis for Portuguese power. Portugal was the only European nation to make any real impression on an Asian society before the nineteenth century.

By 1700, however, the Portuguese empire had virtually ceased to exist. Most bases had been taken by the Dutch or British, leaving only Goa, Diu, part of Timor in the Archipelago, and Macao, off Canton. After 1700 only two ships a year sailed from Lisbon for Goa, and return cargoes were about a fifth of their sixteenth-century volume. Some new developments occurred after 1750. Religious toleration was allowed for non-Christians; manufactures and cotton growing expanded at Goa; the Macao trade increased with the European demand for tea. Yet in 1780 Portugal was making a net loss on her eastern colonies. Her place had been taken by newcomers.

Spanish control of the Philippines – their only possession outside America – was a relic of an early project for an eastern empire. The 1494 Treaty of Tordesillas excluded Spain from trade or territory east of a line drawn north and south through the western Atlantic. The question was how far east this Portuguese sphere extended, and whether earlier papal grants to Spain enabled her to invade it by sailing west from Europe. On the assumption that they did, Magellan, a Portuguese now in the service of Charles v, sailed west from Spain to claim territory in the Far East in 1519.

The Philippines were the result of this expedition. Magellan had intended to reach and claim the Moluccas; but he sailed to the north of them, reached the Philippines and was killed. Under Del Cano his two surviving ships reached the Moluccas and left a small garrison at Tidore, whose sultan welcomed Spanish support against Portuguese domination. Prospects seemed good, and Spanish occupation of Mexico provided a convenient base for regular contacts. But, although further expeditions were sent to the Archipelago in 1524, 1526 and 1527, little more was achieved. The Pacific wind system made the return to America apparently impossible, and Portuguese power in the east was too strong. In 1529 Charles v, on the verge of insolvency after his Italian campaigns, decided to sell his claims to the east while they had value. By the Treaty of Zaragoza he accepted 350,000 ducats and an arbitrary line of demarcation in the Pacific seventeen degrees east of the Moluccas.

The Philippines lay within the Portuguese sphere, but they were occupied by a Spanish expedition under Miguel Lóez de Lagazpi in 1564. This was a Mexican rather than a Spanish enterprise, an early example of colonial 'sub-imperialism'. The return route to Mexico was discovered the following year by Andrés de Urdaneta, who had visited the Moluccas with Del Cano and was now a monk. This made regular trade possible, and Spaniards in New Spain hoped to use Manila as a base for illicit trade with the Moluccas. The Portuguese surprisingly showed no resentment at Spanish occupation of the Philippines, but reacted strongly to such interloping. The Mexican enterprise would have proved pointless, for the Philippines offered little themselves, had a trade in silk not developed with Canton, which was carried in Chinese junks and organized by Chinese merchants. At its peak in about 1597 it was as valuable as the official Spanish transatlantic trade. The silk was sent from Acapulco in Mexico either to Old Spain, or to Peru which provided the silver to pay for it. But from the viewpoint of Madrid the trade had disadvantages. It drained silver to the east instead of to Spain; Mexican and Peruvian markets were invaded by eastern manufactures in place of those of Spain or Europe. The Manila trade showed signs of detaching Mexico and Peru from their assigned place in the Spanish imperial system of trade and linking them to the east. Finally Manila silk coming by this devious route could not compete with silk imported direct by Portugal and was of no economic value to Old Spain. Controls were therefore imposed. In 1631, trade between Mexico and Peru was forbidden in order to close the Peruvian market to eastern goods. Serving only Mexico, the Manila trade declined. In 1720, further restrictions permitted only two galleons with defined amounts of specie to sail each year, and they could not bring back silk fabrics. Quantities of silver and permitted return cargoes were increased in 1734, and the trade thereafter expanded as New Spain became more prosperous. It was the only commercial link between the New World and the east before the start of a trade in furs from the north-west coast of America to Japan and China in the 1780s.

Spanish government in the Philippines was almost incidental to these commercial functions, and Spain showed little interest in it. For the most part the Spanish-American system was adopted unchanged. Manila had a governor-general and normal Spanish colonial administration. The laws of the Indies were applied, including rights for non-Europeans. All land was claimed by the Crown, which allotted it to lay and ecclesiastical colonists on the *encomienda* principle. The islands consisted of vast semi-feudal estates, loosely supervised by the royal government, which never revoked these grants as it did in America. Within this framework Filipino social and political forms survived intact. The most important Spanish influence on the natives was exerted by the Catholic church. As in the frontier regions of Spanish America, friars and monks were the real colonizers. They converted most of the Filipinos, built churches and created a European system of parishes and church schools. The Philippines became a theocratic society. Little was done to develop the economy, and Manila remained primarily an entrepôt. By the eighteenth century the islands were a back-water, a museum piece of sixteenth-century Spanish methods of colonization, lacking sufficient non-clerical settlers to develop along the lines of 'mixed' colonies in Spanish America. Yet it was the only substantial area outside America in which Europeans had then succeeded in assimilating a large alien population to their own religion and ways of life. Spanish rule survived the loss of continental America until it was destroyed by the United States in 1898.

Dutch, English and French Companies in the East

Until the suspension of the French *Compagnie des Indes* in 1769 and the transfer of its bases to the Crown, no North European state owned colonies in the east. The previous hundred and fifty years were the heyday of the chartered companies who shared the Portuguese inheritance and extended it. The field was left open to them because governments lacked the resources to undertake colonization: the east, whose value to Europe was commercial, was well-suited to exploitation by private joint-stock companies. Company control was liable to end only in two circumstances. If a company became financially insolvent the state had to support it or take over its establishments. Alternatively, transformation of a company through its very success into a great territorial power might tempt or force a government to reclaim its political powers. During the eighteenth century the Dutch and French companies failed financially and their assets were vested in the United Provinces and France. The English company, despite changed circumstances, survived as the government of India until 1858; but by 1784 it was under close supervision by the British government. By contrast, although chartered companies were used by the British and Germans in the late nineteenth century, the later European empires in Asia and Africa were established and governed by the states of Europe.

These three great companies had common features. Each exercised a monopoly of the trade between its own country and the east. Each was initially created to end competition between merchants within the same country. All were founded with private capital, though the French company of 1667 and its successor of 1718 were heavily dependent on state support; and all were run by a virtually independent board of directors in the metropolis. None was imperialist in its attitude: their aim was to acquire wealth through trade.

The Netherlands East India Company

The Dutch company, founded in 1602, typified these attitudes. Its function was to break into the Portuguese monopoly of the oceanic trade with Asia and to unite the resources of the several Netherlands towns which were already taking advantage of war with Spain and Portugal to trade in the east. Its internal structure reflected the federalism of the United Provinces. It was governed by a college of seventeen directors – the Seventeen as they were called. But these controlled only general policy, appointing senior officials, organizing fleets and setting the price at which imports were sold in Europe. Real power lay with the directors of the six local chambers, one for each commercial centre. Directors were elected for three years, but in practice formed oligarchies which held office in rotation. Chambers organized cargoes, hired ships, sent contingents of troops, and nominated officials. The two chambers of Amsterdam and Zeeland, which nominated eight and four of the Seventeen respectively, and whose towns had most of the trade, dominated the company just as they dominated the States General. The States General had little control over the company. It examined its accounts and periodically renewed its charter, but made no attempt to influence policy. Greater state control was expected from the appointment of the Stadholder William IV as Director-General of the company in 1749 with considerable powers; but his death in 1751, and the minority and lack of interest of his successor, William V, made this innovation ineffective.

Initially the company avoided territorial responsibilities and acquired only such bases as were essential for trade and establishing a monopoly of certain commodities. They had to conquer the main Portuguese forts, since these were the keys to the east; but the pursuit of monopoly led them to occupation of places never used by Portugal. By the early eighteenth century they held the Cape of Good Hope; Calicut, Cochin and smaller factories on the Malabar coast of India; Negapatam and Pulicat on the Coromandel coast; Masulipatam and other factories farther north and in Bengal; and Ceylon. In India they had rivals, but in the Indonesian Archipelago, which was their main commercial centre, they had a virtual monopoly. Batavia, in Java, was the capital of the whole eastern empire, which it controlled through lesser bases or alliances with native rulers. Malacca gave control over the Malay Straits; the west coast of Sumatra was supervised from Padang. Macassar dominated the Celebes. Most states in Indonesia were tied by treaties which bound them not to make foreign alliances or allow other Europeans to trade, and often involved payment of tribute in local products such as pepper or spices. Farther east the Dutch had trade but no political power, with factories in Cambodia, Siam, Tonking, Mokja and Japan. The only important exceptions to the policy of avoiding territorial commitments were the Banda Islands and Amboyna, where rivalry with the British and desire to force the production of nutmegs led to full occupation; and Ceylon, where control proved necessary to preserve the cinnamon monopoly.

The company's administrative system conformed to the principle that it should trade rather than govern. All bases and factories centred on Batavia; only Ceylon could correspond direct with the United Provinces. The Batavian government consisted of a governor-general, a director-general who controlled commerce and finance and was second in command, and a council of officials. In theory the governor-general was only president of the council and was unable to act without its consent: in practice he was an autocrat, always supported by the Seventeen in disputes with his council. With the council's assent he could make laws, control commerce, supervise justice and declare war on non-European states. The other important body was a council of justice, staffed by lay officials serving in rotation, with jurisdiction over all servants of the company but not over Asians. This simple governmental pattern was repeated on a smaller scale in other centres of government. Trading factories were run by a civilian administrator and assistants who had no political or judicial powers.

Government in the Dutch Indies was virtually autonomous, and entirely run by officials. Autonomy was inevitable because of the distance from Holland and the limited interests of the company. Government by officials was natural because these were not settlement colonies, and in theory only Europeans and Asians in company employment lived in them. The absence of settlers and the inconvenience of sending officials so far for short periods produced an eastern service which became characteristic of all European administrations. Recruits from the Netherlands entered for life – though their contracts had to be renewed regularly – and formed an exclusive corps, whose members could reach the highest posts by seniority. This made for continuity and experience and might have produced efficiency. In fact, it did not. The company always grossly underpaid its servants. It banned private trading, but assumed that it existed and would compensate for low salaries. These facts constituted a vicious circle. Employees took every opportunity to make their fortunes at the expense of company profits or native peoples. The company found it impossible to check them; instead it calculated salaries at false rates of exchange, kept back half the amount due until the end of each period of service, and increasingly employed foreign Europeans who would accept lower nominal salaries.

Such governments were intended only to control the internal affairs of commercial centres: they were unsuited to the government of large numbers of Asians. Dutch policy was to leave indigenous rulers, forms of government and laws unchanged, even where, as in much of Java, the company had effective power. Elsewhere they preferred to make treaties with local rulers rather than take over their functions. Their attitude resembled what was later called 'indirect rule': they governed through indigenous authorities and native forms. Attitudes to religion and native culture were in line. The Dutch were tolerant, and Calvinist ministers sent out by the company showed no strong missionary tendencies. Roman Catholics were excluded from office as a reflection of the European struggle against Spain; other religions were allowed full freedom. The company made no attempt to assimilate natives by offering Netherlands citizenship or by education. Conversely, they showed marked racial consciousness. Dutch officials were forbidden to marry Asians under penalty of losing their pensions, and relatively little miscegenation took place. They thus saved themselves much trouble and possible hostility: but if they had abandoned the east in the late eighteenth century they would have left few traces of two hundred years of occupation.

The aim of the company was to make profits out of trade, and in this they succeeded. Exact figures cannot be estimated, since the annual accounts presented to the States General dealt only with assets and liabilities in Europe, and excluded Batavian balances. Dividends did not necessarily relate to current workings. Yet the company must have run at a profit for most of the century and a half after 1623. Dividends were distributed in all but seventeen years, all of them during wars. Decennial averages were never less than 11·25 per cent (in 1623–32) and reached a peak of 36 per cent in 1713–22. But from 1737 onwards, though dividends were always above 12·5 per cent, this was made possible, in the face of reduced profits or deficits on current account, only by borrowing. Thus by 1781, although the company had not increased its original share capital of 6·5 million florins, it owed 22 millions in debentures and floating debts on which increasing rates of interest had to be paid. By 1795 consolidated debts amounted to over 119 million florins, and three years later the company was wound up.[1] This failure is difficult to explain: there was no decline in the volume of trade, and no major wars between 1713 and 1793. A possible cause lay in the increasing costs of administration in the east as territorial responsibilities grew: yet political power could also increase profits by producing a tribute in local products – such as cinnamon from Ceylon, or coffee from Java. Peculation and inefficiency among company servants may have contributed. But the most likely explanation is that the company was trying to distribute too high a dividend in relation to its actual profits: no other eastern company gave comparable dividends. Prices gained from the sale of eastern goods were declining, for there were now other suppliers, and consumers resisted artificially high prices. Dividends should have gone down proportionately. The attempt to maintain them ultimately led to bankruptcy in 1795.

Yet the Netherlands East India Company had done much for the United Provinces as well as for its shareholders. It had contributed heavily to taxation. After 1750 eastern trade constituted about a quarter of the country's entire external commerce. Eastern goods helped Dutch trade throughout Europe. The company was a major employer of labour, spending an average of more than 14·6 million florins a year in the 1770s on goods and services in the United Provinces. Repatriation of private fortunes made by the company's employees in the east – though largely at its expense – brought in an average of more than 3·7 million florins a year between 1770–9.[2] Although the company died, the United Provinces inherited vast eastern possessions and interests along with its debts. It was a good bargain: during the nineteenth century Holland benefited greatly from possession of Indonesia.

The English East India Company before 1757

In the first half of the eighteenth century the English East India Company resembled its Dutch rival. It too was founded in 1600 to eliminate competition at home and break the Portuguese price monopoly. It took far longer, however, to reach its final corporate form or to acquire comparable possessions or trade. Until the new charter of 1657 its capital was subscribed only for one voyage at a time: thereafter its capital was permanent, but its monopoly insecure. At various times the Crown gave charters to rivals. In the 1690s it was under constant political attack by Whigs, who disliked its Tory affiliations, and by independent merchants who resented exclusion from eastern trade. In 1698 Parliament put its monopoly up for auction. The company was outbid by a rival consortium, which was to take over its monopoly in 1701. In fact, in 1702 this 'New Company' agreed to link its capital with the capital, experience and eastern assets of the 'Old'; in 1709 they were fused as the United Company with a parliamentary charter and monopoly.

The United Company survived until 1858. Provided it remained solvent its monopoly and powers were in danger only when its charter was due to be renewed and grievances could be vented against it. Until 1773 renewal was irregular and normally uncontested, though governments took these opportunities to extract loans for the Treasury. Thereafter the charter was renewed every twenty years, each renewal producing a grand parliamentary inquest and major changes.

During the first half of the eighteenth century the company was a respectable and conservative commercial body, connected with City banking and the Stock Exchange. It was run by a Court of twenty-four directors, who elected a chairman and deputy chairman – who in turn really ran the company – and were the policy makers. There was also a Court of Proprietors, consisting of holders of at least £500 of stock, each of whom had a single vote in electing the directors and could move for changes in company policy. While the directors produced satisfactory dividends and kept clear of parliamentary politics, internal rows or governmental intervention were unlikely.

Oligarchy did not mean inefficiency. Between 1661 and 1691

shareholders received an annual average dividend of 22 per cent on the face value of their stock. Eighteenth-century dividends were less impressive: 10 per cent from 1711–12 to 1722; 8 per cent until 1732; 7 per cent until 1743; then 8 per cent again until 1755.[3] These were lower than those of the Dutch company but honest, reflecting real profits over short runs though not necessarily for any one year. The volume of trade was increasing. Imports were about £500,000 early in the century; over £1,000,000 by the 1750s, and £1,700,000 in the 1770s.[4] Exports of British goods were worth far less, and the balance had to be made up in bullion. This was an inevitable feature of eastern trade by all European countries, since there was very little demand in the east for European products. But the volume of imports from India was far smaller than the company would have liked, and this was due to British regulations. Many Indian goods were excluded by acts passed in the interest of British manufactures. After 1720 the company could still import raw silk, cotton yarn, plain calicoes and a wide range of minor Indian manufactures; but promising lines in silks and printed calicoes had been stopped, and had to be smuggled in by private merchants from Holland. The result of such restrictions was that the company increasingly relied for its profits on selling Chinese tea rather than Indian goods in London. India became mainly a source of goods for sale in Canton and thus paid for part of the tea. The acquisition of territorial revenues in India after 1757 enabled the company to buy these Indian goods without sending money or goods from England: but in 1815 it was still necessary to make up the balance in Canton with silver.

During its first century and a half the English company avoided territorial responsibilities, relying on permission from eastern rulers to set up fortified trading posts or factories (warehouses) wherever profitable. The English had initially expected to trade throughout the east, but by 1700 they were almost entirely restricted to India. All that remained of their efforts in Indonesia was a derelict base at Bencoolen in western Sumatra, whose main function was to attract goods from local rulers who wished to evade their treaty obligations with the Dutch. This contraction of their sphere of operations was forced on them. The Dutch were well established in Indonesia by 1619, and the English company never matched their naval resources there.

Although the company did not want territory in the east, it had to have firm bases to develop a substantial trade: oriental conditions were dangerous for merchants without secure retreats. English aims were accurately defined by Sir Josiah Child, Governor of the company, in 1687. In view of increasingly lawless conditions and the inconvenience of being vulnerable to the importunities of any Indian ruler, it was necessary

> to establish such a politie of civill and military power, and create and secure such a large revenue to maintaine both ... as may bee the foundation of a large, well-grounded, sure English dominion in India for all time to come.[5]

This did not imply extensive territories: Child took as his model the Dutch system of occupying small bases of high strategic and commercial value, with a small hinterland to give both physical security against attack and revenues to offset administrative costs. His statement did not indicate a lust for empire in India.

By 1717 the company possessed only three such fortified places in India. Bombay was the centre for the west coast, and the only territory held by Britain in full sovereignty. It had been ceded by Portugal in 1661 and was transferred to the company in 1668. It was a fortified island with institutions characteristic of most British colonies of settlement, though without any representative assembly. It was a flourishing centre, attracting many Indian settlers by the security it gave, and controlled the company's trade at a number of factories on the Malabar coast and at Surat. Madras was the centre for the Coromandel coast, with a string of subordinate factories at Masulipatam, Cuddalore and elsewhere. Madras was held by permission of the King of Golconda which was renewed by the Mogul emperor after he had conquered Golconda in 1690 in return for a symbolic quit rent. The company's centre in Bengal, the most valuable commercial area in India, also depended on imperial authority. After previously possessing only unfortified trading factories, the company was given permission in 1698 to occupy Fort William, which it had just built at Calcutta. It also received the *zamindari*

– the right of tax collection on behalf of the emperor – in three villages in return for payment of 1,200 rupees a year. Fort William was, however, the least secure of the company's bases, and the company hoped that the new *farman* they obtained in 1717 from the emperor, after long negotiations and much bribery of officials, would increase its safety. The *farman* continued their *zamindari* rights and also exempted company servants from all Indian customs and other taxes in return for an annual payment of 3,000 rupees.

British power in India remained on this narrow basis until the later 1750s. The company's possessions were small and, except Bombay, physically insecure. There was no reason to think they were a dynamic nucleus from which British power would cover the sub-continent. The company remained commercially minded. Its main worry was that its servants, who were recruited and treated in much the same way as those of the Dutch company, similarly made their profits from illicit private trading and peculation at the company's expense. There was no confidence that such practices could be eradicated; nor did the company foresee the consequences of abuse by company servants of their exemption from trading duties in Bengal.

From the 1750s, however, events in India and Britain radically changed the character of the company and its power. Its later history is the history of the growth of the British empire in India and the east.

The French Compagnie des Indes

The French *Compagnie des Indes* was a state concern rather than a private enterprise receiving state support: otherwise its policy and activities closely resembled those of other companies. France also wanted trade rather than empire.

The company founded by Colbert in 1664 was heir to a number of privileged ventures which received little public support and failed to achieve anything except to create Fort Dauphin in Madagascar as a port of call. Colbert took the initiative because he wanted to stop the drain of bullion used to buy eastern goods from the Dutch and English and to open up new fields for trade. He hoped that a company launched by the state would evolve into a self-supporting corporation; and he modelled it on the Dutch pattern, decentralizing power among a number of provincial chambers which elected a Grand Chamber of twenty-one directors at Paris. The company had full powers of government including the right to make war and peace with non-Europeans: but the Crown retained the right to appoint the governor-general and senior judges, giving naval support, preferential customs duties and a considerable capital sum in return.

As a commercial body the company failed. The public subscribed only under governmental pressure, and many shareholders later refused to meet calls for further subscriptions. Only 7·4 million (£472,000) out of a nominal capital of 15 million livres (£960,000) was subscribed; and of this the Crown put up 4·2 million (£268,000). A few dividends were distributed, but these were issued on governmental orders and did not reflect working profits. Yet the company did not fail for lack of capital, or because it was a state enterprise masquerading as a joint-stock company, but because of the difficulty of breaking into a highly competitive trading system against three established European competitors, and the crippling effects of war with Holland from 1672–8 and with Britain and Holland for most of 1689–1713. After 1713 peace should have enabled it to prosper; but its debts amounted to over a million livres (£64,000) and its assets were unrealizable. It had tried unsuccessfully to go into liquidation in 1708, and had leased out its commercial monopoly to private traders. After 1714 it therefore remained inert.

The second phase of French activity began in 1719 when Colbert's company was incorporated into the new company formed by John Law to take over virtually all French colonial trade. The *Compagnie des Indes* emerged from the wreck of Law's company in 1723. It was now primarily a holding body for 56,000 shares in Law's company and was obliged to pay interest on them at the rate of 150 livres a share; but it received about enough to do this from the Crown since it was servicing what were in fact public debts. Thus, like the English South Sea Company, the French company was a financial organization which was also given a monopoly of the eastern trade, and that of Louisiana, San Domingo and West Africa. Its central organization reflected its quasi-official character. It was run by a body of directors in Paris who were appointed for life by the Crown but replaced by others elected by the shareholders. Royal interests were guarded by inspectors (later called commissioners) who reported to the Controller-General. The shareholders' interests were watched by syndics, elected annually, who eventually acquired the status and salary of directors. The administration in Paris was really part of the royal civil service, and resembled a nineteenth-century colonial office rather than a contemporary trading company. Clerical work was divided between departments like those in the Ministry of Marine; the Lorient base, to which all Indian ships came, was like a royal dockyard; and in 1753 the Paris establishment had more than a hundred employees.

Yet there was no reason why the company should not have created a commercial empire in India. Most of its metropolitan staff were employed on internal finances rather than trade, and their salaries were covered by Crown subsidies. Eastern trade was profit. The official status of the company strengthened its credit, and royal support was valuable. The company inherited substantial assets. By 1723 the Madagascar base had been given up, but in Ile de France (Mauritius) and Bourbon it had an excellent entrepôt for the Indian Ocean. Pondicherry, on the Coromandel coast, was held by treaty with the local ruler, and was the capital of the company in India. It had factories on the Carnatic, in Bengal, on the Malabar coast and at Surat, and many trading and political contacts had been made. International peace and the absence of unconsolidated liabilities after 1723 gave the company an excellent opportunity.

Until the later 1760s it succeeded. The overseas organization was simple and cheap and worked well. The governor-general at Pondicherry controlled all Indian bases, helped only by a *conseil supérieur* and a few commercial and military officials. Since this was not a royal colony, there was no intendant. Lesser centres, like Ile de France, had a director-general; still smaller ones had *directeurs particuliers* and provincial councils, or merely a *chef de comptoir*. Service in the company resembled that in other companies. Military forces were directly employed by the company, but naval protection was provided by royal ships.

By the mid-eighteenth century the company had extended its bases in India, but had not ventured farther east except to Canton. Mahé had been established on the Malabar coast, and there was a *comptoir* at Moka on the Red Sea. The company had developed a considerable trade in the normal Indian manufactures; though like the English it was prevented from importing printed calicos and manufactured silk. In return it exported French wines, brandy, textiles, and hardware: but like everyone else, it had to make good a large adverse balance with bullion. Imports to France showed an impressive profit margin: 96·1 per cent on imports sold in France for just under 100 million livres (£6,400,000) between 1725 and 1736; 93·1 per cent on 120 million livres (£7,680,000) from 1743 to 1756. Imports from China made a profit of 104·5 per cent on 18·9 million livres (£1,209,600) in the first period, 116·6 per cent on 41·7 million livres (£2,668,800) in the second. Commerce reached a peak in 1740–4, when between sixteen and twenty-five ships were sent out each year. Even after 1763 trade was brisk, and in the company's last year of full working, 1768–9, fifteen ships went to India and a profit of 11 million livres (£704,000) was made.[6]

This was an impressive commercial record; and the company remained true to its commercial aims as long as it was allowed. As late as 1752 the directors told Dupleix, the governor-general of Pondicherry, that

> *La Compagnie craint toute augmentation de domaine. Son objet n'est pas de devenir une puissance de terre, le parti que nous devons prendre est celui d'une exacte neutralité.*[7]

Two years later Dupleix was recalled for his continued and eventually unsuccessful intervention in Indian politics and his plans to eject the British from the Carnatic. Between 1744 and 1748, and again between 1756 and 1763, the company had reluctantly to fight the British in India. Defeat and the temporary loss of its bases convinced it that politics would be its ruin: thereafter it concentrated on trade alone.

Why, then, did the French company fail in 1769? It was still potentially strong, with the five main bases and lesser *comptoirs* which were returned to it in 1763, and treaty rights to trade with

India and China. It lost no time in reviving its trade, though the profit margin was down to 58·5 per cent in 1763 as a result of greater foreign competition. But it was ruined by its financial obligations in France. Loss of ships during two wars, and the costs of intervention in Indian politics without the compensation victory would have given, left it in 1769 with floating debts of 82 million livres (£5,248,000) and consolidated debts of 149 millions (£9,536,000). Assets then amounted only to 136·8 millions (£8,755,200). The company could have been saved only by the Crown. Instead, the government, influenced by growing French hostility to trading monopolies, appointed the Abbé Morellet to investigate the company's situation. His report reflected his liberal economic beliefs. It stated that the company was too indebted to survive, and recommended that its bases be made royal colonies to which all Frenchmen could trade. The company was suspended in 1769 and in 1770 lost its charter, continuing only as a financial agency for distributing the fixed dividend still paid by the Crown to its shareholders.

A new company was formed in 1785 to revive the commercial monopoly, but did not govern the Indian bases. Vergennes hoped that it would revive French contacts and check the growth of British power in India: but it was also argued that French trade had declined since 1769 and that individual merchants would not take part in it. The new company lasted until 1793. It prospered by buying Indian goods from the British, but failed to develop its own trading network. It did at least show that political control was not essential for profitable trade in the east, and that British predominance did not exclude France from a share in Indian commerce.

The French had failed in India by 1769 because the company had fallen between two stools. As a commercial company it prospered; but it could not avoid implication in Franco-British struggles and ruined itself in two wars. On the other hand if Dupleix' policy had succeeded, and if France had become dominant in India, the company might have saved itself financially, as the British company was able to do, by gaining control of Indian revenues. The Anglo-French struggle was a gamble for both companies in which the stake was financial ruin or immense profit.

The Growth of Territorial Empires in the East

Throughout the seventeenth century, and for much of the eighteenth also, no European power deliberately tried to establish a territorial empire in the east; the chartered companies which had divided Portugal's inheritance were organized for trade rather than conquest or government. Yet by the early nineteenth century the Dutch directly controlled much of Java and other smaller territories in Indonesia and had held most of Ceylon until they lost it to Britain in 1796. By 1818 the British ruled or controlled all India except the Punjab, Sind and the north-west frontier. So striking a development, which meant the beginning of the modern European empires in the east, can be explained by no single formula. But before surveying the growth of Dutch and British territorial possessions, it is convenient to isolate some of the situations which tended to lead to European control of foreign states in Asia.

The most common cause was a change in the indigenous political situation. Hitherto Europeans had acted according to the political conditions they found. For the most part they relied on obtaining special privileges for their trade, extra-territorial jurisdiction over their own servants to protect them from local courts, and grants of land on which to build warehouses and fortifications. These were the rights normally obtained by merchants trading to foreign states in Europe and the Middle East: British merchants in Cadiz had much the same position as the East India Company in Bengal, except that they had no fortified headquarters. Such rights depended on maintenance of the local *status quo*: radical change in the political situation, particularly a weakening of indigenous authority, made them useless. If, as happened in India, a previously stable empire disintegrated, Europeans had to fend for themselves. They might come to terms with smaller successor states, or alternatively become more independent of native authority. Conflicts between the new states offered opportunities for profitable alliances: often foreigners had to take sides; and once involved in local politics, it was difficult even for a peace-loving trading company to withdraw,

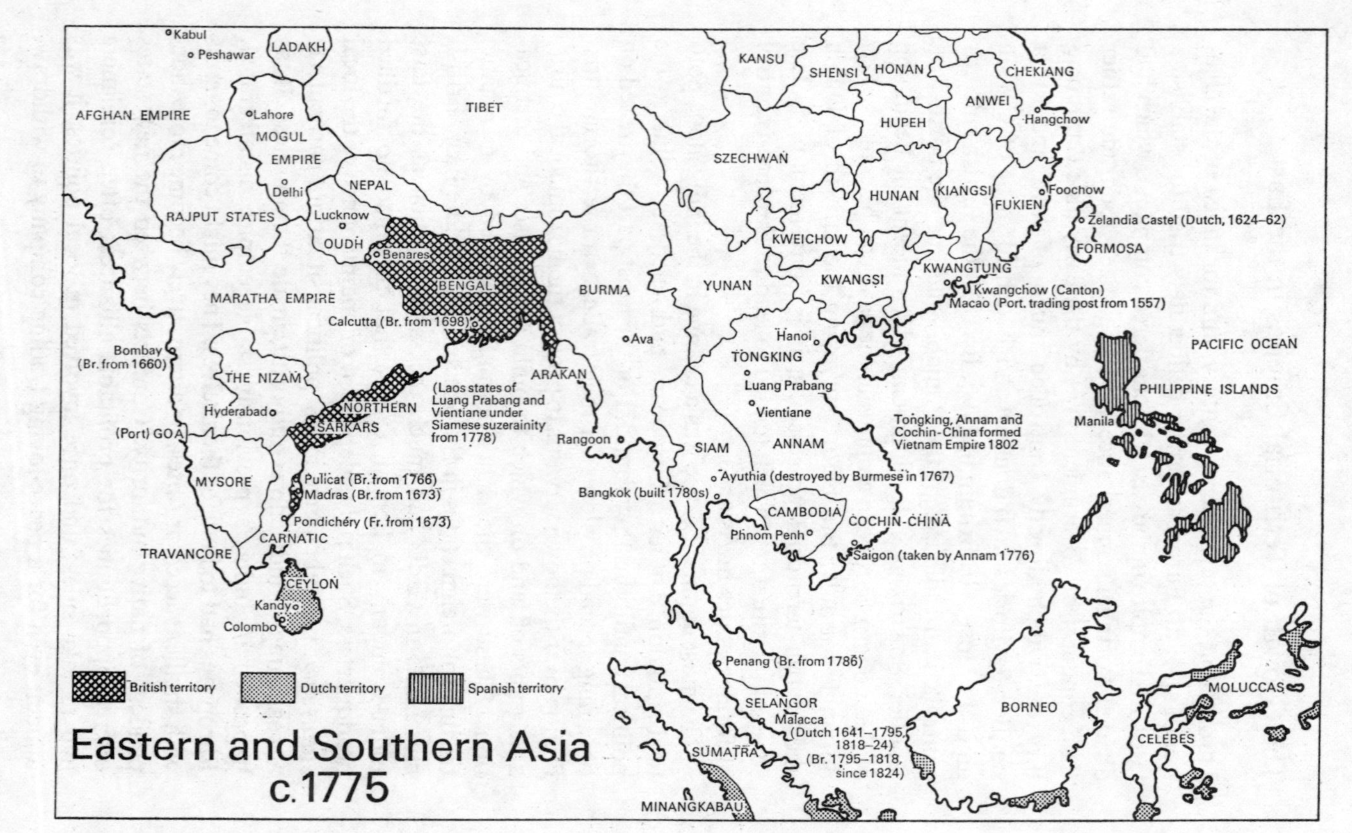

Eastern and Southern Asia c. 1775

for its future depended on victory for its allies. Provided native states remained strong, such involvement might still not lead to dominance. But European intervention tended to intensify political conflicts and to create a political vacuum in which Europeans had to take control. Thus the most likely cause of European expansion in Asia was the crack-up of an indigenous political system leading to an unplanned and initially unwanted access of political power.

But once the native authority against which Europeans had leant began to totter, two secondary factors stimulated further action. Inter-European rivalries, which were unimportant while an Asian power could keep all under control, became significant if it seemed possible for one European country to exclude a rival. European jingoism stimulated conflicts for power among the ruins of Asian states: fear of exclusion generated aggression which ambition might not have done. The other secondary factor was realization that political power might be more profitable than trade. The companies existed to provide dividends. These would be increased if the goods they sold in Europe did not have to be paid for; if, that is, they were given as tribute from dependent Asian rulers. Alternatively full territorial government by Europeans gave them Asian revenues, which could be used to pay for goods transmitted to Europe. Ultimately, a company might rely on political power to pay for its trade; and the tribute which had previously supported indigenous rulers would be transferred to stock-holders in Europe through the medium of unrequited exports. In addition, the desire of individual servants of trading companies to make personal fortunes through plunder, or by blackmailing Asian rulers, was an important factor making for further political intervention.

Such problems and ambitions might lead to the first territorial acquisitions. Thereafter the impulse to extend them was almost irresistible. The search for security on the frontiers led inexorably from the first British and Dutch possessions in India and Indonesia to European dominance throughout South-East Asia. In America colonies expanded with the moving frontier of European settlement: in Asia European dependencies expanded into their frontiers of insecurity.

The Dutch in Ceylon and Java

The growth of Dutch territorial power in Ceylon and Java during the later seventeenth and eighteenth centuries was a classic example of expansion due to European relations with native states rather than competition with other Europeans. In about 1667 the Dutch possessed sovereignty only in the Banda Islands, Amboyna and a small area round Batavia. Effective control over Ceylon arose out of conflict with the kingdom of Kandy, which possessed suzerainty over the island. The company inherited from the Portuguese control of most ports and the areas in which cinnamon was grown. They did not want more: but their existing interest depended on satisfactory relations with Kandy. Between 1739 and 1765 quarrels with the Raja over the cinnamon monopoly led to war and the capture of his capital. He was left in power as the nominal ruler of Ceylon, but had to pay tribute. The company administered most of the island, but used native intermediaries as far as possible. The reward of this new political power was a supply of cinnamon for which they did not have to pay.

In Java a similar but more complex process led to full Dutch occupation. They built their capital at Batavia and controlled a small area round it: they relied on treaties with native sultans to provide security and a monopoly of spices at low cost. The most important Javanese rulers were the Sultan of Bantam and the Sultan of Mataram, whose family had acquired paramountcy over most of Java and used the title of Susuhunan (overlord). In 1646 the Dutch made an alliance with the Susuhunan, Amangkurat: thirty years later the reigning Sultan invoked their help against an attack from Madura which threatened his paramountcy. The Dutch had to support him or risk losing their position. Simultaneously, the Sultan of Bantam, contrary to treaties, was allowing the French and English companies to set up factories in his territory and hoped to acquire land near Batavia. The Dutch defeated Bantam, and by a new treaty with the Sultan in 1684 reduced him to vassalage and acquired the monopoly of his trade. More important, they helped the Susuhunan and later restored his successor to full paramountcy. The treaty he had to sign in 1677 made him virtually a Dutch puppet

He granted the company control of several ports and the sole right to export opium and cotton cloths. The Dutch acquired territory in the Preanger, adjoining Batavia, and later expanded into Cheribon. These successes produced new commitments. Preservation of the Mataram dynasty involved them in two succession wars between 1704 and the 1720s, and these resulted in further extensions of Dutch territory. By the 1740s they controlled all the coastal districts of Java, and no island power could challenge their authority.

The use made by the Dutch of their political power had two peculiarities. Where possible they preserved native dynasties and ruled through them: even in areas now under company rule the existing native chiefs, known as regents, were retained as intermediaries. Conversely, in areas under Dutch sovereignty, the right to tribute inherited from indigenous rulers was used in a special way. Regents were made to develop coffee plantations on which peasants had to work for fixed periods each year without payment: the produce constituted tribute to the company. This system of forced renders showed the advantage of territorial power, since it provided unrequited exports to Holland. It was abolished by the British when they occupied Java after 1811 and replaced by taxes in money based on assessment of the productive capacity of each village. But it was revived by the Dutch in a different form as part of the so-called 'Culture System' in the 1830s.

At the end of the eighteenth century the Dutch had full territorial power only in Java and Ceylon: they still controlled the rest of Indonesia through treaties with native states supported by naval power and a few strategic bases, and lacked the desire or the resources to extend their territorial possessions. But during the following century their political and commercial interests throughout the Archipelago constantly forced them to take more positive action until ultimately they ruled the whole of Indonesia.

The British in India before 1818

The growth of British power in India was a far more surprising and complex process than Dutch expansion in Java. Indonesia was a maritime region relatively easy to control with European naval resources: India was a sub-continent within which sea-power had little effect. The rulers of the Archipelago were weak: in the early eighteenth century India was a great oriental empire, second only to that of Peking. Even after the weakening of Mogul power in Delhi many of the successor states were larger and more populous than Britain itself. How could a joint-stock trading company, several months sailing away from its own country, gain control over so vast an area?

British power grew as a parasite on the decay of the Mogul empire. The Moguls had been at their peak in the sixteenth century, and remained strong throughout the seventeenth; though revolts of provincial rulers became endemic, and a serious threat to imperial power emerged in the Deccan, where the Hindu bandit, Sivaji, created a robber empire based on Poona. The power of this Maratha empire increased steadily, though control passed from Sivaji's successors to their hereditary prime ministers, the Peshwas. But to the groups of European merchants trading on the periphery the Mogul empire seemed impregnable, the precondition of their activities.

Yet the Mogul empire was in decay. Its strength lay in the military and administrative abilities of a Muslim people invading India from beyond the Oxus. It was obeyed for its power and tolerated because it gave stable government and respected indigenous Indian religions and customs. Late in the seventeenth century it was becoming less efficient and less tolerant. Aurangzeb, the last great emperor, failed to conquer Maratha fortresses, and provincial rulers became more independent. Moreover Aurangzeb, as a pious Sunni, stirred up opposition by destroying Hindu temples and reimposing the poll-tax on non-Muslims which Akbar had abolished in the later sixteenth century. This provoked Hindu reaction and gave Maratha plundering raids a specious nationalist character. It also weakened the loyalty of the fighting races of northern India, Rajputs, Sikhs and Jats, whose refusal to support Delhi against Marathas and Pathans had serious consequences.

The half-century after the death of Aurangzeb saw the virtual dissolution of the Mogul empire. Successive emperors were puppets of court factions. The Marathas ignored imperial authority in the six provinces of the Deccan and attacked other provinces in search of loot, imposing their two main taxes, *chauth* and *sardeshmukh*. By the 1740s they were invading Hindustan itself, and the Nawab of Bengal, Ali Vardi Khan, had to cede them part of Orissa and pay *chauth* for Bengal and Bihar. Other adventurers took their chance. The Sikhs became an independent military power in the Punjab. A Persian army plundered Delhi in 1738–9. Afghan tribes raided Hindustan at will, and in 1761 defeated a large Maratha army at Panipat.

As imperial authority declined, the provinces, though still acknowledging allegiance, became independent states. Some, like Hyderabad and Oudh, were ruled by imperial officers; others like Rohilkjand, north of Oudh, and Mysore, by captains of armed bands. Subdivision of imperial provinces was common. In the south the Nawab of the Carnatic threw off the authority of the Nizam of Hyderabad; the Raja of Tanjore and the Coromandel powers became petty sovereigns. Even the Maratha empire began to split after Panipat. The Peshwas could not claim the same authority as the descendants of Sivaji, who were now only rajas of Satara: their lieutenants carved out semi-independent states, such as Dhar, Indore, Gwalior and Baroda, linked only as a loose military federation. India was no longer a unity but a continent of autonomous states.

This fragmentation made British domination possible; but it was not inevitable nor, from the Indian point of view, necessarily desirable. The alternative was a period of endemic conflict, causing great destruction, but leading ultimately to a new states system dominated by the most powerful successors to imperial power. This had occurred in Europe after the disintegration of the Carolingian empire and in South-East Asia, where the decline of Chinese imperial authority led to autonomous states still recognizing the theoretical overlordship of Peking. The importance of British intervention was not that it saved India from chaos (for the wars which lasted for sixty years after Plassey in 1757 were probably as destructive as purely Indian struggles would have been) but that it prevented the imminent Balkanization of India and for a century and a half saved her from the internecine wars which have followed the disintegration of every other great empire.

Imperial disintegration reduced the disproportion between the power of India and the resources of European companies. Yet many of the new Indian states were powerful and the companies operated on small financial and military margins. Why did the British emerge dominant?

Britain was not necessarily stronger than India, for there was never a confrontation between their economic and political potential, and the British company won India by using Indian resources. Nor was military technology decisive, for Indians rapidly adopted European arms and tactics. On the other hand European military discipline enabled small bodies of trained Indian soldiers – sepoys – to rout large armies fighting on traditional Indian lines: parade-ground tactics have seldom proved more effective. The discipline and determination of European civilians in moments of danger was also important. But in the last resort the British succeeded by using Indian resources and playing Indian politics more effectively than their opponents. Every conquest produced tribute, plunder, or control of taxes which financed further victories. By contrast, few Indian rulers succeeded in mobilizing their potential resources. Their financial and military systems were not designed for this sort of struggle, and perhaps only Haidar Ali of Mysore and his successor Tipu Sultan really solved this problem. Yet military success alone could not have stabilized British conquests. In the long run British domination depended on at least negative assent; tolerance of every aspect of Indian life and religion, except what concerned taxation, made such assent possible. Unlike the Portuguese the British for long showed no missionary zeal and made no distinction between Muslim and Hindu. Indian laws and customs were left intact. In this respect British rule resembled Mogul authority: a neutral shield under which most Indians could remain as they were.

The question of motives remains. Why did the East India Company, and similarly the French company, drop their long-established policy of avoiding territorial responsibility in India? The answer is different for each of two periods: from 1741 to 1763, when the first breaches occurred in the non-intervention policy; from 1763 until 1818, when limited possessions were extended to dominance of almost the whole sub-continent.

Two elements of the earlier period have already been noticed: the presence of small but firmly established British and French bases on the coast, and the weakening of Mogul authority. Their conjunction might have tempted either company to dabble in Indian politics. Two events forced the British company to do so against their inclinations: war with France in the Carnatic, and an unexpected attack on Calcutta by the Nawab of Bengal in 1757.

The crisis in the Carnatic began in 1744. Both British and French companies had tried to maintain peace in India, despite war between their governments in Europe. War in the east was precipitated by an attack made by a British naval commander, who was not under the company's control, on French merchant ships in the Indian Ocean. The French government ordered La Bourdonnais, governor of Ile de France, to send a fleet to the Carnatic. This reinforcement, and the temporary absence of the British fleet in 1746, gave Dupleix, governor-general of Pondicherry, the excuse and opportunity to try out his long-planned policy of attacking British bases on the Carnatic. He allied with Indian princes and used trained Indian troops. His capture of Madras showed both sides the advantages of his methods; and peace between England and France in 1748 and the retrocession of Madras did not stop the struggle in the Carnatic. Dupleix was convinced that it was no longer possible for both companies to compete in the same area or to rely on a political framework provided by Indians. Growing disorder made it essential for Europeans to gain political power, and one of them must become dominant. In principle he was right: but the struggle from 1748 to 1754 was won by the British, who possessed greater military and financial resources and played Indian politics as effectively as Dupleix. In 1754 he was recalled, and the French company tried to revert to a policy of peace and non-involvement.

This was now out of the question, for both companies were embroiled in Indian politics. The Seven Years War from 1756 to 1763 completed the process begun in 1744. The new French governor-general, the Compte de Lally, tried to fight the British along European lines and was defeated by lack of adequate naval support. France's main Indian ally, the Nizam of Hyderabad, lost faith in French prospects and made peace with the British. In 1763, France was given back her five main Indian bases, but only on condition that they were unfortified. This ended the possibility of French domination of India. Until 1815 Frenchmen dreamed of reversing this verdict, relying on increasing dislike of British power among Indian princes. But success depended on evidence that France could give her potential Indian allies effective support; and this in turn depended on French naval supremacy in the Indian Ocean. This was acquired briefly in 1782–3 by de Suffren, and opened immense possibilities for France: but the Peace of Paris in 1783 wasted the opportunity, and it did not recur.

The importance of this Anglo-French struggle was that it launched the British company on a policy of Indian alliances and territorial expansion from which there was no return. But had this been the only new factor, expansion elsewhere in India might have been long-delayed. The war with France was concentrated in the Carnatic, which was a peripheral and relatively poor region. The real centre of Indian politics and wealth was Hindustan, and the decisive event, which was complementary to events in the south, was the occupation of Bengal after 1757.

The crisis in Bengal grew out of unsettled Indian politics and Indian fear that Anglo-French rivalries in the south might lead to intervention in the north. In 1756 the new Nawab of Bengal, Siraj-ud-daula, decided to strike at all rivals to his power, including members of his family and the British in Fort William; almost incidentally he attacked and captured Calcutta in contravention of the imperial *farman* of 1717. The British could not fail to react; yet no one intended the consequences of sending a small force from Madras under Robert Clive, a company servant who had distinguished himself in the Carnatic war. Clive had learnt his Indian techniques from Dupleix. By allying with local enemies of the Nawab he secured his political position: at the battle of Plassey in 1757 his force of 800 Europeans and 2,200 Indians scattered the Nawab's army of some 50,000 with a cannonade. Almost by accident the British were masters of Bengal. They replaced Siraj-ud-daula with a puppet. When he proved restive they replaced him with another, who in turn rebelled and was defeated at the far more decisive battle of Baksar in 1764. The Mogul emperor himself was now in British hands and their tool. His authority was preserved, and the company chose to regard itself as his servant, extracting the *diwani* – the right of tax-collection – of Bengal. Another puppet nawab was set up to rule Bengal on the company's behalf. The East India Company was now ruler of Bengal and one of the great powers in India.

After 1764, therefore, the issues changed fundamentally, and three problems faced the East India Company and the British government. The primary question was whether the British should avoid further territorial conquests or complete their occupation of India. In the 1760s the question seemed open, since British possessions were small and a system of treaties with Indian states appeared preferable to expensive and possibly unsuccessful wars. Whatever future policy was adopted, however, existing possessions in Bengal and the Carnatic posed urgent questions. Could a joint-stock trading company be allowed the same freedom from state control now that it was a great territorial power, able to commit the British government to major operations in the east? Again, how should the company administer its new dominions in Bengal and the Carnatic?

At the start the British company and government hoped to avoid further territorial expansion, for the mental habits of 150 years died hard, and the cost of the military effort seemed prohibitive. Three forces eventually destroyed this conservatism. Constant fear of French intervention made precautionary alliances essential. The need to defend existing possessions in the jungle of Indian politics made isolationism impossible. Security for each British centre entailed alliances with Indian neighbours, which in turn led to involvement in local politics and Indian wars. Victories produced additions to British territory and a consequential new alliance system to protect them. This process was not planned by London and was for long unwelcome to it. It was expensive and seemed to offer no hope of permanent stability. By about 1800 it became clear to servants of the company in India that a patchwork of regional alliances would never produce peace while any Indian powers remained outside British control, for Indian politics had become inherently unstable. The alternative was to create a single security system for the whole of India based on British power. Soon after 1800 London began to accept Calcutta's view that the occupation of India must be completed, as an investment in future peace and economy.

There was, however, an additional incentive for expansion. Conquest produced private loot for servants of the company and thereafter revenues for the company itself. Even if a state was not annexed, alliance with its ruler could entail subsidies in return for protection. Revenues and tribute made the company rich and lifted it above the financial margins of a trading concern. The English company outlived its French and Dutch rivals because it no longer depended entirely on the limited profits of selling Asian goods in Europe.

Even so, the conquest of India after 1764 was undertaken reluctantly, without planning or continuity. Company policy was for long to avoid further war or acquisitions, and no new British territory was acquired in Hindustan until the end of the century. But events in the Carnatic forced the company's hand. Haidar Ali, a Muslim military adventurer who had conquered Mysore, hoped to dominate the whole south of India with French support. In 1780, in alliance with Hyderabad, the Marathas and the French, he attacked Walajah, the Nawab of the Carnatic, now a British puppet, and overran the whole area before he was checked in 1780 and deserted by his Indian allies. Peace between Britain and France in 1783 left him alone, and his son, Tipu Sultan, made peace in 1784. He inherited his father's ambitions, however; and in 1789 was provoked into attacking the Raja of Travancore, a British ally. With the Nizam of Hyderabad and the Marathas this time as allies, the British had defeated him by 1792, and were undisputed masters of the Carnatic. They did not, however, annex Mysore. Instead they created a model for future dealings with defeated Indian states by annexing its peripheral provinces or giving them to allies such as Hyderabad, leaving Mysore weakened and cut off from possible allies. They also imposed a large indemnity and a treaty involving future tribute. Mysore was harmless, and provided profits; but the company was not obliged to administer it.

The final settlement of southern India came in 1801, and now reflected deliberate policy rather than a response to events. In face of renewed threat from France after 1793, Wellesley's argument that Britain must either rule or have firm control over all Indian states temporarily convinced the British government and company. In 1798 Hyderabad was forced to expel French officers and troops, and to sign a 'subsidiary' treaty under which the Nizam paid annual tribute, gave up control of foreign relations and accepted British troops and a resident. Mysore was treated similarly in 1799. Tipu had again allied with France. He was attacked and killed. The previous Hindu dynasty was restored on the basis of a subsidiary treaty like that forced on Hyderabad, and more territory was added to company possessions. Finally, in 1801, the Nawab of the Carnatic was removed and his possessions taken over. By that year the whole of India, south of Goa and the Kistna, was directly governed by the British, excluding only Mysore, Travancore and Cochin, which were tied by subsidiary treaties.

Settlement of the south cleared the way for dealing with the many powerful independent states in Hindustan, the Deccan and the west. Oudh was forced to sign new subsidiary treaties in 1797 and 1801 which deprived it of further territory and made it subordinate. War against the Maratha powers from 1802–5, nominally in support of a claimant to the Peshwa's lands and title, incorporated large areas into the company's estates, including Cuttack, the Doab, Delhi, Agra and other land in the Deccan and Gujarat. But the war failed to break Maratha power; and when Wellesley was recalled in 1805 the British were still not secure in central India. For the next seven years his project for imposing a *pax Britannica* on India was suspended while Britain concentrated on securing the Indian Ocean and Indonesia against the French and their allies, the Dutch. It was revived after 1812 by the new governor-general, Lord Hastings. Between 1816 and 1818 he undertook the largest military operations in Indian history. By 1818 he had defeated all Maratha forces and was able to impose a general settlement. Its principle was that the company should take all land necessary for security, but that elsewhere Indian rulers should be left in power, provided they signed treaties accepting residents and protection by British military forces. The Peshwa's lands were entirely confiscated, but the other Maratha states survived. The small Rajput states were bound by treaties, but did not have to accept British forces. The territorial settlement of India was for the moment complete. Britain either directly governed or indirectly controlled all India to the boundaries of the Punjab and Sind.

Long before this time the East India Company had ceased to be primarily a trading company. Given the radically changed position in India it might well have lost its governmental functions altogether: but, by a compromise typical of eighteenth-century British attitudes to corporate rights, it continued to administer India under governmental supervision.

State control was imposed gradually, each step resulting from company weakness. Its autonomy was first weakened by internal conflicts. Between 1758 and 1765 Clive and others who had made fortunes in Bengal attempted to control the Court of Directors by buying shares and 'splitting' them into as many voting units of £500 as possible. This led to internal feuds and so to governmental intervention. Clive's acquisition of the *diwani* of Bengal was expected to make the company immensely rich. In 1767 it was induced to offer £400,000 a year to the Treasury and an act was passed to restrict its dividends. Ironically, however, it was company poverty rather than affluence which led to formal control. By 1772 its servants in India were making fortunes, but the company was financially embarrassed by high military costs in Bengal, unexpectedly low selling prices at home and a banking crisis. It appealed to the government for a loan, and in return had to accept Lord North's Regulating Act of 1773. The company remained independent, but the government obtained the right to be informed on all financial, administrative and military affairs in India, and to set up a supreme court in Calcutta. In 1784, after a political uproar reflecting rumours of scandals in Indian government, Pitt's India Act extended state control as far as was compatible with leaving the company to administer India. It retained its commercial rights and functions, and controlled all appointments; but a body of royal commissioners, including members of the government, could now see and amend any despatches sent to India by the company, and send positive orders to the governor-general through a secret committee of the company. This dual system was illogical, but worked well and lasted until 1858. The commissioners became known as the Board of Control, and their president acted as if he was a secretary of state with a seat in cabinet. All major policy decisions came from or were approved by the government, which in effect used the company as a civil service to administer India on its behalf. The company continued to distribute dividends; but, as these were restricted by law, it had no temptation to use political power to enrich its shareholders. Dual control wasted time; but it incidentally protected India from the vagaries of British politics.

Perhaps the most surprising result of this compromise was that the company carried out its administrative duties so well; for it had no model for government of millions of Asians, and its own record was unpromising.

Administrative honesty was essential. The acquisitive habits characteristic of all servants of European companies in the east had proved disastrous when applied on the grand scale by Clive and his associates in Bengal. Reform came gradually, forced on the company by scandalized English public opinion. The Regulating Act of 1773 attempted to ensure honesty at the top by making the governor-general dependent on his council. He regained his supremacy in 1786, but thereafter the normal, though not invariable, policy of appointing governors-general from outside the Indian service tended to increase their sense of responsibility. The most important reform was reconstruction of the Indian service, undertaken between 1786 and 1793 by Lord Cornwallis. A clear distinction was at last made between government and commerce. Administrators lost all commercial functions and were forbidden to take part in trade or accept presents from Indians. They were paid good salaries and pensions, and so became less open to temptation. These reforms created the Covenanted Indian Service, which offered a good career rather than the chance to make an illicit fortune. It quickly developed an *esprit de corps* and sense of moral obligation to India. For all its many defects, particularly its increasing lack of direct contact with Indians, it supplied India with honest impartial government for a century and a half. It was the first specially organized and properly trained professional administration in European colonial history.

There remained the question of how to administer India. Two alternatives were open: to rule through Indian agents and Indian forms, as was done in Bengal in the 1760s and 1770s and as the Dutch did in Java; or to govern directly through expatriate officials, using whatever forms seemed convenient. The British never completely adopted either alternative. By 1818 a primary distinction existed between British India – those areas actually owned by the company – and the rest. British India was ruled 'directly' through the company's servants; the rest 'indirectly' through Indian princes, controlled by treaties, troops and resident advisers. This distinction remained to the end of British rule. Even within British India methods of tax-collection and government varied between the three main presidencies – Bengal, Madras and Bombay, to which all newly acquired lands were annexed. Bengal, for example, adopted the *zamindari* method of collecting taxes through hereditary Indian collectors who were liable for a fixed sum as laid down in the 'Permanent Settlement' of 1793. Madras and Bombay ultimately adopted either village or individual (*ryotwari*) assessments, according to local conditions. Similar variations existed in other fields of government and law.

By about 1818 the most formative phase of British activity in India was over. A commercial company had acquired control over one of the two greatest indigenous empires in the east. It had overcome the immense practical and moral difficulties of its first period of power, and had evolved systems of government which enabled it to exercise complete power without driving Indians to resistance. British dominance had so far brought few if any benefits to Indians and had riveted on them taxes heavier than they had known before. Three-quarters of a century of constant wars and plundering by British, Marathas, Persians and Afghans had reduced vast areas to a wilderness. But the worst period was over. During the century after 1818 India received some of the benefits of alien rule – internal peace, increased economic activity, better communications, and the intellectual stimulus of European literature and ideas.

For the future development of the European colonial empires British occupation of India had huge consequences. For the British it involved concern for Indian security, and so almost continuous frontier expansion in the north, north-west, Burma, South-East Asia, and ultimately even in East Africa and the Middle East. India was the nucleus from which much of the new British empire grew. For other European countries British success in India was both a defeat and a challenge. France and later other states believed that Britain drew much of her power from India. They saw that she had used Indian resources to occupy India and that it was possible to govern so large a territory with very few expatriate 'sojourners' at no cost to the metropolis. The occupation of India was to influence and stimulate the course of European imperialism during the nineteenth and twentieth centuries.

In terms of colonial history the significance of India after 1818 was that it was unlike any previous European dependency. It was not a colony of settlement, nor a trading base and it offered little incentive to establish plantations on the American pattern. No European power had hitherto ruled millions of a foreign race of comparable civilization, who could not be converted to Christianity nor assimilated to European culture. The British ruled India as guardians, not as settlers or planters. Power came from Indian sources, but was wielded by a few hundred British expatriates supported by a predominantly Indian army. India was the first great European dependency which was not also a colony in the true sense. The Spanish and Portuguese created prototypes for the first European empires in America: Britain made the model for the modern empires in Asia, Africa and the Pacific.

[illegible]

[illegible]

[illegible]

PART TWO

The Colonial Empires after 1815

9

The Second Expansion of Europe 1815-82

During the first quarter of the nineteenth century the colonial empires were in retreat. When the Spanish and Portuguese colonies in America had gained independence they were smaller than at any time since 1700. Moreover, there seemed no likelihood that they would expand again in other parts of the world, for the conditions which had previously seemed to make colonies worth while evaporated with the American empires. Commercial monopoly, the theoretical foundation of 'mercantilist' empire, was no longer practicable, for most of America was now free to trade as it chose. Britain responded by opening her remaining colonies to foreign ships and goods in the 1820s, though retaining the monopoly of shipping between her own and colonial ports until 1849. Most other imperial powers followed her example. On British initiative there grew up a web of international commercial treaties which destroyed high tariffs, preferences and other obstacles, so that by the mid-nineteenth century international trade was largely free. This made the old arguments in support of empire meaningless, for the end of *l'exclusif* was logically the end of empire.

Political conditions after 1815 also militated against imperialism. European rivalries were damped down for half a century. Colonial empires were no longer useful diplomatic counters or necessary for wartime strategy. Most important was British predominance. Until the 1890s Britain had unchallenged naval power: she was also the only state still to possess a large overseas empire. She could acquire any part of the world accessible by sea and deny it to others; and the main reason why a new European expansion seemed unlikely after 1815 was that Britain showed no desire to build a new empire. She was not so much 'anti-imperialist' as unconvinced that new colonies would be of value. Canada and Australia could absorb any of her emigrants who chose not to go to the United States. Colonies were no longer wanted as monopolistic markets, for her industrial supremacy opened those of the whole world. During the seventy years after 1815 Britain was the chief exponent of leaving the independent parts of the world alone.

Yet European empires expanded faster during the century after 1815 than at any previous time. Between 1800 and 1878 Europe added some 6,500,000 square miles to its claims; between then and 1914 another 8,653,000. In 1800 Europe and its possessions (including ex-colonies) covered about 55 per cent of the land surface of the world; in 1878, 67 per cent; and in 1914, 84·4 per cent.[1] Expansion continued; by 1939 the only significant countries which had never been under European rule were Turkey, parts of Arabia, Persia, China, Tibet, Mongolia and Siam. In addition to new colonies, there were new colonial powers – Italy, Belgium, the United States, and Russia. Far from being the end of empire, 1815 had marked a new beginning.

Why did this second expansion take place? Why did so many European states take part? It is convenient to divide the period at 1882, treating the first seventy years as a period of expansion, the rest as an age of partition and redivision.

Before about 1882 one obvious reason for renewed expansion of Europe can be ruled out: it was not due to a revival of European imperialism – the urge to acquire colonies to serve metropolitan interests. It is, of course, historical nonsense to divide history into 'imperialist' and 'anti-imperialist' epochs, for there have always been some who favoured and others who distrusted the possession of colonies. But if ever most European states were undeniably unenthusiastic about acquiring new colonies, it was between 1815 and 1882. Indeed, it is only a slight exaggeration to say that no colony was acquired during this period primarily as a result of calculated desire for it in Europe. Occasionally a metropolitan pressure group might demand occupation or retention of some territory in which it had a particular interest, as the

French Catholic party did for Tahiti and the Marquesas in the 1840s and Cochin-China in the 1860s, or as British supporters of E. G. Wakefield did for New Zealand in the 1830s. But these were primarily responses to situations on the circumference which invited a choice between acquisition and rejection: they did not necessarily imply an abstract demand for colonies. In fact, no European government, political party or social group strongly or consistently demanded new empire-building before the 1880s.

Thus, imperial expansion during this period was almost entirely unplanned by Europe: the momentum came from the periphery. This distinguished it very clearly both from the first expansion of the fifteenth and sixteenth centuries, and to some extent from events after 1882.

By the early nineteenth century Europe was unavoidably linked with the still-independent countries of Africa, Asia and the Pacific in many ways. The growth of European technology and industry rapidly extended trade with all parts of the world. Steamships generated types of commerce which would once have been unprofitable. Christian missions were establishing stations everywhere, and explorers mapped 'dark' continents. Europe was now an immense power house, radiating energy indiscriminately, stumbling into closer contact with all independent states. Such contacts were the solvent of a 'hands-off' policy. Improved European military and naval equipment and techniques were reversing the old power balance. Islamic and other civilized states, hitherto able to resist Europe, could no longer withstand attacks by quite small forces, as the British defeat of China in 1839–42 dramatically showed. In the past colonization had often been made possible by the skilful use of small resources against great odds, as in India. Now it was almost too easy. Indigenous states, previously formidable obstacles or valuable buttresses to European activities, now crumbled to the touch. These were the causes of the new expansion of Europe.

Thus the great majority of new colonial annexations after 1815 occurred not because they were planned but because some European interest on the periphery made them inevitable: many grew directly from some existing European possession and expressed its local interests. This 'sub-imperialist' process took differing forms. Colonies of white settlement in Canada, South Africa, Australia or New Zealand, expanded internally and into their peripheries as a result of colonists' land-hunger, bullion prospecting, trading, or labour recruiting. Non-European colonies of occupation, like India, Java, or Algeria, expanded because the local government felt an incessant urge to deal with frontier insecurities. Even small possessions, such as the West Africa trading bases, grew by making treaties with neighbouring native states. In weak non-European societies, such as those of the Pacific Islands, a few missionaries or white planters might so disrupt indigenous society that European intervention became necessary. These events lay on the circumference: but action had ultimately to be sanctioned by a metropolitan government. European statesmen frequently tried to avoid taking full responsibility for new territories. Evasive devices were used, such as protectorate treaties, which gave some political control over native states but not full possession. Sometimes, also, international complications made annexation impossible. But usually annexations occurred because the metropolis found it easier to approve the actions or policies of men on the spot than to denounce or reverse them.

Colonial expansion was thus the result of two main forces: the general impact of industrial Europe, and the local power of existing European nuclei. Occasionally a colony was positively wanted in Europe: more often it was taken because the alternative seemed impracticable. By 1882 the new empires, reflecting their origins, consisted very largely of colonies which their owners did not want and could not use for any imperial purpose. The partition of the next thirty years merely exaggerated this peculiar characteristic.

The Growth of European Power in Africa

In 1815 Africa seemed an unlikely field for European colonization. The Mediterranean coast was attractive for trade or settlement, but was barred to colonization by Islamic states under varying degrees of Turkish suzerainty. The west coast was more accessible: there were full colonies in Senegal, Gambia, Sierra

Leone and Angola, and numerous trading bases. But the decline of the slave trade, though it did not altogether cease until the 1860s, reduced European interest. Trade in ground-nuts and palm-oil eventually took its place. But for long it was relatively small in value; and because these goods were supplied by African middlemen, the trade itself was not necessarily an incentive for colonization. The Portuguese were too weak to extend their territory in Mozambique, and there were few European interests or bases elsewhere on the east coast. Only in southern Africa, where the European settlement at the Cape was expanding to the east, was it predictable in 1815 that new territory would be acquired.

The Mediterranean Coast

The most surprising acquisitions made by Europe in Africa before 1882 were Algeria, Tunisia and Egypt, for these were all Islamic states able to offer formidable resistance.

The occupation of Algeria by France, begun almost as an historical accident, was one of the most significant events in the growth of European power in northern Africa. Conquest had been considered by Louis XIV and by Napoleon, but it was not a profound French ambition in 1815. Occupation began in 1830, when Charles X, partly to suppress piracy, partly to gain a spectacular success for his unpopular government, sent a naval expedition to occupy Algiers. The Restoration monarchy fell in that year; but its successors felt bound to complete the occupation of the coast, and so suppress piracy, by capturing Oran and Bone. France had still no desire to occupy the rest of Algeria. She was forced to do so – with the alternative of evacuating altogether – by the Islamic revolt of 1834 which lasted intermittently until 1879. At the start France had little to lose by evacuation, except that the French army felt its honour was at stake; but by 1882 Algeria was fully occupied by French forces, and there was a sizeable settler population near the coastal towns. Algeria thus became the first of the modern hybrid colonies, occupied for no good reason of economics or strategy, but because a limited initial foothold escaladed into complete colonization.

The establishment of a French protectorate over Tunisia in

1881 and the British occupation of Egypt in 1882 followed similar patterns. Tunisia was the first Islamic state to lose its independence through over-indulgence in the amenities offered by European bankers. The Beys, who had been subordinates of the Sultan of Turkey, obtained French financial help in the 1830s to make good their independence. The danger was that Tunisia, as neighbour of Algeria, might exchange one master for another; but for long the Beys skilfully used diplomatic support from Italy and Britain to offset French influence, at the same time borrowing heavily in Europe to modernize the administration and economy. By the 1850s, however, debts to French and other bankers were too great for the Bey's revenues to service; and in 1857 the British and French consuls obtained supervisory powers over the Bey's government, which were later shared also by Italy. In 1869 an international finance commission was set up, representing these three creditor states, to reform Tunisian finances. By virtue of her greater financial interest, and her consul's skill in allying with the Tunisian finance minister, France gained the upper hand. Yet she had no desire to annex the country for the cost of conquering Algeria still rankled, and a repetition in Tunisia would have been politically ruinous for any ministry which undertook it. France's hand was forced by Italy, who made it clear that she intended to acquire Tunisia herself. To prevent such a take-over, the Algerian army was sent over the border in 1881: even so France's aim was only to sign a protectorate treaty and withdraw her forces. Once again a nationalist rebellion forced her to undertake full occupation. An Islamic rising broke out against French intervention and the Bey's excessive involvement with infidels: in suppressing it France occupied the whole of Tunisia. Vestiges of her limited first intentions could be seen in the fact that Tunisia remained a protectorate and in the use of the Bey as the nominal government; but in effect Tunisia became a French possession.

Financial failure in Turkey coincided with that in Tunisia; but its different outcome demonstrated the sort of international situation which might check the expansion of European colonization. By 1876 the Sultan owed about 200 million Turkish pounds (£183 million sterling) and was insolvent. The revolt of Bosnia in

1875 and Bulgaria in 1876 led to Russian intervention which might have given her control of Turkey itself. In fact Russia surprisingly failed to take Constantinople in 1877 and made peace with Turkey at San Stefano in March 1878; but her intervention forced other states to shore up Turkish independence, since Turkey was too important in the strategy of the Middle East and the Balkans to be dominated by any one power. At the Congress of Berlin in 1878, the first international concert on a quasi-colonial issue, Turkey was reprieved, and her financial problems were alleviated. She remained politically free, but was now a corpse propped up to serve the needs of diplomacy, providing a wonderful field of activity for the European financiers and concession hunters on whose help she now entirely depended.

Egypt was less fortunate because less important to the powers. She had become independent of the Sultan of Turkey under Mehemet Ali between 1811 and 1847; since when he and his successors had modernized the country by constructing canals and roads and developing the economy with western technicians and capital. Egypt's mistake was to grant a concession in 1854 to De Lesseps, the former French consul, to construct the Suez canal, since this made the Khedive responsible for part of the costs, and increased international interest in Egypt's future. France gained a dominant interest both in the canal and in Egyptian loans; but Britain was equally interested because the canal was critical for the route to India.

The crisis came in 1878 when the Khedive Ismail had to suspend payment on treasury bills. An international body representing both his creditors and shareholders in the canal was set up to supervise his finances; and when, in 1879, he tried to evade their control he was deposed and a more pliant Khedive, Tewfik, set up. Egypt was now governed by two commissioners who were appointed by France and Britain as agents of a new international Debt Commission, the system being known as the Dual Control. Egypt's nominal independence seemed secure, since no one foreign power would allow another to take sole control. But, as in Tunisia, a nationalist rising destroyed this balance. The revolt expressed general resentment at infidel intervention; and under Colonel Arabi the insurgents had gained control of most of

Egypt by 1882. Only effective military action could have restored the Dual Control; only joint action could have preserved its international character. In 1882 the French parliament refused credits for the proposed French expedition, and Britain was left to act alone. In August 1882, Sir Garnet Wolseley defeated Arabi, reinstated Tewfik and effectively controlled Egypt. This marked the beginning of unilateral British control. Gladstone wanted to withdraw British forces and restore the Dual Control. But the French would not send troops; without European forces the nationalist movement would have gained control again; and the *jihad* begun by the Mahdi, Mohammed Ahmad, in the Egyptian Sudan menaced Upper Egypt. The British had to stay, prisoners of their own success. But their presence in Egypt had momentous consequences. France remained intensely jealous, for she thought Egypt was primarily her own sphere of interest, and was ready to embarrass Britain in other colonial spheres. British diplomacy was hamstrung because, to run Egyptian finances, she depended on majority agreement in the Debt Commission; and this gave Germany, one of its members, the chance to bargain for her vote. Egypt, therefore, became a key fact in the diplomacy of colonial partition after 1882; for Britain, hitherto the arch-exponent of a 'hands-off' policy, had broken the ring and taken one of the plums before others had staked their claims. Egypt did not cause the partition of Africa, but its occupation by Britain significantly influenced the later course of events.

Tropical West Africa

In Mediterranean Africa the roots of European expansion were the financial weakness of debtor sultans and the reaction of Islamic nationalists to alien encroachments. In West Africa also there were powerful Islamic and pagan kingdoms; but none collapsed through financial insolvency in this period. European investment was spiritual and geographical rather than financial. European explorers had charted most of West Africa by the 1850s, and by the 1870s were concentrating on the Congo region. They aroused wide public interest in Europe which showed in subscriptions to geographical societies and to the costs of expeditions. The missionary movement also was in full flood. Missions of all denominations moved inland from the coasts, and some missionaries, like David Livingstone, were major explorers. But neither explorers, missionaries, nor their supporters expected formal European occupation. They were concerned to lighten the dark continent, not to govern it. Commerce was desirable as an alternative to the slave trade: but European commerce was thought to be compatible with the independence of enlightened African states.

The roots of European expansion were the European bases in West Africa. Until the 1860s their importance was in suppressing the slave trade with America, and there was little desire in Europe to expand their hinterlands. Yet even such weak nuclei of European power showed a remarkable capacity to expand by their own exertions. Three forces were at work. First, a respectable trade was developing in vegetable oils for the manufacture of candles and soap. Ground-nuts came mainly from the Gambia and from the Scarcies and Melecourie region to the south; palm-oil from most parts of the coast. Neither product required European plantations, for they were grown or collected by Africans: but both trades involved extensive commercial contacts, and led to rivalries between French, British and eventually German firms. Before 1882 these activities resulted in a number of new trading factories and many commercial treaties with African rulers: but the real period of commercial rivalry tending to territorial control came later.

A more immediate cause of expansion was the problem of jurisdiction which commercial contacts created. Security for and control over foreign nationals trading in West Africa required agreements with indigenous rulers to give European states jurisdiction over their subjects outside their small coastal possessions. Such treaties were widely made. In principle they did not affect African independence; but they contained the seeds of future control, for if African states failed to fulfil their agreements, or collapsed, Europeans felt bound to step in. Since, moreover, treaties often contained preferential trading clauses, by about 1882 West Africa was covered by a network of British and French spheres of interest. The French were dominant in the Senegal area and between the Gambia and Sierra Leone; the British on the Gold Coast and around Lagos. But their interests overlapped at many points, such as in Porto Novo near Sierra Leone and on the Niger; and it was already probable that such conflicts would lead ultimately to clearer demarcations of their respective spheres. In changed circumstances this occurred after 1882.

A third cause of territorial expansion was the financial weakness of all these West African bases. France and Britain retained them in the interests of traders and anti-slaving naval forces, but did not wish to subsidize them. The colonies were poor because small, and depended on customs duties for revenue. Since traders could by-pass their ports, and so avoid customs, colonial governments had an incentive to expand their coastal frontiers so as to control all alternative points of access. Hence both British and French tried to canalize trade through their own ports, or to impose the same duties on other independent ports. The British sealed up the Gold Coast by acquiring the Danish forts in 1850 and Dutch Elmina in 1872. They acquired Lagos in 1861, and then extended their control westwards. Annexation was not, however, usual. Both countries preferred to make customs treaties with coastal rulers. The French did so around Senegal, in Guinea and on the Ivory Coast; the British round Sierra Leone, the Gambia and near Lagos. By 1882 these two powers seemed likely to control all points of access in West Africa primarily to make their original possessions viable.

These extensions of territory and influence implied neither metropolitan imperialism, nor deliberate empire-building by local colonial officials. But in Senegal expansion inland had definite imperialist aims, which reflected the views of Dakar – the new capital – rather than Paris, and was inaugurated by Louis Faidherbe, who was governor between 1854 and 1865. His argument for expansion was basically that the colony could only pay its way if it took in the neighbouring regions which produced groundnuts, and also encouraged plantation production by Africans as a cash-crop. But he also expounded a concept new to West Africa. As an ex-officer in the Algerian army he assumed that it was impossible to live at peace with powerful Islamic states, and in particular with the Tucolor empire which had been established up the Senegal by El Hadj Omar; and on this assumption France stood committed to indefinite conquests in the western Sudan. Faidherbe only began the work, defeating Omar's forces in 1857–9. Neither his successors at Dakar nor the French government shared his views, and after his retirement they were not revived until the 1880s. Yet this brand of Senegalese imperialism had important consequences during the partition, for it provided later imperialists with the vision of a French empire in West Africa stretching from Senegal to the Niger, enclosing or absorbing all the foreign settlements along the coast.

Equatorial West Africa

In tropical West Africa European expansion was still almost imperceptible by 1882, and what there was did not spring from European imperialism. But in the Congo a situation had developed which reflected a deliberate desire for colonization and owed nothing to existing colonial nuclei.

The Congo was within the region claimed, but not effectively occupied, by Portugal. It had been investigated by explorers such as H. M. Stanley in the 1870s, and Europe was deeply interested in it. The project for colonizing the Congo was, however, the brain-child of Leopold II, King of the Belgians. Belgium had no colonies and did not want them; but Leopold's study of other empires convinced him that the application of European capital and skills to tropical possessions would make them immensely profitable. His model was probably Dutch Indonesia, where the Culture System had produced the only cash dividend received by any imperial power in the first half of the nineteenth century. After various other projects had failed, Leopold decided to establish a colony in the Congo. He had no claim; his government would not support him; and the great powers would certainly have opposed his project if it had been made known. He therefore acted circumspectly. In 1876 he called an international geographical conference at Brussels, and through it founded the African International Association (AIA) to raise money for exploration in the Congo region. Within this framework he created in 1878 the *Comité d'études du Haut Congo*, a corporate body with privately subscribed capital, to undertake further exploration. By 1882, Leopold entirely owned this company, and through it he employed Stanley, who for long thought he was working for a philanthropic organization, to make treaties giving the *comité* sovereign political authority and commercial rights along the south bank of the Congo. This was to be the basis of a new Belgian colony.

Such activities generated rivalries. The French with their stake in Gabun, were suspicious; and Brazza, a French naval officer, made parallel treaties on the north bank of the Congo, nominally in the name of the French branch of the AIA, but actually to reserve French interests. Britain too was trying to protect her commercial interests on the Congo against a possible foreign monopoly; and in December 1882 she explicitly recognized Portuguese claims to the mouth of the Congo. Thus, simply by injecting a new factor into the colonial situation, Leopold had created an international crisis. If others followed his lead and began to stake out claims for colonies in Africa or elsewhere the whole international situation would be changed. The Congo was a major factor in the Berlin Conference of 1884, and in the genesis of the partition of Africa.

South Africa

The Congo situation was exceptional before 1882 in its artificiality. In southern Africa European expansion took place naturally, as a predictable result of the situation there in 1815.

As always since the mid-eighteenth century a triangle of forces operated in the Cape and its environs. First there was British policy. The British had no desire to expand and felt little interest in the Cape as a settlement colony; but they felt obliged to impose their moral principles on the predominantly Dutch settler population by protecting Hottentots from the abuses they suffered as tied servants, and by abolishing slavery in 1833. Second, there were the Dutch settlers, whose tendency was to expand east and north in search of new grazing lands and away from authority. By the 1830s these instincts were intensified by the new British regulations on servants and slaves, and the presence of British missions. Finally there were the Bantus to the east of the Great Fish River. For long they had been pressing south and west; now their movement was intensified by the effects of Zulu power in the Natal region behind them, which was forcing other Bantu tribes to move either south or north to escape their depredations, and so increased the pressure on those tribes nearest the Cape to move westwards, against the advance of the Europeans.

Boer expansion and Bantu counter-movement made it impossible for the British to restrict the boundaries of the Cape. By 1882 two areas had been occupied by Europeans. In the east the frontier of settlement had moved steadily forward, checked only by recurrent wars with the Xhosas, Tembus and Pondos and by British attempts to renounce acquisitions made as a result of victory. By 1882 only a small area – Tembuland, Galekaland, Bomvanaland, and Pondoland – remained nominally independent, though actually under informal British control. Beyond them Natal also was a British colony: but its settlement was the result of the Great Trek inland which began in 1836. The trek differed from the eastward movement only in that it was a partly organized exodus of some 10,000 Boers to escape British rule and to set up independent republics. The trekkers went north over the Orange River, some to the Transvaal, others to Natal, setting up two small republics. The British were never certain how to deal with them, or with the later Orange River Colony. The Boers were British subjects and could not legally establish autonomous republics. Their presence in these regions had repercussions on the eastern frontier of the Cape because they disturbed Bantu tribes elsewhere. Yet Britain did not want to govern these distant areas, and alternated between annexing them and leaving them alone. In 1842 she occupied Natal and in 1848 the other Boer settlements. Natal was never given up, but in 1852 Britain recognized the Transvaal and in 1854 the Orange River Colony as sovereign states. Twenty years later this policy was again reversed in the hope of imposing a single native policy throughout southern Africa. The Transvaal was annexed in 1877, but was given qualified independence in 1881.

In 1882 the future of British power in South Africa was still uncertain; but a new factor was now drawing the British into Central Africa. The discovery of diamonds in Griqualand West led to its annexation in 1871, despite the claims of the Orange Free State and the Transvaal to the region. The diamond fields were controlled by Cape businessmen, and a new Cape imperialism evolved which wanted to expand from Kimberley, the diamond centre, into Bechuanaland and Central Africa in search of more diamonds or precious metals. During the next thirty years this ambition immensely complicated Britain's position in Africa and was an important factor in the eventual partition of Central Africa.

European Expansion in Asia

By 1882 far more important developments had taken place in the east, where European power had expanded in Central Asia, China, India, South-East Asia and Indonesia. But in no case was expansion the outcome of a deliberate plan in a European capital to acquire new possessions.

Russian Expansion in Central Asia and the Far East

Russian expansion occurred in Central Asia and northern China. In each case it was the result of problems arising out of existing Russian possessions, and was carried out on the initiative of men on the spot.

In the Far East, Amur Province was acquired from China. Russia already stretched across Asia to the Pacific; and throughout the nineteenth century the colonization of Siberia continued, bearing some resemblance to the westwards expansion of the United States, though the occupation of Siberia was more the result of transportation than of voluntary emigration. There was truth in the quip that in Russia the knout followed the flag. Amur was not necessary to eastern Siberia, but it was easily accessible from it. It was occupied by the Russian governor-general of Irkutsk in the 1850s on his own initiative, because the defeat of China by Britain between 1839 and 1842 had demonstrated Chinese weakness, and because it offered Russia improved access to the Pacific. Russian control was accepted by Peking in an informal treaty in 1858. It was ratified by St Petersburg in 1860 and the area further extended. The subsequent foundation of a port at Vladivostock made Russia a Pacific power. The occupation of Sakhalin Island in 1875 was a logical consequence, and brought Russia into close contact with Japan. In the 1890s both new acquisitions were of great importance.

The other Russian acquisition was Central Asia. This too was unplanned, but bore a closer relationship to real Russian needs. The previous southern frontier of Siberia ran from the northern shore of the Caspian up the river Ural to Omak, Semipalatinsk and then to the Chinese frontier. To the south was the unstable and thinly populated Kazakh steppe, and further south the powerful Islamic khanates of Khiva, Bokhara and Kokand. Russia had several motives for controlling this area. Settlers, merchants, and administrators in Siberia were affected by chronic disorder to the south; the steppe lands were attractive for settlement; and after the British attack on Afghanistan in 1839–42 the Russians feared British expansion into Turkestan. Central Asia was a dangerous vacuum which Russia felt obliged to fill. Yet occupation was slow and hesitant, owing more to soldiers and administrators on the spot than to St Petersburg. By 1864 the steppe lands had been conquered, and St Petersburg tried to call a halt. As always, however, there were unanswerable reasons for pressing on. To the south lay three khanates with whom it was impossible to establish a stable relationship. By 1880 they had been dealt with. Bokhara and Khiva were reduced in size but left nominally independent, under protectorate treaties. Kokand was fully incorporated into the new Russian province of Kazakh.

By the later 1870s, Russia had occupied all Central Asia as far as Merv, and stood on the borders of Afghanistan, distrusting British intentions. These fears were mutual, for the British had advanced from the other direction for similar motives. Fears on both sides were resolved after the failure of the British expedition to Afghanistan in 1878–80 and the crisis of 1884–5, when a Russian general occupied Pendjeh and the British feared an invasion of Afghanistan. Thereafter the powers agreed to delimit the northern frontiers of Afghanistan, which remained independent and neutral. Persia, however, still worried them for the same reasons; but the agreed settlement of her frontier with Afghanistan in 1888, and the subsequent informal division of the country into Russian and British spheres of influence, solved this problem without formal partition. The Anglo-Russian entente of 1907

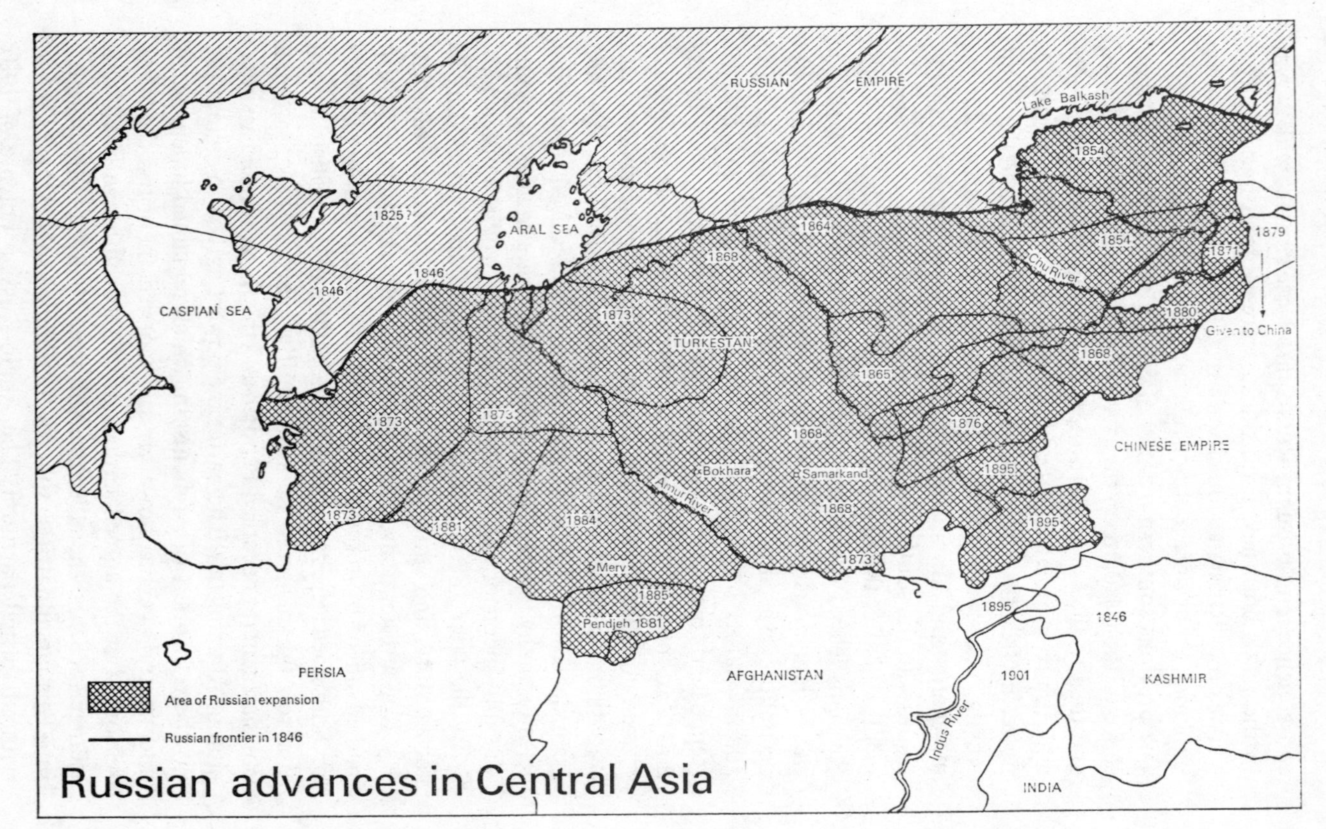

Russian advances in Central Asia

cemented the compromise and enabled Persia to share with Afghanistan the honour of never being made a European colony.

British Expansion Within and Around India

British expansion within and on the frontiers of India after 1815 was a classic example of unplanned expansion. The settlement of 1818 made the British dominant within India. But it left a number of Indian princes semi-independent; it did not extend to the Punjab, Sind or the north-west frontier; and it did not secure the eastern border. In addition there were problems connected with Indian trade in the Archipelago and to China. The expansion of British power in response to these problems was the result of Indian interests and policies rather than of British policy. The Indian government in Calcutta was not independent of London; but it had its own point of view and its own army, paid for out of local taxes. In most cases London assumed that what Calcutta thought necessary was also in the interests of Britain.

Internal expansion meant incorporating more Indian states into British India. Until Lord Dalhousie became governor-general in 1848 there was no general desire to do this, and states lost their independence only when they proved rebellious or were badly governed. Coorg was taken over permanently, and Mysore temporarily, in 1831 on these grounds. Dalhousie, however, believed that direct British government was better than government by princes, and looked for excuses to annex. By applying the doctrine of 'lapse' – the principle that the British could repudiate an adopted heir to a Hindu state under Hindu custom – he took over Satara, Jaitpur, Sambalpur, Baghat, Udaipur, Jhansi and Nagpur. Oudh, a Muslim state, was absorbed in 1856 for bad government, and Hyderabad was forced to cede Berar for failure to pay subsidies due under treaty. The outbreak of the Mutiny in 1857, which may have been influenced by these annexations, led to a new policy. Thereafter individual princes were sometimes removed for misdemeanours, but no Indian state was permanently annexed.

The north-west frontier presented the same problem to the British as Central Asia to the Russians. The Punjab, providing access to Afghanistan, was the key. The death in 1839 of Ranjit

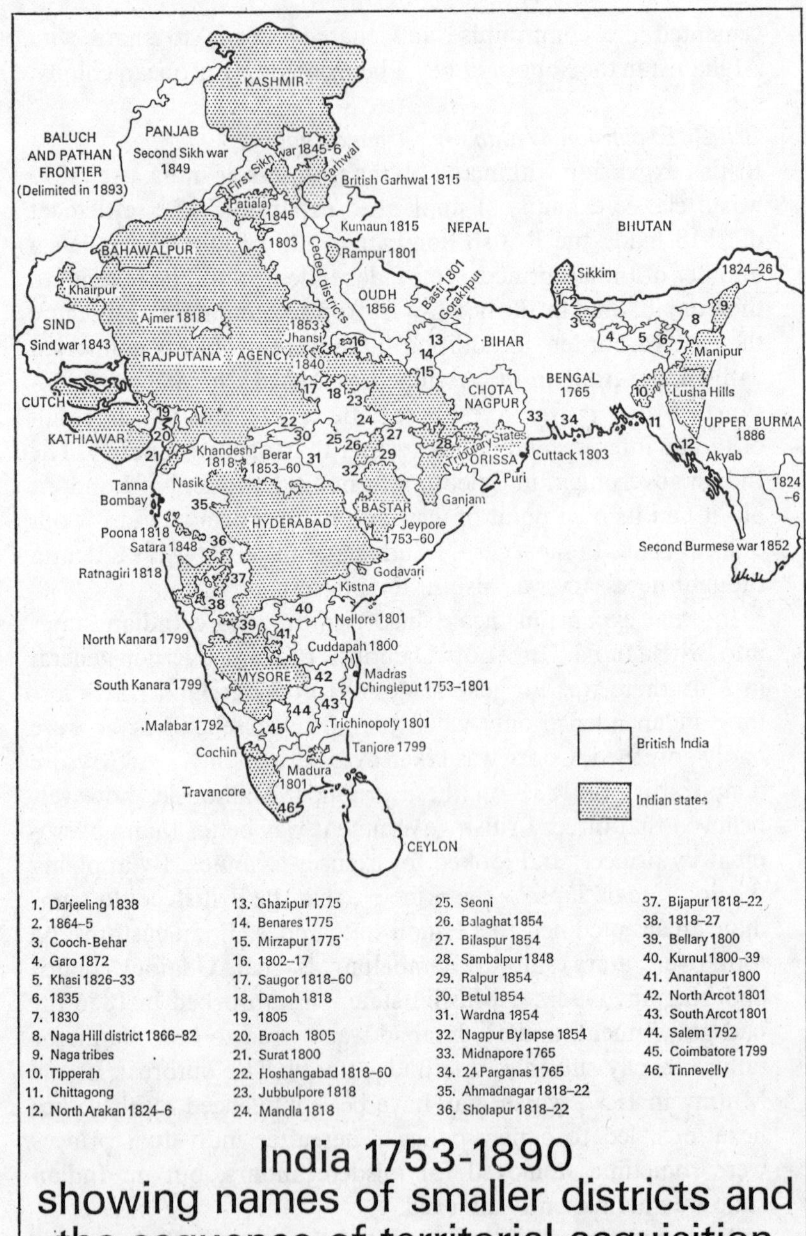

India 1753-1890
showing names of smaller districts and the sequence of territorial acquisition

Singh, who had created this Sikh state, produced internal chaos. The British had to act. In 1845 the Sikhs attacked British protected territories across the river Sutlej and were defeated. An attempt to create a stable Sikh state under British protection failed; and after a second revolt in 1848 the Punjab was annexed to British India in 1849. Sind was absorbed for less compelling reasons. It was a congeries of small states, tied by British treaties, but otherwise independent. Temporary occupation during the abortive British expedition to Afghanistan in 1839–42 showed its importance as the best route to Kabul, and in 1842 Karachi, Sukkur and Bukkur were retained permanently. When the remaining Amirs revolted against new treaty conditions in 1843, they too were annexed. Neither annexation was justified by the facts: Sind suffered for British failure to control Afghanistan.

Afghanistan was the one region in the north-west which retained its independence. In 1839–42 the British attempted to control it by placing a puppet ruler on the throne of Kabul, but failed. A second attempt was made in 1878–80 because a later Amir refused to accept and obey a British resident. This also failed; but it had the secondary result that a protectorate was imposed on Baluchistan and Quetta annexed. By this time better relations with Russia made the north-west frontier seem less dangerous, and Afghanistan thereafter provided an admirable buffer state. Britain was left to impose order on the unruly frontier provinces between her and the Punjab, and this was a problem she never satisfactorily solved.

British expansion on India's eastern frontier was due not to imperialism, greed, or fear of a European rival – at least before the 1880s – but to bad relations with an Asian state. In 1815 Burma was ruled by the Konbaung dynasty, whose ambition was to create an empire throughout South-East Asia. Since 1782 Burma had conquered Arakan and become a neighbour of Bengal. Consequent frontier problems and Burmese suspicions that the British were supporting Arakan rebels made King Badawpaya determined to conquer Assam and Bengal. Assam was occupied in 1817. In 1824 the Burmese attacked Cachar and prepared to invade Bengal through Chittagong. To prevent this, the British landed forces at Rangoon and captured the new Burmese capital of Amarapura in 1826. Under the Treaty of Yandabo they acquired the territories recently conquered by Burma – Arakan, Tenasserim, Assam and Manipur. Their policy was to establish a secure buffer zone rather than to gain territory, and they gave up the valuable areas they had conquered in Pegu. Such clemency did not lead to better relations, and Burmese rulers refused to work with British residents. By 1851 Indian traders were being attacked in Pegu, and Dalhousie decided to act. In 1852 Pegu was occupied and a treaty made with the new and more amenable King Mindon. Upper Burma remained independent, but lost Pegu. She was thus cut off both from India and the sea: there seemed no possible ground for future conflict and no reason why the British should want to occupy Upper Burma.

The final stage came as the result of a radically new situation in 1885–6. Now that France controlled Indo-China, the Burmese court hoped to get French support for a bid to escape British overlordship. In 1885 reports that Jules Ferry had promised Burma financial and military support coincided with Burmese provocation against British firms trading in Upper Burma. British demands for redress of grievances and a new protectorate treaty were rejected, and in 1885 an Indian army occupied Upper Burma, almost without fighting. The British could find no suitable candidate for the Burmese throne, so they annexed Burma to India.

The British occupation of Malaya was also the outcome of local problems which seemed otherwise insoluble. The peninsula consisted of small states in which neither the local sultans nor their suzerain, Siam, could maintain order. Pirates swarmed along the coast and attacked shipping on the route to Indonesia and China. Chinese settlers from Singapore, many of whom had British nationality, complained that they could get no protection for their trade or tin mining. The British colony of Penang depended for its food on Kedah and suffered from local conflicts for power. The British tried to avoid involvement, on Stamford Raffles' principle that Britain had no interest in acquiring territory on the mainland; but after 1867, when the Colonial Office took over the British Straits Settlements (Penang, Malacca and Singapore) from the India Office, limited interference was decided on. The aim was merely to make treaties with the Malay states under which they would receive residents and accept their advice on the pattern of the Indian states. In 1874 the Pangkor Engagement was made with the leading chiefs of Perak, which obliged the successful claimant to a disputed succession to the sultanate to receive a British resident 'whose advice must be asked and acted upon in all questions other than those touching Malay religion and custom'. Similar arrangements were made with Selangor and Sungei Ujong in the same year; with Pahang in 1888; the rest of Negri Sembilan in 1895; and with Kedah, Perlis, Kelantan and Trengganu when they were transferred from Siamese suzerainty to British protection in 1909. Johore did not accept a British adviser until 1914.

British occupation of Malaya was intended to be informal: these were 'protected states' like those in India, not full British possessions. In fact, protection and the advice of residents soon became effective occupation and real government.

British occupation of Labuan and Sarawak was as unplanned as that of Malaya. They came under British control through the action of James Brooke, an ex-naval officer, who took service with the Sultan of Brunei in 1841, and was given Sarawak in full sovereignty in 1846. In the same year Britain acquired the island of Labuan as a coaling base on the route to China. Borneo remained independent, but the Dutch later imposed authority on all but these two British possessions and the other territories belonging to the Sultan of Brunei.

China was the other sphere in which British expansion was related to the needs of India. British interests were purely commercial. The China trade was important to British India because the East India Company used the credits it acquired in India to sell Indian goods in Canton and buy tea for sale in Britain. Unfortunately the most saleable Indian commodity was opium. The Chinese government not unnaturally wished to keep it out, and banned importation in 1800. For long this ban was evaded by smuggling; but in 1838 a new imperial commissioner at

Canton closed all foreign factories and seized over 20,000 chests of opium. This was a blow to the British, who also had a long-standing grievance at being forbidden to trade with any Chinese port except Canton. Britain had no moral or legal case; her decision to act was characteristic of the frequently low moral standards of European dealings with other countries during the nineteenth century. After a decisive naval struggle between 1839 and 1842 the Chinese government accepted the Treaty of Nanking. The British received Hong Kong in full sovereignty as a trading base, and were permitted to trade at four additional 'treaty ports', Amoy, Foochow, Ningpo and Shanghai. British subjects were exempt from Chinese jurisdiction in these ports, and Chinese import duties were restricted. Foreign Christian missions were allowed in certain areas. This treaty began the forcible opening of China to the west. The United States, France and Russia quickly obtained similar rights, and further concessions were extracted in and after 1855. Yet in 1882 China remained independent, and had lost only Hong Kong and Amur. Her future depended on whether she could reorganize her attitudes and forms of government to meet the challenge of western infiltration. The fact that Japan, which had similarly been forced by the United States to open her ports to foreigners in 1854, did so, and even became a major international power, showed that this was not impossible.

French Expansion in Indo-China

British expansion in Asia before 1882 sprang from territory and interests Britain already possessed; but the first phase of French expansion in Indo-China is difficult to explain in terms of the expansion of an existing nucleus. Like French power in Algeria it was partly accidental, partly the result of metropolitan decisions.

In 1815 the five unfortified trading bases in India were France's only possessions in the east, and her trade was small. Her contacts consisted of Catholic missions and naval forces; yet between them these generated French power in Indo-China and the Pacific.

French missions in Indo-China were established in the later

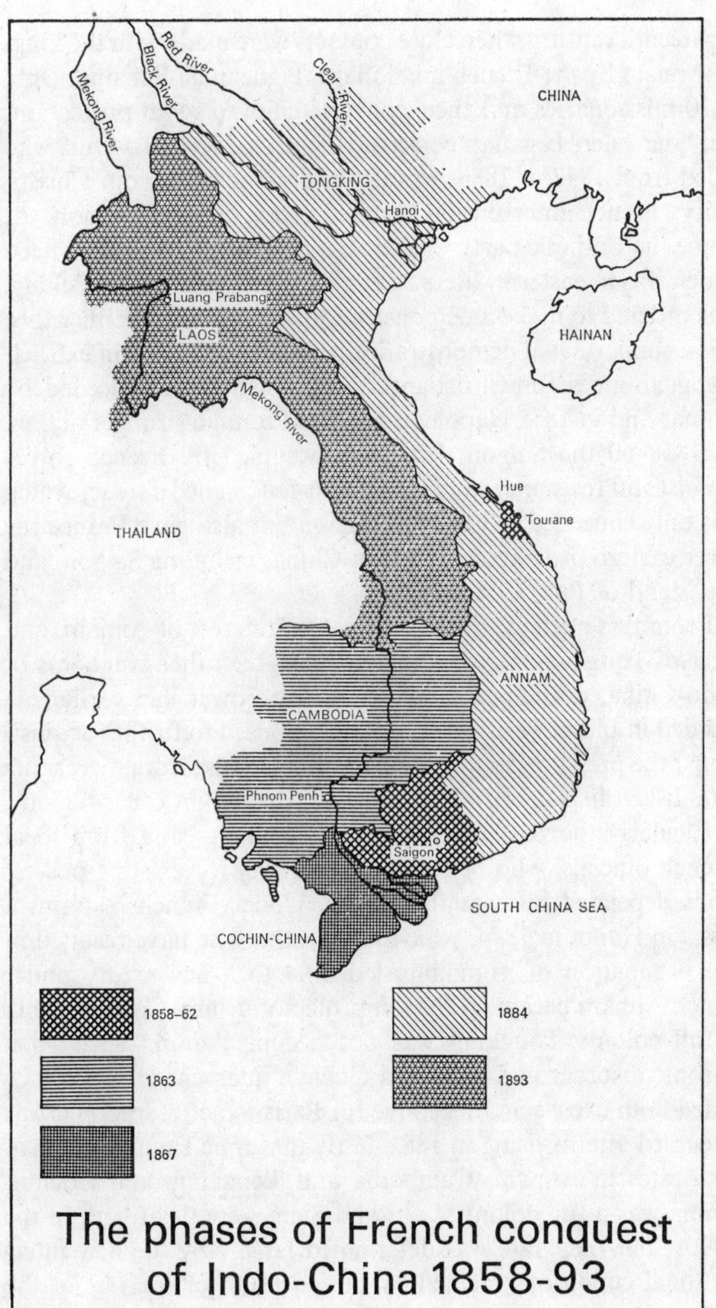

The phases of French conquest of Indo-China 1858-93

eighteenth century when close contacts were made with the kings of Annam by the French missionary, Pigneau de Béhaine. Until 1820 missionaries and their converts enjoyed royal protection; but later rulers began to persecute them, and King Tu-Duc, who ruled from 1847 to 1883, was determined to stamp out Christianity. French intervention resulted from this persecution. At home the Catholic party was strong; and in 1847 a French fleet, which was in eastern waters to extract treaty rights from Peking, was ordered to make a demonstration off Tourane. Neither this, nor a similar naval demonstration in 1858, succeeded in extracting guarantees for Christians such as had been conceded by China; and in 1858 Napoleon III agreed to take stronger action. In 1858–60 the Saigon delta was occupied by French forces against stiff resistance; and in 1862 Tu-Duc signed a treaty which not only conceded religious toleration but also gave France the three eastern provinces of Cochin-China, including Saigon, and the island of Pulo Condore.

From this nucleus, the occupation of the rest of Annam, and later of Tongking, Cambodia and Laos, the other kingdoms of Indo-China, developed much as British power had earlier expanded in India. Paris was normally opposed to further acquisitions: the pressure came from French missions; from merchants established in Saigon, who wanted to operate in other regions, particularly the Red River area of Tongking; and from local French officials, who believed that security for existing possessions depended on extending them. Under French restraint a crisis in Hanoi in 1874, which might otherwise have resulted in the occupation of Tongking, led only to a new treaty under which Annam became a French protectorate and Cochin-China a full colony. Tongking was not occupied until 1884, when chronic disorder and increased Chinese intervention there provided both excuse and incentive for Paris to act. Cambodia was occupied after a rising in 1884–6. By that time France had protectorates in Annam, Cambodia and Tongking, and Cochin-China was a full colony. Laos and Siam were dealt with in the 1890s; but their fate was determined largely by the new international conditions created by the partition of the rest of the independent world.

Dutch Expansion in Indonesia

By contrast, the extension of Dutch power in Indonesia after 1815 merely continued a process which had operated within Java for some two centuries.

The end of the Napoleonic wars and the settlement of territorial disputes with Britain in 1824 left Indonesia as a recognized Dutch sphere of interest; but only parts of Java, the Banda Islands, Amboyna, and a number of forts and trading bases were actual Dutch possessions, and elsewhere their influence rested on treaties with independent rulers and on naval forces. Effective occupation was forced on them by three factors. Piracy was dangerous to trade. Revolts of Indonesian rulers against Dutch overlordship led to retributory wars and more complete control. The economic interests of Dutch nationals and of the government of Batavia were an incentive to occupying areas which produced tin, coffee, coal or other commodities. By 1882 Java was almost entirely under direct Batavian rule: the two surviving states, Djokjarkta and Surakarta, had lost most of their land and were politically powerless. Bali was annexed in 1850 after a revolt; part of the Celebes in 1858–9 to suppress piracy; Billiton for its tin mines. The Sultanate of Banjermasin in Borneo was annexed in 1859–63 after a revolt against Dutch overlordship. Sumatra came gradually under Dutch control; and in 1882 a major war with Acheh, the last surviving powerful state, was still in progress and lasted until 1908.

Effective Dutch occupation of Indonesia was, therefore, carried out piecemeal and was the work of Batavia rather than The Hague. It was not complete in 1882; but by 1914 the Dutch effectively ruled Borneo (apart from British areas), the Celebes, part of New Guinea, Java, Sumatra and most of the smaller islands.

European Expansion in the Pacific

European occupation of the Pacific came late. It was fully charted only in the later eighteenth and early nineteenth centuries, and discovery showed that it offered little of value to Europe. Since it was also far from other European settlements and off the major trade routes, occupation was undertaken very hesitantly.

Colonization in the Pacific grew from a few local nuclei, and reflected the interests of Europeans in the region rather than those of Europe itself. During the period before 1882 Australia was the most important source of activity; but Australia itself became a British colony almost by chance. The first British base at Sydney in 1788 was a penal settlement, chosen because of its remoteness. Colonization of the rest of the continent followed slowly and without British planning. Free settlers were first encouraged to settle in New South Wales to support the penal colony. Shortage of land round Sydney led to search for grazing land for the sheep which had become the basis of the Australian economy. In due course sub-colonization by graziers, which resembled the South African trek rather than the consolidated frontier of settlement in North America, produced the daughter colonies of Victoria and Queensland. The other inhabitable parts of the continent would probably have been occupied in due course as part of the same process; but settlement was accelerated by two private colonizing ventures coming from Britain itself which were reminiscent of seventeenth-century enterprises in North America. One created a colony in Western Australia in 1829; the other, organized by E. G. Wakefield to demonstrate the virtues of his theory of 'systematic colonization', founded South Australia in 1836. Australia was thus in many ways a reincarnation of the earlier British colonies of 'pure' settlement in America, the product of private initiative rather than state planning.

Australia was the dominant influence in the Pacific for most of the nineteenth century: British expansion there was primarily the result of Australian 'sub-imperialism'. From Sydney traders, whalers and missionaries spread through the islands. Minor trades were profitable for Australians, or others using their ports, which would not have been worth while if conducted from Europe. New Zealand was the first Pacific group to be seriously affected. By the 1820s a considerable colony of Europeans were settled there, engaged in sealing, whaling and selling European goods to the Maoris. Their impact on Maori society was serious, a foretaste of similar situations in other parts of the Pacific. Europeans formed lawless communities, outside effective British jurisdiction. They sold guns and liquor to the Maoris, disrupting their social and political systems, and bringing retributive attacks on themselves. By the 1830s it was obvious that Britain ought to take formal authority over islands in which British subjects were causing such problems: but the government, under pressure from missionary headquarters in London, was reluctant to do so. Its hand was to some extent forced by Wakefield's decision to establish another 'systematic' colony in New Zealand, since the incursion of thousands of new settlers was certain to exacerbate existing racial problems. The decision to assert British jurisdiction over part at least of New Zealand was taken before the first of Wakefield's settlers sailed in 1839; but as a consequence of their arrival the British commissioner, Captain Hobson, declared full British sovereignty over both islands in 1840, just forestalling a French project for a small whaling base at Akaroa.

The British had thus reluctantly acquired another possession. At first it was seen as a colony of occupation, in which British officials would rule a Maori majority and control a settler minority. By 1870, however, after increased British immigration and the grant of responsible government to the settlers, New Zealand had become virtually a 'pure' settlement colony, in which Maoris, like North American Indians, were pushed to the frontiers of European settlement. Thereafter New Zealand constituted another dynamic nucleus for British expansion in the Pacific.

By 1843 the French also had Pacific possessions. This was surprising, for France had no reason to colonize the Pacific – no existing bases in 1815 and little trade. In 1840 her only interests were Catholic missions, whaling ships coming from Valparaiso, and a few naval vessels which charted the Pacific and protected French nationals. But in conjunction these three elements generated colonies. French missions had no more desire to found colonies than had other missions in the Pacific; but in most places they found Protestant British or American missions strongly entrenched. Island chiefs were often reluctant to permit rival missionary establishments, and the French challenged this principle of *cuius regio eius religio*. In Tahiti and the Marquesas they were so effectively supported by visiting French naval officers, acting on their own initiative, that the rulers of these groups had to sign French protectorate treaties. This development embarrassed Guizot, the Anglophile French Prime Minister. But French and Catholic prestige were at stake; in addition, these islands would provide France with the ports of call which her whalers and naval vessels needed. France stuck her ground, and by the Declaration of London of 1847 Britain recognized these two protectorates. Others made by French naval officers were denounced, and several island groups were stated to be barred to British or French occupation.

The Anglo-French agreement was intended to prevent further annexations in the Pacific by removing competition. Since the United States was then the only other foreign power with significant commercial or other interests there, it seemed possible that further colonial expansion could be avoided. France took New Caledonia in 1853, but this was only as a penal colony and the British government made no objection. Yet by the 1860s it was evident that further European colonization was bound to take place. European economic activity was increasing rapidly. The earlier marginal trade in sandalwood and sea-slugs – both for the Chinese market – was being replaced by a more important trade in coconut oil – the Pacific equivalent of West African palm-oil – and guano, the accumulated droppings of sea-birds, which was in demand as a fertilizer in Europe and America. The growing demand for vegetable oil led to the establishment of European-owned plantations in several island groups, and so to small European settlements. As earlier in New Zealand, these alien groups further disrupted politically unstable Polynesian and Melanesian societies. Competition between Europeans of different nationalities caused complications. The demand for labour for the plantations led to extensive 'blackbirding' in other islands, and widened the area of disturbance. By the 1860s the situation in Fiji, Samoa and other island groups was deteriorating, and native governments were beginning to crack under the strain.

European governments, reluctant to undertake political responsibilities, for long tried palliatives. Consuls were used to control European nationals and prop up native régimes. In the 1870s the British created the Western Pacific High Commission with jurisdiction over British subjects throughout the western Pacific. But in the end effective occupation was unavoidable. The British were the first to admit this. In 1874 they accepted the repeated requests of the would-be King of the Fiji group and annexed it. Fiji became the headquarters of the High Commission. Samoa was equally ripe for annexation; but there the balance between British, German and United States planters and traders was so close that unilateral action was impossible. A compromise was attempted in 1878–9 when each of these powers signed treaties by which they recognized the native king, Malietoa Lauppa, and acquired commercial and juridical rights for their nationals. The experiment amounted to an informal condominium, but by 1882 it was clear that one power must take full control, or the group be divided. Two other native states proved more capable of standing up to European pressures. Hawaii and Tonga, the first under United States influence, the second under British and German, retained their independence into the 1890s.

By 1882, there had been few formal annexations in the Pacific, apart from Australia, New Zealand, Fiji and a few small islands held as penal settlements or ports of call. But the growth of European influence had already made effective rule over the rest desirable on moral grounds, and growing rivalry between the four western powers concerned made partition into spheres of influence inevitable. In no other part of the world was the partition of the next twenty years a more natural outcome of earlier European expansion.

The seventy years before 1882 proved, despite the initial probabilities, to be one of the great periods of European expansion. The record of formal acquisitions was formidable. Yet little of this expansion had been planned in Europe or was the result of metropolitan imperialism. Europe was not 'anti-imperialist' in that the imperial powers wanted to be rid of their existing colonies: on the other hand they showed little desire, on economic, political or jingoistic grounds, to acquire new colonies. The powers acted when a strong case was made out by European interests at the circumference or by metropolitan groups with special interests there. As a result annexation was highly selective, regional, lacking an overall pattern: annexations in one place did not necessarily affect the situation elsewhere. Behind it all was the general assumption that areas which no one power chose to annex would remain independent, and that even those that were annexed would remain open to the commercial or other activities of all other countries. This psychology of the 'open door' was the precondition of avoiding an international partition.

The contrasting feature of the period of partition was that these conditions changed. Annexations might still result from problems on the periphery: they were no longer dealt with individually, but as part of general international settlements. The future of Samoa, for instance, came to depend on the diplomatic position in Africa. Global settlements left no room for areas of non-annexation: to hold back might mean exclusion by a rival. The statesmen of Europe could no longer wait for their hands to be forced by pressures on the colonial frontier – they had to make precautionary claims to regions in which they had no pressing interest. These facts marked the transition from the second expansion of Europe to the second partition of the world between the powers of Europe.

10

Expansion, Partition and Redivision, 1883–1939

Three features distinguish the thirty years between 1883 and the outbreak of the First World War. The rate of imperial expansion increased considerably: more colonial territory was acquired than during the previous three-quarters of a century. Annexation was no longer usually or necessarily the outcome of strong pressures from the circumference on reluctant European governments. The number of European powers concerned was multiplied by the revival of Spanish and Portuguese interest and by the intervention of states with no previous colonial tradition – Germany, Italy, the United States and King Leopold II of the Belgians. These facts were of sufficient importance to distinguish the period of partition from that of expansion: yet by no means all was new. There was no break in the continuity of European expansion, and the forces already making for imperial growth continued. The fundamental question after 1883 is why selective acquisition by a few states as a response to problems on the periphery became headlong partition of the world among so many.

Four basic interpretations have been provided: two assign one overriding cause for the new imperialism. The first alleges that partition was due to economic necessity. The industrialization of continental Europe and the revived protectionism of the last quarter of the century made tropical colonies necessary as never before to provide markets for manufactures, fields for the investment of surplus capital, and an assured source of raw materials. Colonies were deliberately acquired to fill these needs, and were circumscribed by tariffs and monopolies to ensure the advantage of the metropolis. This economic approach was given a specialized form by liberal-socialist writers like J. A. Hobson and by Marxists such as V. I. Lenin. Lenin emphasized the need of industrial capitalism in Europe to invest overseas, on the principle that the growth of 'finance capital' and monopoly within Europe resulted in ever-declining profit margins for new investment. Thus tropical colonization was a means of staving off the eventual sterility of European capitalism and the coming of the socialist revolution.

Another single-cause explanation regards imperialism as an expression of European nationalism. By the 1870s the unification of Germany and Italy, the defeat of France in 1870–71, and the growth of jingoism in all countries generated a degree of international rivalry unknown since 1815. Colonies became sources of national power and symbols of prestige. Pressure of the uneducated mass vote in this first phase of European democracy forced aristocratic statesmen to acquire colonies; competition produced partition.

The weak points of these explanations cannot be examined in detail. Basically, both fall down on chronology. The phenomena on which they concentrate existed at one time or another, but developed too late to have been critical in the vital period before 1900. The great age of 'finance capital', international cartels, banking trusts, etc., was after 1900 and still more after 1920. Britain, Russia, Germany, Italy, Spain, Portugal, and France were not seriously affected by them during the period of partition. Jingoistic imperialism also came late, reaching its peak in the 1920s: certainly there is little evidence that European statesmen were acting under such pressures in the 1880s and 1890s; more usually they had to stimulate public enthusiasm for acquisitions they had already made. In short, the colonial partition cannot be explained as the result of any one novel phenomenon within Europe.

A third approach assumes that partition was no more than a continuation of trends evident in the past half-century. Europe still did not hunger for new colonies; but the option was no longer open. Growing pressures on non-European societies now produced crises, similar to those in Tunisia or Fiji, in which indigenous governments cracked up or local nationalism reacted against 'informal' alien interference. Thereafter 'informal' control was no longer feasible: annexation became the alternative to evacuation. General partition was necessary both because older imperialisms had reached points of collision in West Africa, the Pacific and South-East Asia; and because more European states now had commercial or other interests in the colonial world which had to be accommodated. There are elements of truth in this theory: it rightly stresses that many new acquisitions can be explained in terms equally applicable to the previous half-century and were the result of pre-existing situations. Yet it is not a full explanation of the partition. It is satisfactory only in certain cases. It cannot explain the new speed or extent of European expansion, for there were no irresistible local stimuli to European action in many places made colonies in the twenty years after 1882.

The fourth interpretation denies that Europe needed tropical colonies for economic reasons or that there was a great public demand for them. It recognizes that previous trends were accelerating, and were likely to generate full occupation and partition of certain regions. But it maintains that the suddenness and speed with which Africa and the Pacific were divided after 1882 were not fully explicable in these terms, and looks for new influences. It sees the answer in new diplomatic patterns within Europe, and pinpoints Bismarck's sudden claim for German colonies in 1884–5 as the genesis of the new situation. Bismarck treated colonies as undifferentiated diplomatic pawns which any great power could claim and use as bargaining counters. By staking large claims in Africa and the Pacific, and by bringing colonial disputes in West Africa to an international conference table, he created a stock-market in colonial properties which none could thereafter ignore. Any power which failed to make its own claims, however unsubstantiated, was liable to find itself ultimately barred from further expansion. Thus the essence of the partition was that a central-European statesman imposed continental methods of procedure on maritime powers who had hitherto treated colonies as their special preserve. Only along these lines is it possible to explain the sudden partition of Africa and the Pacific, or contemporary events in South-East Asia after 1882.

This last interpretation seems to fit the known facts most closely, and will be adopted in this survey of events between 1883 and 1914.

The Paper Partition, 1883–90

The eight years after 1883 were the most important in the second expansion of Europe. By 1890 the greater part of Africa and the Pacific had been claimed by one power or another as spheres of influence or full possessions; the partition of South-East Asia was almost complete; and it was predictable that the rest of the independent world would soon come under European rule.

The crisis which led to partition had its roots in the Congo situation and Anglo-French disagreement over Egypt; but it was made explosive by Bismarck. Leopold's Congolese claims could have been dealt with as a local issue. French resentment at British occupation of Egypt in 1882 was likely to stimulate French activity wherever she already had points of contact with Britain – in West Africa, South-East Asia and the Pacific. But it takes more than friction between two powers, who had no intention of fighting over such marginal issues, to generate a partition of the world. Partition could have come only if other major European powers entered the field. The entry of Germany as a claimant for colonies in 1884–5 was the cause of the new phase of European expansion.

The motives which led Otto von Bismarck, the German Chancellor, to claim colonies remain a matter of debate. It seems unlikely that he was convinced by the propaganda of theoretical German imperialists, or by German commercial groups with interests in Africa and the Pacific, that Germany needed colonies for economic reasons. He recognized that Germans needed protection in these places, and suffered from the absence of German bases; but it seems unlikely that Bismarck ever thought colonies intrinsically worth while. He remained a central European: security against Russia and France was infinitely more important than the dubious commercial advantage of possessing colonies. On the other hand by claiming colonies he might achieve strictly tactical political objectives on two fronts. Probably the more immediately important of these was to win the support of the National Liberals in the 1884 Reichstag elections by contriving a demonstration of national power in the colonial field. Certainly this policy succeeded, leading first to National Liberal support in 1884 and then to their coalition with the Conservatives in 1887. But the new colonial policy can also be linked closely with Bismarck's international calculations. His specific aim in 1884–5 was to mollify France by supporting her over Egypt and in West Africa. At the same time he wished to demonstrate to Britain the desirability of her working with rather than against Germany. He could achieve both objects by claiming colonies in areas which would not outrage France but would inconvenience Britain; claims which would, in fact, constitute weapons like the existing 'Egyptian baton' which he could wield to bring Britain into line. Probably Bismarck had no long-term plan for using such colonies as diplomatic counters, though his successors in fact later did so. Devious though such motives may appear, it remains likely that the entry of Germany into colonial politics was in part the result of domestic political needs, in part, as has been said 'the accidental by-product of an abortive Franco-German entente'.[1]

Bismarck's action in 1884–5 blew up half a century of imperial arrangements like a land-mine. In May 1884 he declared a protectorate over Angra Pequena, in South-West Africa, where there was already a private German claim to land. By July the German explorer Gustav Nachtigal had obeyed Bismarck's instructions to declare protectorates over Togoland, west of Lagos, and the Cameroons. In December Bismarck imposed a protectorate over the northern coast of New Guinea, on the basis of treaties made by a new German plantation company. Earlier a German warship had forced King Malietoa of Samoa to sign a new treaty giving Germany predominance in the Samoan group. Finally, in February 1885 Bismarck accepted treaties made by the German explorer, Carl Peters, imposing German protection on part of the East African coast opposite Zanzibar.

Tentative though these claims were – none amounting to more than a protectorate which could later be denounced – they set the tone for European expansion for the next quarter-century. Bismarck had demonstrated that any power strong enough to support its claims with authority could acquire colonies without occupying them: a few ambiguous treaties with native chiefs were all that was required. Once such lines had been drawn on the map they had considerable importance, for they could be erased by rivals only if they made counter-concessions to Germany. This demonstration had two consequences. It induced other states to make counter-claims for fear of losing their chances for good, or having later to pay too high a price for territory reserved by someone else; and it freed them from the need actually to occupy their claims. The first partition was, therefore, only an exercise in cartography by the chancellories of Europe, who were often hard put to find in the gazetteers the more remote places they now possessed. Yet it had serious consequences. The first claims could be relatively uncontroversial; there was still much to choose from. Taste grew with indulgence: by the 1890s the instinct to partition was stronger, yet had to be satisfied from a much reduced supply. The growing international bellicosity of the later 1890s and 1900s was a product of the bloodless partition of the 1880s.

The chronology of partition before 1890 will be described briefly by regions. There was never a general international conference to distribute the prizes: claims were made unilaterally and ratified by treaties with every other interested party. The nearest to a general settlement was made by the Berlin Conference of November 1884–February 1885, summoned jointly by Germany and France as a product of Bismarck's new policy of friendship. Its achievements were limited. It recognized Leopold's claims on the Congo, which became the Congo Free State; but the conventional region of the river Congo was made a free trade zone open to all. French claims on the north bank of the Congo also were recognized. This settled the Congo question. There was no attempt, however, to solve the equally controversial West African question, for there only two major powers were involved. Germany's protectorates were taken for granted, but British and French claims to predominance were recognized and they were left to thrash out their differences, provided that freedom of navigation on the river Niger was preserved. Other parts of the world were left alone, but the conference tried to define conventions for making future claims in Africa. These were to be notified to all signatories of the 'Act' drawn up by this conference; claims to territory on the coast implied 'effective occupation' and responsibility for protecting all Europeans there; freedom of trade was to be preserved, though there was no ban on customs or preferences. These principles had little practical importance. 'Effective occupation' was required for full colonies, not for protectorates or spheres of influence, and it related only to the coasts – most of which were already claimed. Since the later partition was concerned with continental Africa, the Berlin Act had little effect on it.

The conference settled little, but was an immense stimulus to colonial expansion. By drawing up rules it declared the game in progress. During the next five years there was feverish colonizing activity throughout the non-European world.

In West Africa British, French and Germans quickly staked out claims which would have seemed incredible three years earlier. The British concentrated on the Niger, where the bulk of their trade lay; thus sticking to the old-fashioned principle of selecting only colonies which served a genuine interest. In 1885 Britain declared a protectorate over the coast from the Cameroons to Lagos, which extended inland to Lokoja on the Niger and Ibi on the Benue. British prospects farther inland and up the Niger were left to the new Royal Niger Company, whose charter enabled it, like seventeenth-century companies, to make treaties, govern in the name of the Crown, and monopolize British trade on the Niger above the protectorate. The ultimate size of British Nigeria depended on the capacity of this company to make more treaties than the French and establish some form of government as proof of British occupation.

The rest of West Africa was virtually left to the French and Germans. Germany showed little interest in extending her initial claims, for Bismarck was discouraged by finding that no German company would undertake the government of Kamerun and Togoland. The French were very active. Enthusiasm for expansion came from soldiers and administrators in West Africa rather than from Paris; but chronic French hostility to Britain after 1882 gave the men on the spot the support they needed. French policy broadly followed Faidherbe's principles: France must extend Senegal and her other small possessions until they covered the whole hinterland of West Africa from Algeria to the Congo. In 1890 the French had not yet dealt with the major Islamic states which barred the way to full control of the Western Sudan; but they had occupied much of the region between Senegal and the Gold Coast, and were poised for a double thrust to the Upper Volta and the Middle Niger. French predominance was reflected in the conventions made with Britain in 1889 and 1890 which defined the coastal boundaries of their possessions, and in part the inland boundaries of the Gambia and Sierra Leone. The Sudan, north of a line drawn from Say, on the Middle Niger, to Barruwa, near Lake Chad, was declared to be a French sphere. Nevertheless much still remained to be decided: how the hinterlands of the British Gold Coast and Nigeria were drawn depended on the success of French and British treaty-makers on the spot and the military force they could rely on.

In East Africa the period 1885–90 was more decisive, because Britain and Germany were able to come to satisfactory agreements with little difficulty. Italy had acquired Assab, on the Red Sea, and wanted to build an empire for prestige reasons in the Horn of Africa. She was weak, but she was a member of the Triple Alliance, and this entitled her to German sympathy and stimulated Britain to offer counter bribes. Bismarck had little interest in East Africa, beyond the welfare of Carl Peters' East African Company. Bismarck supported him in whatever treaties he made with Africans to extend his company's claims provided these did not produce a serious quarrel with Britain. Britain, in fact, had the greatest stake in East Africa: but her interests were typical of the involuted diplomacy of partition. There were British missions in Uganda, and the Scottish shipowner, William Mackinnon, was trying to establish a trading empire between

Mombasa and Lake Victoria, including control of the inland possessions of the Arab Sultan of Zanzibar. Mackinnon was given a charter for his Imperial British East Africa Company to enable him to compete with Peters in treaty-making: but in fact British statesmen regarded both missions and company as expendable. The vital British interest was India; and Indian security was rather obscurely thought to depend on British naval predominance in the Indian Ocean and the Middle East. German control of the coast would endanger the first; German or other control of Uganda or the Upper Nile would threaten Egypt and the Suez Canal. Ironically, therefore, British statesmen felt bound to stake more on East Africa, the least attractive of all colonial lots at auction, than in other places where real bargains were to be had. Until 1898 this fact dominated the diplomacy of partition.

The key dates were 1886 and 1890. In 1886 Lord Salisbury forestalled possible German claims to Uganda by recognizing the German protectorate over Dar-es-Salaam and Pangani, and by implication also over Witu and the coast fronting it, in return for a provisional British sphere of influence north of a line from Wanga to Lake Victoria. Zanzibar, which was under British control and became a full protectorate in 1890, was to control a long stretch of coast to the depth of ten miles. By 1890 Salisbury was clear that Britain would remain in Egypt indefinitely. This made control of Uganda fundamental and a more definite division was made by the so-called Heligoland treaty. Britain recognized a German protectorate running from Portuguese Mozambique to Lake Nyasa, Lake Tanganyika and the boundary of the Congo Free State west of Lake Victoria, but stopping short of Uganda. Germany was given Heligoland, which most Germans thought a better acquisition than Uganda. In return, Germany recognized a British sphere of influence stretching north without a break from the previous demarcation line, and also the British protectorate over Zanzibar.

This 1890 treaty virtually fixed the pattern of colonial East Africa. It remained to decide whether Britain would convert her sphere of influence into a formal protectorate or colony, or merely keep Germany out of it; what boundaries would be drawn between Uganda and the Congo Free State; whether the Congo would cede a corridor west of Lake Tanganyika, so that Uganda and Egypt could be linked with Central Africa; and finally, whether France or Italy would dispute British predominance in the Egyptian Sudan.

The partition of Central Africa also was complete in principle by 1890. The vital decisions were taken in Europe; but they were complicated, as nowhere else in Africa, by the 'sub-imperialist' ambitions of British settlers in the Cape and Natal.

In 1884 Central Africa was a political vacuum with a mere scattering of European missionaries, traders and prospectors, into which Europeans were poised to advance from all sides; Germans from South-West and East Africa; Portuguese from Angola and Mozambique; Transvaalers and Cape colonists from the south. Britain herself had few interests there – only the Scottish missions on Lake Nyasa and the Lakes Company which supported them: but she had to stake claims to satisfy the Cape colonists, who saw this as their main sphere of expansion, and expected to find gold fields in Matabeleland to match those recently discovered on the Rand in the Transvaal. The lever they could use on London was the British fear that the Transvaal might engulf the Cape if her new wealth was not balanced by the extension of Cape wealth and territory; or that a disgruntled Cape might throw its lot in with the Transvaal and so deprive Britain of her naval base at Simonstown. Thus British policy in Central Africa was ultimately – and grotesquely – linked, like that in East Africa, to the security of the sea routes to India, the crux of all British imperial thinking.

By 1890 the eventual pattern of partition in Central Africa was visible. Britain established a protectorate over Bechuanaland by stages in 1884, 1885 and 1890, eventually turning the southern area into a full colony; but her aim was simply to preserve a route to the north and east, where interest had been aroused by the discovery of gold in Matabeleland. Yet this region of Zambezia was not included in the British protectorate, for Britain had no effective claims there and lacked the diplomatic capital to bar German or Portuguese ambitions until such claims were established. As in West Africa, a chartered British company was created to compete with the two German companies and the Portuguese government. In 1889 Cecil Rhodes' British South Africa Company was given a blank cheque to occupy and govern any areas north of Bechuanaland and the Transvaal, outside the limits of German and Portuguese occupation. To avoid international complications a British sphere was defined in the 1890 German treaty and Portuguese treaties of 1890 and 1891; but to be safe this area had to be occupied by Rhodes. The only place so far declared a British protectorate was the region south of Lake Nyasa, where the missions and the Lakes Company did not want to be absorbed by Rhodes. This British Central African Protectorate, as it was called after 1893, was probably the only British possession acquired during the partition primarily to protect a British missionary enterprise, though the missionary factor had some influence also on the Uganda protectorate declared in 1894.

The Partition of the Pacific, 1884–90

In the Pacific as in Africa the bull-like entry of Germany in 1884 produced partition, as other powers attempted to cordon off German claims. But here, more than in East and Central Africa, partition was closely related to earlier trends, providing the opportunity for Europeans to resolve existing conflicts and undertake overdue responsibilities for government of island territories.

The main settlement took place in 1885–6 and produced very little friction. In 1885 Britain and France both recognized the German protectorate over part of New Guinea and New Britain. Germany recognized British occupation of south-east New Guinea and French protectorates, dating from 1880, over Raiatea and the Leeward Islands. The Germans thus accepted France's right to annex any island in the Eastern Pacific. The British recognized that this was probably inevitable, but were not prepared to abrogate their 1847 agreement with France, which guaranteed the independence of a number of these islands, until they had made diplomatic use of it. Meanwhile, the Anglo-German agreement of 1886 defined their respective spheres of influence. It excluded Britain from the Northern Solomons and the still Spanish Carolines and Marshalls, but gave her a free hand in the Gilberts and other islands south of the line of demarcation.

These agreements left unresolved conflicts between Britain and France over islands near Tahiti and the New Hebrides. Britain had little interest in them; but her subjects in New Zealand and Australia, concerned for their trade and missions, wanted a line of British islands as a defence against French or German aggression. Australia was already furious that Britain had disallowed the annexation of southern New Guinea by Queensland in 1883 (since such action was beyond the legal capacity of a colony), and so allowed the Germans to stake their claim. Britain therefore opposed French annexations as far as was diplomatically convenient. Rapa, since 1867 a French protectorate unrecognized by Britain, was given away; but the Cook Islands were made a British protectorate in 1888 on the condition that New Zealand, who had interests in them, paid for a resident. Over the New Hebrides, where there were strong Australasian Presbyterian missions, a compromise was reached after four years of intense triangular correspondence. In 1888 a joint Anglo-French Naval Commission was created which gave unsatisfactory government to the islands but satisfied British colonial susceptibilities.

This completed the main partition of the Pacific. The future of Samoa, Tonga and Hawaii was not decided until the dissolution of the Spanish Pacific empire in 1898 offered a second opportunity for a general Pacific settlement.

The Partition in South-East Asia

By contrast with Africa and the Pacific, the period of partition brought no new forces into play in South-East Asia. Events still depended primarily on the relations of Britain and France with indigenous states and with each other; and the main novelty was increased Franco-British hostility.

The most important development was the French conquest of Tongking, which began in 1884: but this had been planned as early as 1881, and was the product of chronic disorder in the

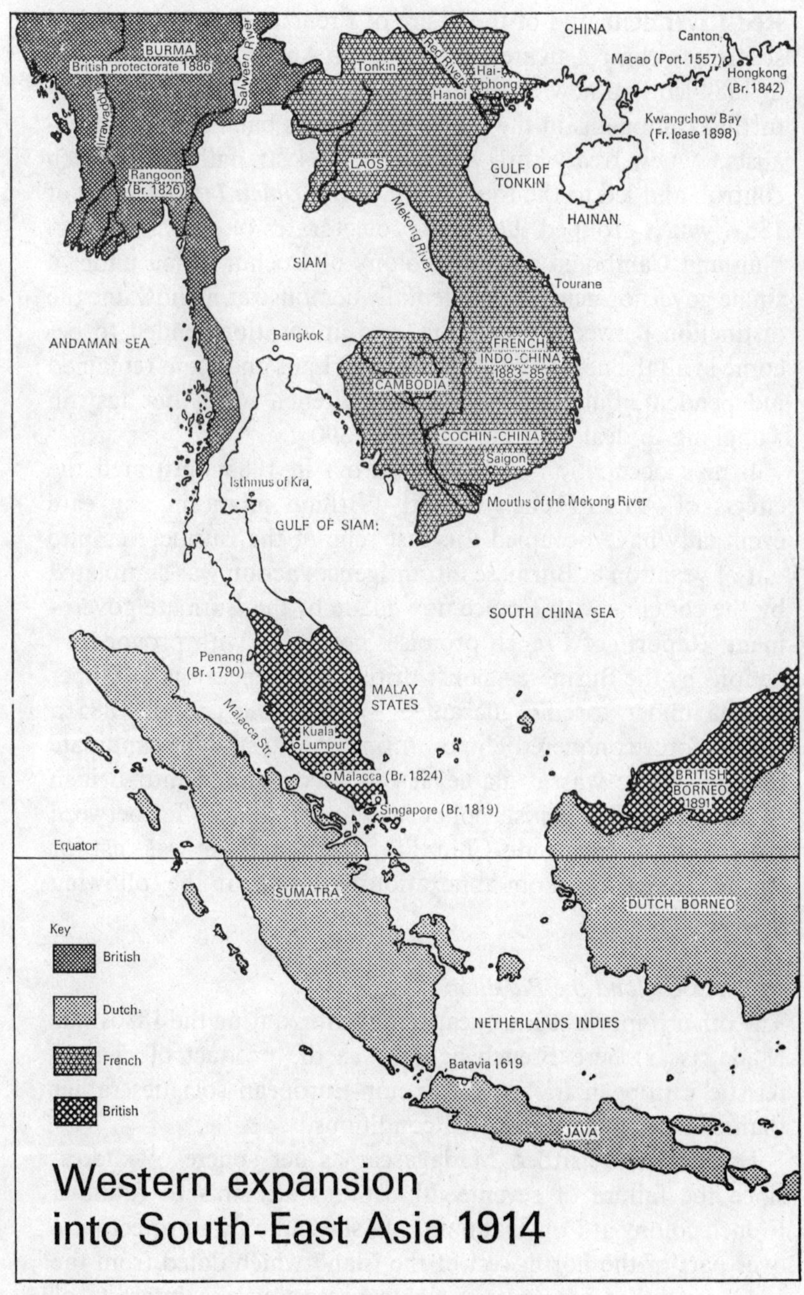

Western expansion into South-East Asia 1914

Red River delta and of the desire of French administrators and soldiers to control an area contiguous to Annam. Initial disasters in 1884 led to a new expedition and victory in 1885; but also to further campaigns in the north to suppress bandits and nationalists. A new treaty with Annam in 1884 strengthened French control, and led to the foundation of the *Union Indo-chinoise* of 1887, which grouped the three protectorates of Annam, Tongking and Cambodia with the colony of Cochin-China under a single governor-general; incidentally demonstrating how fine the distinction between 'protection' and annexation tended to become in all the new colonial territories. Laos and Siam remained independent, but only because the French were too busy in Tongking to deal with them before 1890.

British occupation of Upper Burma in 1885 illustrated the effects of Anglo-French hostility. Britain might in any case eventually have occupied this last relic of the Burmese empire out of vexation at Burmese intransigence: action was stimulated by the contacts with France now made by the Burmese government. Reports of French promises coincided with provocative actions by the Burmese against British firms operating in Upper Burma under specific guarantees; and at the end of 1885 a British force conquered Upper Burma. As no suitable candidate for the throne was available, it was incorporated into British India. Thereafter British policy was to create a buffer between Burma and French Indo-China: the fact that Siam was cast for this role saved her from annexation by France in the following decade.

Madagascar and the Partition

The other important European acquisition during the 1880s was Madagascar: here French action was the product of characteristic European frictions with non-European societies rather than of the new international conditions.

France had regarded Madagascar as her sphere of interest since the failure of seventeenth-century attempts to found a French colony at Fort Dauphin; but she had only a protectorate over part of the north-west of the island which dated from the 1840s, together with treaty rights protecting the interests of

French nationals. The British were quite as influential, and their Protestant missionaries, soldiers, teachers and financiers were more popular with the Hova dynasty which claimed to rule the whole island. French intervention was primarily a response to a deliberate anti-French campaign begun by the Hova rulers after 1880, which forced France to retaliate or allow her subjects to be deprived of treaty rights. A naval expedition sent to frighten the Hovas in 1883 produced a protectorate treaty in 1885; but it gave France little real power, and her position remained unsatisfactory. Britain recognized the protectorate in 1890, ignoring the chance to capitalize on Malagan preference for the British connexion; and in 1898 the French seriously undertook the conquest of the island. It is possible that Franco-British hostility after 1882 made it easier for French governments to get credits from the Chamber for these extravagances: but essentially the French occupation of Madagascar was part of the expansion of Europe as it had operated before the partition began.

Partition and Effective Occupation, 1890–1914

By about 1890 the first phase of the partition was over and the outlines of the modern colonial empires were visible. The second phase, which lasted until 1914, was an inevitable consequence. Whereas the paper partition had been easy, cheap, and relatively amicable, the sequel was difficult, expensive and generated much international heat.

The period had two main features. First it was necessary for all who had taken part in the preliminary scramble to occupy their provisional spheres of interest – on pain of seeing them claimed by someone else – and to impose effective European authority on indigenous peoples who had hitherto met only a few individuals touting treaties. Occupation meant fighting. These were 'little wars'. They were expensive in money and lives, and in their effects on native societies, but they were inevitable. Apart from international dangers, each colonial power felt the financial burden of its new possessions. As in India and Indonesia in the past, and more recently in West Africa, the need to raise local revenues made it necessary to impose full government.

There was also the incentive to 'pacify' states on the periphery of existing colonies. Given metropolitan readiness to pay, there was now no military difficulty in doing this. The Maxim gun was the symbol of the second phase of the partition as the diplomats' cartography had been of the first.

By 1914 most of the new colonies had been pacified and occupied. The French fought long and expensive wars against the embattled Islamic states of the Western Sudan and in Dahomey, Madagascar, and Indo-China. Morocco had to be conquered as Algeria had been in the past. The British fought major campaigns against Ashanti, and the Khalifate of the Egyptian Sudan, and smaller campaigns in the Niger region and in East Africa. Rhodes' company fought the Matabele in 1893, and the British the Transvaal and Orange Free State from 1899–1902. The Germans had to suppress the Hereros rising in South-West Africa in 1904–7 and the Maji-Maji rising in Tanganyika in 1905–6, gaining an unjustified reputation for exceptional cruelty. The Belgians carried out a systematic conquest of the Congo region. Only the Italians were unsuccessful in their claim to rule 'backward' peoples: in 1896 they were routed at Adowa by the Abyssinians, and had to give up their protectorate.

The other feature of this period was a growing bellicosity between the great powers which had various roots. After about 1904 it was primarily a reflection of European tensions and had little to do with colonies. Such jingoism was extended to the colonial sphere partly by its relevance to international diplomacy, partly by the growing imperialist enthusiasm evident in most European states. Though generated too late to influence the constructive phase of partition, such imperialism undoubtedly exacerbated its later stages, and embittered conflicts for the few remaining colonial lots. The fact that little of the world remained to divide gave it affinities with the last phase of the distribution of church properties in England during the 1550s, of which it was later said that

> Such who had mannerly expected till the king carved for them out of abbey-lands, scrambled for themselves out of chantry-revenues, as knowing this was the last dish of the last course, and after chantries, as after cheese, nothing to be expected.[2]

The Final Partition of Africa

The final stages in the partition of Africa produced inter-European crises in Nigeria, the Egyptian Sudan, Morocco and South Africa, but a major war only in the last.

The settlement of West Africa between Britain and France concerned the hinterlands of the British coastal possessions and the Upper Niger. The French were committed, for military, financial and jingoistic reasons, to build a continuous block of territory from Algeria to the Congo and eastwards across the Sudan – the French equivalent of Rhodes' Cape to Cairo dream. They were intensely active in West Africa, hemming in the British coastal possessions with treaties and military expeditions, and at last coming to grips with the Islamic empires in their path. Until after 1895 the British did little to counter this French drive, for they were preoccupied with East Africa; and Sir George Goldie's Royal Niger Company lacked the resources to match the French state-supported enterprise. The appointment of Joseph Chamberlain as British colonial secretary in 1895, however, injected a last-minute urgency into British West African policy, for, unlike most British contemporaries, he really believed in the economic possibilities of tropical colonies, and may have adopted his ideas from continental theorists such as Jules Ferry. For the next three years the British matched the French in treaty-making and fighting. Ashanti was conquered; the hinterland of Sierra Leone occupied. To protect the Middle Niger region Chamberlain created the West African Frontier Force which reached Borgu in 1898 and put a stop to French expansion there. The final demarcation of 1898 gave Britain a large area in Northern Nigeria and a reasonable hinterland for the Gold Coast on the Upper Volta. France was left with the lion's share; but, as Lord Salisbury unkindly pointed out, much of it consisted of the light soils of the Sahara.

In East Africa also 1898 was a year of decision between France and Britain. French intervention here was new, for she had only small bases at Obok and Jibuti in Somaliland. By 1894 Britain had imposed a protectorate on Uganda and had tidied up its frontiers with neighbouring German, Italian and Congo Free State territories. She was in no hurry to deal with the powerful

Khalifate in the Egyptian Sudan, and this gave the French the excuse to interfere. Their aim was to establish a base on the Upper Nile, and so demonstrate that British occupation of Egypt was contingent on French acquiescence: moreover the defeat of the Italians at Adowa in 1896 left Abyssinia open to French influence, and made possible an advance to the Nile from the east as well as from the Western Sudan. The result was a slow-motion race between the British and the French to establish an adequate military force on the critical upper reaches of the Nile between Lake Victoria and Khartoum. The French sent expeditions from the Congo and Abyssinia; the British intended to approach from Uganda and Egypt. All were hampered by immense distances and hostile African powers. In the event a small French force under Marchand, coming from the Congo, reached the Upper Nile at Fashoda on 10 July 1898. No French force came from the east. The British failed to launch an expedition from Uganda; but Kitchener arrived at Fashoda with a large army on 19 September, having defeated the Khalif at Omdurman on 2 September. The French were there first, but the British had an immensely greater military force. War between the two countries was a real possibility; but the British position was impregnable, and late in October 1898 Marchand left Fashoda on his own initiative. The Franco-British agreement of March 1899 wound up the Sudanese and East African questions. France kept the Sudan from the Congo and Lake Chad to Darfur, but was excluded from the Nile. Britain controlled the Eastern Sudan under the form of a condominium with Egypt.

The failure of France in the Eastern Sudan and Italy in Abyssinia had the surprising but closely connected results that France acquired Morocco and Italy took Tripoli. France had an obvious interest in Morocco as neighbour to Algeria and the most valuable property still unclaimed in Africa. Italy coveted Tripoli as compensation for her failure to get Tunisia. Both Morocco and Tripoli were barred to annexation by earlier international treaties relating to the integrity of the Ottoman empire; and Franco-Italian jealousies had prevented both from resolving these diplomatic obstacles. France's humiliation in the Sudan, and her desire to detach Italy from her Triple Alliance with Germany and Austria, led first to a rapprochement and then to a secret agreement in 1900 by which Italy was given a free hand in Tripoli in return for accepting French claims in Morocco.

It remained for both to obtain the agreement of other signatories of the treaties. Britain agreed to French occupation of Morocco as part of the general settlement of 1904. Spain made no objection, provided her own rights were preserved. Germany remained uncommitted; but, with the genuine excuse that deteriorating political conditions within Morocco were creating disturbances on the Algerian frontier, France decided to act unilaterally. In 1902 a first treaty with the Sultan of Morocco gave France control of the Algerian frontier region and the collection of customs there, and also the right to make loans to the Sultan. In 1905 France demanded control of police, public banking and public works, which would have amounted to a French protectorate. At this point Bülow, the German Chancellor, intervened by sending Kaiser William II to Tangiers to announce Germany's interest. Bülow's aim was to bring France to heel in Europe by demonstrating that she could not rely on the British entente in a crisis. In this he succeeded, for Britain gave France no promise of support; and an international conference was summoned at Algeciras in January 1906 to deal with Morocco. The conference accepted French predominance there, provided the Sultan's nominal independence was preserved; but by the Algeciras Act guarantees were given for an 'open door' for foreign economic activities; an international bank was established at Tangiers; and Spain became jointly responsible with France for the police force.

Under cover of this arrangement France cautiously advanced her control over Morocco, taking advantage of growing internal disorder. In 1907–9 French forces occupied Casablanca and its hinterland. The Germans complained that the Sultan was forced to grant banking and railway concessions to France, though in fact German interests were not affected. The crisis came in 1911. The French sent forces to Fez to protect the Sultan (at his own request) against rebels, and the Germans sent the gunboat *Panther* to Agadir, and announced that the Algeciras Act had been nullified by French action. Their aim was once again to humiliate France and demonstrate that Britain would not support her: but this time the British government supported France, and Germany had to come to terms. By a treaty of November 1911 Germany agreed to a French protectorate over Morocco, in return for the cession of a considerable part of the French Congo to Kamerun. This cut off Gabun from the French Sudan and was seen by Berlin as the first step to the acquisition also of the Belgian Congo. The French protectorate over Morocco was declared in 1912.

The crisis of 1911–12 made possible the final partition of North and North-West Africa. Italy occupied Tripoli; and Spain, which had established a protectorate over the Rio de Oro, south of Cape Bojador, in 1885, extended it to the southern frontier of Morocco in 1912.

The other major crisis in Africa was the Boer War of 1899–1902. This was not part of the expansion of Europe, but a by-product of the increasing European bellicosity of the last phase of partition. It arose out of the long-term rivalry between the Cape and the Transvaal, intensified by the discovery of gold in the Transvaal in the 1880s. Ten years later this was the richest and most powerful unit in South Africa. Rhodes' failure to find comparable gold deposits in Rhodesia – the renamed British sphere in Zambezia – destroyed British hopes that the Cape might become strong enough to balance the Transvaal, and suggested that the whole of South Africa would eventually be dominated by the two hostile Afrikaner republics. Apart from her obligation to her own subjects, Britain's concern was with control over Simonstown, and the effect Afrikaner dominance might have on it. From about 1895 the British government hoped that the influx of British and other European settlers – *uitlanders* – on the Rand goldfields would convert the Transvaal into a pro-British state; but this would occur only if these immigrants received full political rights, which Kruger, the Transvaal President, seemed determined to refuse them. In 1895 Rhodes, with British connivance, tried to overcome Kruger's hostility by sending a military force to Johannesburg under his lieutenant, Dr Jameson. The

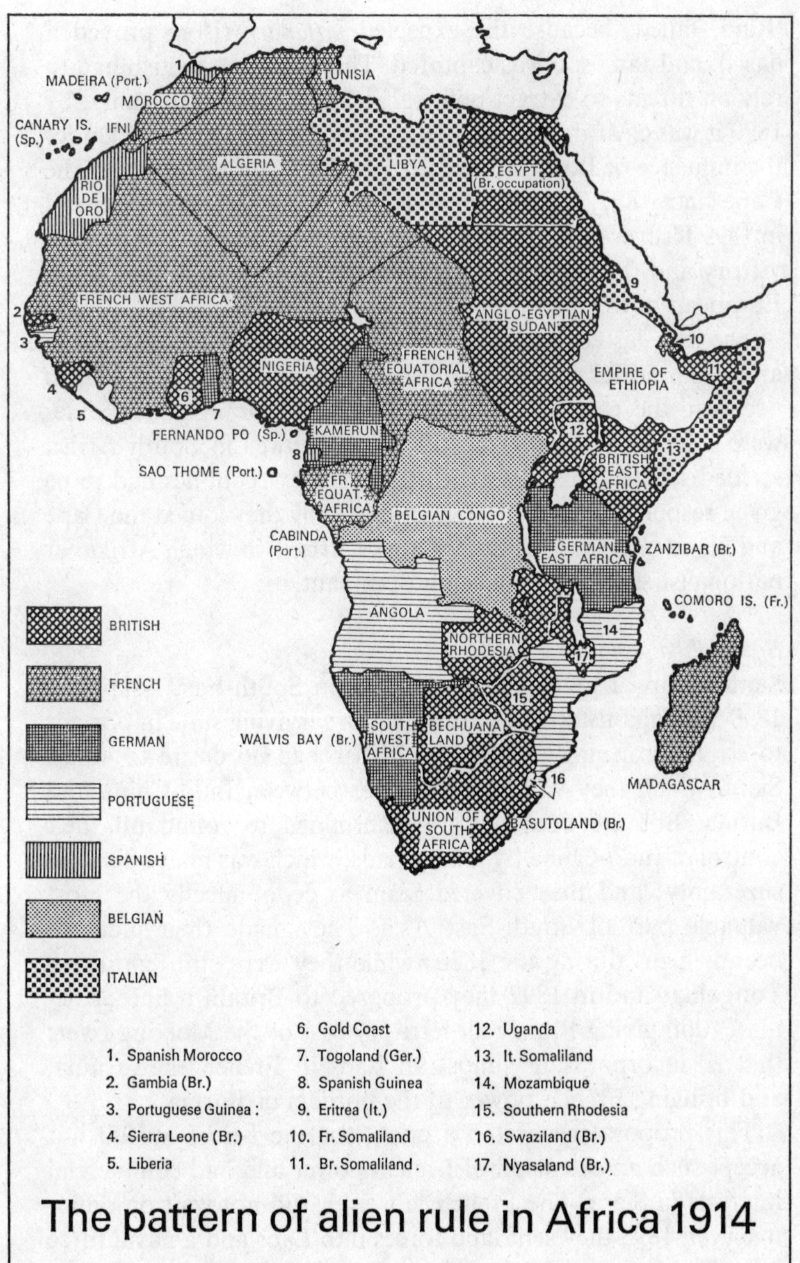

The pattern of alien rule in Africa 1914

'Raid' failed, because the expected *uitlander* rising proved a fiasco, and Jameson was captured. Thereafter the British had to rely on threats to extract political rights for the immigrants; by 1899 it was clear that Kruger felt strong enough to refuse. Under the influence of Lord Milner, British High Commissioner at the Cape since 1897, British demands became more belligerent; and in 1899 Kruger declared war, confident that he could win a quick victory and that he would get support from Germany or other European powers.

The war lasted until 1902. Europe remained inactive; and, after a far stiffer struggle than they had anticipated, the British occupied the republics. The Transvaal and Orange Free State were once again annexed, and British power in South Africa seemed secure. This was an illusion. The ex-republics had to be given responsible government; and in 1909 they joined the Cape and Natal in the new Union of South Africa, in which Afrikaner nationalist sentiment was soon dominant.

South-East Asia after 1890

Siam occupied much the same place in South-East Asia after 1890 as Afghanistan in Central Asia; a surviving state important to rival European powers. The British had no desire to annex Siam, which they valued as a buffer between Indo-China and Burma. But the French were determined to round off their control of Indo-China by taking Laos, which was under Siamese suzerainty; and they coveted Siam as economically the most valuable part of South-East Asia. They made their plans to occupy Laos during the 1880s while they were still fighting in Tongking; and in 1892 they proposed to Britain a line of demarcation giving France all territory east of the Mekong river: that is, incorporating almost all Laos in French Indo-China, and bringing French power to the borders of Burma.

This proposal generated a crisis, for the British would not accept such an extension of French power and had commercial interests in Siam. The French, however, did not wait on diplomacy: in 1893 they sent land forces into Laos and a naval force into the Menam river, leading to Bangkok. When the Siamese fired on these ships France had an excuse to state her demands, which were for the cession of virtually all Siamese territory east of the Mekong, including most of Laos, and the return of the one-time Cambodian provinces of Battambang and Angkor. Siam could have refused only with full British support: Lord Rosebery, the British Prime Minister, reluctantly refused to give it, for he regarded Egypt as more important than Laos, and wanted to avoid a crisis with France in Europe. The French got what they demanded.

Britain did not save Laos, but she did save Siam; for France recognized that she had reached the limits of British tolerance, and in 1896 signed a treaty by which Britain recognized French control of Laos but guaranteed the independence of the rump of Siam. The Anglo-French entente of 1904 froze this agreement. It was followed by the French-Siamese treaty of 1907, which adjusted several boundary questions, and the Anglo-Siamese treaty of 1909, by which the British took control over Siam's Malayan dependencies in return for giving up British rights to extra-territorial jurisdiction in Siam. These treaties completed the partition of South-East Asia. Siam had lost her empire, but she remained independent for the same reasons as Afghanistan and Persia.

China and Partition, 1890–1914

The Chinese empire also survived the expansion of the European empires; and the fact that she did so throws considerable light on the forces operating during the partition. China was an obvious target for European ambitions. She was large, relatively rich, politically weak; an inviting opportunity for European states who wanted new colonies for trade or investment. Four major European states, the United States and Japan were directly interested in her future. Why, then, was she not partitioned?

The critical period began in 1895, when Chinese forces were ignominiously defeated by Japan in Korea. Thereafter the vultures quickly gathered round what they thought was a dying empire. By about 1900 Britain, Russia, Germany, France, Japan and, to a lesser extent, the United States and Italy, had staked their claims. All had obtained general rights to trade and invest at the 'treaty ports'; to reside in international settlements with

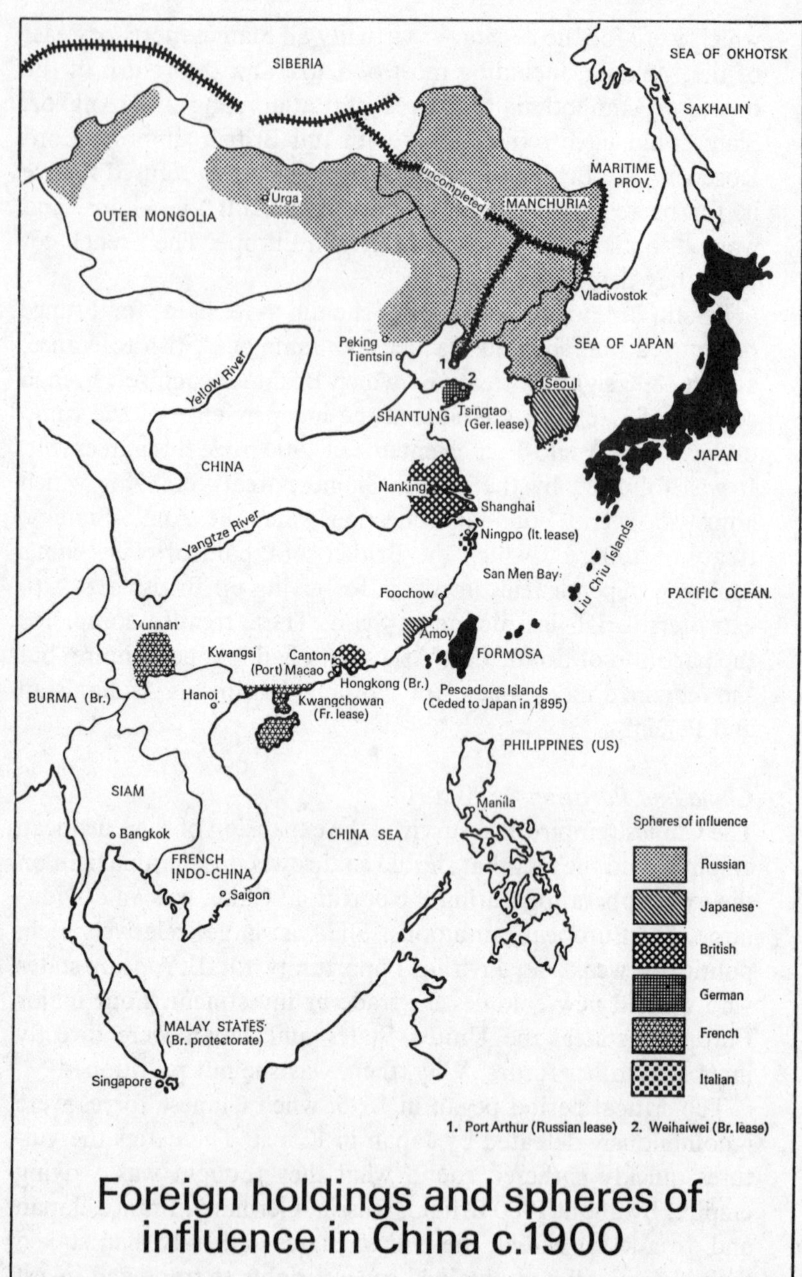

Foreign holdings and spheres of influence in China c.1900

freedom from Chinese courts of law; to maintain Christian missions; and to pay tariffs of not more than 5 per cent on their imports. In addition most of them had small bases leased for 99 years and much larger spheres of interest. The Russians occupied northern Korea, had a lease of Port Arthur in Manchuria, and dominated the north and the Peking area. The Germans had a naval base at Kiao-Chow and dominated most of Shantung. The British had a lease of the port of Weihaiwei, opposite Port Arthur, and spheres of influence in the basin of the Yangtze, including Shanghai, and at Canton. France had obtained frontier 'rectifications' with Tongking, and dominated Yunnan. Japan had a protectorate over southern Korea and a small sphere of influence south of Shanghai. Even Italy had a little sphere of influence. Only the United States took nothing.

These were obvious first steps to formal partition. Why did they go no farther? The explanation lies partly in the Chinese reaction, partly in European rivalries. A central fact was that the imperial government at Peking and its provincial governments went on functioning under these incredible strains. This probably saved China, since there was never a real necessity for Europeans to take over government, as they had to do in other places when indigenous systems collapsed. After 1902 Peking even became politically stronger. Europeans may also have been frightened by the Boxer rising of 1898–1900, which demonstrated a wide nationalist hostility to alien intervention, and suggested that European rule would be difficult. But ultimately China was saved by the conflict of interest between the foreign powers. Japan and Russia wanted Chinese territory, for both were local powers and feared each other's ambitions. The rest were determined that neither of these should gain political control of any important part of China, but did not themselves want substantial Chinese territories. Their interests lay in trade, opportunities for commercial investment and the chance to make loans to the imperial government. None was strong enough to gain a monopoly of the whole of China: the alternatives were partition or the 'open door'. At one stage partition into protectorates seemed a natural result of the spheres of influence, but in fact full partition was impossible without international friction. The spheres did not exclude economic or other activity by all Europeans: partition would have led to preferential tariffs and the monopoly of investment and other opportunities by each protecting power. No partition could have given all a fair share. The plums were the Yangtze and southern Manchuria, for in 1902 14 per cent of all regional foreign investment was in Shanghai alone, and 27·4 per cent in southern Manchuria. Excluding general investments, only 22·5 per cent was invested in all other regions of China.[3] Thus partition would have given most of the prizes to two competitors: the 'open door' was the only generally acceptable solution. It was made more attractive by the fact that the most rewarding European economic activity was lending money to the bankrupt Peking government at exorbitant rates and on the security of Chinese customs. It was obviously preferable for Europeans to share the loans among themselves, and use the imperial civil service to collect taxes to service them, rather than to undertake this unpopular activity themselves.

China was thus a sphere in which 'economic imperialism', acting through 'informal' control of an indigenous government, could survive in its common mid-nineteenth-century form. Between 1899 and 1905 the 'open door' was made safe. It was proposed by the United States in 1899 and accepted in principle by all the powers except Russia. In 1900 an Anglo-German agreement bound both not to acquire territory unilaterally and to maintain the 'open door' in their possessions and spheres of influence. The Anglo-Japanese treaty of 1902 included a Japanese promise not to take Chinese territory, in return for British guarantees of neutrality or an alliance with Japan if she were attacked by one or two powers respectively. The defeat of Russia by Japan in 1904–5 ended the Russian, and also the French, threat to the integrity of China. Until 1914 China remained politically secure under the patronage of Britain, Germany and the United States. She was exploited by foreign financial interests, but had the opportunity to rebuild herself and meet the western challenge.

The Pacific Settlement, 1890–1914

The eight years after 1890 saw no major territorial changes in the Pacific; the powers consolidated the spheres of interest they

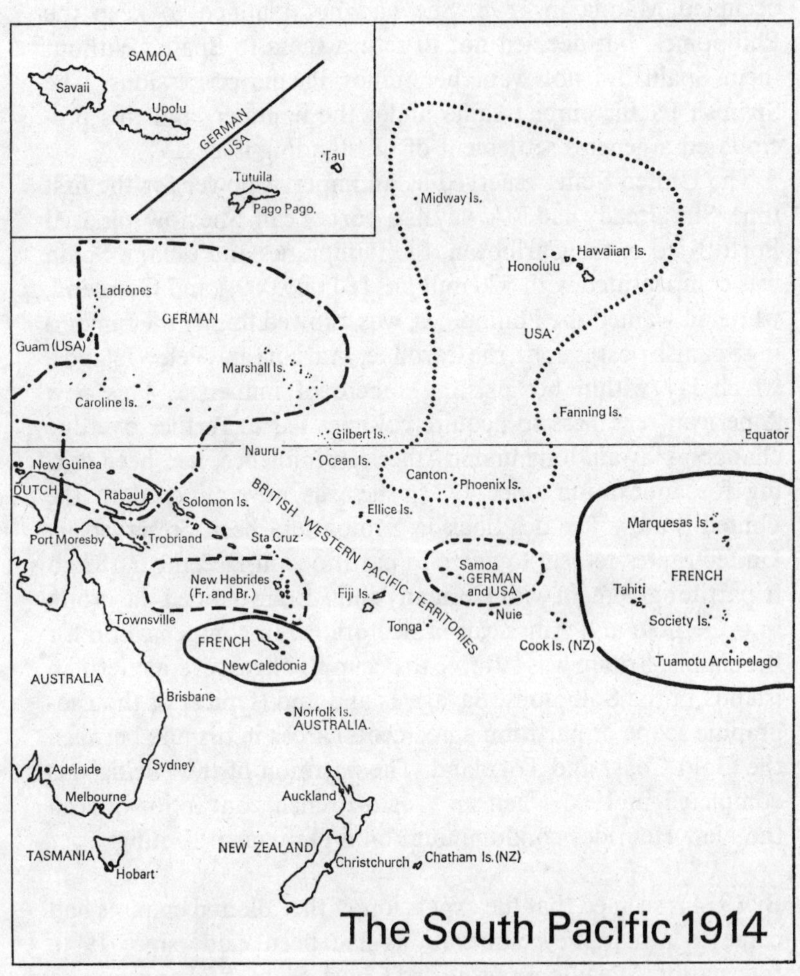

The South Pacific 1914

had already obtained. The final settlement occurred after 1898 as a direct result of the war between the United States and Spain.

The war began in the Caribbean, as a result of the situation in Cuba; but the United States, attacking Spain in two oceans, occupied Manila in 1898. She had not planned to keep the Philippines, but decided not to return them to Spain. Without them Spain did not want her minor Pacific possessions. The Spanish Pacific empire came under the hammer, and this precipitated a general settlement of outstanding issues.

The United States emerged as an imperial power for the first time. She already had Midway as a port of call. She now annexed Porto Rico in the Caribbean, the Philippines and Guam. Spain was compensated with $20 millions (£4,000,000); and Germany, who had wanted the Philippines, was allowed to buy the remaining Spanish possessions, the Caroline, Mariana and Pelew Islands, which lay within her existing sphere of influence. This new American readiness to acquire colonies led to further overdue changes. Hawaii, long under American influence, had been asking for annexation since 1893; she was now annexed to the United States. The deadlock in Samoa had been preserved by United States refusal to agree to partition: in December 1899 a tripartite agreement with Germany and Britain divided the group into German and American protectorates. In compensation for her claims, Britain was left free to occupy Tonga, several German islands in the Solomons, Savage Island and (typical of the geographic scope of partition agreements) areas in dispute between the Gold Coast and Togoland. The partition of the Pacific was completed in 1906 when an Anglo-French convention placed the New Hebrides condominium on a permanent footing.

By 1914 it seemed that the expansion of the colonial empires had come to a halt. Few annexations had been made since 1900. International deadlocks protected China, Siam, Afghanistan and Persia. The United States dominated the Caribbean and Latin America, barring them to European predators. Only the Ottoman empire in the Middle East remained undealt with; but there too the balance of international interests in an area so vital to many barred formal division or unilateral annexation. Germany acquired the upper hand. A German company had obtained the right to build a railway to Baghdad in 1899; German officers were training Turkish troops; German diplomats and financiers dominated the Sultan's court. Yet Germany knew that she could go no farther. The Turkish empire survived by virtue of its weakness and its importance.

Redivision and the Last European Expansion 1914–39

The First World War resolved the deadlock which had checked the expansion of the colonial empires. It began not as a war for imperial redivision, as Lenin alleged in 1916, but for dominance within Europe. Yet, because two of the defeated belligerents, Germany and Turkey, had dependencies, their defeat in 1918 led to the first major colonial redivision since 1815.

During the war all German and most Turkish possessions had been occupied by the allies. They had not included annexation of enemy property among their war aims, but after 1918 there seemed good reasons for keeping them. There was an unanswerable case for not returning Turkish possessions, for it would have been impossible to rebuild the Ottoman empire, so long kept alive only by artificial stimulants. Arab nationalism had grown. Arabs had been promised independence in return for support for the allies; and the British had further complicated things by promising a 'national home for the Jewish people' in Palestine as a reward for Zionist support. There was no comparable case for not returning German colonies, and the allies fell back on the false assertion that the German colonial record proved that she was unfit to govern dependent peoples.

It was easier to keep German and Turkish dependencies than to decide how to allocate them. After much horse-trading Togoland and Kamerun were divided between their British and French neighbours, France receiving the greater share of both. South-West Africa went to the Union which had conquered it; Tanganyika to Britain; Ruanda-Urundi was later passed on to Belgium. German Pacific colonies were divided between Japan, New Zealand, Australia and Britain. Of the Turkish possessions in the Middle East, France got Syria and Lebanon, Britain Palestine,

Transjordan and Iraq. Italy received a strip of Somaliland, including the port of Kismayu, from Britain. The United States virtuously took nothing.

This old-fashioned spoils system was justified to a world increasingly suspicious of 'imperialism' by adopting the principle of 'trusteeship': these transferred colonies were to be governed under international supervision for the good of their inhabitants. The idea had an honourable ancestry stemming from the Berlin Act of 1885, the General Act of the Brussels Conference of 1890, the General Act of the Algeciras Conference of 1906 and the later arguments of liberals in all countries. Article 22 of the Covenant of the League of Nations therefore stated that these territories were to be granted not as full colonies but as 'mandates' under the supervision of the Permanent Mandates Commission of the League. They were divided into three categories. 'A' mandates (Syria, Lebanon, Trans-Jordan, Palestine, Iraq) were to be prepared for independence in the near future. 'B' mandates (the Cameroons, Togoland, Tanganyika and Ruanda-Urundi) were to be treated as normal colonies, subject to certain moral, economic and political obligations, but could not be permanently incorporated with other colonial possessions. The 'C' mandates (the Pacific Islands and South-West Africa), differed in that no political or economic restrictions were attached to them.

By 1923, when Turkey accepted the loss of her provinces by the Treaty of Lausanne, the impact of the war on the colonial empires could be assessed. Three results stood out. Germany had been altogether excluded from the imperialist ranks. The Middle East had been opened to full European activity and Britain was politically dominant there. She gave Iraq full independence in 1932 and freed Egypt in 1936; but her real harvest was the virtual monopoly of oil supplies whose importance had been totally unforeseen when she conquered these areas. Finally the war seemed to have exhausted the imperialist instincts of the main powers. Confidence in the moral justification of imposing alien rule was waning; socialist ideology eroded nationalist enthusiasm. The elimination of Germany, the renewed isolationism of the United States and the internal preoccupation of Bolshevik Russia combined to destroy the political tensions which had

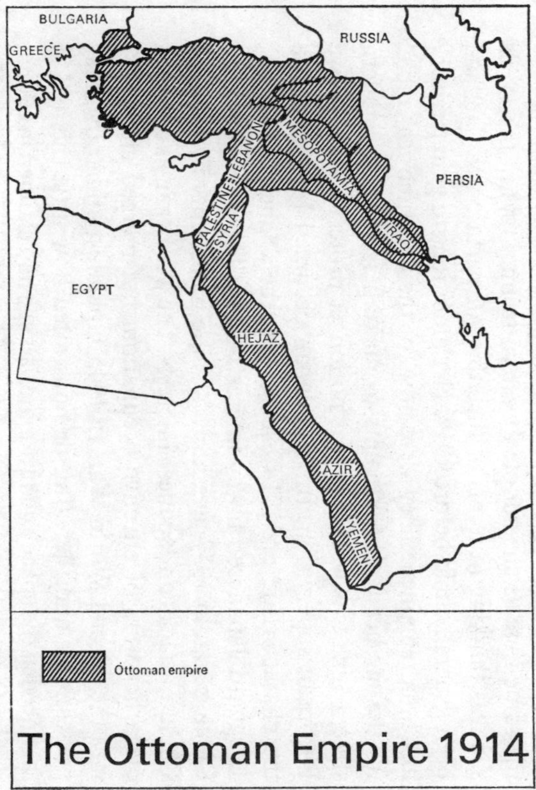

The Ottoman Empire 1914

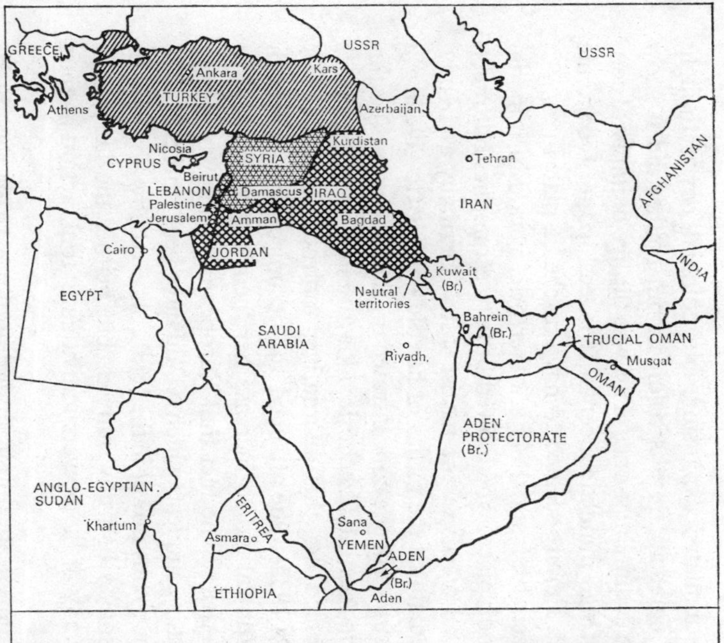

South-West Asia: political divisions after World War 1

previously stimulated expansion. No colonial power thought seriously of emancipating its colonies, but neither did it show any desire to acquire new ones. This was the age of imperial consolidation, of high-minded concepts of trusteeship and of economic development. Empire seemed to have reached a plateau.

Yet between 1931 and 1945 another brief period of imperial expansion took place, which owed little to economics but much to the political creeds of the fascist states, Germany and Italy. Germany demanded the return of her old colonies to give her 'a place in the sun'; but she concentrated on acquiring a more valuable empire in Austria, Czechoslovakia and Poland. Italy, whose weakness denied her this alternative, returned to her earlier ambitions. In 1935–6 she attacked and occupied Abyssinia both to avenge Adowa and to increase her 'neo-Roman' empire in North-East Africa. The fact that European opinion was deeply shocked by this conquest, which would have been unremarkable if undertaken by any power in the 1890s, showed how far opinion in other countries had now moved: but neither the League of Nations nor any of the powers individually took action against Italy.

The most important empire-building of the 1930s was in the Far East. Japan had learnt her imperialism and its methods at the same time as she adopted western technology: in the 1930s she was thinking in terms of the ethics of partition as they had been generally held before 1914. Her ambitions to gain territory in China remained. They were now for the first time realizable, for despite her recent attempts to make herself into a modern state, China was weak and was no longer protected by effective European supervision. In 1931 Japan occupied Manchuria on the characteristic pre-1914 excuse that the Chinese could not safeguard Japanese railway interests there. The final attack on China began in 1937, again given some plausibility by growing Chinese attacks on Japanese interests. The war began as a replica of earlier wars of effective occupation, but merged after 1941 into the Second World War. In 1945 Japan lost all her overseas possessions; and thereafter demonstrated how little she had in fact needed the space and raw materials she had claimed in China.

The Second World War had fewer immediate effects on the

colonial empires than that of 1914–18, though Italy lost Abyssinia. The main beneficiaries were Russia, which turned the whole of eastern Europe into a Soviet protectorate, and the United States, which emerged with bases and informal control throughout most of the non-Communist world. But after 1945 the concept of empire was again weakened by wartime idealism; and the post-war international balance of power prevented new empire-building. The United Nations took over the mandates as 'Trust Territories', and embodied the principle that all subordinate peoples had the right to ultimate self-determination. The post-1945 period became the age of decolonization.

The importance of examining the process by which the modern colonial empires evolved from 1815 to 1939 is that knowledge of how and why a particular colony was acquired is essential for understanding its character and functions as a colony. From this survey one overriding conclusion emerges: during this whole period remarkably few colonies were annexed as the result of a deliberate assessment of their economic potential by an imperial power. Some, like the British settlement colonies in Australia, New Zealand, Canada and South Africa, were developed by private settlers for much the same reasons as America had been occupied in the past: they were wanted for Europeans to live in and create replicas of their own societies. Other colonies were annexed because they were necessary to the security or convenience of existing colonies, such as India, Java or Russian Siberia. A few colonies reflected calculated jingoism in Europe, the United States or Japan. But the great majority of the post-1882 annexations were the product of complex processes in which the influence of existing European interests in the periphery which might eventually have led to annexation was overshadowed and twisted by the pressures of international diplomacy and nationalist fear of exclusion by a rival. In short, the modern empires lacked rationality and purpose: they were the chance products of complex historical forces operating over several centuries, and more particularly during the period after 1815.

The character of these colonial empires reflected their haphazard origins. Essentially they were museums which bore record

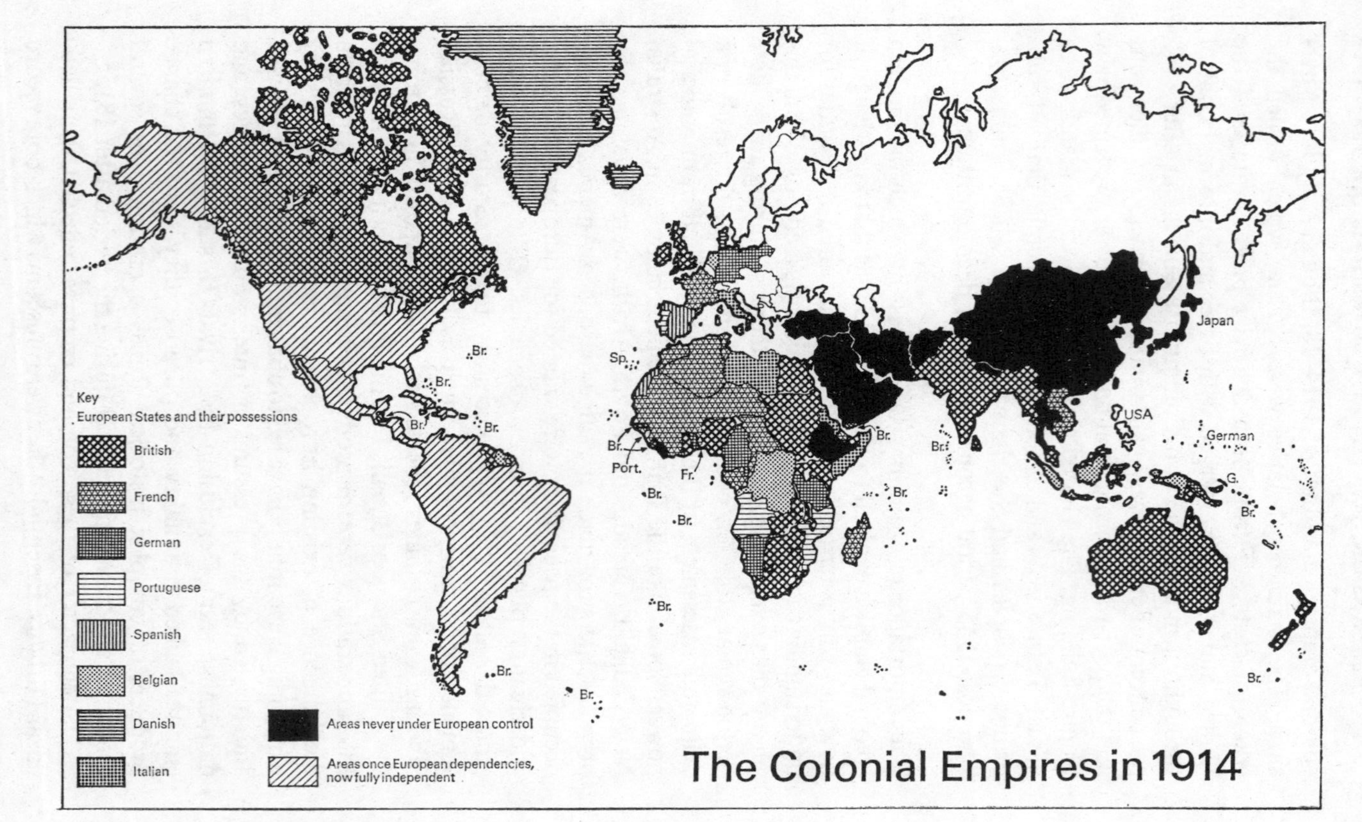

The Colonial Empires in 1914

to the transient ambitions or political situations which had once generated them. Most colonies served no demonstrable imperial purpose, and can therefore only be described as 'colonies of occupation'. Some acquisitions, of course, turned out to be really valuable. It would have been impossible for Europeans to acquire, as they did between 1800 and 1914, some 30 per cent of the earth's land surface, in addition to previous claims and holdings, without making some lucky strikes: copper in the Congo and Northern Rhodesia, diamonds in South-West Africa, gold and diamonds in Central Africa, petroleum in the Middle East and Indonesia, the possibility of growing rubber and other valuable crops in many tropical regions. These prizes have dazzled the eyes of observers, giving the impression that colonial empires were so many Eldorados. They were not. The selectivity of colonial expansion before 1883 reflected in part the knowledge that much of what was rejected was not worth the taking. The indiscriminate partition of the next thirty years was a lucky dip in which there were few prizes, and those mostly well hidden when the draw was made. Most participants in fact acquired only white elephants to which their most enthusiastic efforts could give little future value. Such unpalatable facts were to dominate the history of European colonial policy and administration during the century and a half after 1815.

11

The British Empire after 1815: I

Two primary features differentiated the modern British empire from any other and from its own past. The first was its size and diversity. At its peak in 1933 it covered some 12·2 million square miles – 23·85 per cent of the world's land surface – with a population of nearly 502 millions,[1] nearly a quarter of the world population. This immense agglomeration was the product of three centuries of expansion during which every place the British had occasion to annex, apart from the United States, had been preserved in the imperial museum. As a whole it had no unity of character or function. Its original unity, constitutional and geographic, was broken after 1763 by the addition of conquered foreign colonies and India, and the expansion of the nineteenth and twentieth centuries accentuated its prodigious variety. Such a multiplicity of possessions had nothing in common but their subjection. They constituted three or more distinct empires, according to whether they are classified by geography or political status. In the following account they will be grouped into three parts as the empire of settlement, the Indian empire, and the dependent colonial empire.

The other novel and distinctive feature of the British empire was that after 1830 it became free trading. No other empire escaped entirely from 'mercantilist' restrictions: but for a century free trade exercised a vital formative influence on British imperial policy and the British colonies.

Imperial Organization

In so disparate an empire, co-ordination had to be imposed by the metropolis. Were the British equipped with metropolitan institutions and constitutional principles adequate for their imperial role? During their first period of colonization they lacked both, for they made no formal distinction between overseas colonies and dominions within the British Isles. By the mid-nineteenth century the British had clarified their constitutional principles and possessed special metropolitan agencies to govern the colonies; yet they never made their empire as rational or as centralized as the Spanish had been. Colonial affairs were never entirely insulated from domestic agencies of government; apart from the Indian empire, colonies were never regarded as separate kingdoms under the same Crown, though this is what the 'Dominions' in fact became after 1931. Before at least the 1920s they made no attempt fully to govern the colonies from Whitehall: decentralization remained a hall-mark of British imperial organization.

Clarification of constitutional principles came first. The old doubt whether the British parliament, being a domestic body, could or should make laws affecting the internal affairs of colonies with representative assemblies, was laid to rest by the Declaratory Act of 1766 and the Colonial Laws Validity Act, 1865. By the first parliament had unlimited right 'to make laws and statutes of sufficient force and validity to bind the colonies ... in all cases whatsoever';[2] by the second colonial laws which were inconsistent with any British acts, past or future, were inoperative to the extent of their repugnancy. Such authority was indestructible: neither the British act of 1778, which declared that parliament would not impose taxes on a colony for imperial purposes, nor the 1931 Statute of Westminster, which freed the self-governing Dominions from obeying British acts unless they wished to do so, could reduce the authority of parliament. The hierarchy of legal authority in the empire was thus made clear. It descended in succession from British acts of parliament to colonial acts, prerogative instruments of the Crown (orders in council, letters patent, etc.) to the common law and executive orders given by the British government to its officials.

Clarification of authority was accompanied by new readiness to contrive forms of government for particular colonial conditions. After 1765 Britain no longer automatically gave colonies her own constitutional forms, for most new colonies required special treatment. By 1939 there were six distinct types of colonial possession: (1) The original Caribbean colonies retained their seventeenth-century constitutions unless they had agreed to change them. (2) Newer colonies of white settlement had different types of representative government; and those in Canada and Australia were grouped into federations. (3) Most other possessions had 'Crown Colony Government' – that is, autocratic rule – but differed in their legal status. In colonies conquered from another imperial power the Crown had unlimited authority to rule autocratically. But most new colonies in Africa and the east were acquired by 'settlement', having never had a European master. They were legally entitled to British laws and representative assemblies: but since these were thought unsuitable for indigenous peoples, parliament passed settlements acts enabling the Crown to govern them as conquered colonies. (4) Protectorates and protected states were legally foreign states, governed by their indigenous rulers, tied to Britain only by treaty. Parliament, however, passed foreign jurisdiction acts which enabled the Crown to govern them as if they were conquered colonies. Only the fact that their inhabitants did not become British subjects distinguished them from other Crown colonies. (5) After 1919 they were joined by 'mandated territories', held under supervision by the League of Nations and governed as if they were normal colonies. (6) Finally the Indian empire was in a category of its own.

Control of this complex empire required specialized agencies, and the institutions of domestic British government played little part in imperial affairs. Parliament was normally content to leave the empire to the executive. There was never a strong colonial party, and consideration of colonial business normally emptied either house. Colonial crises or scandals sometimes produced parliamentary debates and select committees to investigate; but for the rest parliament dutifully passed such acts as the government required. The privy council was no longer an effective part of the constitution. Its executive functions were held by the cabinet; but this was usually too preoccupied with domestic and foreign affairs to supervise the empire. The one surviving function of the old privy council was to hear legal cases on appeal from the colonies. To rationalize its jurisdiction, and to prevent colonies from blocking such appeals, British statutes were passed in 1833 and 1844 to define the powers of the new Judicial Committee of the Privy Council, giving it the right to hear appeals 'by special leave' at its discretion. In an empire with a multiplicity of laws and legal systems the Committee was an important unifying force.

Day by day imperial administration was therefore left to secretaries of state. Characteristically, there was never a single secretary or department for the whole empire. The Colonial Secretary dealt with colonies and eventually with the protectorates and mandates. The Foreign Office controlled protectorates in their early phase, since they were technically foreign states; but found quasi-colonial administration a nuisance, and transferred all but Iraq, Egypt and some small territories in the Persian Gulf to the Colonial Office. India was under the East India Company and the Board of Control until it was transferred to the new India Office in 1858. For most of this period, therefore, the British empire was administered by the Colonial and India Offices.

By the mid-nineteenth century the Colonial Office, as the focus of colonial administration, had succeeded in excluding other British departments of state from its preserve. The Treasury still supervised its finances, and the service departments had an interest in colonial defence. But all correspondence between Britain and the colonies went through the office, and other departments lost their right of interference and patronage. The office achieved full independence only in 1854, after being yoked with the War Office under a common secretary since 1801. In 1925 it was formally divided, the self-governing Dominions being transferred to a new Dominions Office, though the latter only acquired its own secretary in 1930. In 1961 a new Department of Technical Co-operation was formed to co-ordinate the economic and social services provided for the ex-colonies which became the Ministry of Overseas Development in 1964. In 1963 the Colonial and Dominions Offices were again placed under a single secretary, as colonial business was reduced by decolonization, only to be separated again the following year.

The character of much of the modern British empire, consisting for the most part of tropical dependencies without representative government, seemed to invite intensive supervision from the centre; and modern communications, especially the telegraph, at last gave London the ability to keep colonial governors under close control. In fact, however, the British ran the empire on eighteenth-century principles until at least the 1920s. This was the result partly of reluctance to do otherwise, but partly also of the character of the Colonial Office. It was run by a secretary of state and a parliamentary under-secretary, both politicians, who seldom had detailed knowledge of or strong opinions on colonial matters. A few were doctrinaires or enthusiasts; two secretaries had been civil servants in the office, and one a viceroy of India. The rest relied very heavily on their permanent officials, and these set the tone of the office. They were *grands fonctionnaires* in the tradition of European bureaucracy under the *ancien régime*, though now appointed on merit, and by competitive examination after the 1870s. They were well-informed and efficient, but legalistically inclined and concerned to prevent trouble rather than to make policy; to process the torrent of paper which flowed on to their desks, not to decide what to do with the empire. Their procedures were slow and cumbersome; they never had time to think ahead. They lacked specialized knowledge of most of the colonies with which they were dealing, and relied on external committees for expert advice on matters such as tropical medicine, agriculture, emigration, defence, etc. Only in the last phase of British colonization, between about 1920 and 1960, was the office and its auxiliaries really ready to tell the colonies what to do. Thereafter central direction was cut short by the emancipation of most of the colonies.

The surviving assumption that colonies ran themselves under remote supervision left great responsibility with the British officials in each colony: since the majority of colonies were now ruled autocratically, these had immense power. It is therefore surprising that, until 1930, there was no general colonial service to train and distribute officials. India had its own service; Ceylon, Hong Kong and the Straits Settlements had career services which were eventually linked. But all other junior officials were recruited in Britain for a particular post, sent out without any preparation, and normally left there for the remainder of their official careers. This did not mean that governors and their subordinates were inefficient: in course of time higher administrative standards evolved than were common early in the nineteenth century, when most governors were army officers on half-pay. But governors moved quinquennially from colony to colony, more concerned to avoid errors and to earn pensions than to improve their temporary charges. Their subordinates acquired proficiency on local matters, but lacked general knowledge of colonial problems and practices. Many showed a dangerous ignorance of the indigenous societies they controlled, and serious mistakes were made in dealing with complex problems such as native land tenures, social customs and laws. Preliminary training for African officers began only in 1909; after 1920 all recruits were given a six-month 'Devonshire Course' at Oxford or Cambridge, and a refresher course later on. Only in the last forty years of its history did the Colonial Office therefore provide the colonies with officials with the training and *esprit de corps* which the Indian service had had since the 1790s.

India, by contrast, was efficiently and tightly governed; but not from London. The abolition of the East India Company's political functions in 1858 left the Crown solely responsible. It could have put British India under the Colonial Office; but the tradition that India was separate was too strong. The functions of the company and the old Board of Control were fused in the India Office with a separate secretary of state. The two offices were similar in structure; but the Indian secretary was encumbered with a council which had no executive authority but whose advice and agreement were necessary on a number of important matters. The India Office attempted even less than the Colonial Office to administer India in detail: it was run by the governor-general in Calcutta, who was almost an independent sovereign.

The function of the office was to act as his agent in Britain, forming a link between the governments of India and Britain. Until after 1919 the costs of secretary and office were paid for entirely out of Indian revenues, as were the offices of the agents general – later High Commissioners – maintained in London by the self-governing colonies. Only in moments of crisis, or when major changes were in prospect, did the India Office, the British cabinet or parliament, interfere in Indian affairs.

British reluctance to govern dependencies from the centre was partly an old tradition, but it owed something also to the other major feature of the nineteenth-century empire – free trade. In the past British political control over colonies had been necessary to enforce commerce regulations: now this was no longer necessary. By 1830 Britain had opened her colonial trade to all foreign states and colonies which gave her reciprocal advantages, retaining only the monopoly of the direct carriage of goods between Britain and the colonies until 1849. By the 1850s all restrictions had gone: *l'exclusif* was dead.

The end of 'mercantilist' controls necessarily altered British attitudes to empire. Colonies were now part of a world economic system: they gave Britain no special advantage. This did not imply that they should be cast off, but that the imperial connexion favoured the colonies rather than Britain, and made it less necessary to control or subsidize them. Tariff preferences on colonial goods entering Britain were retained for a time, but were increasingly unpopular. Imperial preference was an unrequited tax on the British consumer to help the colonial producer; and the end of protection for British farmers in 1846 led also to the abolition of colonial preferences. Preferential tariffs on coffee were ended in 1851; on rice, cotton, wool, and some other goods in 1853; on sugar in 1854; on timber and all other colonial products in 1860. Conversely colonies were free from 1846 to abolish the preferences they had hitherto been forced to give British goods. During the 1860s the British took free trade to its logical conclusion, binding themselves by treaties with Belgium and the German *Zollverein* not to give or receive preferences within the empire which were not also available to these two countries and, as a result of treaties giving 'most favoured nation' rights, to the rest of the world.

Britain remained free trading until 1932. But her self-governing colonies were permitted to have protective tariffs, even against Britain herself; and after the abrogation of the Belgian and German treaties in 1898 they were free to give Britain preferences if they thought it worth while. Free trade had immense consequences. Empire could no longer mean economic exploitation of the 'mercantilist' sort. On the other hand it condemned the poorer colonies to whatever standards their own unaided economic efforts provided. The sugar colonies inevitably declined after 1854 without the protected market they had been built to serve. India suffered from being compulsorily opened to British manufactured textiles. Colonies were expected to live on their own revenues, without imperial grants in aid, since Britain felt no obligation to subsidize colonies which gave her no special economic advantage. At the same time colonies received significant advantages from the imperial connexion. They could import capital on favourable terms, since their political stability gave them sound credit in the City of London. The open British market and her increasing demand for foodstuffs and raw materials stimulated the development of colonial resources. British shipping, insurance and banking were of considerable value to them. Conversely Britain benefited from the tendency of colonies to buy from her rather than her foreign competitors because the imperial system provided the best facilities. In short, the British experiment in running an empire as a free international market was probably in the best long-term interests of all parties.

Britain dropped free trade in 1932 as an emotional reaction to the world slump; a new system of preferential tariffs and quotas was built up between Britain, the self-governing Dominions, and the dependencies. The old arguments in favour of empire on the principle of economic monopoly revived and coincided with the new British readiness to subsidize economic and social development in the colonies. The creation of the Colonial Development Fund in 1929 and its extension by the Colonial Development and Welfare Acts of 1940 and thereafter, meant that Britain was now applying to the colonies current British ideas on the social functions of the state at home. Welfare socialism in Britain meant more intensive government. Welfare in the empire at British expense also led to imperial intervention in colonial affairs. Moreover, the return to 'mercantilism' resuscitated old-fashioned ideas of making the empire self-sufficient and of developing its resources for the common good. By coincidence improvement in communications and the development of the colonial administrative services at last made positive imperial government feasible. The Dominions were by now too independent to be affected; but after about 1930 the dependent empire was more tightly governed, largely in its own assumed interests, than at any previous time. The return to protectionism had partly destroyed the liberalism of the period of free trade.

Colonial independence after 1945 ended this paternalism; but protectionism and colonial welfare survived into the post-colonial era, giving an irrational twist to the character of the expanded Commonwealth. Colonial subordination and 'mercantilism' had been logical bed-fellows; free trade and colonial autonomy had also been rational; but colonial independence, coupled with continuing preferences and financial subsidies, was a logical aberration which would have astonished imperialists of any other age.

The Settlement Colonies and Responsible Government, 1815–1914

During the century after 1815 the self-governing colonies of 'pure' settlement were the unique British contribution to European colonial history. Hitherto British colonies had differed in degree rather than in kind from other plantations or 'mixed' colonies in America: once the Spanish colonies became independent there were virtually no foreign settlement colonies, except for Algeria, which ultimately became a 'mixed' colony of the Spanish-American variety. Thus the surviving British colonies in North America and the new settlement colonies in South

Africa and Australasia maintained the first traditions of European expansion, as true reproductions of European society. They had nothing in common with the majority of new tropical colonies of occupation in Africa, Asia, and the Pacific.

Even in their origins the nineteenth-century British settlement colonies reflected the first phase of colonization; for they were developed – sometimes founded – by individuals and groups, on their own initiative and for their own advantage. After 1815 Britain possessed areas adapted to settlement on the American pattern almost by accident. Canada was the by-product of the Seven Years War, acquired to safeguard the old thirteen colonies. South Africa was an appendage of the Cape, taken in 1805 to secure the route to India; New South Wales the ignoble product of transportation. New Zealand was initially an informal sub-colony of New South Wales. The British governing class saw no point in developing these vacant properties. It had been disillusioned by American revolution, and agreed with Turgot that settlement colonies were like fruit and would drop away once they were ripe. The dawn of free-trading principles made colonies unnecessary as monopolistic markets or sources of raw materials. There was therefore no official desire to build a new settlement empire.

The colonies were founded or developed by individuals and groups in Britain who wanted to emigrate, or to build new British societies overseas, reproducing the best of the Old World. Emigration was stimulated by contemporary economic and social conditions: a rapidly rising population, increased social mobility, unemployment, and pauperism provided a reservoir of potential emigrants. But there was no necessary connexion between emigration and the founding of new British colonies. Most emigrants cared little whether they settled in a British possession or not: they went where the passage was cheap and the prospects good. For most this meant the United States or Canada. Settlements in South Africa or Australasia were attractive only to those who could afford to choose their destination or who wanted to found new societies for the sake of doing so.

The will to colonize was private, as it had been two centuries before; but the British government had an important secondary role to play. It did not take the initiative; but it seldom obstructed others from doing so, though it tried to prevent large-scale settlement in New Zealand until 1840 and indefinite expansion in South Africa, in each case because of predictable clashes with non-Europeans. Government dutifully declared British sovereignty wherever it was strongly demanded for settlement; granted charters to companies; contrived constitutions; set up governments; rescued private ventures which got into financial difficulties; and defended the nascent settlements against foreign threats and native attacks. In the 1820s ministers even caught the emigration fever, sending settlers to the Cape in 1820, and subsidizing pauper emigrants to the Cape and Canada in 1823 and 1825. These efforts were exceptional: thereafter no government supported emigration with public funds until 1919. Paradoxically the greatest official contribution to the new settlements was transportation of British convicts to Australia. When it stopped in 1868 more than 130,000 convicts had been sent – more than the total of emigrants sent by all the private colonizing companies by the same date. This represented an immense capital investment and was crucial in getting these new settlements over the first most difficult phase.

Voluntary settlement in the colonies took three different forms. First there was emigration of individuals from Britain, most of whom went to North America. Second there was internal colonization on the classical North American pattern. This was most important in Canada where the westward movement of the settler frontier from the older provinces on the St Lawrence eventually established the mid-western provinces – Manitoba, Saskatchewan and Alberta, linking them with British Columbia which began as a gold-rush area in 1858. The internal frontier was important also in South Africa and Australia. In the former it produced the provinces of the eastern Cape and the two boer republics – the Transvaal and Orange Free State; in Australia movement away from Sydney established Victoria and Queensland. But in Australia and New Zealand there was a third factor at work: the seventeenth-century British colonizing company was revived. As before these companies ingeniously combined idealism – secular now rather than sectarian – with the profit motive. Profits were expected from the sale of land by early claimants to later immigrants at greatly enhanced prices. The idealism consisted in relieving British social problems by encouraging and subsidizing emigration and in building new Anglo-Saxon societies.

The first of these companies established Western Australia in 1829. It was a simple commercial body without dogmatic principles; and it disappointed its supporters and emigrants because there were too few emigrants to raise land values and inadequate markets for its produce. Western Australia was saved by convict labour and extensive sheep-runs. Other British companies tried to avoid these problems by 'systematic' methods of founding new settlements. Their principles derived from E. G. Wakefield, whose *Letter from Sydney* (1829) and *Art of Colonization* (1849) put forward quasi-scientific principles, deriving from Benthamite thought, on how to maintain a ratio between land and the labour supply. Wakefield's doctrine was that land should not be given away but sold at a 'sufficient' price – low enough to ensure that it could be bought by the small settler with some capital, yet too expensive to be pre-empted in vast blocs before there was labour to develop it. This became the gospel of colonization in the 1830s and 1840s. To demonstrate his principles Wakefield founded or inspired a number of colonizing companies: for South Australia (1836); the Cook Straits of New Zealand (1837–8); Canterbury and Otago in the South Island of New Zealand in the 1840s. His theory was never applied in every particular, for it was found impracticable: all these settlements turned to sheep-rearing rather than intensive agriculture. None of the companies was a financial success, and all were soon dissolved. Grazing land was leased rather than sold freehold. Yet these ventures achieved solid results. They planted colonies and brought out substantial bodies of settlers; their capital and planning saw the new settlements over their first critical phase.

But the most important consequence of Wakefield's enthusiasm for settlement colonies was that it changed British attitudes to this type of possession. In this era of free trade he and associates like William Molesworth and Charles Buller were able to justify new colonies on the grounds that they employed British capital more profitably than on the marginal lands still available in Britain; that they relieved British unemployment; were financially self-supporting; provided markets for British manufactures; and enabled emigrants to remain British subjects rather than become citizens of the United States. These arguments carried conviction. Until late in the nineteenth century the British regarded such colonies as second in value only to India, the real core of the empire. The voluntary and self-sufficient character of these colonies had also an important influence on British attitudes to their government. Since 1763 most new dependencies had been conquered or had been colonies of occupation, inhabited by non-Europeans. In each case non-representative government seemed inevitable; and the British had become accustomed to governing colonies autocratically. 'Crown Colony Government' was automatically applied even to these new European settlements. Yet colonies founded by British settlers because they wished to re-create Britain overseas had an undeniable right to British legal and constitutional institutions, on the same principle as American colonies two centuries before. Since Britain had no 'strategic' reason to control the new Australian colonies; since transportation was about to dry up in New South Wales (1840) and Tasmania (1852); and since trade was now largely free, there were no good arguments against granting these and similar colonies self-government in the old tradition. These arguments were strongly pressed by Molesworth and other 'colonial reformers' in the 1840s and 1850s. They were eventually accepted, and led to the grant of representative government to all the settlement colonies. In these at least Britain had gone back to the principles on which her first empire was founded.

The principle that colonists should govern themselves through representative assemblies had never been entirely lost. It survived in the remaining British colonies in the Caribbean, which kept their seventeenth-century constitutions; and in Nova Scotia and New Brunswick, which were given the same institutions in 1783. Even the old French province of Quebec had been given representative government in 1791, after an influx of 'loyalist' settlers from the United States had made the authoritarian constitution of 1774 unsuitable. Yet in none of these places was the representative system working smoothly in the 1830s and 1840s. In the Caribbean sugar islands, New Brunswick, and Nova Scotia traditional clashes between executive and legislature continued. Governors were independent of their assemblies, but hamstrung by reliance on them for money. Assemblies used governmental poverty to gain *de facto* control of policy. Such government gave liberty but not efficiency: it survived because it was traditional, not because it was good. In Quebec, divided into the separate provinces of Upper and Lower Canada in 1791, there were different problems. Here the British had deliberately tried to avoid the conventional defects of representative government by constructing a 'system' – their first calculated essay in adapting the British constitution for export to a colony. By giving the governors independent sources of revenue and greater powers of patronage, and by creating a large nominated upper house consisting of conservative-minded colonial notables, they hoped to strengthen the executive against the legislature and preserve British authority. To the extent that the governments of Upper and Lower Canada could carry on despite conflicts with their assemblies this scheme succeeded. But it failed to give good government. Governors were unable to get additional funds for important public works; official bills were blocked; it was impossible to form stable governmental parties in the assemblies; assemblymen could not enter the executive councils without being regarded as traitors to the popular cause. Neither side could dominate the other, and bad government and political tension were the result.

Matters were brought to a head in 1837 by two minor risings in Upper and Lower Canada. Although in origin local, they were of importance throughout the British empire because they led to the first reassessment of the principles on which such settlement colonies should be governed since 1791. At this point the new enthusiasm for colonization in Britain and the principles propounded by the colonial reformers led to the adoption of a new form of colonial self-government.

The need was to find a better formula to combine imperial

authority and colonial autonomy – *imperium* and *libertas*. The solution lay in adopting two new principles. The first was that on which 'cabinet government' now operated in Britain: the sovereign could stand aside from government, entrusting his powers to a ministry of members of any party in parliament which could normally obtain majority support for its actions. The second principle, which owed much to Benthamite thinking, was that the subject matter of government could be divided into compartments. In the colonial context this implied a distinction between 'imperial' and 'colonial' interests. The former could remain under the exclusive control of the governor and the British government; the latter could be transferred to a cabinet of colonists. So logical does this solution appear in retrospect that it is necessary to emphasize that it was not available before the later 1830s. Cabinet government in this mature form was a recent growth in Britain, hardly admitted to exist before 1835. Similarly the internal affairs of a colony could not be cordoned off from 'imperial' interests until free trade and the absence of vital 'strategic' questions made it unnecessary for the metropolis to control colonial administration. Cabinet government – normally called 'responsible government' in the colonies – and 'diarchy', the division of colonial government into reserved and transferred subjects, had not been suspended before the unseeing eyes of British governments for an indefinite period before 1837; they were both new possibilities.

Their rapid adoption owed much to Lord Durham, a Whig ally of the colonial reformers, who was sent to Canada as governor-general in 1838 to sort out the causes of the two rebellions. His famous *Report* of 1839 was a manifesto of the advanced school of thought on colonial matters. Fusion of the two Canadian provinces was proposed to alleviate local problems, on the assumption that the French were more prone than English settlers to obstruct government and would be outnumbered in a combined legislature. But the significance of the *Report* was that it proposed some form of cabinet government, tempered by diarchy, as a formula for the government of settlement colonies. Durham took the virtues of cabinet government in a sovereign state for granted. It could be used in a colony without weakening imperial authority or British interests by transferring to a colonial ministry only those fields in which the metropolis had no interest. The British government and the governor should retain full control only over four areas:

> The constitution of the form of government, – the regulation of foreign relations, and of trade with the mother country, the other British colonies, and foreign nations, – and the disposal of the public lands....[3]

The *Report* eventually became the bible of the new British settlement empire, but its proposals were not adopted at once. Upper and Lower Canada were duly joined in 1840; but British statesmen could not believe that the governor of a colony could, in Lord Russell's words, receive 'at one and the same time instructions from the Queen, and advice from his executive council totally at variance with each other'.[4] To accept Durham's principles required an act of faith: it was made by Lord Grey, who was a disciple of the colonial reformers and became Colonial Secretary in 1846. In 1846 Lord Elgin was made governor-general of Canada and in the following year told that he was free to act on Durham's principles if he thought fit. Other Canadian governors were given similar liberty. The first true colonial cabinet was formed in Nova Scotia in 1848; but Elgin's acceptance of a similar ministry later in the same year, and his signature of their Rebellion Losses Bill, obnoxious to him and most English-speaking Canadians because it compensated rebels who had suffered damages during the suppression of the 1837 risings, really marked the full adoption of 'responsible government'. Elgin assumed that this was a purely Canadian question: he had acted on the advice of his responsible ministers and had put diarchy into operation.

This first experiment in 'responsible government' in Canada and Nova Scotia raised questions of policy which dominated the history of the British settlement empire for the next three-quarters of a century. Could this system be applied to all other British colonies, re-creating the constitutional uniformity of the seventeenth century, and ending the new contrast between settlement colonies and autocratically ruled dependencies? Was the arbitrary list of 'colonial' and 'imperial' subjects made by Durham satisfactory or capable of being maintained indefinitely? Was 'responsible government' a permanent solution to the problem of imperial authority versus colonial nationalism, a way to prevent the secession of mature colonies?

In considering whether 'responsible government' was applicable to any particular colony after 1848 British statesmen took three main questions into account. Was the colony primarily a metropolitan interest? If it was a military garrison, like Gibraltar, or a penal settlement, as Tasmania still was in 1849, it was automatically disqualified. Alternatively, was the colony capable of running its own affairs? If it was too small, too poor, or inhabited mainly by non-Europeans, it was unlikely to qualify. On this principle the new tropical colonies, including India, were excluded. Finally there was the question of mixed race. In the past the British would never have hesitated to give representative government to small European groups, even if it enabled them to dominate non-European majorities. Nineteenth-century humanitarianism added a complication. Should the imperial government retain full control over 'mixed' colonies in the interests of non-Europeans? If so, the Caribbean sugar colonies, the Cape and New Zealand would be disqualified from 'responsible government'.

These criteria prevented the universal application of 'responsible government'. Far from reuniting the empire in a single constitutional tradition, it divided the colonies into three distinct streams. The majority of British possessions were disqualified from self-government on the first two criteria. 'Crown Colony Government' became the formula for small colonies and those without substantial European populations. The older West Indian colonies, which already possessed representative institutions dating from their seventeenth-century foundations, were on the border line. Unlike the newer conquered colonies, like Trinidad or Mauritius, they had a constitutional right to British institutions, and their white settlers were predominantly of British stock. They had possessed assemblies for two centuries: the transition to ministerial responsibility would have been simple, and might have ended the endemic conflicts between governors and assemblies. Yet none of them received 'responsible government' before the 1940s. British motives were mixed. Few Caribbean islands had enough educated inhabitants of any race to provide an efficient ministerial system. But perhaps the racial question was more important. The electoral systems of these islands gave the vote only to property-owners, the great majority of whom were whites or mulattoes. In 1864 the Jamaican electorate was 1,903 in a total population of 450,000, the majority of whom were emancipated slaves. To give full political power to this tiny minority was inequitable: to enfranchise the illiterate majority offended mid-nineteenth-century British political principles. 'Responsible government' was therefore not applicable to these islands.

The 1860s were the watershed for the British West Indies. Until then they were left with their old institutions because the British were reluctant to deprive them of their rights. As an alternative to full 'responsible government' an experiment was made in Jamaica and some other islands after 1853 by which an executive committee was chosen from members of both legislative houses to represent the governor in each but not to constitute a cabinet. This experiment failed because these committees could not serve both masters, governors and assembly, without losing the confidence of both. Failure posed the stark alternatives of continuing the older system with its inefficiency and inconvenience and pressing 'Crown Colony Government' on to reluctant white assemblies. A minor negro rising in Jamaica in 1865, unjustifiably dignified by the term 'rebellion', offered Britain an opportunity for action similar to the Canadian 'rebellions' of 1837. Jamaica and later most other West Indian assemblies were persuaded to give up their constitutions and were converted into 'Crown Colonies'. Barbados, Bermuda and the Bahamas clung to the seventeenth-century constitutions, and British Guiana kept its special Dutch constitution until 1928. The rest were thereafter ruled autocratically by a British governor, legislative and executive councils and a few officials.

There remained the new colonies in which British settlement was creating white societies big enough to govern themselves on the new principles. Once they were financially self-sufficient the only obstacle to 'responsible government' was the problem of race relations. The Canadian colonies offered no such problems: the Amerindians were simply ignored. New Brunswick, Prince Edward Island and Newfoundland therefore received 'responsible government' between 1851 and 1854. The western provinces were given it later as they became mature, but as provinces within the framework of the quasi-federal Dominion of Canada which was created in 1867. In Australia the only obstacle was transportation, which constituted a special 'imperial interest' so long as it lasted. No convicts were sent to New South Wales after 1840 or to Tasmania after 1852. In 1855–6 these, together with South Australia and Victoria, received representative constitutions in place of their old 'Crown Colony' governments and ministerial responsibility followed automatically. Queensland followed suit after being detached from New South Wales in 1859. Western Australia had to wait twenty-two years after transportation ceased in 1868.

This left three British settlement colonies – New Zealand, Natal and the Cape. Natal was disqualified from representative government until 1893 by its poverty, lack of settlers and the Zulu danger. In the others the question was whether Britain would give full political power to white settler minorities, who might use it to deprive non-Europeans of land and liberty. Had the question arisen in the 1830s, when the British humanitarian movement was at its height, the answer might have been no. By the 1850s humanitarian influence on British colonial policy had been overshadowed by the 'Manchester men', disciples of Cobden and Bright and the free trade school, who demanded economy in governmental expenditure and denounced unremunerative expenditure on administering colonies. To deny self-government to the Cape and New Zealand – or even to allow them to refuse it when offered – left Britain to pay for native wars in both places. The price of protecting native interests as an imperial responsibility was too high: both colonies must be given full ministerial government to relieve the British taxpayer.

On these arguments New Zealand and the Cape joined the ranks of the 'constitutional colonies', as those with ministerial responsibility were often called. New Zealand got representative institutions in 1852 and a responsible ministry in 1856; but, since the governor refused, on his own initiative, to transfer native affairs to his ministry, Britain retained responsibility for the Maoris and the cost of fighting them. The outbreak of a major war in 1860 showed how expensive such responsibility was: in 1863 the British government forced a reluctant colonial ministry and assembly to take full responsibility for native affairs and to pay for future wars. The Maoris were left to take their chance, and were in fact as nearly assimilated to European society as Amerindians had been in Spanish Central America.

The Cape also was ultimately brow-beaten into accepting 'responsible government'. It was given a representative assembly in 1853; but it was reluctant to accept full ministerial responsibility. The majority saw that this would saddle them with the costs of wars against the Bantu on the eastern frontier; settlers in the east feared that a ministry dominated by the more populated western region would fail to protect them; only a small western party under J. C. Molteno supported 'responsible government'. In the end responsibility was forced on to the colonists to save British military expenditure: the Cape formed its first ministry in 1872.

By 1872 it was therefore clear that Britain would grant 'responsible government' to any colony which had sufficient Europeans to run it, and was financially self-sufficient: large non-European populations without the franchise were no bar. These principles survived until 1923 when they were applied for the last time to Southern Rhodesia, which was given 'responsible government', with some ineffective safeguards for native interests, the moment it was taken over from the British South Africa Company. Thereafter British policy changed, as 'trusteeship' principles gained acceptance. Kenya, whose considerable minority of white settlers were anxious to obtain at least representative, if not full 'responsible' government, was refused both, on the principle that African interests must remain 'paramount'. No other colony with a white minority could qualify where Kenya did not.

The greater part of the new British empire had been excluded from 'responsible government' on the principle that non-Europeans could not run a parliamentary system, partly because they were uneducated, partly because they were not European. By 1920 these principles were weakening. Britain was now a full democracy: the electorate was no longer necessarily qualified by status or education. Racialist theories were under attack. Why, then, should Indians and other dependent peoples be refused self-government? There was no theoretical ground for refusing, though habits of mind, bred by absolute authority, made the British reluctant to apply their own political principles in these dependencies. A start was made in India in 1919, when the provinces were given ministerial responsibility on the diarchical principle, much like Canada in 1848. From then until the end of the British empire in the 1960s it was only a question of time before all colonial territories, whatever their apparent political capacity, also obtained cabinet government. Thus, at its very end, the British empire was momentarily united in common constitutional forms which reflected the political tradition of the parent state.

At every stage from 1848 to 1964 the concession of ministerial responsibility to a colony posed a contingent question. Could the distinction between 'imperial' and 'colonial' fields of government be sustained? If not, and if one 'imperial' interest after another was transferred to the colonists, when would Durham's principle crack? When, in fact, did a colony become a sovereign state? The essential fact after 1848 was that the British never stood on diarchy, for if they had done so, they would have forced ambitious colonial statesmen to opt for independence. The British preferred to throw out of the window all that they had once thought vital to their own interests in a colony in order to retain at least some formal connexion with it. In process of time this infinite pliability transmuted the empire, in which Britain had power, to a Commonwealth, in which she had only a temporary influence.

Of Durham's four 'imperial' subjects, two were quickly seen to be expendable, and were handed over to colonial ministries. 'Public lands' (waste land), which he had thought important because he was a disciple of Wakefield, were transferred in Canada in 1852 and in other colonies on the grant of ministerial responsibility. Control of colonial trade was surrendered when imperial preferences were abolished in and after 1846 and of shipping when the navigation acts were repealed in 1849. In 1859 Canada was permitted to stand the system on its head and protect her own nascent industries against British exports; other colonies followed her example. Native affairs, though not one of Durham's reserved subjects, were given up as soon as possible in New Zealand and the Cape.

Transference of these areas of government left two of Durham's reserved subjects. Foreign policy seemed necessarily an imperial question, for a dependency could not, by definition, have independent relations with a foreign state. Colonial constitutions were more ambiguous, for the particular way in which a colony was governed was not necessarily important to Britain provided her own interests were not damaged. The constitutions of the self-governing colonies were mostly based on acts of parliament, and could not be altered without another British act. Colonial governors were bound by their royal commissions and instructions to use far more personal discretion than the Queen in practice exercised at home: for example, in granting pardons to condemned criminals and in refusing assent to bills passed by the local assembly. Moreover the British government had power to disallow or refuse assent to colonial bills within two years of their passage. These and other practices clearly differentiated 'responsible government', even within its defined field of operation, from the government of a sovereign state such as Britain. Would the colonies indefinitely accept these elements of 'colonial status'?

During the sixty years after 1850 most of these survivals of the imperial past disappeared. Two erosive processes were at work. First, the British normally accepted colonial demands for changes in statutory colonial constitutions or those prerogative instruments, such as the royal commissions and letters patent, which defined the governors' powers. Second, the effective power of a governor to act independently of his ministers automatically became unusable, without the need for formal alteration, as the logic of ministerial responsibility worked itself out. No governor could stand on his nominal powers if his ministers had a firm political position, and threatened to resign if their advice was not accepted. By 1914 colonial governors were normally acting much as the sovereign acted in Britain; that is, as heads of state in their colonies rather than as the agents of imperial authority. As in Britain, some functions of the prerogative could never be fully surrendered to ministers: for example the decision to grant a parliamentary dissolution out of time, or the choice of a new prime minister; and other functions, such as the grant of honours, were implicitly reserved for the British sovereign. But ministerial control of government had gone as far as it could without breaking the letter of British statutes or provoking resistance by the British government. The adoption of the term 'Dominion' in 1907 to describe the 'constitutional colonies', though it made no concrete change, reflected their new-won status. Though technically still colonies, they were virtually sovereign states within their domestic field. Few then wanted to obtain more.

Imperial Federation and the Growth of the Commonwealth

The evolution of 'responsible government' beyond the limits prescribed by Lord Durham raised an issue of fundamental importance for the future of the British empire. Well before 1900 the balance he had devised between imperial authority and colonial autonomy was tilting heavily toward the colonial side. Britain retained two basic elements of authority which demonstrated that the colonies were less than sovereign states; though in practice, these also were losing their force. British statutes still bound the colonies; yet it was now conventional that parliament would not pass acts affecting the colonies without their agreement, and would accept requests to modify existing acts which displeased them. Parliamentary supremacy was thus becoming a legal dogma rather than a fact of empire. Again, the colonies could not act as international persons: they had no power to pass laws with force outside their territorial limits, to make treaties or declare peace or war. Yet, in practice, they were allowed to opt out of, or later to withdraw from, newly made commercial treaties; colonial representatives were often associated with treaty negotiations affecting their colony; and colonies were not obliged to play a positive role in wars entered into by Britain. In short, the last obstacles to full colonial sovereignty were already tottering by about 1900. Durham's system had not provided a permanent imperial balance.

The history of European colonization provided no precedent for this situation, but logically it seemed to have only two alternative consequences. The most likely was that the colonies would eventually secede, knowing that Britain would not prevent their doing so. Alternatively, they might use their freedom to become more closely associated with Britain and each other, no longer as subordinates but as full partners; sharing Britain's authority in legislation, foreign policy and defence, turning the self-governing empire into some form of federation. These were the rational alternatives: they could be avoided only if the meaning of words and principles was changed. But, if colonial 'allegiance' no longer implied obedience to Britain, and if full colonial sovereignty was somehow made compatible with imperial authority, the Dominions could remain within the imperial framework and yet act as sovereign states. Such a solution would make nonsense of 'empire', but it would have the advantage that the colonies could obtain the liberty they wanted without formally breaking their historic links with Britain and each other.

The crucial period, during which these options were still open, was between the 1880s and perhaps 1919. Secession was never seriously considered, for only the Afrikaner-dominated Union of South Africa after 1909, and the post-1922 Irish Free State, both Dominions despite themselves, might have chosen it. For the rest the choice was between closer imperial integration and loose association.

The idea of closer association between the 'constitutional colonies' and Britain was born in Britain and remained primarily a British concept. It became influential in the early 1870s, as a defensive reaction to the assumption that self-government must result in colonial secession; and its original motives were sentimental. The new 'imperialists', as they were called, held that the settlement colonies were an extension of Britain, not separate entities: secession would deprive the mother country of her own stock. Their approach was summarized by Lord Rosebery when addressing a Sydney audience in 1883. The colonies, he said, were

> connected by a golden thread of affection and of descent. They are cemented ... more closely than anything by the fact that there are few of us in England who have not got relations or kinsfolk among you here.[5]

More material grounds were, however, soon put forward to support arguments based on the ties of blood. The colonies provided a reserve of land for emigration; they were expanding markets for British manufactures. In a period of growing international tension and vast continental armaments they might share the cost of the British navy, and supply man-power for the British army. From these roots the 'imperial federation' movement drew its strength.

The chief propaganda agency of these ideas was the Imperial Federation League, founded in 1884. It had branches in several colonies and included many leading British statesmen. Yet it was never able to produce an agreed platform for positive action. The difficulty was that 'imperial federation' could not be expressed in precise terms equally acceptable to Britain and the colonies. Britain was free trading, the colonists protectionist. Britain wanted open markets in the colonies, but would not adopt protection to give them preferences. Conversely the colonies offered preferences to Britain, but gave them by raising their existing high tariffs against foreigners, not by lowering them to help the British importer. Hence an imperial *zollverein* – customs union – was never possible.

In the field of defence there were similar difficulties. Australia, New Zealand and the Cape agreed to pay small subsidies to the British navy after 1887, but Australia and the Union of South Africa dropped them in or after 1909. No colony was prepared to maintain a regular expeditionary force to fight in Britain's wars, or to allow Britain to dictate on its local defence problems. Colonies sent small contingents to South Africa during the Boer

War, and large forces to Europe and the Middle East after 1914; but they would never commit themselves to fight in advance, and could not be regarded as part of an imperial defence system.

Political integration proved equally unobtainable. Britain would have dominated an imperial legislature or council, so that any form of federation must have deprived the colonies of some part of their freedom. Yet the concept of political association left the imperial conference system as a by-product. It began informally with 'Colonial Conferences' in 1887 and 1897 to celebrate the Queen's jubilees; thereafter conferences became regular. From 1907 they were known as 'Imperial Conferences' and were formal meetings; from 1937 they were known as conferences of Dominion (later Commonwealth) Prime Ministers, and were private and informal. Few concrete decisions were reached, but as round-table discussions of common problems they generated a sense of common interest. The nearest such meetings came to the ideal of the federationists was in 1917–18, when Lloyd George added colonial representatives to his existing War Cabinet, calling it the Imperial War Cabinet, and used it to make major decisions on the strategy of war and peace. Enthusiasts for federation like Lord Milner hailed this as the nucleus of a permanent imperial executive; but the tool broke in their hands. After 1919 the Dominions did not want to involve themselves in Britain's international diplomacy, and by 1923 the conferences were back to their pre-war form.

The failure of attempts to create closer union made possible the evolution of the modern Commonwealth as a loose association of equals rather than an empire or a federation. The tremendous military effort put out by the Dominions between 1914 and 1918 entitled them to claim their reward. In 1919 they demanded the right to sign the international peace treaties, illogical though this was for dependencies who were also bound by the signature of the British plenipotentiary. In 1923 the Canadians insisted on signing a treaty with the United States on their own account; the Imperial Conference of the same year established the right of all Dominions to make treaties, provided they informed all other parts of the empire. Thus the war had blown up the first barrier to Dominion sovereignty, and with it the diplomatic unity of the empire.

The second obstacle went down in 1926. As a result of pressures from Canada, Ireland and South Africa, each of whom had domestic reasons for wanting to emphasize its formal independence, the Imperial Conference agreed to a new definition of the status of the Dominions. In the words of Lord Balfour's famous draft, they were now stated to be

> autonomous Communities within the British Empire, equal in status, in no way subordinate one to another in any aspect of their domestic or external affairs, though united by a common allegiance to the Crown, and freely associated as members of the British Commonwealth of Nations.[6]

These quasi-theological phrases were intended to mean anything Britain or the Dominions wanted: their only clear significance was that the Dominions were now sovereign states, yet were not foreign because they gave allegiance to the Crown. A more practical step taken by this conference was to redefine the position and functions of governors-general – as all governors of Dominions were called after 1907. These were to hold 'the same position in relation to the administration of public affairs in the Dominion as is held by His Majesty the King in Great Britain....'[7] That is, they were no longer agents of the British government, but viceroys, acting for the King alone; substitute heads of state, appointed on the recommendation of each Dominion government. Since governors-general would no longer act as agents of the British government in the Dominions, the British sent High Commissioners to all Dominions to perform the same quasi-diplomatic functions there as Dominion High Commissioners performed in London.

But even these changes did not alter the fact that while the Dominions remained subject to British statutes, they were not fully sovereign. In 1931, the Statute of Westminster, evolved in discussions during the previous two years, freed the Dominions from parliamentary supremacy as far as each wished to be free. Those who accepted it – Ireland, Canada and South Africa at once, Australia in 1942 and New Zealand in 1947 – were not bound by any past or future British act unless this was specified in the 1931 statute, or unless a subsequent act expressly stated that the Dominion had 'requested, and consented to, the enactment thereof'.[8] Conversely, no Dominion act was invalid simply because inconsistent with any future or previous British act. Dominion laws acquired full force outside their territorial limits. Future changes in the royal succession or royal titles required the assent of Dominion parliaments. Membership of the Commonwealth – as the inner group of Britain and these Dominions had officially been called since 1926 – was conditional only on the Dominions giving allegiance to the common Crown.

The Statute of Westminster completed the evolution of the Dominions and gave the British Commonwealth a definite legal basis; but until 1947 the Commonwealth remained an exclusive club forming only a small part of the still vast British empire. Its ultimate importance was that these settlement colonies had created a framework into which other parts of the empire could be fitted when they too acquired full self-government. Any organization which imposed precise obligations would have been unacceptable to the new Afro-Asian states: the Commonwealth offered advantages without any concomitant obligations. On this basis India, Ceylon and Pakistan chose to become full members in 1947–8 on achieving 'independence' – as Dominion Status was now for the first time called. Other colonies followed as they gained 'independence'; Burma was the only colony to refuse membership, though the Irish Republic left the Commonwealth in 1948.

The entry of these new states not only changed the character of the Commonwealth by making it multi-racial and immensely larger: it also raised the question of the minimum qualification for membership. In 1931 'allegiance' to the Crown had been obligatory. In 1949 India decided to become a republic; and as her citizens would no longer be subjects they could not give allegiance. This proved a small gnat to swallow. In 1949 the Conference of Prime Ministers agreed that India could remain a member of the Commonwealth even though a republic; and in due course many other new states took advantage of this precedent. But the 1949 procedure implied that each state must reapply for membership on becoming a republic. As a result South Africa, although one of the founding fathers of the Commonwealth, was forced to resign in 1960 as a result of strong criticism of her racial policies.

The Commonwealth was the end-product of three and a half centuries of British empire-building; but it was not the old empire in a different form, an ingenious device by which Britain retained informal control over emancipated colonies. Members were entirely independent, and Britain had no power over them whatever. There was no system of Commonwealth defence, diplomacy, law or currency: even economic links, such as the sterling area, whose members used London as their international bank, and tariff preferences were only bilateral arrangements, and were equally available to non-member states. In short, the Commonwealth did nothing as a whole and performed no necessary functions. It had no homogeneity, since some members were monarchies, others republics, and the old division between colonies of settlement and colonies of occupation was reflected in continuing contrasts of language, culture and approach. The Commonwealth existed only to preserve and make use of certain common interests which were the alluvial deposits of varying periods of common subjection to Britain. But as an experiment in international co-operation and consultation it had much to offer its members, if they wanted it, in economic aid, preferential trade, defence, information and consultation.

12

The British Empire after 1815: II

The Indian Empire, 1815–1947

The British always thought of and treated India differently from any other possession. This was partly due to the historical accident that it was first occupied and governed by the East India Company; yet India in fact required special treatment because it was unique. It had nothing in common with the settlement colonies because the British were there as alien 'sojourners'; it differed from all other colonies of occupation in its vastly greater size and population. But the fundamental difference lay in its function as a British possession: it provided Britain with political and military power. India was very large and had a population of about 200 millions in the 1860s. In some ways it was a poor country, but its resources were harnessed to support a great military empire before the British arrived. The British had only to preserve and improve what they inherited from the Moguls to become one of the two great powers in the east. It was as though they had acquired a continental state like Russia and were free to use its resources. This was true of no other European dependency in the modern period.

These advantages were not obvious during conquest and were not its purpose; the British acquired India by defending their trade and consolidating initial footholds. But, once the conquest was complete, the function of British rule, and its particular rewards, were grasped. Conventional attitudes to colonization were discarded. European settlement was improbable, plantation culture unnecessary. Commercial monopoly was both undesirable and unenforceable. The company lost its Indian trade monopoly in 1813; Indian ports had already been opened to foreigners; Britain was soon to adopt free trade. India was a very valuable market, but was part of a multilateral trading system. Nor had the British any strong desire to change or improve India. Some in Britain wanted to 'assimilate' Indians to European culture, but in practice colonial policy aimed to train Indians for subordinate roles in government rather than to make them into Europeans. Christian missions were allowed after 1813 but had a very limited impact. In short, the British governed India as a great eastern country over which they had fortuitously gained control. Their reward was a harvest of political power which centred on and was symbolized by the Indian army.

The importance of the army can be seen only in the context of Britain's international position during the nineteenth century. She was the greatest naval power of all; but militarily she was negligible and her regular army of about a quarter of a million had to garrison a world-wide empire. India made her the greatest territorial power in the east, maintaining an army of some 150,000, which could rapidly be expanded in time of war. This was a net profit to Britain, for it was paid for entirely out of Indian revenues: by contrast, the puny contributions the imperial federationists hoped for from the self-governing colonies after 1880 would have been insignificant. India enabled Britain to play a role in world affairs which the British tax-payer would not have been willing to pay for: to take a major part in the partition of East Africa and South-East Asia, and to conquer much of the Ottoman empire during the First World War.

The history of British rule in India is therefore dominated by two main questions. How did the British govern India so as to make full use of the power it offered them? Why, in the end, did they lose India? The first implies a study of methods of governing a vast dependency through a small alien administration; the second of the growth of a type of nationalism very different from that in colonial America.

The study of administration is complicated by the division of

India into two parts which were treated very differently. British India was under 'direct rule'; the Indian states under 'indirect rule'. In no other British dependency was there so great a contrast.

The government of British India was an essay in professional administration based on an efficient civil service, army and police force. It was absolute government on the pattern of the *ancien régime* in Europe, for long uncomplicated by constitutional principles or political pressures. The theoretical basis of British power caused little concern. It was possible to justify it legalistically by claiming that the British sovereign inherited Mogul authority in 1858 when the old empire was declared defunct. This romantic notion, made still more romantic when Disraeli gave the Queen the title Empress of India in 1876, served to give Britain the paramountcy which the Moguls had enjoyed over the independent Indian princes. Nevertheless, even while adopting Mogul symbols, the British, with their own constitutional tradition, had to justify absolutism to themselves. They did so on two different grounds. The first was that Indians, unlike British colonists, had no claim to representative government, since this was a special British product with no relevance to India. Indians could establish a moral claim to it only if they showed themselves fit to run a parliamentary system. Liberals, like T. B. Macaulay, felt bound to keep this possibility open: in his famous speech of 1833 he admitted that

> It may be that the public mind of India may expand under our system till it has outgrown that system; that by good government we may educate our subjects into a capacity for better government; that, having become instructed in European knowledge, they may, in some future age, demand European institutions. Whether such a day will ever come I know not. But never will I attempt to avert or retard it.[1]

This did not, however, imply deliberate intent: self-government was merely the logical outcome of the current policy of educating Indians so that, to quote Macaulay again, there might emerge 'a class of persons Indian in colour and blood, but English in tastes, in opinions, in morals, and in intellect'.[2] Such conditions were not fulfilled before the end of the century: until then the British felt morally justified in ruling absolutely.

By then, however, many British observers had adopted a second and more basic argument against sharing power with Indians. As expressed by Sir John Strachey in 1888, it reflected current civil service attitudes after the Mutiny:

> although I suppose that no foreign government was ever accepted with less repugnance than that with which the British Government is accepted in India, the fact remains that there never was a country ... in which the government of foreigners is really popular. It will be the beginning of the end of our empire when we forget this elementary fact, and entrust the greater executive powers to the hands of Natives, on the assumption that they will always be faithful and strong supporters of our government.[3]

This was to expose the bare bones of British rule. Empire depended on power: to liberalize it would destroy it altogether, for when a despotic government makes concessions it is about to abdicate. The question was whether the conditions which made absolute rule possible would always continue.

Absolute government meant that power descended from the top and was concentrated in few hands. Ultimate authority lay in the British parliament and Crown; in practice it was exercised by the governor-general, who was also viceroy for the Indian states. For a century after 1815 he was practically an oriental despot, a worthy successor of the Moguls. He had to obey the British parliament, the East India Company (until 1858) and then the India Office. But these were remote: even the arrival of the telegraph from Britain in the 1860s had little effect on the independence of Calcutta. Within India there was little to check him. His executive authority was unrestricted except by a small council of officials. In 1833 he gained for the first time power to legislate for the subordinate presidencies – Madras and Bombay – as well as Bengal, when acting with an enlarged council. This body was gradually extended by the inclusion of more officials, judges and nominated unofficial members in 1853 and 1861; in 1892 quasi-elected and in 1909 properly elected members were added. It thus became the nucleus of an all-Indian parliament and potentially a real check on the governor-general's absolute powers: but until 1921 it was little more than a debating and petitioning body, with no capacity to initiate legislation or obstruct government.

The total centralization of legislative power which resulted from the 1833 changes did not last. In 1861 the two original presidencies regained their legislative functions, and when other provinces were created they also were given legislative councils. Like the Calcutta council these became partially representative by stages and had elective majorities after 1909. By 1935 there were eleven full provinces (in addition to Burma) which had legislatures, and four Chief Commissionerships and the Agency of Baluchistan without them. This pointed to a federal system of government for India. But before 1921 the councils did little to diminish the power of the governor-general, for they depended on Calcutta for finance, and their decisions on the local matters left to them were subject to approval by the central government. India remained a centralized state in which certain municipal functions were allocated to subordinate agencies.

The unity of British India was cemented by the existence of a single civil service for the whole country and eventually by the unification of the Indian army and police forces. These were the tools of British power, the reason for its success.

India had to have a centralized professional administration, contrary as it was to all British traditions, because Britain was an alien occupying power, and because the Indian tradition itself had known no self-governing units above the level of the village community. The quality of British government was determined by the Indian Civil Service, which was the first administrative corps of its kind in British or European colonial history. As the Covenanted Service it was created by the Charter Act of 1793 and Cornwallis' reforms in the 1790s. It was purely administrative, with no commercial functions. Members received adequate salaries, good promotion and pensions; and these attracted able men of good family as an alternative to the conventional professions – the bar, the church, medicine, education and the armed forces. Recruitment was by patronage until 1853, thereafter by open examinations; but this made little difference to the character of the service, for its traditions were already formed. It was an *élite* corps, tending to inbreeding and conservatism;

but it brought to India the devotion and often the idealism expected of the professions at home. Its members were probably the first colonial administrators who regarded their work as a calling rather than simply a means to profit.

The service set the tone of British rule in India: autocratic and alien, but just and anxious to improve the country. The fact that it was common to all British India made for unity of outlook and practice. Yet the Covenanted Service was numerically only a small part of the Indian Civil Service: in 1893 only 898 out of a total of 4,849 civil servants. The rest were members of the Uncovenanted Service, remodelled in 1889 into the Provincial and Subordinate Services. The vast majority of these officials were Indians; but since they were subordinate, this did not weaken the British monopoly of power. The problem was whether Indians should be allowed into the inner circle of the Covenanted Service, and so share real responsibility. In 1833 they were for the first time made eligible; but in fact no Indian entered the service until 1864, for there were practical obstacles facing Indian candidates, such as having to take the post-1853 entrance examination in Britain. Under pressure of Indian demand various devices were tried to improve their chances; but by 1915 there were only sixty-three Indians in the service, 5 per cent of the total. Simultaneous examinations in Britain and India began in 1922; by 1935 Indians constituted 32 per cent of the service, and 'Indianization' thereafter proceeded rapidly. Yet to the end the Covenanted Service retained its alien and British character.

The Covenanted and Uncovenanted Services undertook three main functions of government: revenue collection, general administration and law. The first two were combined in the same men, but there was a special judicial branch to staff the courts and so to maintain the vital distinction between government and law. The other main services were separate. The Political Service provided residents in the princely states and diplomats to foreign countries. The Public Works Department, the Forestry Department, the Indian Medical Service and the Police were recruited separately and did not form part of the Covenanted Service. Of these the police were the most important, but for long were inferior in quality. Until the 1860s the British maintained the system they inherited, based on unpaid and traditionally corrupt village officials, supervised by British ex-army officers called Superintendents. The first professional police forces were created, on a provincial basis, in the 1860s, with senior officers recruited in Britain. The first all-Indian Police Service was created by Lord Curzon in 1905. Its members took the higher posts in the provincial police forces and formed an exclusive corps comparable to the Covenanted Service. In addition, an all-Indian Department of Criminal Intelligence was set up, specializing in political conspiracy and *Thagi*.

All branches of the civil administration were vital to British power in India; but the army was its real basis, for alien rule ultimately depended on force. From the 1740s the British relied on a predominantly Indian army, for an entirely British force would have been too expensive. Such an army required careful organization, and Britain nearly lost her control over India in 1857 because the company allowed the quality of its army to deteriorate. In 1857 there were about 16,000 European troops in separate regiments and about 200,000 Indian sepoys with Indian officers to company level. In addition regular British regiments were sent to India on occasion. The Mutiny showed that this system was defective: in particular, the ratio of British to Indian troops was too small. Thereafter radical changes were made. The three presidential armies remained distinct until they were united to form the Indian Army in 1893. But the balance of European to Indian soldiers was fixed at one to one in Bengal – the danger area of the Mutiny – and one to two in Madras and Bombay: in 1885 there were 73,000 British and 154,000 Indians in the three armies. The distinction between British and sepoy regiments remained. The former were now British regiments serving in India in rotation at Indian expense; the latter had Indian officers to company level and British 'staff' officers above, for Indians held only commissions from the Viceroy until 1917, after which they could hold the King's commission and rise to higher commands. Partly to secure the loyalty of Indian regiments, partly because they were the best fighting troops, sepoys were recruited almost entirely from the traditionally 'martial' races in the Punjab, the North-West Frontier, Kashmir, the United Provinces, and the independent state of Nepal. The army thus became more than ever a professional force, detached from Indian politics. It proved its political reliability by loyalty during the civil disturbances of the inter-war years, and its military value in both world wars. It was the most satisfactory military force ever drawn from a dependent empire, and was potentially the equal of the professional armies of Europe.

The ultimate basis of British rule in India was force; and the Mutiny had demonstrated that it could be destroyed by a mutinous army. Yet force alone was insufficient: an army of some 200,000 could not have held down a rebellious population of 200 million. British power therefore depended on the passive or positive acceptance of alien rule by Indians: it lasted for so long because this was normally given. In retrospect Indian subservience may seem surprising: in context it was not. The British assiduously cultivated Indian acquiescence by making very few changes in the basic structure of Indian life, and by providing good government.

The British were conservative wherever possible. They preserved Indian social and legal customs, protected all religions, made no major changes in land tenures and went far to maintain the forms and terminology of the Mogul empire. They would have liked to use the hereditary Indian governing class as agents, and did so in the princely states. But elsewhere the landed aristocracy, who were preserved as *zamindars* in Bengal, proved unsatisfactory associates: they lacked real power in their own society and were reluctant to acquire European administrative techniques. The alternative was the Indian middle class of merchants, bankers, and the professionally literate. These were generally ready to work with the imperial power, but were too few to rule on its behalf. As 'mendicants' – beggars for a share in power – members of all these established social groups gradually obtained places in the expanding civil service: but they did so as subordinates and not by virtue of their natural social position or influence. In the last resort the British had to undertake full 'direct' rule: their achievement was not to allow absolute power to corrupt them; to tax India to support alien rule, but to give good government in return.

The primary function of British government was to collect taxes to support administration; all else flowed from this. By 1815 the British no longer exacted tribute from India, as in the chaotic early days of Clive. The East India Company's dividends were fixed by statute and were a minor burden. Payment for other British services – the cost of British regiments, the servicing of loans, pensions to civilians and army officers – have been criticized as a 'drain' of Indian resources to Britain. Yet the real burden on the Indian taxpayer was not payment of debts to Britain but the cost of the Indian government and army. Although small in numbers they were a heavy burden on a poor country, and for long left no surplus for other purposes: the army took 42 per cent of total Indian revenues in 1891–2, 36 per cent in 1911–12, and 31 per cent in 1929–30.[4] By contrast Britain spent 38 per cent of her total budget on defence in 1890 but only about 14 per cent in the 1920s.[5]

British tax policy was conservative: the British inherited ample fiscal rights and saw that it was politically dangerous to innovate. Land revenue was the largest source of income, providing about 40 per cent of total revenues for most of the nineteenth century.[6] British theorists claimed it was a rent rather than a tax, since Britain had inherited the Mogul claim to own all land: James Mill argued that the government was entitled to take any proportion of the net value of each land holding without injustice or economic harm to the cultivator. In practice they took much less: perhaps a third of the gross product during the nineteenth century, much less as prices for agricultural products rose after 1900. Forms of assessment and collection were never uniform: by 1858 there were three distinct principles. Bengal and Bihar paid under the Permanent Settlement of 1793, by which *zamindars* – hereditary Indian officials – contracted to pay a fixed sum for a given area, and made their profit by collecting more. The defects of this system, which was inherited from the Moguls, were so obvious that it was not adopted in the other presidencies. Throughout the rest of India the basic principle was that each peasant holding should be carefully assessed from time to time and that the tax should be fixed and revised according to capacity to pay. In Madras payments were made by individual cultivators to agents of the collectors, under the so-called *ryotwari* system. Fair though this was, it weakened the village *panchayats* – the traditional authorities – and in most other provinces variants of the Madras system were used by which villages or estates – *mahals* – were made responsible for payment of the gross amount at which their individual holdings were assessed.

As compared with land revenues, other taxes were light. The most productive were the monopolies of opium and salt, both inherited from the Moguls, which produced 13·4 per cent and 14·5 per cent respectively in 1891–2; though the former declined when the opium trade to China was abolished after 1907. Customs duties produced little, since India was virtually a free trade country: 2·86 per cent of total revenues in 1891–2. At the same date internal excises on luxury goods produced 8·6 per cent of the total. Income tax was levied intermittently from 1860. It became permanent in 1886, but only gradually became an important source of income.

The land tax, therefore, was fundamental to Indian finance: its collection moulded the pattern of civil administration. The British undertook the direct government of India reluctantly, and mainly to obtain revenue. They divided the areas they controlled into fiscal districts and entrusted them to 'collectors'. These districts became the units of administration as governmental functions expanded. By the end of the nineteenth century there were some 250 of them, with an average area of 4,500 square miles and a population of a million. The collectors were in effect governors of provinces, supervising a growing bureaucratic machine, but also possessed judicial powers as magistrates in minor criminal cases. They were helped by assistants, the most junior of the covenanted servants, who were in charge of a subdivision of the district. Below them were many smaller units run by Indian members of the Uncovenanted (later the Provincial and Subordinate) Services.

District administration was 'direct' rule in its classic form. Although the majority of officials were Indian, they were salaried bureaucrats rather than hereditary leaders of the communities they supervised. Local self-government was very limited. The village retained some minor functions; from the 1870s there were local rural committees to raise money and advise on local amenities; there were a few municipalities in the major towns, some of which had corporate governing bodies. But self-government above village level was alien to the Indian tradition: everything rested on the professional British administration, and as a result it became intensely paternalistic. It began by collecting taxes and ended by supervising virtually everything from methods of agriculture to personal indebtedness. This was characteristic of benevolent autocracy: collectors and assistants had much in common with the intendants and sub-delegates of pre-revolutionary France, agents of despotic power, who tempered autocracy with humanity and affection for their own districts.

The analogy between British India and France during the *ancien régime* could be extended in many fields; but there was one major difference. In India the law was supreme. Government never deteriorated into tyranny, and officials could not use administrative law or special courts to enforce their will. This predominance of law over government was the most characteristic British export to India, reflecting the intense legalism of the British constitution. Separation of administrative and judicial powers began in the 1790s, and in Bengal even deprived collectors of their magisterial powers from 1793–1831 and again from 1837–59. Even without this nice observance of British principles, the judicial branch of the Covenanted Service constituted a separate and independent corps; and at every level Indians had the right to appeal from administrative decisions to the law.

The institution of a comprehensive legal system in India posed difficulties. What laws should the courts enforce? Should they apply equally to Indians and British? It was the classic problem of governing an alien society without assimilating it. Until 1861 the British avoided the issue. British residents were under British law, enforced by supreme courts in the three presidency towns. Indians were under Hindu custom and Islamic criminal law, enforced by the two *Sadr* courts in each of the presidencies and a parallel hierarchy of courts descending to village level. These were mostly staffed by British judges, who applied Indian law and custom to the best of their ability with the help of Indian *pundits*. This experiment was unsatisfactory because of its dualism and because customary law as interpreted by Indians through British judges was uncertain and variable. The need was for a single system of courts enforcing codified laws. The courts were unified by a British act of 1861. The law they enforced was embodied in the three great codes – the Code of Civil Procedure (1859), the Penal Code (drafted by a commission under Macaulay in the 1830s, enacted in 1860), and the Code of Criminal Procedure (1861). Indian civil custom was gradually codified later in the century. By the end of the century India possessed a corpus of law and procedures which compared with the Napoleonic codes in France, blending British statutory and common law and procedure with Hindu custom. It was possibly the greatest British achievement in India.

A striking feature of British rule was the contrast between British India and the princely states. In the first there was intensive 'direct' rule by Europeans, in the second 'indirect' rule through hereditary princes. During the nineteenth century there were some 600 states, mostly small. They survived because before 1818 it had been politically convenient to make treaties rather than occupy them, and because the later policy of assimilation was thought to be one of the grievances behind the Mutiny. In effect they were British protectorates; but only about a tenth of them had formal treaties with Britain, and the British in any case claimed to have 'paramountcy' over all by inheritance from the Moguls. The result was a complex of relationships which, as Lord Curzon said in 1903, had

> no parallel in any other country of the world. The political system of India is neither feudalism nor federation; it is embodied in no constitution; it does not always rest upon a treaty; it bears no resemblance to a league. It represents a series of relationships that have grown up between the crown and the Indian princes under widely differing conditions, but which in process of time have gradually conformed to a single type.[7]

There were, in fact, only two basic features common to all the states: their foreign relations were in British hands; and they had autonomy in fiscal, legal and administrative matters, subject to supervision and advice by British residents. But in course of time they became more closely integrated with British India through improved communications, the education of princes at British schools and universities, and their use of civil servants trained in British India. Reforms of all kinds were encouraged by the residents accredited to the states from the Political Service, many of whom always held that the princely state was the ideal form of government since it could supply the amenities of modern society while maintaining the traditional style of India. Their views may have been tinged with dislike of the western-style politicians then emerging in British India, who seldom existed in the states: but the achievements of the better-run states were undoubtedly comparable with those of British India, and were a strong argument in favour of 'indirect rule' through the princes.

By the later nineteenth century the British had achieved much in India. They had imposed law and order on a sub-continent which had been in chaos. They had given India an advanced system of centralized government, well-calculated laws, honest courts, an improving police force and a first-class army. In the economic sphere they had built the best system of roads, railways and canals in Asia, uniting the country physically and making large-scale industrial and agricultural growth possible. By imposing free trade they had ruined older Indian domestic industries such as textiles, but had encouraged new export staples and made India part of a world economy. They had created an educational system based on the European model, which may have concentrated excessively on the teaching of English and on European subjects, and was perhaps too closely linked with examinations for the public services; but which nevertheless provided the educated classes with a common language and gave them a window on to the outside world. Yet British rule was characterized more by its cautious conservatism than by its innovations: during nearly two centuries of power it made surprisingly little impact on Indian civilization. Hindu religion and the caste system remained the basis of Indian society; only a very small minority of Indians were affected by western ideas and habits. The British *raj* was an umbrella under which Indians retained their own identity.

In the later nineteenth century British authority seemed impregnable, founded on efficient use of power and intelligent limitation of aims. Yet within half a century India was an independent republic. India had proved that European empire was not invulnerable and had showed other dependent peoples how to unseat their rulers. Why was this?

The short answer is that the transitory conditions which had enabled Britain to conquer and rule India gradually disappeared. Conquest was made possible by Indian disunity; subordination depended on passive acquiescence and co-operation with alien rule. By 1900 India was united as never before; and a new hostility to alien rule was eroding obedience. This hostility was not due to British exploitation or bad government: it can be explained only in terms of a growing sense of Indian nationality incompatible with subordination. The British could rule India so long as it remained a mosaic of unrelated fragments which had nothing in common except subordination; they could not do so once India felt it was a nation.

The origins of Indian nationalism can be interpreted in one of three ways. It may have been artificially generated by the impact of European liberal ideology, encouraged by the policy of education in English, which produced a small élite of educated Indians who demanded a share in their own government, formed the Indian National Congress in 1885, and eventually infected the masses with European concepts of national self-determination. Alternatively, nationalism may always have existed, expressed first in resistance to conquest and then in the Mutiny of 1857. But because it was based on traditional institutions and loyalties, nationalism could not express itself once these were destroyed. Imported liberal ideas gave it a new language, and the model of European mass political parties the means of action. After 1920 Congress used these devices to focus nationalism on its modern objective of gaining full self-government under British forms, and succeeded in 1947. The third interpretation is more concerned with social phenomena. By about 1900 India was no longer the same country that had docilely accepted alien rule before 1818. Urbanization, expanding population and the first phases of an industrial revolution were creating a landless proletariat and intense pressures for social and economic change. British rule was conservative, supporting the possessing Indian classes. It had to be swept away not only because it was alien but because it was part of the *ancien régime* in India, an obstacle to social evolution.

None of these interpretations can stand by itself: collectively they explain why the British could not maintain power in India. Concessions were necessary by the 1890s, when the nationalist movement first became embarrassing. But the retreat from empire was slow, for overwhelming pressures did not build up until Gandhi took control of Congress after 1920. For long the British assumed, in Lord Dufferin's phrase, that only a 'microscopic minority' were aggrieved, and tried to buy them off by 'Indianization' of the services and by giving ambitious individuals scope to play politics harmlessly. To this end, but also to get useful co-operation in government, they created and encouraged local self-government in towns and rural areas from the 1870s. In 1892 the Indian Councils Act brought a minority of Indians, nominated by corporate bodies, on to the provincial and central legislative councils. The Morley-Minto reforms of 1909 went further, putting a minority of elected Indians on to the all-Indian legislative council and a majority on to the provincial councils: but in neither could they do more than debate government bills and ask supplementary questions on matters such as finance. Beyond this the British could not go without breaking the first principle of their system – the need to preserve ultimate authority. The First World War forced their hand. In 1917, under pressure of renewed disorder in India and gratitude for the immense Indian war effort, the secretary of state, Edward Montagu, defined as the new goal 'the gradual development of self-governing institutions with a view to the progressive realization of responsible government in India as an integral part of the British Empire'.[8] This was a crucial admission, for it immediately transferred India from a permanent dependency to a future Dominion. It remained only to phase the transfer of power: but, even while conceding the principle, the British were determined not to do this until Indians had proved themselves capable of sustaining the system they had built and of which they were justifiably proud.

The process of imperial withdrawal was therefore slow. In 1919 the Montagu-Chelmsford reforms gave Indian ministries in the provinces full responsibility for certain 'transferred' subjects on the same principle as Durham's proposals in 1839. The 1935 Government of India Act gave full ministerial responsibility in the provinces and began 'diarchy' in the all-Indian government. Dominion status could now follow simply by transferring to an all-Indian ministry the last reserved powers of defence and foreign policy: but this did not take place before 1939 partly because the British remained distrustful, partly because the federal system of government which the 1935 act envisaged was made impossible by the refusal of princes representing a majority of Indians in the independent states to join it. Once again war forced the British to advance beyond their inclinations. Congress refused to support the British war effort, and revived its civil disobedience campaign of 1930–2. To rally Indian opinion in the crisis caused by Japan's entry into the war, a British mission under Sir Stafford Cripps promised India full Dominion status immediately after the war in 1942. In 1945 Britain still had the power to govern India, but the war and continuing Indian unrest had broken her will to rule: India became fully self-governing in 1947. But it did so as two separate states. The Muslim minority, which had originally co-operated with the Hindu-dominated Congress, had become frightened of Hindu majority rule and insisted on forming the separate Dominion of Pakistan from those regions which had a Muslim majority. Thus, at the last, the main British achievement in India – the imposition of political unity – was broken. It remained to be seen whether the other benefits of alien rule would survive decolonization.

The Dependent Empire After 1815

Considered without the white settlement colonies and India, the rump of the British empire after 1815 was still immensely large and diverse, but it was no longer unique. This 'dependent empire', as it may conveniently be called, was similar to the French empire of the same period in size, geography and historical origins, and individual British colonies had much in common with those of minor European empires in the same regions.

The British colonies fell into eight groups. The oldest were in or near the Caribbean: Jamaica, the Bahamas, the Bermudas, the Leewards, the Windwards, Trinidad, British Guiana and British Honduras. These were all relics, acquired before 1815, and thereafter of little importance to Britain. The sugar boom which had once made them prosperous ended early in the nineteenth century; the end of commercial monopoly in the 1820s deprived them of their imperial function; the abolition of slavery in 1833 and the withdrawal of imperial preferences after 1846 completed their economic decline. What had been the pride of the British empire were now its slums.

In the Mediterranean Britain possessed territories whose origins and value lay in naval strategy. Gibraltar, Malta and the Ionian Islands were acquired before 1815; Cyprus was taken in 1878; Egypt was occupied four years later to safeguard the route to India. Palestine, Iraq, and Jordan were conquered during the First World War and kept as mandates to buttress Egypt and the approaches to India. All retained their strategic importance until at least 1945. Iraq also provided a rich harvest of oil which had not been foreseen when it was conquered.

British possessions in West Africa were similarly a product of contrasting British interests over several centuries. The Gambia reflected pre-1815 commercial interests; the Gold Coast the slave trade before 1807; Sierra Leone late eighteenth-century humanitarianism; Lagos the growth of the palm-oil trade in the mid-nineteenth century. The hinterlands of these coastal colonies were acquired during the secondary phases of British activity, products of slow expansion before 1880 and the sudden partition of the next twenty years. For most of the nineteenth century the older coastal possessions seemed as valueless as the Caribbean islands, but by the end of the century they were increasingly valued as demand for their products grew. They exported palm-oil, palm kernels, hardwoods, ivory, gold, ground-nuts, cocoa, cotton and lesser commodities, and were growing importers of British manufactures. By 1911–14, British West Africa had a total overseas trade of £26,418,000[9] which later increased considerably, giving Britain an important economic interest in the region.

In Central Africa Britain possessed two protectorates – Rhodesia (divided in 1923 into the protectorate of Northern Rhodesia and the colony of Southern Rhodesia) and Nyasaland. For long both seemed valueless to Britain; Nyasaland remained so. White settlement made Southern Rhodesia a 'mixed' colony with a thriving agriculture, and copper made Northern Rhodesia one of the richest African colonies. In Southern Africa, apart from the self-governing colonies, there were the British protectorates of Bechuanaland, Basutoland and Swaziland. These were products of transient historical needs and gave Britain no long-term advantage. They were retained only because British humanitarians were unwilling to transfer them to the Union of South Africa, whose native policies they abhorred.

British possessions in East Africa, consisting of Uganda, Kenya, Somaliland, Zanzibar, the Egyptian Sudan and, after 1918, Tanganyika, were also unrewarding. They were products of the partition and the First World War, acquired to safeguard the Indian Ocean and Egypt. Despite the encouragement of peasant crops in Uganda – cotton and coffee – and the growth of European farming in the Kenya highlands, they had little economic value, and created intense political and financial problems.

Near East Africa, and in the Indian Ocean, were a number of dependencies originally taken for strategic reasons: Aden, the Persian Gulf Protectorates, Mauritius and the Seychelles. Like the Mediterranean colonies, they retained their political importance in the twentieth century, and the Persian Gulf territories also provided oil. Ceylon had been acquired because the harbour of Trincomalee was needed as a naval base, though this was later transferred to Colombo. Ceylon presented the same administrative problems in microcosm as India, but gave Britain a far smaller reward.

British possessions farther east were equally mixed in character. Burma, Malaya, Singapore, parts of Borneo and Hong

Kong had been acquired for divergent reasons, many of which soon lost their force; but these colonies offered new advantages as they lost their original functions. Burma, conquered to protect the Indian frontier, produced oil, teak, rice and other important exports. Malaya, occupied to protect the trade route to China, became valuable for its tin and rubber. Borneo, product of suppressing piracy, provided oil and rubber. Hong Kong and Singapore remained what they were originally intended to be – the chief emporia of British trade in the east.

British possessions in the Pacific were excellent examples of colonies without imperial function. Britain had annexed them either for humanitarian reasons or to serve the special interests of Australia and New Zealand rather than her own. She continued to administer Fiji, Tonga, and some smaller island groups, but Australia was left to control eastern New Guinea and mandated German islands to the east, and New Zealand was given responsibility for the Cook Islands and mandated Western Samoa.

Merely to list the components of the British dependent empire is thus to indicate its dominant features. It had absolutely no unity of character and no necessary imperial function. Some colonies were valuable economically, especially those which produced internationally saleable commodities such as rubber, tin, copper, or oil, and thus helped Britain's balance of trade. The richer colonies were also useful markets for British exports. But many produced and consumed little; and British free trade before 1932 in any case gave her no special advantage over foreign rivals. Economically valueless colonies were not, of course, necessarily useless, for some gave Britain strategic advantages in vital regions, enabling her to deploy her power. Yet, when all allowances have been made, it is likely that if the British had ever made a short list of intrinsically worthwhile colonies, they would have written off a considerable part of the empire.

Why did they never do so? The answer is that, even when counting-house criteria were applied to the empire, as in the mid-nineteenth century, the obstacles to abdicating power always seemed insuperable. Before 1918 evacuation would often have led to occupation by another European power; and this might have created the very political or economic problems British occupation was intended to avoid. Moreover, transference to another power was strongly resisted by local inhabitants whenever it was mooted. After 1918 League of Nations supervision made it conceivable that liberated colonies might keep their independence but by then other obstacles to decolonization had arisen. Most of the larger units were political artifacts, created by diplomatic cartography and the convenience of colonial administration. They lacked geographical or ethnic unity and had no apparent capacity to govern themselves as nation states. Once they had been through the imperial mill they could not return to their earlier social and political forms: to qualify for independence they had to evolve further along western lines. The British were probably too slow to admit that India and Ceylon were capable of autonomy: in most other places the facts supported their continued power as late as the 1950s. Alien rule was therefore not a device to exploit nations struggling to be free but a burden incurred by Britain as a result of past interests and actions. Empire was a holding operation without a terminal date.

Britain shared these problems with other modern imperial powers, for tropical colonization was a great leveller. Comparison turns on different methods of dealing with similar situations rather than with fundamental contrasts of principle. Apart from divergent metropolitan organizations and economic policies, the subject-matter of modern colonial history centred on two points: the political relationship between a colony and the metropolis, and the methods used to control non-European subject peoples – 'native administration'.

The political pattern of the British dependent empire after 1815 can be summarized as uniformity, subordination and local autonomy. The first two features were shared with most contemporary empires; colonial autonomy, though not unique, was the special inheritance of British dependencies from the older British tradition.

The apparent uniformity of British colonial government reflected the general application of the institutions and principles of 'Crown Colony Government'. This uniformity was surprising because it concealed vast diversity in the status of different possessions. By the 1920s Britain held possessions on four distinct juridical principles. Some were 'settlement' colonies (in law though not in the sense that they were established by emigration), which were entitled under common law to British laws and representative institutions. Others were obtained by conquest or treaty from a European power, and had the right to retain any earlier institutions which were specified in the terms of capitulation or cession, but not to British laws or institutions. Protectorates and protected states were not true colonies, but foreign states under British protection, retaining their own nationality and forms of government. Finally there were the League of Nations mandates. 'A' and 'B' mandates remained foreign states, but 'C' mandates were fully incorporated, and their inhabitants became British subjects.

The variety of governmental forms to be expected from these differences of legal status and origin was increased by the revival during the later nineteenth century of the chartered company as a means of administering British spheres of influence or protectorates. During the later nineteenth century there were four: the Royal Niger Company, the Imperial British East Africa Company, the British South Africa Company and the British North Borneo Company. Like the early seventeenth-century chartered companies, each had full authority to govern the area granted to it. Two of these exotic alternatives to normal metropolitan rule did not last for long. The IBEA Company gave up its charter in 1893; the Royal Niger Company in 1900. But the British South Africa Company continued to govern Rhodesia until 1923; and the British North Borneo Company survived until the Japanese invasion of 1942. Hence only Rhodesia and North Borneo had company rule for any length of time: Northern Nigeria and East Africa were transferred to royal government almost as soon as British occupation was complete.

From this diversity the British gradually moulded a largely uniform system of colonial administration. Legal peculiarities were ironed out by British statutes. Settlement colonies which did not obtain 'responsible government' were mostly deprived of their right to representative institutions by the settlements acts; some in the West Indies gave them up voluntarily. Only Bermuda, the Bahamas and Barbados kept representative assemblies without full ministerial responsibility: the rest were given 'Crown Colony' institutions, joining the conquered colonies. These conquered colonies also gradually lost the peculiar institutions they inherited from their European founders, on the assumption that time eroded the promises made on conquest or cession: though British Guiana retained its constitutional oddities until 1928, and in others various foreign laws and minor institutions survived.

Protectorates and protected states also were gradually assimilated to 'Crown Colony' status. Some, like Ashanti, Kenya and Southern Rhodesia, were transformed into full colonies by act of parliament. The rest remained technically protectorates and therefore foreign; but the foreign jurisdiction acts enabled the government to administer them as if they were colonies. There was no legal obstacle to annexing them, but the fact that their inhabitants did not become British subjects, and so were not entitled to British institutions or legal rights, was a convenience to colonial administration: for example native law could be retained and British officials could have virtually unlimited police and quasi-judicial powers. Apart from such matters, however, most protectorates were governed as if they were normal 'Crown Colonies'.

The exceptions were the protected states, such as Egypt, Zanzibar, Brunei, the Malay States and Tonga. These retained their indigenous rulers and political forms, but British residents exerted considerable political power, and in some a British bureaucracy ran administration. They were never formally under British 'paramountcy'; otherwise these states closely resembled the princely states of India.

A similar division survived between different types of British mandate. Britain had no 'C' mandates. The 'A' mandates – Palestine, Iraq, and Jordan – were treated as protected states; 'B' mandates – Tanganyika, Togoland, and the Cameroons – as protectorates. The first was administered as a separate 'Crown Colony'; the other two were attached to the Gold Coast and Nigeria.

Uniformity within the dependent empire thus became almost but never quite complete: ultimately the most important difference was between protected states and 'A' mandates and the rest. The former retained some national identity and at least the façade of self-government; the rest were merged in the generality of 'Crown Colony Government'. Subordination to British power was universal. Settlement colonies had constitutional rights because they were full dominions of the Crown: 'Crown Colonies', because they were conquered, or had lost their rights through the settlements or foreign jurisdiction acts, had not. Their constitution and laws could be changed simply by order in council; their domestic affairs were subject to dictation from Whitehall. Colonies of continental powers had always known such subordination: it was new to the British imperial tradition.

Yet British 'Crown Colonies' had considerably more autonomy than most foreign contemporaries. This was due partly to the continuing older tradition that colonies governed themselves, partly to the inability of the Colonial Office to administer so extended an empire in detail. Thus 'Crown Colonies' could pass laws through their legislative councils or 'ordinances' through their executive councils if they had no legislature. They had the initiative on all domestic matters and drew up budgets. They retained revenue surpluses, contracted loans for public works and developed social services. In all these spheres Colonial Office approval was necessary, as it was not in the colonies with 'responsible government'. Provided no British interest or principle was offended assent was normally given; but the price of autonomy was financial solvency. A rich colony could do much: a poor one, especially if it relied on imperial grants-in-aid, was strictly controlled.

Such autonomy was administrative rather than constitutional: it did not necessarily imply control of government by colonial subjects. Legislative councils normally included some nominated or elected unofficial members; but, until Jamaica regained a fully elected assembly in 1944, only Ceylon (from 1923 to 1931) and British Guiana had elected majorities on their councils. 'Local' action was therefore that of the British officials and nominated local notables who controlled the legislative councils; and these usually did what they were told by the governor. He in turn was subject to pressures from local interests and the colonial press; and some governors tended, chameleon-like, to adopt the attitudes of the people they governed. But, in the last resort, colonial autonomy meant no more than devolution of authority to agents of the imperial power rather than direct control by Whitehall.

'Crown Colony Government' was a convenient device, but did not in itself supply an answer to the special problem of modern tropical empires – how to govern large non-European populations.

In older British dependencies – the Caribbean islands, the pre-1815 conquered colonies and the small West African colonies such as Sierra Leone, the Gold Coast and Lagos, before they acquired large hinterlands – this was no great problem. The older sugar colonies had substantial white populations and the non-white majority of ex-slaves were assimilated to European modes. The inhabitants of small early nineteenth-century colonies in West Africa and elsewhere were British subjects, using British or European law. Local affairs were run by municipalities or justices of the peace; European principles of land tenure operated. In short these maritime colonies consisted of individuals conforming to European patterns and required no special form of colonial administration.

But this was no longer true of the majority of British tropical possessions by the later nineteenth century. They had very few European residents and were in any case too large and populous to be assimilated easily to European modes of life. Indigenous society was based on the tribe, village or small kingdom; and the individual, all-important in European law, had no defined status. Older models of government were therefore inapplicable: Northern Nigeria could not be treated like Lagos. Yet some form of government had to be imposed; not to do so endangered British control and the need to raise taxes involved administration. The problem was to decide what methods of government were best suited to these special conditions.

The need to administer large non-European societies was not new: by the later nineteenth century there were at least five models, four of which have already been described. They were relevant to all the modern tropical empires, but may conveniently be listed here.

Two were Spanish. 'Spanish assimilation', used in parts of America where there were numbers of colonists, implied the incorporation of Amerindians into European society as full subjects. By contrast Spanish policy in remoter regions of America and in the Philippines left non-Europeans as far as possible under their hereditary chiefs. Under this 'Spanish frontier' system they were supervised by *corregidores*, and might be liable for labour services, but remained unassimilated: their main contact with Europe was through Catholic missions.

This 'frontier' approach to native administration was only a holding operation. Other models were more positive. The Dutch provided two. Not wanting a territorial empire, they controlled most parts of Indonesia 'indirectly' through treaties with protected states. They left indigenous rulers with full internal power, but controlled their foreign relations and demanded tribute and other positive advantages in return for protection. This system was also used by Britain in the Indian states. But in Java, where the Dutch acquired full control and wanted to stimulate export staples like coffee, they used another method which may be called 'Javanese indirect rule'. No change was made in native law and social custom and indigenous chiefs were preserved as regents; but they were supervised by Dutch officials, and these were the real rulers. The system was cheap and prevented social disorders; but it was also positive and led slowly to the adoption of European habits. Shorn of its 'exploitive' features, such as the forced render of crops, it offered nineteenth-century colonial rulers a convenient and morally attractive method of administering new dependencies.

Finally there was 'Indian direct rule' in British India. It was the first method devised in modern times to govern and tax a vast non-European population by means of a small alien civil service; but it was applicable only under three conditions. A colony must be sufficiently rich to support a large number of professional administrators; sufficiently civilized to produce educated non-European subordinates; and sufficiently individualized – 'detribalized' – for the people to accept government other than through traditional chiefs and local customs.

One at least of these models was suited to any of the new British tropical dependencies; and until about 1900 Britain applied whichever seemed most adaptable in a particular situation: that is, they had no calculated 'native policy'. Other Europeans did the same. Britain's claim to originality was that she eventually contrived a hybrid form of native administration known as 'Indirect Rule', which was fundamentally 'Java indirect', but reflected the new and essentially moral approach to colonial affairs characteristic of the early twentieth century, embodying the paternalistic concept of 'trusteeship'.

Until the end of the nineteenth century most British possessions in Africa were loosely regulated under a 'frontier' system similar to that used by Spain in America. It was first applied in South Africa as the colonial frontiers expanded. But here, and later in Central Africa and Kenya, there was the danger that white settlers would deprive Africans of most of their land. The British therefore created native 'reserves' on the Cape's eastern frontier, in the southern protectorates, in Rhodesia, and eventually also in Kenya, which were supervised by British or colonial officials, operating on tiny budgets. The reserves policy achieved its aim of protecting the native right to land: but it was only a substitute for a sound 'native policy'. Reserves could not become self-sufficient economic or political units because they were artificially carved out of the indigenous units of native society, and their inhabitants tended to rely on employment in European settlements. In South Africa they were the roots of the *apartheid* policy adopted by the Union government.

In West and East Africa, where there were for long virtually no white settlers, land reserves were unnecessary. Early British administration was restricted to treaty-making, suppressing revolts, preventing slave trading and imposing nominal authority. It was in these large regions that more intensive methods of administration had eventually to be devised to obtain sufficient taxes to support the colonial government.

Conditions in other new British dependencies were different from those in Africa. In Ceylon and Burma the British were able to use 'direct rule' on the British Indian pattern: both were at one time provinces of British India, though Ceylon was separated in 1801 and Burma in 1937. But in Malaya and Borneo, where Britain had only protectorates, the indigenous sultanates provided a natural framework for the loosest form of 'indirect rule' similar to the princely states of India. Malaya was divided between the Straits Settlements (Penang, Singapore, Malacca) which were full colonies with British law, etc.; the Federated Malay States, which were nominally protected states with British residents, but by 1914 were run as a unit by a British bureaucracy; and the Unfederated Malay States, which retained their identity but were increasingly influenced by British residents. In North Borneo there were similar divergences but no direct British administration. Brunei and Sarawak both became protectorates in 1888. The former was governed by the Sultan as a protected state, supervised by a British resident. Sarawak was ruled autocratically by the descendants of the British Rajah, James Brooke. The north-east was controlled by the British Borneo Company. In Malaya and Borneo there was therefore no need for a 'native policy', for in form at least these states retained their identity under British supervision.

In the Pacific divergent conditions produced wide contrasts of policy. All British protectorates and colonies, other than Fiji and possessions of Australia or New Zealand, were under the general supervision of the British High Commissioner in Fiji. The Gilbert and Ellice Islands Colony and the Solomon Islands Protectorate were supervised by resident British commissioners, who made little attempt to change indigenous social and political forms. Tonga remained a protected state governed by its own dynasty – one of the few native states anywhere in which alien protection did not lead to close administrative interference. The New Hebrides remained under the Anglo-French condominium, jointly administered by British and French resident commissioners. Only Fiji was closely governed by British officials. It was a full colony; but, since it was annexed only because the native dynasty proved unable to maintain its own power against

Fijian rivals or to control the considerable European settler population, only loose British supervision was to be expected. In fact, through the accident that the first British governor, Sir Arthur Gordon, had studied Dutch methods of 'indirect rule' in Java, and had a deep interest in native welfare, a special form of 'indirect rule' was created, in which intensive control by British officials was combined with calculated preservation of native tribal institutions and the authority of Fijian chiefs. Its special feature was that Gordon and his successors aimed to preserve indigenous culture and social institutions as morally more desirable than gradual assimilation to European forms; yet used their supervisory powers to introduce 'improvements' in many spheres. Initially Gordon's system was merely expedient, since both alternatives of 'direct' and 'protected state' rule were impracticable. Yet, as a system, it proved well adapted to the needs of a primitive society and was capable of application to analagous areas of Africa after the first phase of occupation was over.

By about 1900, the problem of devising a 'native policy' for British tropical dependencies was limited to Africa, for methods of administering or supervising non-European societies in Asia and the Pacific were now well established. The initial probability was that some form of 'direct rule' on the British Indian pattern would become general, since few indigenous governments were large or efficient enough to be treated as protected states, and existing 'frontier' or loose 'indirect' methods gave inadequate control. 'Direct rule' was applied to British East Africa – Kenya and Uganda – and to other colonies such as Sierra Leone, where a network of British commissioners and African officials was built up. The British often acted through indigenous agencies, but regarded hereditary rulers, or the 'warrant chiefs' appointed to replace them, simply as paid members of an imperial civil service. Ultimately these regions were ruled in much the same way as British India, though administration remained much less complex.

The same process was going on in other parts of British Africa, and would probably have become universal had it not been for

F. D. Lugard, High Commissioner in the new protectorate of Northern Nigeria from 1900 to 1906 and governor of Nigeria – which now included the colony of Lagos and the protectorates of Southern and Northern Nigeria – in 1912–19. Lugard's system of native administration was evolved during his period in Northern Nigeria, where the power of the Muslim Emirs was so great that some form of 'indirect rule' was inevitable. Lugard accepted this, but wanted more. Like Gordon in Fiji, whose ideas had been introduced to Southern Nigeria after 1899 by his former subordinate, Sir W. MacGregor, Lugard wanted to maintain the social and political structure of African society as a means of preserving it from the worst effects of European influence. At the same time the British had a mission to 'improve' Africa by eliminating practices which seemed morally objectionable and introducing useful European exports, such as education and honest administration. 'Direct rule' was too harsh, even if practicable, since it destroyed self-government and social organization; conventional 'indirect rule' was too weak because it gave Europeans inadequate power or influence for good. Lugard's solution was to combine the close supervision of 'direct' with 'indirect' rule's tolerance of indigenous rights. He worked out his system in Northern Nigeria, tried to apply it throughout Nigeria after 1912, and publicized it in *The Dual Mandate* in 1922 after his retirement. His first principle was that African colonies should be supervised by strong central British governments, but that actual administration should be left to 'native authorities', preferably hereditary chiefs, who must be both 'unfettered' and yet 'subordinate'. 'Unfettered' meant that they were largely autonomous, with their own treasuries, courts, laws, etc. 'Subordinate' implied that they lost control over foreign relations, obeyed laws made by the colonial government and the orders of British officials, and contributed part of their revenues to the colonial treasury. Thus the system tried to balance native autonomy and imperial authority, enabling non-Europeans to take an active part in their own government without weakening British control.

Lugard's principles and the precise rules he laid down to realize them were widely publicized and carried by disciples to other parts of Africa. Adaptation to different environments by other exponents produced some changes of which Lugard did not approve: Sir Donald Cameron, for example, applied the system to Tanganyika with many variants. Hence the wider influence of 'Indirect Rule' as defined by Lugard lay in its general approach to 'native policy' and non-European areas rather than his own detailed prescription. It pleased humanitarians, aroused by reports of the horrors of the 'pacification' process in British and in foreign colonies, because it emphasized the right of indigenous peoples to proper respect. It was compatible with the new anthropology which was challenging the age-old assumption that all non-Europeans were barbarians, unfit to govern themselves and best served by being fully assimilated to European modes of government and life. It also solved the moral problem of how Europeans could act as 'trustees' for other races, for it enabled these to retain their identity under the shelter of alien authority. Finally, it satisfied the demand for economy in colonial government, since 'native authorities' were financially self-supporting. Lugard's success therefore owed much to the coincidence of circumstances: he provided solutions to acutely felt problems.

The result was that between 1920 and 1945 the process of intensifying British control over African dependencies took the form of 'Indirect Rule' through traditional native agencies rather than 'direct rule' through professionals. Few places were as well adapted to it as Northern Nigeria: in many, tribal institutions and chiefs had deliberately to be created to fulfil the formula and act as 'native authorities'. In East Africa the new doctrine was reflected in the addition of 'native councils' to the existing colonial bureaucracy of 'direct rule', and the adoption of a 'two-pyramid' theory of European and African development. Even in Southern and Central Africa it was invoked to justify leaving Africans to their own devices within their reserves. In the years between 1920 and 1939 'Indirect Rule' was the most important single influence on British policy in tropical Africa.

By the later 1940s the long-term results of the two fundamental features of British rule in tropical dependencies – 'Crown Colony

Government' and native policy – could be assessed. On the credit side British rule, after its destructive first phase, was honest, humane and tolerant. In many places and under widely differing forms, it preserved the best of indigenous institutions, laws, land tenures, and cultures. It stamped out slavery and many customs which offended western sensibilities. It introduced western amenities – communications, medicine, education, improved agriculture – and created the infrastructure of a modern state. It could certainly not be said that British rule meant tyranny or exploitation.

Its obvious defect, as it appeared after decolonization, was that it was too negative. It was based on two assumptions which later became unfashionable. First, it demanded colonial self-sufficiency in finance; so that Britain had done little before the 1940s to 'develop' her dependencies. Poor colonies remained poor and only naturally rich colonies could afford the amenities of modern civilization. Second, the British assumed that empire was permanent and that tropical colonization was an indefinite holding operation: colonial powers had no concern to train their colonies to become independent states. It was in this field that the significance of 'Crown Colony Government' and 'Indirect Rule' was most evident. The first provided a simple government by expatriates which offered no scope for aspiring colonial politicians to learn the business of government; the second, by preserving traditional aspects of indigenous government and society, was an obstacle to the growth of a modern state, unified, progressive, offering the career open to talent. Both devices were admirably adapted to governing dependencies: neither, despite protestations made in the period of decolonization, was in fact a useful seed-bed for eventual independence.

The result was that during the twenty years after 1945, when the demand for colonial independence suddenly became irresistible, British policy had drastically to be changed. 'Crown Colony' institutions were transformed into proto-parliaments by expanding the representative element in legislative councils; non-Europeans were admitted into executive councils; rulers of protected states were forced into federations and had to adopt democratic institutions; non-Europeans began to be trained to take over key administrative and other positions. 'Indirect Rule' and 'direct rule' alike had to be discarded. Elective local authorities replaced traditional chiefs and non-European officials; differing regional customs, land laws, etc., were fused into national systems of law and courts. Democracy replaced traditional autocracy. In short, the apparatus laboriously constructed during long periods of colonial rule had to be discarded in two decades.

By 1964 the process was nearly complete: the great majority of British dependencies were sovereign states. Although in this last phase the British were often reluctant to transfer power as quickly as Africans and Asians demanded, this was due to conservatism and a realistic appraisal of the problems facing these artificial nations rather than because Britain herself stood to lose by decolonization. It has been emphasized that in most of these colonies British interests were fully served by the exclusion of other world powers and the maintenance of political stability as a prerequisite to economic activity. Empire itself was an unrewarding obligation, though the taste for it grew with consumption. If colonies could stand as free states and run their own affairs, Britain had little or nothing to lose by their independence. Strategic interests had changed since the period of partition: most military and naval bases were no longer vital, though some were retained after decolonization by agreement with the new states. Economic interests might be damaged if political security was destroyed; but new states were in no position to deny their products to the western world, and decolonization was unlikely to deprive Europe of tropical foodstuffs and minerals. Thus the British dependent empire, unlike the colonies of settlement, was a transient phase, product of special British needs under particular world conditions. Tropical empire meant only occupation, which could be terminated without significant loss: but colonization was indelible, even when the colonies became sovereign states. In the post-colonial era this was the main residual difference between British colonization in America and Australasia and her occupation of territories in Africa, Asia and the Pacific.

13

The French Colonial Empire after 1815

The modern French empire, with an area of 4,776,000 square miles and a population of about 108,153,000 in 1933,[1] was smaller than the British and contained no dependencies comparable in importance with India or similar in type to the self-governing British Dominions. Yet the two empires were alike in many ways, standing apart from their contemporaries. Both were complex world-wide systems, balancing each other at many points; both included territories characteristic of every stage of European colonization since the early sixteenth century.

France's American colonies were the clearest evidence that she was an old imperial power: she retained the sugar colonies of Guadeloupe, Martinique and French Guiana in the Caribbean and the fishing bases of St Pierre-et-Miquelon off Newfoundland. Her African territories, on the other hand, demonstrated the leading role she had played in nineteenth-century expansion and partition. In North Africa she had Algeria – her one 'mixed' colony – and the protectorates of Morocco and Tunisia. In tropical Africa she had a huge bloc, larger than that of any other power, stretching from southern Algeria to the Congo and east to the borders of the Egyptian Sudan. This immense area was administered as two federations, subdivided into colonies, whose structure and names varied from one time to another. In 1939 the Federation of French West Africa contained the colonies of Mauretania, Senegal, Guinea, the Ivory Coast, Dahomey, French Sudan, French Guinea, Upper Volta and Niger. French Equatorial Africa consisted of Chad, Gabun,

Middle Congo and Ubangui-Chari. Also in West Africa were the ex-German mandated territories, Togoland and Cameroun. Other French possessions in or near Africa were French Somaliland, Madagascar, Réunion and the Comoro Islands. The parallels between British and French Africa were obvious. Each contained Islamic territories in the north, a tropical bloc, 'mixed' colonies of settlement and islands in the Indian Ocean. These possessions had been acquired at the same time and for much the same reasons and posed similar problems of policy and government.

This dualism was repeated in other parts of the world. In the Middle East France had mandates over Syria and Lebanon. In India she had five small bases as a memento of her eighteenth-century ambitions. In South-East Asia she had the Union of Indo-China, a federation consisting of the colony of Cochin-China and the protectorates of Annam (Vietnam), Tongking, Cambodia and Laos. In the Pacific she possessed New Caledonia, island groups centred on Tahiti (Oceania), and a condominium with Britain over the New Hebrides.

The character of this French empire reflected the way in which it had grown during the nineteenth century. Like the British, it was largely unplanned and had no unity of character of function. Many French colonies were the product of unplanned expansion by existing nuclei: Senegal and much of West Africa grew out of local commercial interests and problems of jurisdiction. Tunisia was the child of French banking enterprise and rivalry with Italy. Indo-China grew from the difficulties of French missions and a first foothold in Cochin-China. Oceania was also the offspring of missionary enterprise and French naval officers' intervention. To this extent the French empire was as much the product of circumstance and problems arising on the periphery as that of Britain.

Yet there was a difference. In 1815 France had few colonies which might tend to generate expansion in their vicinity, and her overseas trade was too small to give her strong incentives to acquire territory. France could probably have avoided a second colonial empire: the British could not. France had no persistent desire for glory through colonization, and metropolitan imperialism was intermittent. Yet on a number of occasions pressures within France led to colonial acquisitions which could have been avoided, or were larger than a crisis on the periphery made necessary. Algeria was initially the product of the Restoration monarchy's desire for spectacular success; its full occupation reflected the French army's professional ambitions. Indo-China grew from the minor crisis of the early 1860s partly as a result of metropolitan enthusiasm. Many African territories acquired after 1884 reflected French hostility to Britain and growing enthusiasm for tropical possessions. Morocco was primarily a means of saving face after Fashoda.

The modern French empire was therefore more deliberately acquired than the British: the French were aware of this, and took their empire seriously. This was one reason why they specialized in theories of colonial policy. But there were others. France was a continental power for whom colonies were of marginal importance. Colonial enthusiasts had to justify the empire in continental terms: after 1871, in particular, to demonstrate that it would help France eventually to regain Alsace and Lorraine from Germany. Before the 1870s the empire was small. Guizot's claim that France needed '*points d'appui*' justified the minor trading stations, and Bugeaud's argument that she needed settlement colonies covered Algeria. But tropical colonization on the grand scale, with its concomitant expense, required other excuses; and once colonies were acquired, theorists quickly produced arguments in their favour. Adopting Leroy-Beaulieu's classification of colonies into three types – '*les colonies ou comptoirs de commerce, les colonies agricoles ordinaires ou de peuplement, et ce que l'on a appelé les colonies de plantations ou d'exploitation*'[2] – they held that most French possessions except Algeria (a 'mixed' colony) fell into the last category. The need was to define their particular 'use' to France, and two advantages were claimed. Tropical colonies were markets for French exports, employed her surplus capital and provided raw materials: they would make her rich and powerful within Europe. In addition they would provide manpower for her armies to offset her inferiority to Germany and Russia. It was never, of course, proved that colonies produced these benefits: the belief that they would do so enabled the colonial enthusiasts to get their way.

The other root of French rationalism on imperial organization was her political and philosophical tradition. Post-revolutionary France inherited egalitarianism and concern for the principles of political liberty from the enlightenment and the revolution; administrative centralization and autocracy from the *ancien régime* and the First Empire; precision in constitutional and legal matters from Roman law and the Napoleonic codes. The modern French empire reflected each of these influences. In theory it was liberal, but in practice centralized and authoritarian; and its administration showed the impress of precise legal thinking and a passion for symmetry. Many French historians have overstressed the purely theoretical features of their empire, but this attempt to impose rationality and uniformity on an empire almost as diverse as that of Britain gives French colonial history its special interest.

French attitudes to empire centred on its economic functions. They never escaped the rigid assumption of the *ancien régime* that colonies must be economically profitable for the metropolis, and clung to the old principle of *l'exclusif*. France could not profitably adopt free trade because Britain had the advantage in most manufactures and in shipping; until 1861 'mercantilism' therefore survived practically unchanged. Colonies could sell only to France, import only from or through France, and had to use her ships. France then became temporarily free-trading, not because she wanted to be, but partly because the Second Empire wanted improved relations with Britain and partly because French colonies in West Africa and the Caribbean were economically dependent on imports of British manufactures. The Anglo-French treaty of 1860 committed her to open her colonial markets as well as reduce her own tariffs. The Caribbean islands were given commercial freedom in 1861, Guiana and Senegal in 1864, Algeria in 1867, and in 1868 a general edict abolished the composite laws which had constituted the old *pacte colonial*. But in the 1880s conditions again changed. France was at loggerheads with Britain; Germany and other European states were adopting heavy protection; the new French colonies were expensive and had to be justified to French critics.

Colonialists automatically reverted to *l'exclusif*: as Eugène Etienne, doyen of the colonial party, put it in 1891:

> We do indeed believe ... that since France must incur the obligations involved in a colonial domain, it is just and proper that this domain should be reserved as a market for French products.[3]

The retreat from free trade was rapid. It was never complete, for French colonies remained open to foreign trade and ships: but France attempted to put a ring fence of tariffs round the empire. The new system divided the colonies into two categories, those which were theoretically assimilated to the metropolitan tariff system and were an integral part of it, and those which were not. In 1884 and 1887 Algeria and Indo-China respectively were given French tariffs. In 1892 the Méline tariff imposed the first general protective tariff on France and extended it to all colonies except those in West Africa, the Congo and the Pacific, which could not be included because those in Africa were covered by international treaties and those in the Pacific depended on trade with nearby British possessions. Each therefore had a separate fiscal '*régime*', but in all of them French trade received preference. This dual system remained virtually unchanged until 1945, but was never satisfactory to either party. Those colonies which were integrated with the metropolis suffered from the fact that the system was one-sided. France retained revenue-producing duties on a number of tropical products even though her market was theoretically entirely open to colonies assimilated to her own tariffs; and at one time it even seemed likely that she would protect her own industries from colonial competition. Yet France failed to get the monopoly of her colonial trade. Foreign imports to French colonies were never less than half the imports from France in value, and were about two-thirds in 1926. Exports from French colonies to foreign states increased from less than half those to France in the 1890s to about the same value in the 1920s. The proportion of France's total overseas trade with her colonies remained small and constant: about 10 per cent in 1897 and 12·7 per cent in 1927.[4] In short, the French colonies were never an exclusive French preserve and were never of primary economic importance to her. Economic facts triumphed over the theory of empire as an economic utility.

In the field of colonial government and law the fascination of French imperial history lies in the contrast between the rationality and universality of French theory and the variety of practices which had eventually to be adopted.

The French approached the constitutional relationship between colonies and metropolis with an assumption derived from the republican principles of 1789. The republic was one and indivisible: colonies were an intrinsic part of it, and should ideally be assimilated to it in every particular. *Assimiliation* was therefore the French imperial ideal during all periods of republican government at home: that is, apart from the years 1815–48 and 1852–71. It has been defined as 'that system which tends to efface all difference between the colonies and the motherland, and which views the colonies simply as a prolongation of the mother-country beyond the seas'.[5] This meant not only a single tariff system, but application of the metropolitan pattern of local government and laws, representation of colonists in the French assembly, and full cultural assimilation. The French never admitted that any other relationship was theoretically desirable. *Assuejetissement* – full subordination, characteristic of the *ancien régime* – was incompatible with the Rights of Man; autonomy on the British pattern was inconsistent with the unity of the republic. Practical problems forced them ultimately to recognize *Association* – the principle that colonies should retain a separate identity and be governed pragmatically – as a necessary expedient; but it remained an inferior substitute. The French imperial mission was to mould their colonies into replicas of France and eventually to incorporate them with the metropolis.

Translated into administrative practice, these principles gave the French empire two of its characteristic features – intense concentration of power in Paris, and lack of autonomy in the colonies.

The supreme central authority was the French assembly, which had power to legislate for any part of the empire. In practice this brought the assembly into line with the British parliaments: in theory its power had different roots, for the French colonies were represented in the assembly and so assented to their own laws, at least during the republican period, 1848–52, and continuously after 1870. Thus the presence of colonial deputies satisfied republican principles; but it did little else. Only full colonies – those in the Caribbean, Senegal, Algeria, Réunion, Cochin-China, India and the Pacific – sent deputies; the rest, being protectorates or mandates, and not part of the republic, did not. Colonies were grossly under-represented: there were only 8 colonial delegates in a chamber of 750 in 1848, 20 out of 612 in 1936, and 80 out of 600 between 1946 and 1958; too few to form a party or influence legislation. Until 1946 electoral limitations meant that they were not even representative of their colonies as a whole; yet they were held to commit their colonies to obey all French laws.

In fact, the French assembly played as small a part in imperial government as the British parliament. Real power lay with the executive. From 1800 to 1848 first the Emperor and then the King had control over legislation as well as administration. Thereafter the President or Emperor could make decrees which were fully binding on the colonies, and were inferior only to laws made by the assembly, though in the 1850s a clear legal distinction was made concerning the type of legislation which applied to French dependencies. In the last resort, then, the empire was run by the government of the republic; that is by the French ministry and the responsible minister.

Yet, for a centralized and highly bureaucratic state, France was slow to develop a full colonial minister or office – even slower than Britain. There were three obstacles. First, many republicans held that *assimilation* made a colonial office unnecessary, since colonies were overseas departments and should be dealt with by the normal French ministries according to subject matter. Second, there was the French tradition that any ministry could interfere in the colonies. Finally there were for long too few colonies to warrant a full ministry, and the Ministry of Marine had a long tradition of controlling all colonies. Hence, from 1815 to 1858 colonial business was dealt with, as before 1789, by a sub-department of the Ministry of Marine. Algeria, then the only important colony, was first run by the War Office, then fully assimilated to France in 1848 by the system known as '*rattachement*' of Algerian business to French ministries. A full colonial ministry was created by Napoleon in 1858, primarily to provide an office for his nephew, Prince Napoleon; but it was abolished when he lost interest in 1860. Algeria reverted to *rattachements* and the other colonies to the Ministry of Marine.

By 1883, however, the empire had expanded greatly, and a colonial ministry became necessary. From 1883 to 1894 the colonies were under their own Under-Secretary, who was neither subordinate to the Minister of Marine nor himself responsible to the Chamber. The desire to make him susceptible to parliamentary criticism therefore led to the creation of a full Colonial Ministry in 1894, but its power remained limited. It never took over Algeria, which was still assimilated to the metropolis, nor Tunisia, Morocco and the post-1918 mandates, which were run by the Foreign Office. The Colonial Ministry had to work with the Army and Navy on defence matters, and its annual budget had to be approved by the Chamber. The minister was supposed to be guided by special committees representing colonial interests: the *Conseil Supérieur des Colonies*, created in 1883 and lasting until 1939; the *Haut Comité Méditerranéen*, set up in 1935; and, after 1946, the *Haut Conseil* of the Union, representing the governments of member states. But these were only advisory bodies with no real power. Despite republican theories the French empire was run as autocratically by the Colonial Ministry as any other dependent empire.

The hall-mark of French colonial government was autocracy and centralization. Centralization had two facets: the power held by the metropolis and the limitations of self-governing institutions in the colonies. The controlling powers of the centre were overwhelming. Colonies were bound by laws made by the assembly and decrees made by the President on the advice of the minister. Governors had extensive powers, but were under tight metropolitan control. After 1894 colonial officials were trained in the *École Coloniale*, and in course of time they formed part of a special *cadre* imbued with habits of obedience. From 1887 there was a special organization called the *Inspection des Colonies* to investigate colonial administration. Policy on all matters was drawn up or had to be approved in Paris; proposals made by the various colonial councils or other advisory bodies were always subject to metropolitan disallowance. The tightest control was exercised over colonial finance, the key to local autonomy. The French would have liked to assimilate colonial budgets entirely with that of France, leaving colonies only the minute freedom possessed by French departments and municipalities. In practice they had to allow greater local initiative, but tried to limit it narrowly. Tariffs were in any case imposed by Paris. Until 1841 the Antilles and Réunion were left to raise their own taxes and pay their expenses; but this liberal experiment proved a failure, for the local assemblies refused to vote enough money, and France had to subsidize their governments. Thereafter metropolitan control was steadily tightened, and by about 1900 colonial finance had been divided into three categories. France defined the amount to be raised locally to pay for obligatory services. She undertook the cost of colonial defence and services relating to the colonies in France, but had power to demand colonial contributions towards them. The colonies were free to raise additional taxes for other purposes, but only when obligatory expenses had been met, and subject to metropolitan approval. The result was that only the minority of colonies which had *conseils généraux* had any degree of fiscal liberty.

The object of this strict budgetary control was that the colonies should not be a burden on the metropolis. In fact they always were. At constant pre-1914 values for the franc, net metropolitan expenditure on the colonies rose from 110·19 millions (£4,400,000) in 1875 to a pre-war peak of 558·14 millions (£22,300,000) in 1913. Thereafter it declined, but was still 378 millions (£15,100,000) in 1930. The greater part of this, however, represented military activity; civil subsidies were only 40·67 million francs (£1,600,000) in 1895[6] and these declined steadily. Wars in Tongking in the 1880s, in West Africa in the 1890s, and thereafter in Algeria and Morocco made the French empire very expensive. Centralized budgeting certainly never enabled France to make a fiscal profit out of her empire as Spain and Portugal had done in the eighteenth century.

The obverse of centralized control by Paris was autocracy in the colonies. Effective power lay with the governors or governors-general, who, as direct agents of the President, held plenary powers in their territories. There was no technical difference in status between governors and governors-general; but the governors-general of the three federations (West Africa, Equatorial Africa and Indo-China) were given greater freedom of action than other governors, and much more than the governor-general of Algeria, who was harried by the War Office and the other French ministries directly concerned with Algerian affairs. In appearance French governors were autocrats. Outside Algeria all could control their own administrations, the police, the armed forces, native administration and the judicial system. They could covertly evade French laws and decrees by failing to promulgate them. Yet their effective powers were tempered in many ways. They had to obey orders from the ministry and were watched by its inspectors. Their old rival, the intendant, was abolished after 1815, but he was replaced first by an *ordonnateur*, who supervised money supplied by Paris, ratified the budget, and issued his own *ordonnances*, and then, after about 1880, by a colonial secretary. Colonial officials who disagreed with governors could bring cases before special administrative tribunals, with appeal to the council of state in France. Colonial public opinion could influence governors through local councils, the press, pressure groups and even, in certain colonies, by using their deputies in the metropolitan Chamber. Finally all colonies had councils which the governor had to consult on most matters.

The basic advisory body in all full French colonies was the *conseil d'administration*, the equivalent of the British executive council. Normally it was an entirely official body, though it sometimes included a minority of non-officials. Governors-general of federations also had a *conseil de gouvernement* for their whole region and a *commission permanente* of the officials in charge of the administrative services. None of these bodies controlled the governor, for he could ultimately reject their advice; but in each case he had to report his action to the ministry, and thus give Paris the opportunity to review the question.

In all these fields French practice was much the same as British: the difference lay in the absence of a French equivalent to the British legislative council. There was no place in French colonial theory for colonial legislatures, for full colonies were part of a single republic and other possessions were subordinate to it. France could not delegate segments of her sovereignty to dependencies. The nearest approach to a legislature were the *conseils généraux* or *conseils coloniaux* in the four *anciennes colonies* (Martinique, Guadeloupe, Guiana and Réunion), the Indian bases, Senegal, New Caledonia, Oceania, St Pierre-et-Miquelon and Algeria. But even these were only administrative bodies, modelled on the *conseils généraux* of the departments of metropolitan France. Those in the Caribbean had a brief period of glory from 1833 to 1848 when they were allowed to pass laws and fully control local finances: thereafter none had proper legislative powers and their budgetary autonomy was very tightly restricted.

Circumscribed though their powers were, these councils were regarded as an exceptional privilege: the majority of French possessions were not given them, either because they were not full colonies, or because they had too few French citizens. Yet, as these new colonies were consolidated, the need for additional revenues and voluntary co-operation from subject peoples produced tentative experiments along similar lines. Algeria, always the test-bed for colonial experiments, was the pioneer. Before 1898 it had three departmental councils for Algiers, Oran and Bone, but no general council because it was assimilated to France. The need for an effective regional organization then produced two bodies with functions covering the whole of Algeria. The *conseil supérieur* resembled a normal colonial council, but had a majority of elected members. A more experimental device was the *délégations financières*, which formed the lower house of a bicameral system. It consisted of three bodies, sitting apart. One was elected by French citizens with rural property, another by citizens of substance in the towns, the third by Muslims from the northern departments and the southern zone under military rule. Each section produced resolutions on public expenditure, taxation, and public works which were combined and sent to the *conseil supérieur* for further consideration. If approved they were submitted to the governor-general and then to the ministry in Paris for final approval or rejection. Yet this elaborate representative system did not give colonists and subjects real control over government. Their proposals could be quashed; if they refused to vote the compulsory sections of the budget presented to them by the government these could be brought into effect by the French council of state.

This was the furthest France went before 1946 in allowing colonies self-government; and only exceptionally qualified colonies were allowed similar institutions. Neither West nor Equatorial Africa was given an elected council or *délégations*, though both eventually had advisory councils consisting of nominated African notables. Madagascar was given *délégations economiques* in 1924 and Oceania a similar body in 1932. Indo-China obviously qualified for something similar because there were many French citizens there and the indigenous population was highly civilized. Cochin-China, as a full colony, had a normal *conseil colonial*. The four protectorates did not qualify for this, but had partly elective local assemblies, which performed similar advisory functions; except for Laos they had separate sections for French citizens and others. In addition the Union of Indo-China had a federal *grand conseil*, which resembled the Algerian *délégations*. It had separate sections for citizens and others, but met as a single body with citizens in a majority of 28–23. This was a truly federal body, for its members were indirectly elected by the provincial assemblies; but its powers were only those of the Algerian *délégations*, and its proposals could be quashed or modified by the governor-general.

French colonial government at the higher level was therefore autocratic: France accepted only advice from her citizens and subjects in the dependencies. This was none the less consistent with republican principles for France wished to assimilate her colonies to the metropolis, and had no wish to foster autonomous institutions which would have encouraged separation. This same logical desire to assimilate, tempered by *ad hoc* devices to meet practical needs until assimilation was possible, characterized all other aspects of colonial administration.

The character of French colonial institutions flowed naturally from clarity of thought on two important issues – the juridical status of different types of possession and the right to citizenship. French dependencies fell into three groups. *Colonies incorporées* were the equivalent of full British colonies (dominions), though France made no distinction between settled and conquered colonies. Protectorates and mandates were the same for both. Where they differed was on citizenship. Britain had only two categories – subjects of the Crown and protected persons: France had three. Inhabitants of incorporated colonies were automatically French nationals; but the vast majority of nationals were not French citizens. All nationals of the metropolis were citizens, but nationals in other territories who had no claim to citizenship by French blood were *a priori* only subjects and obtained citizenship under conditions which varied from one place to another. At this point the system became arbitrary. In 1833 all free nationals in the Caribbean colonies and Réunion, and in 1880 all inhabitants of Tahiti, were made full citizens. Everywhere else subjects had to fulfil defined conditions before qualifying, which normally involved renouncing non-Christian religions and indigenous social customs and legal rights, and meeting linguistic, educational and other tests. The result was that France had an empire of subjects: in 1939, for example, only 0·5 per cent of the inhabitants of West Africa were citizens.

This fact had important consequences for French colonial administration and native policy. Colonies in which the majority were not citizens were not given the classic public liberties of the metropolis – liberty of the press and public meeting, liberalized penal laws; only the Antilles, Réunion and St Pierre-et-Miquelon possessed these in full. Again, subjects could not vote for colonial representatives in the French assembly; colonies without a substantial number of citizens were not entitled to full colonial councils, etc. Native administration was made simpler by the fact that subjects were not entitled to French law, and so could be dealt with arbitrarily through informal legal institutions – known as the *indigénat* – and were liable for forced labour – *prestation*. In administrative practice, the British acted on much the same assumptions, for most of their non-European subjects were dealt with in the same way as French subjects, though only protected persons differed juridically from subjects in Britain.

The difference was that whereas Britain applied non-British institutions and arbitrary administrative methods pragmatically, France justified these by reference to clear legal principles. This was particularly evident in the three fields of municipal government, law and native administration.

French municipal institutions reflected the juridical status of particular possessions and the proportion of citizens they contained. Fully incorporated colonies, and those with sufficient citizens, were given *communes de plein exercice* on the metropolitan pattern, in which elective mayors, assistants and councils ran parochial affairs under the supervision of the governor, who thus took the place of the metropolitan prefect. Their freedom of action, however, varied. In the Antilles communes were nearly as autonomous as those in France; in Senegal, New Caledonia, Tahiti, Guiana, parts of Madagascar and Cochin-China they were under close supervision. In Algeria the three northern departments had communes with full metropolitan functions, but had double electoral colleges to enable non-citizens to choose a minority of councillors.

Below these full communes there were eventually three inferior substitutes. From 1913 most of Madagascar had *communes de moyen exercice*, elected by double colleges of citizens and subjects, fulfilling the same functions as full communes but with executive posts filled by nominees of the governor. One degree lower were the *communes mixtes* which began in the military zone of Algeria in 1868 and were widely used later in West and Equatorial Africa. In these also official posts were filled by French administrators, but the councils ranged from nominated to fully elective. At the bottom of the ladder were native communes, traditional indigenous institutions formally recognized as local government units by France, though not all indigenous units were thus recognized. In southern Algeria native rulers – *douars* – and their councils – *djemââs* – were recognized in 1868 and survived the creation of mixed communes in 1875. In West Africa many native institutions were used but not formally recognized as communes. In Madagascar the village unit, the *fòkon-'òlona*, was preserved by Gallieni and made a standard substitute for communes where these were not thought suitable. Similarly the village councils of Indo-China were treated as municipalities and allowed to elect a notable to carry out the functions of the mayor in a commune.

Thus local government in the colonies conformed to French principles. In most places it consisted of *ad hoc* indigenous bodies under close official supervision, but these were supposed to be evolving into the ideal of fully elective communes on the metropolitan pattern.

Law and organization of courts followed the same principles. French law was best and should eventually become universal; but only citizens were entitled to it, and subjects could be dealt with on any convenient and ethical basis. Hence the Antilles and Réunion, consisting entirely of citizens, had virtually the full metropolitan system of law: most others had dual systems dealing separately with citizens and subjects. Colonial courts using French law were similar to those in France but offended legal purists by adopting simpler procedures and by having judges who could be dismissed by the executive. There were also administrative tribunals of officials and judges to try officials and adjudicate in cases affecting the government. Courts using French law had exclusive jurisdiction over all citizens, even if one party to a dispute was not a citizen. Subjects also were encouraged to use them as an incentive to qualifying for citizenship; but the great majority were under a distinct system of courts, run by administrators rather than judges, and applying indigenous custom in civil (though not criminal) cases in place of the French codes. Native courts were first developed in Algeria; by the twentieth century there were three main types in the empire as a whole. Some were run entirely by subjects, but these were few; most were presided over by a European official who was advised on native custom by assessors. Finally there were native courts using French procedures but applying native custom. From all of them appeals could be taken to courts of appeal and courts of last resort, normally run by French officials and judges with the advice of native assessors.

The French disliked the dualism of this system: they hoped

ultimately to make French law and procedures universal. But until the empire consisted entirely of citizens this was impossible; and this condition was not fulfilled until 1946.

In native administration French policy flowed naturally from the ideal of *assimilation* and the juridical principle that subjects were not entitled to metropolitan legal rights; but actual practice was influenced more by expediency than by principles. France faced administrative problems as diverse and intractable as those of Britain. No common solution was applicable to the relics of the once powerful kingdoms of the Western Sudan and Dahomey, which had been broken by 1894; the politically fragmented regions of West and Equatorial Africa; protected states such as Tunisia, Morocco, Annam, Cambodia and Laos, whose native dynasties remained in being; Madagascar, whose Hova dynasty proved unsuited to be the agent of French control; and to other parts of Indo-China and the Pacific islands. Moreover, the role of the military during the initial phase of conquest and occupation was crucial, for few soldiers were concerned to preserve native forms, and the practical measures they took had lasting influence. By the early twentieth century the French realized that the universalist assumptions of republican philosophy and the *mission civilatrice* were impracticable; in the end they were driven to pragmatism.

Algeria was France's first laboratory of native administration, and there Muslim resistance made full *assimilation* impossible. Algeria was never assimilated: in 1936 there were only 7,817 citizens who had qualified by renouncing Islam and their place in indigenous society. Algeria was therefore divided. The north became a 'mixed' colony, dominated by white settlers, with a largely submerged but unassimilated Muslim community. The southern region was supervised rather than governed on 'frontier' principles by the French army and the *bureaux Arabes*. This failure to assimilate was repeated in all large French territories acquired during the later nineteenth century. In politically and culturally advanced societies, such as Tunisia, Morocco and Indo-China, it was impossible to convert the majority to Christianity or to replace indigenous social and political institutions.

Experience in Cochin-China before the 1890s clearly underlined the lessons of Algeria: a conquered territory could not be treated as *tabula rasa*, especially where there were few European settlers. In West and Equatorial Africa similar conclusions were reached by different routes. Once the main indigenous kingdoms had been defeated there was no obstacle to full French rule on any pattern, for African society lacked the power to resist shown in Algeria and South-East Asia. Yet the difficulty and cost of imposing full French administration on these huge and relatively poor regions were insuperable. Some alternative to *assimilation* through close French government was necessary.

By the 1890s, in fact, none of the great French pro-consuls still believed in the civilizing mission as a practical short-term policy. Indo-China was the main seed-bed of new practices, for Algeria was complicated by European settlement; and it was there that men like August Pavie, de Lannesan, Galliéni and Doumer worked out the more pragmatic approach to native administration which Galliéni later took to Madagascar and his protegé, Lyautey, to Morocco. Meantime Paul Cambon had made similar experiments independently in Tunisia. Once established in practice, the new approach soon received theoretical expression. Galliéni defined its major concepts in his *Principes de pacification et d'organisation*, published in 1896:

> 1. L'organisation administrative d'un pays doit être parfaitement en rapport avec la nature de ce pays, de ses habitants et du but que l'on se propose.
>
> 2. Toute organisation administrative doit suivre le pays dans son développement naturel.[7]

Other definitions followed: but it was Jules Harmand, another product of Indo-China, who best summed up current attitudes in his *Domination et Colonisation*, published in 1910. The new approach, he wrote,

> wishes to better the lot of the aborigine in all ways, but only in directions that are profitable to him, – by letting him evolve in his own way; by maintaining each in his place, his function, his *rôle*; by touching native customs and traditions with a very light hand only, and ... using their organization to reach these objectives. In a word,

association is the systematic rejection of assimilation, and tends to substitute for the necessarily rigid and oppressive *régime* of direct administration *that of indirect rule*, with a conservation, albeit a well-watched and well-directed conservation, of the institutions of the subject people, and with a respect of its past.[8]

By 1910 these new ideas were accepted in France, and had major effects on her colonial policy. On the one hand they gave practical expression to the ideas of humanitarians who had been shocked by the scandals of earlier French treatment of native peoples: by the *réfoulement* of the period before 1870 in Algeria when the French drove the majority of Algerians off their land; by the treatment of New Caledonia and by the powers given to monopolistic land companies in the French Congo in the 1890s. These and other abuses were not peculiar to French colonization, but they were now effectively checked by the emphasis placed on the moral claims of subject peoples to retain their identity and their property.

The political consequences of the new approach naturally varied greatly, but in the 1920s the French began to conserve rather than destroy those indigenous institutions which still survived. In Southern Algeria they retained loose control over tribal units and their rulers. Tunisia and Morocco were treated as protected states by preserving the nominal authority of the Bey and Sultan, and by retaining indigenous forms of government and law. Madagascar could not be treated as a protected state, for the authority of the Hova dynasty could not be sustained. Galliéni therefore abolished the Hova kingdom and applied 'indirect rule' in forms differing from one part of the island to another. Indo-China again demanded special treatment. In Cochin-China indigenous institutions had been destroyed beyond repair, but the French now used native mandarins as part of their bureaucracy and recognized native laws. In Tongking, however, the traditional administration, destroyed during the conquest, was rebuilt, and the functions of the village communes were buttressed, though French residents played a very active role. Annam remained nominally a protected state, the French acting through the court and the mandarins; though here too their power was very great. Finally Laos and Cambodia were left with the appearance of protected states, but French residents exercised control at all levels.

In the North African possessions (apart from Algeria), in Indo-China and in Madagascar the French had preserved the façade of 'protection' rather than 'direct rule'. In West and Equatorial Africa, and in most Pacific possessions, however, this was not practicable. In New Caledonia and Oceania the French had allowed local authorities to decay, or their authority to lapse, before the later policy of preserving them was adopted: 'direct rule' had therefore to be sustained. In West Africa also 'direct rule' was the norm, but for different reasons. Once the French had broken the power of African states, they made no attempt to preserve them as units of government; in most regions there had in any case been no large political units. The French therefore fell back on something like the 'Indian direct' system in terms applicable to a tribal society. French administrators had full control. They used Africans in many functions, and often acted through chiefs; but these always owed their status to French appointment rather than to hereditary claims: they were like the 'warrant chiefs' of British East Africa, without the private treasuries or judicial authority which Lugard had specified for his 'native authorities'.

It is impossible, therefore, to single out any one French native policy as typical: by the 1940s the French empire contained practices as diverse as those within the British empire. But three features stand out. First, the legal distinction between citizens and subjects provided France with a clear juridical basis for those two common features of modern tropical colonization – forced labour and informal legal systems run by administrators: citizens were exempt from both. Second, the French conscripted non-Europeans for overseas military service. Finally French rule, whatever its form, tended to produce a small assimilated native élite devoted to French civilization. Yet, on balance, similarities between British and French native policies outweighed contrasts. By 1945 both had imposed intensive control over all their territories and adopted the concept of the 'trust' for 'backward' races. Both assumed that empire over tropical dependencies would last indefinitely.

In 1939 the major difference between French and British attitudes to the ultimate development of their colonies was that whereas the French ideal remained assimilation of all overseas possessions, the British possessed in the Commonwealth and the Dominions a model for eventual colonial self-government. The Second World War and the nationalist movements which followed virtually destroyed even this distinction: after 1945 the French also were forced to experiment with methods of devolving power to the colonies as the only alternative to their full independence.

The Second World War had an immense impact on the French empire. In 1940 the metropolis lost control of all her overseas possessions: by 1945 many of them had undergone a transformation. The mandates of Syria and Lebanon claimed independence in 1941 and France was never able to reoccupy them. Indo-China was occupied by Japan from 1941 to 1945. A Franco-Japanese convention of 1940 reserved French rights in principle, but during the occupation the pre-war nationalist movement, Vietminh, increased in power and controlled Tongking and Annam. In 1945 France recognized this 'Republic of Vietnam' as an autonomous state within the Indo-Chinese federation, but hoped to preserve some control over the whole region. In Mediterranean Africa French authority was also sapped. The allies occupied these territories in 1942–3, and the pre-war nationalist parties revived, extending their demands from greater participation in government to full independence. Only in West and Equatorial Africa, and in Madagascar, the Caribbean, and the Pacific was French power not seriously weakened by nationalist movements before 1945.

After 1945 these facts forced France to recast her colonial policy; and she did so in three stages. The first began in 1946 with the transformation of the old empire into the French Union. This was divided into two parts. The first consisted of the metropolis, the existing *Départements d'Outre-Mer* (the Caribbean colonies, St Pierre-et-Miquelon, Réunion and Algeria), and the *Territoires d'Outre-Mer* (West and Equatorial Africa, Madagascar and the Pacific Islands). All these formed a single political entity, the French Republic. They had a common President, government and parliament; and, since their relationships were defined in the new constitution, they could not be changed until the constitution of France itself was altered. All residents of the Republic were French citizens, though not all had electoral rights; all territories were represented in the assembly, though not in proportion to their population. There was a basic distinction between different territories. The 'Overseas Departments' were fully assimilated to the metropolis (all but Algeria losing their local councils); the 'Overseas Territories' remained distinct political units under the renamed *Ministère d'Outre-Mer*. Hence the Republic was in fact part of the old centralized empire under new names, for France still ruled the 'Territories' as colonial dependencies. The only beneficiaries were the one-time subjects in the 'Territories' who, as citizens, were now released from forced labour and arbitrary justice, and received most metropolitan public liberties.

The other part of the Union resembled the British Commonwealth; but existed on paper rather than in fact. In addition to the Republic it included 'Associated States' – the protectorates of Tunisia and Morocco and the old Union of Indo-China. All were recognized as having full autonomy, subject to any restrictions agreed on with France, but without control of their foreign policy: that is, they resembled British Dominions before 1919. The Union was held together by the President of the Republic, as ex-officio head of the Union; the *Haut Conseil*, representing the various governments; and the Assembly, half of whose 240 members came from the metropolis, half from the 'Overseas Departments', 'Territories' and 'Associated States' combined.

The Union was an interesting attempt to combine French imperialism with greater freedom for her colonies; but it proved a failure. The organs of the Union, other than those of the Republic, never functioned. The 'Associated States' seceded: Indo-China in 1954, Morocco in 1955, Tunisia in 1956. France thereafter attempted to establish special relationships with each of these now sovereign states, but largely failed. This left only the Republic: and in many of its 'Overseas Territories' also the forces of nationalism were demanding major changes. The acquisition of power in France by General de Gaulle, who had opposed the principles of 1946, led to the dissolution of the

Union in 1958. It was replaced by the French Community, which was an attempt to make the previous 'Overseas Territories' into 'Associated States'. Algeria was to remain part of the Republic, though still with some legislative and administrative autonomy: all other dependencies not already assimilated with France were given the choice in a general referendum between membership and complete separation. Membership entailed subordination of foreign policy, defence and economic policy to the Community, which had a federal structure of government consisting of a common President, executive council, secretariat, senate, *Conseil Economique et Sociale*, courts of law and common citizenship. All the 'Overseas Territories' chose to join except Guinea, which chose independence, and those places which felt too small or poor to stand as states – the Comoro Islands, French Somaliland, St Pierre-et-Miquelon, New Caledonia and Oceania – which remained *Territoires d'Outre-Mer*.

But even this federal Community was no stopping place. In 1961 Algeria became fully independent. In the same year France dissolved the Community, and all the African states and Madagascar also became independent. All that remained of the French empire were the *Départements d'Outre-Mer*, now fully incorporated into the metropolis, and the few *Territoires d'Outre-Mer*, which were still dependencies. France had generated no organization comparable to the British Commonwealth, and this fact symbolized the contrasts between French and British colonial principles. Yet in practice the vestigial remnants of French imperial power were not utterly different from those of the British empire. One-time French colonies were distinguished by their cultural assimilation to French civilization. France had special treaty relations with many ex-members of the Community which provided for military support, economic aid and assistance with education and other technical services. Several of the African states were enabled, with French support, to become associate members of the European Economic Community. In the end decolonization proved as great a leveller of imperial theories and practices as had the facts of tropical colonization three-quarters of a century earlier.

14

The Dutch, Russian and United States Colonial Empires

Between the British and French and all other modern colonial empires there were contrasts in size so great as to amount to a difference in kind. Britain and France had world-wide empires of immense diversity: the rest were relatively small and geographically localized. Except for the United States empire, each had a single gravitational centre. For Portugal, Germany and Belgium this was in Africa. The Dutch empire consisted almost entirely of Indonesia. Russian colonies were widely spread but were territorially continuous. To maintain correct proportions, these six empires will be described briefly, in two groups. The German, Belgium and Portuguese colonies fall together naturally, since they consisted largely of African territories in a practically contiguous bloc; the others can only be joined in a marriage of convenience.

Three other empires will be ignored: the Spanish empire because it was a moribund relic, almost destroyed in 1898; the Italian empire in North and North-East Africa because it was small and for the most part also short-lived. The Japanese empire in the Far East deserves attention, but was not part of the expansion of Europe.

The Dutch Empire after 1815

The Dutch empire after 1815 was an inheritance from the West and East India Companies, both defunct by 1800. Alone among modern empires it was no larger in 1945 than in 1815, for the Dutch took no part in the nineteenth-century scramble for colonies, content to occupy and develop a region in the East Indies which had been their sphere of influence since the seventeenth century.

The Dutch empire and Indonesia were virtually synonymous. In the Caribbean they still had the poor, thinly populated, sugar colony of Surinam and the trading islands of St Eustacius and Curaçao: all other American colonies had been lost. In West Africa Elmina survived until 1872 as a relic of the slave trade, but was then transferred to Britain. Ceylon and the Indian bases were lost to Britain before 1815 and Malacca and Singapore, implying predominance in Malaya, were given up finally in 1824. Only the Indonesian Archipelago remained, but for nearly three-quarters of a century was one of the most valuable European colonial possessions.

The transfer of Dutch colonies from company rule to the States General began a new phase of Indonesian history but made little difference to colonial administration. The first principle of company rule was that the Indies were governed from Batavia and not from the Netherlands. This survived unchanged: Indonesia was as little dictated to by the Hague as India by Westminster.

The metropolitan agencies which inherited the power of the East India Company closely resembled those of other powers. Until 1848 the colonies were the sole responsibility of the Crown; thereafter the States General had ultimate authority, but made little practical use of it. The States restricted themselves to passing laws on colonial tariffs and currency, calling the colonial minister to account during the annual budget debate, and occasionally demanding alterations in general policy. For the rest colonial affairs were left to professionals. Executive power was delegated by the Crown to the colonial minister and his office, and no other department could by-pass them. Dutch colonial ministers were exceptional in being for the most part specialists rather than politicians, and seldom sat in either house of parliament. Many had held office in Indonesia: nine of the twenty-five governors-general of Indonesia after 1815 were colonial ministers at some time in their career. East Indian affairs were treated by the office as a mystery which only the initiated could understand. This made for expert treatment and gave Batavia the whip hand over The Hague, but it also led to inbreeding of ideas and bitter parliamentary criticism of policies over which the legislature had little influence.

Batavia, then, was the real centre of the Dutch colonial empire, and there the governor-general was the key figure. Although he had to obey parliamentary statutes and orders from the minister, his position was as strong as that of the British governor-general at Calcutta, and as unrestricted by local agencies. He had his own civil service, budget and armed forces. His executive council consisted of five officials whose careers depended on his good offices. His freedom to ignore their advice varied from one time to another: for the most part he had to ask for their assent but was free to reject their decisions. For a century after 1825 he did not have to deal with any representative, or even nominated, legislature. The demand for representative government began only about 1900 and resulted in the creation of a Batavian *volksraad* in 1916, which at first consisted partly of notables nominated by the government, partly of men elected by professional bodies. In its early days it had only advisory powers, associating non-Europeans with government but giving them no control over it. It had to be consulted on the annual budget; it could petition and complain; but it could not legislate. Nevertheless it grew rapidly in size and function. By 1929 it had 61 members, of whom not less than 38 were elected indirectly by separate racial colleges and could legislate within defined limits of subject-matter. But it remained marginal to government. The governor-general could still make laws without its assent, and the States General could bring sections of the Indonesian budget into operation if the *volksraad* did not agree to them by a fixed date. There was no ministerial system, so that initiative always lay with the governor-general. Government in Batavia remained essentially professional; but the Japanese invasion of 1941 cut short an experiment in representative government which might eventually have evolved into something resembling Dominion status within the British Commonwealth.

The distinctive feature of Dutch rule in Indonesia was its approach to native administration and race relations, which was an inheritance from the East India Company. The Netherlands never believed they had a civilizing mission. They took it as self-evident that Indonesians were different, but not necessarily inferior. They made no serious attempt to spread Christianity, the Dutch language or European culture. They were the first European country to assume that in a tropical dependency the interest of the non-European should remain paramount. Hence, despite considerable European settlement after 1815, there was never any question of Indonesia becoming a 'white man's' country dominated by expatriates.

These principles were evident in the four main fields of government – native administration, law, land ownership and social welfare.

Under company rule native administration had been left as far as possible to Indonesians. After 1815 methods gradually changed, but the principles of indirect rule remained, expressed in two distinct forms. First were a large number of native states under treaty; second, regions under full Dutch sovereignty. In course of time the proportion between them changed as political crises and the expansion of European activities led to the annexation of one native state after another. By the 1930s areas under full sovereignty covered 93 per cent of Java and more than half of the 'Outer Islands'.

Until late in the nineteenth century the Dutch preserved the company's methods of administering areas under full control through hereditary native 'regents', aristocrats who had once governed units of indigenous sultanates. Their districts were called regencies, and were grouped into residencies supervised by a European resident. Under this 'Javanese indirect' system regents were installed by Batavia and could be dismissed, but were left alone as far as possible. During the nineteenth century, however, European supervision became increasingly intense, since growing economic activity and European settlement required more effective government than untrained and often illiterate Javanese aristocrats could supply. By about 1900 'indirect rule' concealed highly centralized government by residents and their European subordinates, closely supervised by Batavia. This tendency, similar to that in Malaya, was deplored by the Dutch. The alternatives were full direct rule by Europeans or adaptation of older methods to new situations. They chose the latter. To decentralize government they created a number of larger units and gave them considerable autonomy. To enable Indonesians to take a major share in government they subdivided these into residencies and regencies with varying forms of representative government. By 1939 Java consisted of three provinces subdivided into regencies, and two native states. The Outer Islands were grouped into three provinces, divided into residencies (or governments) and subdivided into districts. At every stage supervision by European officials was intense, but Indonesian participation was preserved. In Java the regents survived as members of the government service and ran regency affairs with elective councils and elected executive committees. Urban areas had elective municipal institutions. Regency and municipal councils elected the provincial council which had power to legislate for the province. In the Outer Islands there was greater variety, and institutions were less westernized. There were no regents, and European supervision extended lower down the scale; but as far as possible existing tribal institutions were used to form 'group communes' and 'ethnic municipalities', with wider autonomy than was possessed by the Javanese regencies. These experiments in decentralization were cut short by the Japanese attack in 1941, but were clearly tending towards a federal system of government throughout the Indies in which Indonesians played a considerable part.

Changes also took place after 1815 in the position of native states. Many were absorbed into government lands. Those which survived were incorporated into the residencies as subordinate units of government. After 1900 a uniform 'Short Declaration' was substituted for long-standing separate treaties when occasion offered to reduce the states' autonomy; and in 1927 Batavia drew up the Native States Regulations to define the status of the princes. By 1941 the surviving states were colonial protectorates rather than full protected states; but the Dutch showed no inclination to eradicate them. They were destroyed only when Indonesia became independent.

In the sphere of law the Dutch preserved the juridical identity of Indonesians by providing different systems for them and for

Europeans. Indonesians could renounce customary law and become subject to European courts without difficulty, but suffered no disabilities by not doing so. This dual system was accompanied by a triple division of courts. About a fifth of Indonesia, consisting mainly of native states, had courts run entirely by Indonesians, which applied traditional procedures and penalties and were linked with the governmental system only by the right of appeal. The majority of Indonesians came under courts run by the government and staffed by Europeans. These applied native custom in civil cases and Roman-Dutch law in criminal matters, and appeals again lay to the councils of justice in the provincial centres and thence to the High Court in Batavia. The only other courts which affected Indonesians were the *landgerechten*, set up in 1914 to deal with minor criminal offences committed by Indonesians and Europeans alike. For Europeans, and also for others (including some Asiatics) who were entitled to use their courts, a third system rose parallel with the native courts from the regencies to the High Court. The Dutch made no attempt to codify law or unite jurisdictions as the British did in India. Their legal system always reflected the principle that like should try like.

Land and labour policy were of immense importance in a 'mixed' society like Indonesia, and in these fields also the Dutch had an unusual and generally good record.

The land policy of the East India Company was to forbid permanent alienation of native land to individual Europeans. It did so in its own interests, to prevent competition; but after 1815 the principle survived on moral grounds. Between 1800 and 1815, however, first the Dutch government and then the British permitted land alienation; so that a considerable area of Java became 'private lands' held in freehold. The return to the older policy then stopped further alienation, but it also created a serious economic problem. European plantations were necessary to produce export staples, and these required land. Two solutions were adopted. The government took over as public domain all native land not actually used by Indonesians – though ignorance of native custom produced much injustice and hardship – and leased it to Europeans in blocs of limited size for up to 75 years. In addition individual planters and agricultural companies could lease land from native princes or village communities. These methods produced large areas for European plantations. In 1928 non-Indonesian land-holdings in Java and Madura contained, in addition to the 552,310 hectares held as 'private lands' in freehold, 690,030 hectares on long government leases and 209,044 rented from Indonesians. In the Outer Islands 2,567,343 hectares were held on government leases or as agricultural concessions, mostly in Sumatra.[1] Thus, despite governmental land policy, Indonesia evolved a typical plantation economy. Europeans produced most of the sugar, tobacco, tea, rubber, coffee, and copra which, together with petroleum and tin, provided the export staples.

The plantation economy generated labour problems. In Java there was ample labour: the problem was preventing its abuse. Most Europeans employed paid workers, but some took advantage of native custom to get forced labour. Owners of 'private lands' were entitled to fifty-two days unpaid work a year from their tenants in lieu of rent. Planters who rented village lands and tenants of government land often contracted with village headmen for compulsory labour to work them. The government tried to regulate these devices, but never succeeded in eliminating them. Its position was in fact weak, since Batavia preserved a *corvée* for public works which it inherited from preceding native rulers. This right was never sub-let to planters and could be commuted for money; but while it lasted it was difficult to forbid private planters from using similar traditional rights.

In Sumatra and other Outer Islands, however, there was an acute labour shortage due to lower population density and dislike of working on plantations. Batavia therefore allowed recruitment of labourers from Java and elsewhere on contract. Other colonial powers used the same system, but Dutch contracts had one feature much criticized by humanitarians: breach of contract by an indentured labourer was a criminal offence.

The Dutch record on land and labour was generally good, given the assumption that Europeans should take a leading part in the economy of a tropical dependency. Yet during the middle of the nineteenth century the Netherlands acquired a very bad reputation among humanitarians on the ground that it exploited its political power in Indonesia to produce profits for the metropolis. Was this justified?

This notoriety was the result of the so-called 'Culture System' as applied to Java between 1830 and the 1870s. At root it was a revival of practices used by the company before 1800. The company obtained spices for sale in Europe partly from its own plantations but also by demanding payment of tribute in kind from protected princes and regents. In Java – though not elsewhere – the British destroyed this system by substituting cash payments by village communities for tribute in kind by the regents, and also began land surveys to provide a detailed assessment of village liabilities. Raffles, who inaugurated the change, hoped it would benefit the Javanese peasants: ironically it was precisely the principle of village assessments that ultimately gave the Culture System its worst features.

From 1815 to 1830 the Dutch retained the new system of taxation in money. The result was an economic and financial crisis. World prices for government-grown coffee and sugar declined; taxation in cash produced revenues but no goods for export. Indonesians showed little desire to grow cash crops instead of rice. To stimulate production of export commodities the governor-general, van den Bosch, suggested a return to payments in kind. As propounded by him in 1830 the system was morally unobjectionable. Existing village tax assessments were commuted into obligation to grow specified crops for the government. No quantity was laid down, but they were to be grown on a defined proportion of communal village lands, with a maximum of a fifth, and peasants were liable for no more labour than would have been required to grow rice on the same land. If a village produced goods worth more than its previous cash assessment, the surplus was to be returned to it in money.

At root this system was sound: trouble arose because van den Bosch's successors and their subordinates inverted his first principle. In place of a defined area to be devoted to government crops they demanded fixed quantities of goods; and these were made unreasonably large by officials of both races who received a percentage on what they collected. By the 1860s the system was under joint attack in Holland by humanitarians and by dogmatic liberals who disliked governmental participation in production and trade. These critics won the first round in 1870, when forced production of all crops ended, though the governmental coffee plantations were continued. Batavia fell back on cash-assessment of the villages and increasingly relied on indirect taxes for its revenues. Staple crops for export depended on European plantations and voluntary peasant production.

The Culture System became a scandal; but it was nevertheless a staggering financial success. Between 1831 and 1877 it enabled Batavia to transmit a total of 823,000,000 guilders to the Netherlands treasury; an average of 18 millions a year when the Dutch budget was about 60 millions.[2] This windfall was used in Holland to pay off debts left by the East India Company, reduce the national debt, and build public works. In addition the carriage of such large quantities of East Indian produce, which was made a Dutch monopoly, revived the Dutch merchant marine and made Amsterdam again the centre of the European spice market. The end of the system therefore meant a considerable loss to Holland. Liberals who claimed that a free economic system would ultimately bring her even greater benefits were wrong. Indonesia boomed, but Holland received little advantage from its increased wealth. The end of the Culture System was accompanied by free trade, and the Dutch share of Indonesian trade dropped sharply. The proportion of exports sent to the Netherlands declined from 76·5 per cent in 1870 to 15·3 per cent in 1930. Imports from Holland to Indonesia declined from 40·6 per cent to 16·8 per cent of the total.[3] After 1877 there were no more fiscal subsidies to the Dutch treasury: Holland had on occasion to make up Indonesian deficits. The Netherlands received considerable advantage from profitable investment in plantations, oil, tin, and other economic activities; from the repatriation of profits; and from the savings of officials. But all these had to be earned. There was no return to the halcyon days when the Culture System whetted the appetite of continental observers like Leopold of Belgium by showing how unrequited profits could be made from tropical colonization.

From the Indonesian point of view, the last period of Dutch rule before 1941 was the best. Aspects of the older 'indirect' approach remained, but the state now took a paternalistic interest in social welfare. Education expanded rapidly, with separate streams for Indonesians and Europeans below secondary level. The civil service was open to all races. Agricultural advisory services were provided to encourage peasant production. Road and rail communications were greatly improved. Population increased from 37 millions in 1905 to 70 millions by 1940[4]; exports from 175 million florins in 1880 to an inter-war peak of 2,228 millions in 1920.[5] The economy was diversified. The burden of taxation was largely shifted from Indonesians to the wealthier Europeans. Dutch Indonesia remained typically 'colonial' in its economic structure and its paternalistic government; but within contemporary conventions of colonial rule the Dutch record was impressive.

The Russian Empire in Central Asia

The initial problem presented by the Russian colonial empire is to distinguish colonies from metropolis. Other empires were divided by the sea, but the Russian empire was a continuous land mass stretching from Poland to the Bering Strait. By 1945 it included regions as diverse as the Crimea, the Volga, the Ukraine, Central Asia, Siberia and Amur; to which might be added the eastern European states occupied by Russia during the Second World War which thereafter closely resembled protected states. Which of these should be treated as colonies? Many might qualify. Siberia was a settlement colony resembling Australia, created by a similar process of penal and voluntary emigration. The Caucasian provinces were clearly non-European dependencies of European Russia. The present study will, however, deal only with Russian Central Asia. It was a product of nineteenth century, rather than earlier, Russian expansion. It presented characteristic 'colonial' problems. The fact that it had not been fully assimilated to the rest of the Russian empire by 1917 makes it possible to compare Czarist with Soviet methods of dealing with colonial situations.

Russian control of Central Asia began as military occupation intended to stabilize an area of disturbance on the southern frontier of Siberia, but developed into full colonization. This process was well advanced by 1917 and was completed by the Soviet Socialist Republic.

The conquest of Central Asia, begun in the 1840s and virtually complete by 1870, presented St Petersburg with complex problems. Central Asia was as large as Western Europe and had no natural unity. Different races had little in common beyond faith in Islam. Three were nomadic: the Kazakhs, who occupied most of the steppe from Siberia to the Syr-Daria river; the Kirghiz to the east, round lake Issyk-Kul; the Turkmen in the south-west, between the Syr-Daria and the Caspian. By contrast the Uzbecks, occupying land south and east of the Turkmen, were a settled agricultural people. The Uzbeck khanates of Bukhara, Kokand, and Khiva were the only strong states in Central Asia. The area was therefore fragmented, a graveyard of past conquests and broken empires. It was economically stagnant, for the international trade routes which had once made it rich had long been choked by political disorder.

Given their limited objectives – security on the Siberian frontier, a barrier against British advance from India – the Russians hoped to restrict government to the barest supervision. The natural solution would have been a system of protected states; but in most areas the lack of suitable indigenous powers made this impracticable. Bukhara and Khiva were preserved, though diminished in size, under protectorate treaties; but Kokand proved unsatisfactory and lost its identity. All other areas had to be placed under direct Russian administration. In 1898 Central Asia consisted of two provinces – Steppe and Turkestan, each under a governor-general. Other parts of the steppe region were absorbed into Siberia.

Government in Steppe and Turkestan reflected the fact that this was a frontier region: it was military, autocratic, centralized. The two governors-general were responsible to the Czar in person (there being no colonial minister), and were free to override advice from their councils of military governors and heads of administrative departments. Similar patterns were repeated in subordinate units of government, which descended from *oblasts* to *uezds* and *uchastoks*. In each, military officers combined civil and military powers, and were responsible also for justice until Central Asia was given the judicial system of European Russia after 1884. Nevertheless some autonomy was allowed in local affairs. The main towns began as military centres, but later had administrative committees of colonists and local officials to organize local amenities. Rural settlements formed by Russian immigrants were given such rights and institutions as Russian villages possessed after the serfs were freed in 1861. They were administered by meetings of householders presided over by an elected elder who also had minor judicial powers. Villages were grouped into *volosts* with similar agencies.

Although European in origin this system of rural self-administration was easily applied to indigenous society. The village elders of Turkestan and the heads of families in Kazakh were given official status and paid salaries by the government. Native villages were grouped into *volosts*, and village and *volost* courts were left to apply Islamic law – unwritten *adat* law in the steppe, written *Shariat* law in Turkestan. This was autonomy, but of an unimpressive kind. Russian officials interfered too much for the indigenous people to act responsibly, yet did not enforce honesty or efficiency. Junior officials were badly paid and corrupt, and were often drafted from Russian regiments for incompetence. Standards had improved by 1914, but Russia never developed a trained corps of professional colonial administrators.

The ambivalence of Russian attitudes to the functions of Central Asia was shown in changing policy on native land rights and European immigration. Until the later 1880s the general assumption was that this was a frontier zone whose native inhabitants should be protected against immigration and thus kept loyal to Russia. Settlement by Europeans was therefore entirely forbidden in Turkestan until 1890, but was tolerated in the thinly populated regions of Steppe, south of Siberia. The change in Russian policy came in the 1880s, when new problems within Russia – increased mobility and land-hunger among peasants, population growth and political radicalism – made emigration seem a universal panacea. For Central Asia the turning point was the Ignat'ev Commission of 1884, which recommended peasant colonization of Turkestan as well as Steppe. Thereafter official encouragement turned the earlier trickle of settlers into Kazakh into a flood, which overflowed also into Turkestan. By 1914 some 40 per cent of the population of Steppe were immigrants, the great majority rural. In Turkestan there were proportionately fewer – 407,000 (6 per cent) out of a total population of 6,493,000 in 1911, about half of whom were rural settlers.[6] Both thus became 'mixed' colonies, but Turkestan retained its essentially non-Russian character.

Immigration necessarily modified Russian native policy. Initially this was fair, conservative and designed to avoid native resistance to alien rule. Full religious toleration was allowed. No new forms of taxation were introduced, though some which were inherited were modified or dropped. There was no poll tax or forced labour, and no compulsory military service until 1916. The indigenous people became full subjects of the Czar; and those who could meet the electoral qualifications were entitled to vote when elections to the central Russian *Duma* were held in 1906. Most important was land policy; and for long this too was just. The Crown claimed all land by inheritance from previous rulers. It kept the right to 'vacant' land, but granted what amounted to freehold tenure, with right of alienation, to all actual occupiers. This constituted a social revolution. Most land in Turkestan had been held in quasi-feudal tenures by the aristocracy, and rented to the peasantry: the Russians converted Turkestan, outside the protected states, into a land of peasant proprietors. It was only when the demand for land for settlers became insistent that Russian land policy seriously damaged native interests. Repeated surveys of 'waste' land in Steppe, which ignored the special needs of a nomadic people, ultimately deprived the Kazakhs of much grazing land and forced them into sedentary agriculture. As in many other 'mixed' colonies, native interests ultimately gave way to those of white settlers.

Tolerance of indigenous society was obviously expedient in the first stage of occupation; but it was inconsistent with Russian traditions. The empire consisted of diverse regions which had been more or less assimilated to European Russia: ultimately Central Asia also should be assimilated. Education was the obvious means of doing so. Different systems were applied in Steppe and Turkestan; but basically all were designed to teach Russian as well as the native language. At the lower levels there were distinct schools for Russian and non-Russian children, though the latter could attend Russian schools if they chose. Higher education was along Russian lines and was integrated. In terms of numbers the impact of education on the non-Russians of Central Asia before 1914 was unimpressive. In 1913 only about 7·5 per cent of the 105,200 children enrolled in Steppe schools were Kazakhs. In the Turkestan *oblast* of Syr-Daria 95 per cent of Russian children received primary education in 1912, but only 2·02 per cent of non-Russian children.[7] These small attendance figures were due partly to native dislike of western education but also to the lack of an incentive such as careers in government administration might have offered them. The vast majority of Central Asians remained uneducated and totally unassimilated; even the small educated minority who had jobs as teachers, junior civil servants, or technicians remained Muslim in outlook, influenced more by the Islamic revival then taking place in the Crimea and Volga regions than by the attractions of Christianity and western culture.

By 1914 Central Asia was thus an increasingly 'mixed' society, in which the majority of non-Russians remained conservative, uneducated, and non-Christian. But Russia had been successful in other ways. There were only two minor risings against her rule, both reflecting conservative Muslim resistance to change rather than hostility to alien rule. It required the challenge of conscription for military service in 1916 to generate major peasant risings in several regions; and these too reflected long-standing grudges against local Russian officials and native notables rather than calculated nationalism.

In economic matters also, Russia's record was good. She created an infrastructure of roads, railways, and other modern services, and revived the decayed irrigation systems of the past. The Russian market stimulated production of many kinds, and the administration followed a constructive paternalistic policy.

Despite the reduced area open to them, Kazakh herds of cattle increased in numbers. In Turkestan cotton growing was encouraged as a peasant activity by tariff preferences, reduced freight rates, and the incorporation of improved strains from America. By 1913 cotton production occupied nearly a fifth of the irrigated area of all *oblasts* except Semirechie, and supplied more than half the agricultural income of Turkestan. Excessive monoculture had some bad effects; for example bad harvests and price fluctuations tended to force peasants into debt and many were forced to sell their holdings. But cotton gave Turkestan its first cash crop and export staple.

In 1917 Central Asia was a typical colonial society, autocratically governed by aliens, with a growing settler population, a vast cultural and linguistic gap between Central Asians and immigrants, and a dependent primary economy. The Bolshevik revolution of 1917 and the destruction of the Czarist empire created new possibilities. Either Central Asia would be liberated from Russian control; or it might be fully assimilated within a Socialist Russian state and lose its distinctive 'colonial' characteristics. In fact, neither of these had happened by 1964. Central Asia remained part of Russia, but it had neither true autonomy nor economic equality with European Russia. It remained 'colonial' in all but concept.

In principle Lenin admitted the right of distinct ethnic groups to secede or to govern themselves: in practice Central Asia was too important to Russia to be liberated. Her barely exploited raw materials and her food and industrial raw materials were vital to the Russian economy. Strategically she was the key to Russian contacts with the Middle East, India and China. Imperialism had therefore to continue under the guise of serving the Central Asian proletariat.

The constitution of the USSR was well adapted to preserve the union while giving the illusion of colonial autonomy. With the constitutional reforms of 1924–5, completed only in 1936, the old empire was reconstituted as a union of federated republics. European Russia, Siberia and Amur formed the Russian Soviet Federated Socialist Republic. The rest became autonomous republics within the Union of Soviet Socialist Republics. This formula bore a close resemblance to the French Union of 1946: the reality was different. The whole of the USSR was united under the Supreme Soviet, one house representing the whole population on a proportionate basis, the other the various republics. The Presidium, elected by both houses, was the executive government of the whole; and the All-Union Communist Party, for whom Soviet and Presidium were mere cloaks, was from the first organized on a unitary, not federal, basis. Centralization was evident also in every aspect of government. Administrative departments in Moscow had wide powers in the republics over their own fields; even the nominally autonomous governments were subordinate to them. Some ministries in the republics were 'all-Union' – directly responsible to the centre rather than to the local government – and these controlled key subjects. Russia was a unitary state in which limited powers were devolved to local agencies. The Czarist empire had become more rather than less centralized.

In Central Asia assimilation of non-Europeans was now adopted without reservations as official policy. The original administrative structure was replaced in 1936 by the five provinces of Turkmenistan, Uzbekistan, Kirghizia, Tadzhikistan and Kazakhstan. Nominally each nationality was now concentrated in a single province: actually this policy was designed to prevent the growth of a common Central Asian nationalism. Every attempt was made to detach the masses from their own upper class leaders and persuade them that they were part of the all-Russian proletariat. Courts of law using Muslim codes were discouraged and finally eliminated from the official legal hierarchy by 1939. Propaganda against Islam was intense. In education the previous policy of assimilation through use of Russian was intensified by the adoption of the Russian alphabet for indigenous languages in 1939, and the increase of literacy and school-attendance was striking. Like other colonial régimes the Russians used education as the most effective solvent of indigenous loyalties and traditions.

In the economic sphere also Soviet achievements were striking, but Central Asia was more subordinated to the economic needs of the metropolis than any other colonial economy. Bolshevik propaganda promised industrialization: but apart from textile manufactures which used local cotton, extractive industries alone developed to any extent before 1939. Russia needed food and raw materials: Central Asia was organized to produce them. Collective farms in place of peasant holdings greatly increased wheat production but led to a further decline in numbers of livestock in the steppes. New crops, such as beet sugar, were introduced and the mechanization of farming began. The obvious link with the colonial past was the staggering increase in cotton production, which was back to its pre-war area of 800,000 hectares by 1928 and rose to 1,446,000 hectares by 1937. Despite considerable immigration of industrial workers between the two world wars, the great majority of non-Europeans remained rural producers of primary products.

The main result of Soviet rule was therefore that Central Asia was one of the only colonial territories with a predominantly non-European population which never became independent. Like the United States in Hawaii, the French in their smaller colonies, and the Portuguese in Africa, the Russians countered colonial nationalism with full integration. Ironically Russian socialists were more successful in holding and using colonial dependencies than the 'imperialist' countries they denounced.

The United States Empire

The United States was the last western power to acquire a colonial empire and the most unlikely imperialist of all. Born in revolution against British imperialism, she made hostility to empire part of her ethic. Republicanism, like Marxism, seemed incompatible with rule over dependent peoples, for the Declaration of Independence stated that 'all men are created equal, that they are endowed by their Creator with certain unalienable rights, that among these are life, liberty, and the pursuit of happiness'. Until 1898 all American territories, except the Pacific coaling station of Midway, were in North America. They had been acquired honestly, either by the settlement of 'empty' lands (at the expense of nomadic Amerindians), or with the consent of their European inhabitants (as in the states bordering Mexico). More important, republican principles had been maintained, for all new acquisitions eventually became full and equal states of the Union, though some, like Alaska, had long probationary periods as dependent 'territories'. The United States had fulfilled her 'manifest destiny', but had not broken republican principles in doing so.

The American colonial empire dated from 1898 and constituted an ideological embarrassment. The United States did not want colonies. There was little expansionist jingoism in the 1890s, and opportunities to take part in the international partition were rejected. Empire grew unsought out of international tensions and political disorder in the Caribbean. The solvent of American isolationism was Cuba, in which Americans had substantial economic interests. Cuba revolted against Spanish rule in 1895. Americans were disgusted by the Spanish methods of suppressing the revolution, and the sinking of a United States naval vessel at Havana in April 1898 was the excuse for intervention. Naval strategy led to occupation of Cuba and also of Manila, Guam and the Marianas: once occupied they could not be returned to Spain, since Americans were convinced that she was morally unfitted to govern them. The alternatives were independence and annexation, either by the United States or some other power. Cuba was made independent, but Porto Rico was annexed to prevent European intervention in the American hemisphere. The Philippines and Guam were annexed as strategic bases for the China trade, but Spain was allowed to sell her other Pacific islands to Germany.

The United States was now an imperial power; and one imperial responsibility bred others. Hawaii, which had long been dominated by American planters and missions and had already petitioned for annexation, was incorporated into the Union in 1898. Wake Island was annexed in 1899 to link Honolulu with Guam. In the same year Washington at last agreed to solve the Samoan deadlock by partition with Germany, and annexed Tutuila and other islands in 1900. The United States thus acquired a major stake in the Pacific. In the Caribbean also new responsibilities bred further power, though of a more informal kind. A direct link with the Pacific was now required to enable the fleet to operate in both oceans: hence Panama was helped to become independent of Colombia. By the treaty of 1904, she accepted American protection and gave her a strip across the isthmus for building a canal. Caribbean stability now became essential to the security of the canal; and the 1904 'Roosevelt Corollary' to the Monroe Doctrine asserted America's right to intervene in any state which became politically or financially unstable. Since instability was chronic, a number of states were brought under American suzerainty. Treaties, variously giving the rights of military occupation or the control of public finance, were made with Cuba in 1903, Dominica in 1904, Nicaragua in 1911 and 1916, and Haiti in 1915. By 1916 Haiti and Dominica were occupied and governed by the United States and Nicaraguan finances were in the hands of American receivers. American forces intervened in Cuba intermittently. To complete American control of the Caribbean, Denmark's Virgin Islands were bought from that country in 1917.

The United States had thus acquired an empire spread across two oceans consisting partly of full dependencies, partly of protected states. This was a conventional colonial empire: but the fact that Americans never used such words as 'colony', 'dependency' or 'protectorate' in describing it provides the key to its later history. The special feature of the United States as a colonial power was that she attempted to fit her colonies into a republican framework; to treat them either as proto-states of the Union and ultimately to absorb them completely, or as sovereign states with whom she was allied and who would finally throw off her tutelage. Not all dependencies could be fitted into one of these categories, but the desire to do so moulded American practice.

The foundations of American colonial policy were the United States constitution and the process by which new states had been added to the Union in the past. No attempt was made to construct principles or institutions suitable for permanent colonial dependencies.

Administrative practice in Washington illustrated this oblique approach. No single agency had exclusive or general responsibility for the dependencies. They were dealt with by any department, on the French principle of *rattachements*; but for convenience the various territories and protectorates were allocated to the Departments of the Interior, War, the Navy and the State Department, which acted as channels for correspondence and undertook administration. In 1934, however, a Division of Territories and Inland Possessions was created within the Department of the Interior to supervise all dependencies except Guam and Samoa, which were left to the Navy, and the Panama canal zone, which was run by the Army; and to act as a Dominions Office for the now virtually independent Philippines. Characteristically the Division had neither a political head nor executive authority. It advised the President, Congress and colonial governments and linked them with other departments; but it never governed the empire.

The American empire never acquired a formal constitution; but its legal structure, as defined by the United States courts, fell into three parts. Caribbean states held by treaties were foreign. Alaska and Hawaii were incorporated into the Union by Congress and came within the constitution. In 1959 they became full states. All others were unincorporated territories – colonies in all but name. Citizenship followed the same distinctions. Inhabitants of incorporated states were citizens of the United States as well as of their own states; others were either 'foreign' (in the protectorates) or 'nationals of the United States' and citizens of their own territories. In practice, however, Congress extended full citizenship more widely; to all Porto Ricans in 1917, Virgin Islanders in 1927 and Guamanians in 1950.

This legal distinction between incorporated and unincorporated states had little practical significance in forms of government: the real contrast lay between colonies thought fit for American self-governing institutions and the rest. In 1917 Hawaii, Alaska, Porto Rico and the Philippines had practically identical constitutions, each modelled on the American constitution, with a governor, bicameral elected legislature, and non-voting delegates in the House of Representatives. Their laws and legal systems resembled those of states within the Union, and appeals lay from regional courts to local federal courts or to the Supreme Court in Washington. These colonies, therefore, appeared to be entirely autonomous: but this was misleading. Under the camouflage of American institutions they remained dependent. Governors were agents of the President, taking orders from Washington. Since the American constitution made the head of state the sole executive authority, governors did not have to act on the advice of their executive councils; and only when they came to be elected did these dependencies gain real self-government. The Philippines reached this stage in 1935, Porto Rico in 1948. Hawaii and Alaska had to wait for full statehood in 1959.

The legislative powers of the colonial assemblies were equally circumscribed. They appropriated taxes; but if they refused to adopt the budget drawn up by the government the previous year's appropriations automatically continued. They could pass laws on any domestic matter; but bills could be vetoed by the governor and again by the President if the governor's vote was overridden by a two-thirds majority. Congress could legislate on any subject and could annul any colonial act. Colonial autonomy thus fell a long way short of statehood in the United States or Dominion status within the British Commonwealth after 1931.

The underlying liberalism of these four colonial constitutions indicated that they would eventually become states of the Union or fully independent. This did not apply to the smaller Pacific dependencies who did not fit American constitutional patterns and had, so to speak, to be swept under the carpet. The United States showed little interest in Guam, Samoa or the other islands except as strategic bases, and left them to the Navy. They were loosely administered by naval officers with autocratic powers, who took such advice as they needed from councils of indigenous notables. The result was a species of indirect rule which preserved the native pattern of district and village administration and did little to assimilate islanders to American ways. But for long American officials lacked experience, and many important changes were made simply through ignorance.

The other formative feature of American colonial policy was its tariff. Again the continental tradition of a common external protective tariff and internal free trade was applied to all dependencies except where international commitments constituted an obstacle. Alaska and Hawaii were incorporated within the American tariff immediately on acquisition; Porto Rico in 1900; the Philippines in 1909, the Virgin Islands on annexation. Of the full dependencies only the Panama zone and Samoa were excluded, the first because it remained foreign, the second because the tripartite treaty with Britain and Germany of 1899 stipulated the 'open door'.

Tariff assimilation made the United States empire the only colonial empire other than the Russian which formed a single economic system; and this gave it exceptional cohesion. But the balance of advantage lay with the colonies. All were primary producers, who found their best markets in the United States and suffered few countervailing inconveniences. Only Porto Rico found incorporation a mixed blessing, for the benefits she received from a favourable sugar quota in the United States were offset by the higher prices she paid for imported food as a result of protection for American producers. For all, economic ties were a strong argument against secession. In 1933 the Philippines temporarily rejected an offer of independence after ten years because it entailed gradual exclusion from American tariffs. Conversely, the United States gained little from her colonial *zollverein*. Some colonial goods competed with domestic products. Colonies normally bought and sold American, but their trade was of marginal importance to the United States. In 1920, for instance, only 3·8 per cent of American exports went to them, and 4·9 per cent in 1925. They were equally unimportant as spheres of investment. They took full advantage of the American capital market, but by 1943 American investments in Porto Rico and the Philippines together constituted only 2·5 per cent of her total overseas investment.[8] Independent states such as Mexico, Cuba or Canada were immensely more important for American capitalists. Even land policy aimed to prevent alienation by indigenous people rather than to benefit American settlers or land companies; though in Porto Rico restrictive regulations were not effectively enforced until 1935. The United States did not need colonies to shore up her economy and did not 'exploit' them. Assimilation to the metropolitan tariff meant only the application of republican principles to new American territories.

The United States could claim to have remained republican rather than imperialist in two other ways. She freed all those dependencies which were either not destined for full incorporation or were clearly unable to stand alone and did not wish to do so. She deliberately rejected the opportunity afforded by her military predominance in 1945 to build a new world-wide empire.

Decolonization took place first in the quasi-protectorates of the Caribbean. On the analogy of other empires, these might gradually have become full dependencies: instead the Americans treated them as temporary mandates, and withdrew their control as soon as fear of European intervention ended; that is, after 1918. Military occupation of Dominica was ended between 1922 and 1924; the right of interference in Cuba in 1925. The Marines were withdrawn from Nicaragua in 1925, recalled by the Nicaraguan President in 1927, and finally withdrawn in 1933. American troops left Haiti in 1933–4. Even the 'Roosevelt Corollary' was obliquely denounced and replaced by F. D. Roosevelt's 'good neighbour' policy. By 1941 the United States no longer supervised the Caribbean states, and left them free to indulge in political chaos and social revolution.

The year 1945 brought the final American rejection of empire. The Philippines became totally independent in 1946, though this had been projected since 1934. Elsewhere the vast military empire which had been created in defeating Germany and Japan was almost entirely dismantled: only the Japanese mandates in the Pacific, the Ryukyu, Bonin and Volcano Islands which were part of Japan, and bases in the West Indies, Iceland, Greenland, the Azores, Tripoli and Arabia were retained, in each case as a result of voluntary agreement by the states concerned. America remained loyal to her own principles and to the promise made in the Atlantic Charter that neither she nor Britain sought territorial aggrandizement. Thereafter, like Britain during the nineteenth century, the United States expressed her immense power through influence and 'informal' empire rather than in territorial possessions. By 1964 she had fully incorporated or entirely released the greater part of her colonial empire. Porto Rico became entirely self-governing, and resembled a British Dominion. Only the small Pacific territories remained true dependencies; and in these the United States found the same apparently insuperable obstacles to full independence as other colonial powers with similar Pacific possessions.

15

The Portuguese, Belgian and German Colonial Empires

The Portuguese Empire after 1815

The modern Portuguese empire abounded in paradoxes which made it difficult to compare with its contemporaries. It was the oldest overseas empire; yet geographically the greater part of it was acquired only after 1884. For centuries it seemed likely to succumb to external attack or Portuguese lethargy; yet it survived all others in the age of decolonization. Portugal was poor and militarily weak, never able to hold the larger colonies against their will; yet after the secession of Brazil in 1822 she lost nothing until India seized Goa and her other possessions in India in 1961. The Portuguese were never as unconscious of race as they eventually claimed, for long making a distinction between Portuguese citizens and all others; yet there was never a colour bar in Portuguese colonies, and in the 1960s she was the only European state which still unashamedly proclaimed the ideal of full integration in a multi-racial state. In fact, Portuguese colonial history differed from that of all north European states precisely because she herself was different. In the modern period only Spain might have followed similar lines: but she had virtually lost what remained of her empire in 1898.

The modern history of Portugal overseas hinges on the 1880s. Until then her empire appeared to be decadent. From the 1580s until 1822 one colony after another was lost. Nothing remained in America after Brazil seceded. In the Atlantic there were the

Azores and Madeira Islands, fully incorporated into the metropolis in 1832; the Cape Verde Islands, decaying with the sugar industry; Portuguese Guinea, which was barely supervised, let alone governed; the islands of São Tomé and Principe, first slaving entrepôts for Angola, then cocoa producers; and finally Angola. Here Portugal effectively controlled little more than the ports of Luanda and Benguela and the slave trade (later the contract labour traffic) from the interior; though in the mid-nineteenth century there was some colonization in the highlands by Brazilian coffee planters, coming to find the African labour no longer allowed to be despatched to them. In East Africa Portugal retained only the island of Mozambique, a few coastal forts, and the virtually independent *prazos* (feudal principalities) up the Zambezi. Further east there were the three Indian territories, Goa, Damão and Diu; part of Timor Island in Indonesia; and the peninsula of Macao near Canton, which survived on the foreign trade with China. These territories were enough to keep the Portuguese imperial tradition alive, but not to make her a significant colonial power.

The partition of Africa during the last years of the nineteenth century might well have deprived Portugal of the little she retained there: in fact it gave her an empire larger than she had possessed since 1822, and forced her to take it seriously. Her interest always reflected that of others. In the 1860s and 1870s British designs on Delagoa Bay showed her the value of Lourenço Marques as a port; the fact that arbitration by the French President in 1875 supported Portugal's claim was a useful precedent for other areas. Yet in the 1880s, when competition became more intense and the powers less ready to accept antiquated Portuguese claims, she stood to lose the vast hinterlands of Angola, Mozambique and Guinea, as she lost most of the Congo in 1884. She was saved by the rivalries of others and by German and French readiness to recognize a continuous band of Portuguese territory from Angola to Mozambique as a bar to British annexation. Ironically it was Britain, Portugal's historic ally, who had supported her claim to the Congo in 1882–4, that dispelled this 'pink-coloured' dream (*mapa cŏr de rosa*). Britain had no better claim to Central Africa; but she was a great power, her missions in Nyasaland protested against Catholic Portuguese sovereignty, and Cecil Rhodes wanted it for the British South Africa Company. In 1890 Lord Salisbury sent Lisbon the famous 'ultimatum' demanding removal of Portuguese troops from the Shire and Mashonaland regions, and then imposed a settlement which placed a British sphere of influence between the two halves of Portugal in Africa. Boundaries were established by the Anglo-Portuguese treaty of 1891 and by treaties made with other colonial powers during the next decade.

Partition had aroused Portuguese hopes only to destroy many of them. Yet in place of mythical claims she now had internationally recognized territories. Portuguese Guinea contained some 14,000 unknown square miles; Angola about 481,000, and Mozambique 298,000.[1] Moreover the shock of rivalry stirred Portugal into awareness of her opportunities, generating a colonial party which held that colonies would be her economic salvation. Portugal as an African power rubbed shoulders with the great north European industrial giants, Germany, Britain, France and Belgium. The question was whether she possessed the political and economic resources to open up and develop such huge tropical dependencies.

Compared with contemporaries, Portugal failed as a colonial power. Although after the 1890s she copied others and benefited from the wealth which the development of southern and Central Africa brought to her own colonies, she appeared incompetent, out of date, and often deficient in moral standards. This had, of course, been equally true in the first centuries of colonization, when Portugal cut a poor figure beside the grandeur of the Spanish empire. Yet, seen in relation to her resources and her place in European civilization, the Portuguese record was reasonable.

Her administrative system and declared aims of policy differed little from those of France: both believed in full integration. The Portuguese National Assembly was the ultimate authority for the whole empire. It was supposed to represent all its components; and from 1930 colonial deputies sat in Lisbon. Effective power, however, was always wielded by the executive – King or President – and the Council of Ministers. Until 1911 there was no distinct colonial office, though at times colonial affairs were handled by a sub-department of the Ministry of Marine and Overseas, which then became the Ministry for Overseas. The ministry was advised on proposed colonial decrees by the Overseas Council, founded in 1643 as successor to the Council of the Indies, and also by occasional governors' conferences and an Overseas Economic Conference. But in fact, after the inauguration of the New State in 1930, colonial affairs were closely supervised by Dr Salazar, as President of the Council.

Colonial government also closely resembled that in French colonies. The smaller territories had governors; Angola and Mozambique governors-general (called high commissioners in the 1920s to emphasize a transient belief in colonial autonomy). All had more autonomy than the principle of integration made likely and drew up their own budgets. But these were closely vetted in Lisbon, and all local affairs were investigated by a special corps of inspectors. Executive government was run on conventional lines by executive councils of officials and bureaucratic departments; but Portuguese colonies also had legislative councils with power to make local laws. Before 1930 these consisted of officials and nominated local residents, and thereafter contained a majority of elected Portuguese citizens. Their consent was theoretically necessary for legislation and budgeting, but in the last resort the governor-general could override opposition. Government in the colonies therefore remained autocratic: in 1964 it still resembled that in British 'Crown Colonies' a generation earlier.

In the past local government in Portuguese colonies had been based on municipalities – *concelhos* – on the metropolitan pattern, but these could not be created in most parts of Portugal's new African empire. The few areas with substantial European populations were given municipalities: the rest were placed under conventional forms of native administration. Angola and Mozambique were divided into districts, each with its own governor, and subdivided into European *concelhos* or non-European *circumscrições*. At first these were merely military districts, but after about 1914 they were run by civilian administrators and subordinate chiefs of post, both Europeans. Africans were used for all lower posts, though as members of the official hierarchy rather than as hereditary rulers. Indigenous chiefs were appointed as '*régulos*' where possible; but these were 'warrant chiefs' in the tradition of British or French direct rule, for Portugal did not accept the premises underlying the preservation of African institutions through indirect rule.

This was the eventual pattern of Portuguese administration in Africa, but it was slow to develop. Portugal was poor, and in Mozambique at least preferred to leave the task of effective occupation to chartered concessionary companies. Three such companies were set up, all with foreign capital, and were given large concessions, formed partly from the old *prazeros* which the Crown had eventually taken over in 1880. All had a monopoly of land, trade, mining, fishing, and the collection of taxes for defined periods. The Mozambique and Niassa Companies undertook full administration, the Zambezia Company did not. None was a spectacular success financially, but all helped Portugal by importing capital for the first stage of economic development and by establishing effective control over Africans. While their concessions lasted Mozambique was inevitably dominated by foreign, especially British, interests; but in the end Portugal reaped the benefits.

To this point there was nothing exceptional in Portugal's record as a modern colonial power in Africa. Her bad reputation derived from her policy on African labour and the fact that a colonial system typical of other empires in the 1920s survived almost unchanged into the 1960s.

The problem of inducing Africans to work was common to all African colonies, but was acute in places like Mozambique where concessionary companies were developing plantations and where taxes on emigrant labour attracted temporarily to the Rand goldfields were vital to a balanced budget. All colonial powers put pressure on Africans to take paid labour: the charge against Portugal was that she used stricter sanctions than most and retained them after others had made labour free. This time lag began early in the nineteenth century, for slave-trading survived legally until 1836 (and in fact for some time longer) and slavery was not abolished until 1876. From then until 1926 labour laws variously forbade or imposed forced labour: but in practice the government always supported recruitment of labour for private as well as public works, and made it a penal offence for an African to break his contract. The result was forced labour on a vast scale under generally poor conditions, and international publicity for its resultant evils led to new laws being made in 1926. Thereafter non-Europeans could be forced to work only on projects of public importance (though these might be carried out by private firms). They had to be paid unless these projects were for their exclusive advantage (local roads, etc.). But criminals and tax-defaulters could be put to work, and the state still acted as recruiter and superviser of contract labour for private employers. Penal sanctions for breach of contract remained.

These reforms brought Portugal nearly into line with other powers: her system now resembled *prestation* for public works in French-African colonies. But the penal clause in private contracts was inconsistent with the International Forced Labour Conventions of 1930 and 1946 and the 1936 Indigenous Workers Convention. Portugal evaded these on the principle that her colonies were part of Portugal overseas rather than normal dependencies, but state supervision of labour practices nonetheless became more effective. In 1960 the penal clause in labour contracts was finally abolished and forced labour was stopped. In 1961 Portugal was exonerated of malpractices by an International Labour Organization Commission.

Portugal had earned her bad reputation by preserving the common evils of the late nineteenth century into the mid-twentieth. This was due less to peculiar malignancy than to her domestic attitude to labour. Portugal had no industrial revolution or humanitarian movement. Her labour laws remained archaic. Her colonies suffered from the extension of metropolitan attitudes to Africa and from governmental poverty, which encouraged the use of every resource.

The same tendency to lag behind other colonial powers occurred in the field of citizenship and law. Citizenship laws resembled those of France, with the same distinction between citizens and subjects and a similar emphasis on ultimate assimilation of all to full citizenship. Apart from a brief liberal interlude after 1832, when all inhabitants of colonies were declared citizens, only those born Portuguese were given full status. The rest were subjects under the *régime do indigenato*. They could qualify as *assimilados*; but by 1950 only 30,089 in Angola and 4,353 in Mozambique had done so.[2] Again such distinctions became unfashionable: in 1961 Portugal abolished the *régime do indigenato*, and all became citizens. Now that forced labour had ended, however, this made little difference, for the old legal distinction between subject and citizen continued. As always, citizens were under laws and courts based on the metropolitan common law and civil and criminal codes; all unassimilated Africans under native custom enforced in special courts. There was nothing intrinsically bad in this legal dualism, for it reflected the undeniable fact of dual societies. Yet in the period after decolonization it offended the sensibilities of new states in Africa and gave credence to the charge that Portugal was still acting as an 'imperialist' power.

In most other spheres Portuguese colonial policy and practice were equally conventional. Land policy assumed the need to provide for European plantations and extractive industries, and so relied on creating native reserves and compensating indigenous people removed from their land. Education policy aimed at ultimate assimilation; but it was left mainly to Catholic missions which received public subsidies, and literacy and school attendance figures were low by comparison with those in the Congo. Tariff policy, after the late nineteenth century, was conventionally 'neomercantilist': heavy preferences for Portuguese imports to the colonies; reduced duties on inter-colonial trade and on colonial goods entering Portugal. Taxation depended on import duties, African poll-taxes, payments by concessionary companies, and, in Mozambique, a levy on labourers going to Rhodesia and South Africa on short-term contracts. After 1930 Portugal adopted paternalistic policies to improve social amenities and communications, though this was made difficult by the New State's reluctance to accept foreign capital, which was thought to produce undesirable 'interference' in her affairs. By the 1960s Portuguese Africa was in roughly the position other African colonies had reached some twenty years earlier.

Logically the next step should have been decolonization: but again the paradox of Portuguese colonial history was evident. Portugal rejected the principle that she should 'liberate' her colonies, arguing that they were not dependencies but an integral part of Portugal overseas. From most colonial powers this claim would rightly have been suspect, but for Portugal it had some substance. She had an obvious material interest in retaining her colonies, for they provided preferential markets and a 'drain' of money to the metropolis through pensions of officials, interest on loans, etc. The foreign exchange earned by Angolan and Mozambique exports of minerals and tropical crops was a necessary support for the Portuguese escudo; and these colonies provided a field for Portuguese emigrants. Such benefits gave credence to attacks made on Portugal as the last of the 'imperialist' powers to hold colonies for exploitation.

Yet Portugal was less cynical than others supposed. She really believed the colonies were integral with the metropolis, and that they would grow, as Brazil had done, into Portuguese societies in close association with the parent state. Moreover she rejected the racialist premises on which African and Asian nationalism was based. Portuguese nationality was no more alien to African citizens than the artificial nationalities constructed by the new states of Africa, and implied no inferiority of Africans to Europeans. Angola and Mozambique were not 'white man's countries', like Southern Rhodesia and South Africa, but multi-racial societies. In short, Russia had assimilated Central Asia without incurring the charge of colonialism: why should not Portugal similarly assimilate her African territories?

In 1964 the balance between Portuguese assimilation and African nationalism was nicely poised. The real test of Portugal's lonely stand for the principle of assimilation was whether her African citizens chose to be Portuguese or something else: whether the nationalist rising which began in northern Angola in 1961 would spread and whether a similar movement began in Mozambique. Provided there was no external attack the choice was in fact theirs, for Portugal lacked the power to hold down some four and a half million citizens in Angola and six million in Mozambique if they became rebels.

The Belgian Empire in the Congo

The Belgian empire consisted of a single territory, the Congo, to which was added the ex-German territories, Ruanda and Urundi. Together they had an area of 942,000 square miles and a population of 13·5 millions in 1933.[3] Although comparatively small and concentrated, this empire was nonetheless important in modern colonial history as a microcosm – almost a caricature – of evolving European attitudes to tropical dependencies. Leopold II acquired the Congo not as a Belgian colony but as a private estate, and supported the assumption that modern tropical colonization was motivated by economic greed by treating it as a mere business investment. He further justified humanitarian complaints that empire meant exploitation of non-Europeans by the scandalous methods he used to govern the Congo and extract its wealth. Yet, after the Congo became a full Belgian colony in 1908, the Belgians again typified the period by creating one of the most efficient and benevolent colonial régimes to be found in Africa. Finally, the disasters which followed Congolese independence in 1960 demonstrated more forcefully than anywhere else how dangerous it was to end imperial control before a dependency was adequately prepared for freedom.

The genesis of the Congo Free State between 1876 and 1885 has already been described. In theory it belonged to the *Association Internationale du Congo* and had humanitarian objectives. But Leopold entirely owned the Association; so that the Congo was a private estate, like those of contemporary chartered companies in Africa, and was run on commercial lines. Leopold created an administrative façade in Brussels with names appropriate to a sovereign state. He had a *Conseil Supérieur du Congo* to advise him and act as a legal court of appeal, a secretary of state and bureaucratic departments. But all power remained in his own hands, and Free State finances were indistinguishable from his own. Government in the Congo was made as cheap and as dependent as possible. There was a governor-general and administration at Boma, but no executive or legislative council. Provincial government was based on large districts subdivided into zones, sectors and posts, each under a European officer. Africans were controlled undogmatically by using any African chief or Arab *condottiere* who was ready to serve: tribal units and native traditions were ignored. By far the most important institution, and the main agent of Leopold's policy, was the *Force Publique*, a mercenary army which by 1905 contained 360 European officers of different nationalities and 16,000 Africans.

In the context of its time – the period of preliminary government and effective occupation throughout tropical Africa – this skeleton administration was not unusual. It was significant partly because its guiding principle of complete centralization of power in Brussels was never dropped; partly because it was too weak to prevent flagrant abuses by junior officials. These abuses made Leopold's system notorious by 1908.

Leopold saw the Congo simply as a financial investment comparable to the Suez canal, and required it to pay dividends. Scandal arose because profits were difficult to extract. The Congo was immensely rich in minerals, but these could yield no profits until they had been investigated and much capital sunk in communications and mines. By 1890 Leopold had exhausted his private resources and could not wait. His solution was to exploit natural resources which required minimal expenditure – ivory, palm-oil and wild rubber. To do this he adopted two well-tested devices – monopoly and forced renders by Africans. Monopoly within the Congo basin was forbidden by the Berlin Act; yet after 1892 Leopold divided the Congo into three sectors, two of which – the *Domaine Privé* and the *Domaine de la Couronne* – were reserved for trading by the state and its concessionaries. Only the third and least profitable area was left open to others. The domain lands were either exploited by Leopold's own agents or let out to concessionary companies in which he had a major interest; the most important of these, such as the Katanga Company, its subsidiaries, the *Comité Special du Katanga* and *Union Minière du Haut-Katanga*, and the *Société Anversoise de Commerce au Congo*, were to be important throughout Congolese history.

The Congo scandal of the early 1900s arose from the way in which these concessionary companies and the state itself used their power to extract the maximum profit. Only African labour could turn natural assets into profitable commodities; and Africans were as reluctant in the Congo as in most parts of tropical Africa to work for the low wages offered. The conventional solution of the late nineteenth century was to adopt the Dutch 'Culture System' (without its sophisticated safeguards) and impose a tax payable in labour or in renders of specified goods. This led to abuses everywhere: in the Congo they were exceptional because no attempt was made to supervise subordinate European and African officials. Reports made by individual foreign observers, such as the American missionary, J. B. Murphy, and two Englishmen, E. D. Morel and Roger Casement, shocked international opinion in the same way as contemporary reports on the Portuguese labour-contract system. In 1904 even Leopold felt bound to appoint a three-man international commission to report. The evidence was conflicting, but the consensus of opinion, as summarized by a Belgian geographer in 1911, was that

> In the rubber districts in place of work the tax was assessed at so many kilogrammes of rubber. If the stated quantity was not delivered to the 'Treasury' there were several methods of enforcing compliance. Chiefs were detained ... until their people furnished their quota of rubber; hostages were taken; women and children imprisoned; the *chicotte* (a raw hide lash) was used on those who had not brought into the post their prescribed amounts of rubber. Sentinels were posted in centres of population to supervise the work of the natives. Refractory villages received visits from military patrols. At times punitive expeditions were sent to mete out exemplary punishment. Villages were burnt.... Savage instincts were revealed....[4]

These scandals blew up the Congo Free State. Catholic and Liberal party opinion in Belgium, which had previously been hostile to colonial responsibilities, now demanded that the Congo be nationalized. Leopold was reluctant to hand over: he was making considerable (though unmeasurable) profits, and wanted to retain the *Domaine de la Couronne* as an endowment for the royal family. He was forced to give way. Late in 1908 the Congo became a full Belgian colony.

The effect of nationalization was not so much to destroy Leopold's system of government or his economic ambitions as to humanize them. As a colony the Congo now benefited from the conscience and efficiency of the advanced industrial democracy which controlled it.

Political centralization remained. Brussels was the effective capital of the Congo, Boma (and later Leopoldville) merely the provincial centre. Metropolitan organization became conventional. Parliament could legislate, and passed a fundamental law known as the Colonial Charter to define the juridical status of the Congo and its constitution, but left normal administration to the Crown. The King, acting on the advice of his responsible ministers, could issue edicts, but these had to be considered by a colonial council similar to those in France and Portugal. The Colonial Minister and Office had normal functions, except that they were also represented on the boards of concessionary companies in which the Crown had an interest. The only distinctive aspect of Belgian constitutional thought was that the Congo remained juridically distinct and had to have special laws in all fields.

Government in the Congo conformed to patterns of other tropical dependencies. The governor-general was under strict control from Brussels, but was otherwise an autocrat. He could make laws for up to six months at a time, and his council of officials and a few nominated Belgians had only advisory powers. There was no legislative council. There were, however, two unusual institutions, both designed to prevent further scandals. Until 1921, the *procureur général*, who was in charge of legal services and was independent of the governor-general, controlled all government officials to protect them from arbitrariness; and he also presided over an Aborigines' Protection Committee which had to report annually on native conditions. The report went direct to the King and had to be published to prevent official concealment of abuses.

Legal administration continued Leopold's skeleton system and elaborated it. There were eventually six large provinces (plus Ruanda-Urundi) each under a vice-governor general, which duplicated the institutions at Leopoldville. They were divided into districts under commissioners and these into sub-districts under administrators. The system was designed to administer Africans, not Europeans, and to do so within their tribal structure. In 1955 there were only three municipalities in the Congo, and even in these the local commissioner kept the initiative, using elected committees of Europeans to raise rates and organize amenities.

This was natural. The Congo was not a settlement colony, and by 1941 it had only 27,790 European residents – 0·27 per cent of the population. Government, therefore, meant native administration. In 1908 the Belgians had everything to learn, but they were ready to follow the best methods evolved by others. After 1908 Indirect Rule as expounded by Lugard was the obvious model and the Belgians adopted it almost without reservation. Policy was to govern through native agencies and preserve indigenous culture. The difficulty was that so much of both had been destroyed during the period of occupation, leaving a multiplicity of petty chiefdoms as fragments of previously larger African states or tribal units. The government regrouped these, forming 432 *chefferies* out of 6,000 odd chiefdoms and 509 entirely artificial *secteurs* from isolated villages. The resultant units had an average population of 12,000 and were big enough to be given some autonomy. They were run by chiefs, assisted by councils of notables, under European supervision. Most had their own secretariat, treasury, court, police force, schools and medical centres. This was indirect rule, but it was largely an artifact.

The one important group of Africans for whom such native authorities did not cater were those who had become 'detribalized' by moving to one of the big towns or to a mining or industrial centre. They too were dealt with on Indirect Rule principles. Large groups were formed into *centres extra-coutumiers* with powers and functions like the *chefferies*. Smaller groups constituted *cités indigènes* with their own chiefs and councils but less autonomy. They were segregated from European social groups; but after 1957 many of these urban units were transformed into municipalities on western lines.

Indirect Rule was consistent with Belgian practice on citizenship and law. Only Belgians by birth were citizens, the rest subjects. These could become *immatriculés* (assimilated), but were not encouraged to do so. Laws and courts followed this division. Africans were under their own courts, run by Africans or local administrators, which administered native custom in civil cases. Europeans had parallel courts, staffed by professional lawyers, applying Belgian law. Africans could use these courts, but were tried in accordance with their own custom.

Labour policy was a compromise between respect for current trusteeship concepts and the practical need to provide workers for plantations and mines. Forced labour could be used only for public purposes, and Africans could be compelled to cultivate specified crops (such as cotton) on communal lands. They could not be forced to work for private European employers, but the government stimulated recruitment on contract by imposing a head tax payable in money and by using chiefs as recruiting agents. These practices were common in Africa between the wars: the Belgians stood out only in the efficiency with which they supervised contracts and working conditions. Limits were set on the proportion to be recruited from any area; new European enterprises were banned in zones whose labour force was already committed; conditions of work and wages were defined and policed; social amenities of all kinds were provided in the mining centres. Probably no other African colony had better labour conditions. The Congo benefited from its capacity to pay for these advantages and from the efficiency brought by a highly industrialized north European state with advanced welfare services.

Education also was provided on an impressive scale, mainly by Catholic missions with government subsidies. By 1959 the Congo had a high primary school attendance (56 per cent), though few went on to secondary schools. There was no attempt at linguistic or cultural assimilation. Emphasis was on practical instruction for, like all aspects of native policy, education was designed to train Africans to live within a colonial framework. This was good trusteeship but a bad apprenticeship for independence.

The Congo was exceptional as an African colony because it so largely fulfilled the economic expectations of its founder. The profits from rubber and ivory lasted only until about 1915. They were then surpassed by profits from minerals such as copper, diamonds, radium and uranium, and from tropical agricultural products such as palm-oil, palm kernels, cotton, copal and coffee. European plantations and farms produced the greater part of these, though the government made great efforts to encourage peasant production, and provided the best advisory and educational services in Africa to improve it. But mining was the basis of the Congolese economy, and this was dominated by a few large concerns. In 1932 there were about 200 companies operating in the Congo, of which 71 owned two-thirds of the capital invested there. These in turn were controlled by four financial groups: the *Société Générale*, the *Groupe Empain*, the *Groupe Cominier*, and the *Banque de Bruxelles*. The first of these invested more than four times as much capital in the Congo as the rest combined; and since the state was a large shareholder, the Belgian government effectively controlled the economy. The *Société*, through its many subordinates, controlled practically the whole production of minerals and had large interests in transport, plantations, electricity and banking. As a Belgian Senate commission remarked in 1934, 'without the group of the *Société Générale*, economic Congo can be said not to exist'.[5]

Thus the Congo approximated closely to Leopold's dream of a Belgian colony of investment: by 1936 it was estimated to have received some £143 million,[6] and by 1960 £1,000 million.[7] Belgium had gained one of the real windfalls of partition. Yet she did not obtain extortionate profits: the average return on total Belgian investment over a long period has been roughly estimated at between 4 and 5 per cent.[8] Higher rates of interest could have been obtained in many European securities. Moreover Belgium made no attempt to milk the Congo by transferring revenues to the metropolitan treasury: on the contrary, before 1937 she frequently subsidized the colonial budget.

In most respects, therefore, Belgium became a model colonial power after 1908. Her record appeared defective only after 1960, when it became clear that she had not prepared for Congolese independence. For too long paternalism seemed enough. Before 1945 educated African *évolués* were given no opportunities in politics or the higher levels of administration. Nominated African notables were given seats in the central and provincial advisory councils after 1947; corporate groups began to nominate to both bodies in 1957; but no direct elections were allowed before 1960 – the year of independence. Similarly, the higher levels of the civil service and responsible posts in industry were opened to Africans only in 1959. The Belgians were so blind to the existence of Congolese nationalism that they were taken aback by the Leopoldville riots of 1959. Then they reacted too quickly. Lacking wider experience, accustomed to think of the Congo as a docile contented dependency, they had no heart for a struggle. Independence was conceded as readily as trusteeship principles had been adopted after 1908. At the Round Table Conference in Brussels in January 1960 they argued for a phased transfer of power over several years, but capitulated to the demand of inexperienced African politicians for immediate withdrawal. The first representative parliament met in Leopoldville in May 1960; independence was declared on 30 June. Within two months the *Force Publique* mutinied; Katanga declared itself independent; the Congo slid into chaos. By September it depended for its unity, probably its very survival, on a United Nations military force. This was the price of paternalism unduly prolonged in the era of decolonization.

The German Colonial Empire

The German colonial empire had the shortest life of all: born in 1884, it was extinguished in 1919. Yet its record is important. It shows that a rich and efficient industrial power, though without any colonial experience, could master the complex problems of tropical colonization within a generation. It also contradicts two commonly held fallacies: that Germany deserved to forfeit her colonies because she had been uniquely irresponsible in dealing with non-Europeans; that the colonies were essential to German economic prosperity. Germany was in fact probably not significantly worse than other colonial powers by 1914, whatever may have been true a decade earlier: and her colonies were of little demonstrable value to her.

The bulk of the German empire was in Africa. Tanganyika contained 384,000 square miles; South-West Africa 322,000; Kamerun 305,000; Togoland 34,000. German possessions in the Pacific were relatively small: 93,000 square miles of New Guinea; the Bismarck Archipelago; the Caroline, Mariana and Marshall Islands; Opulu and Sawaii in the Samoan group; a number of smaller islands; and the lease of Kiao-Chow in China. The empire thus consisted of about a million square miles and had a population of perhaps 15,000,000.[9] It was a typical product of the partition, an empire of occupation offering few rewards. Only a few regions of Tanganyika and South-West Africa attracted German immigrants, and, apart from limited mineral deposits in South-West Africa, it provided no windfall sources of wealth. Germany inaugurated the partition but gained few of the prizes.

The history of German colonization falls into three periods, dividing in 1891 and 1906. The first was one of experiment, the second of effective occupation, the last of maturing policy.

The period from 1884 to 1890 demonstrated Bismarck's idiosyncratic approach to empire. He did not think Germany needed colonies for economic or settlement reasons. He staked his claim only to support German diplomacy and to please minority interests who demanded colonies. He was determined that those who wanted and benefited by his acquisitions should also be responsible for running them. All dependencies were therefore protectorates (to limit imperial obligations), and were to be administered by chartered companies. This should have been a limited liability empire; but it proved otherwise. Chartered company rule was possible only if German investors regarded the colonies as a profitable speculation and formed viable companies to administer them. In fact no company could be formed to run Kamerun or Togoland, and from the start these had to be administered by the government. All others, except Kiao-Chow, were initially granted to companies, but the state had ultimately to relieve all of their administrative responsibilities.

South-West Africa was placed under a company formed in

1885 to take over concessions already acquired by Luderitz; but it was an artifact, most of whose small capital was subscribed (under pressure from Bismarck) by von Hansemann and Bleichroder, two leading bankers who played a major role in all the chartered companies. The company failed to develop profitable mineral deposits and was allowed to give up its administrative duties in 1888, surviving as a privileged trading and land-owning company. The East African Company lasted two years longer. It was founded by Karl Peters, who had made the treaties with Africans on which German control was based, but was taken over by bankers, again under Bismarck's pressure, when the investing public refused to subscribe. It had full sovereign rights but no commercial monopoly, since this was barred by the Berlin Act. It found the cost of suppressing Arab slavers and imposing authority on Africans too much for its finances, and in 1890 the government relieved it of its governmental functions. The company did well for itself in retaining a guaranteed revenue from customs, the monopoly of mining, possession of unoccupied land and the right to establish a bank of issue. But Germany was left with another unrewarding burden.

The two Pacific companies lasted longer. The New Guinea Company was a genuine commercial venture, formed before Bismarck claimed part of the island to give it scope. Yet it could make nothing of its opportunity. It gave up administration temporarily from 1889 to 1892, and did so finally in 1899, receiving financial compensation and 150,000 hectares of land. In fact the Jaluit Company, formed to trade in the smaller islands, was commercially the only successful chartered company. This was probably because it left administration to the imperial commissioner for the Marshalls, paying the small costs involved, and concentrated on plantations and trade. It lost its charter in 1906, after Australia had complained that it was levying differential duties contrary to the Anglo-German agreement of 1886, but survived as a profitable trading concern.

Thus, when Bismarck was dismissed in 1890, his concept of an empire run by chartered companies was already a failure. Germany was left in the position he had tried to avoid, with a dependent empire to organize and pay for.

The second phase from 1890 to 1906 was one of disillusionment; though this did not prevent William II from acquiring further colonies as part of his strategy of world power, with strong support from such patriotic groups as the Navy League, the Pan-German League, and the Colonial Society. The colonies were now seen to be a liability rather than an asset: they had nevertheless to be occupied and 'pacified'. By 1906 this had been done; but in the process Germany had gained a bad reputation.

For all colonial powers effective occupation of Africa entailed a series of 'little wars': the charge against Germany was that she fought them with excessive brutality. There is no doubt that the Herero rising of 1904–7 in South-West Africa and the 1905–6 Maji-Maji rising in southern Tanganyika were brutally suppressed: the attempt to drive the Hereros off their land and to exterminate them was particularly obnoxious. But these horrors must be seen in proportion. Germany lacked experienced colonial administrators and soldiers. Her agents tended to excess through fear. German resources in Africa were severely strained by these simultaneous risings, and reprisals were intended to prevent a recurrence. The Germans had no monopoly of 'frightfulness' in tackling such crises: the French in Algeria and the Western Sudan, the Belgians in the Congo and the British in the Egyptian Sudan used similar methods. There were, of course, individual Germans, such as Leist, acting governor of Kamerun in 1893, who acted barbarously: it is more significant that he was dismissed and condemned by a special court in Germany. German methods of imposing effective authority were crude and harsh: their real qualities as colonial administrators could be assessed only after 1906, when the occupation of the African colonies was complete.

The third phase began in about 1906–7. Criticism of mounting costs and reported brutalities came to a head when the Reichstag rejected a supplementary colonial estimate in 1906. The Chancellor, von Bülow, recognized that change was necessary, and marked it by transferring most colonies from the Foreign Office to a newly created colonial office – *Kolonialamt* – under Bernhard Dernburg. The German empire then entered its mature phase.

Now that the chartered companies were out of the way, the German system of colonial government differed from others mainly because the German constitution itself was peculiar. The Emperor had sole legislative as well as executive authority over the colonies, requiring only the assent of the Bundesrat (the upper house of the federal legislature) to validate his decrees. The Reichstag, the popular house, was limited to voting the annual colonial estimates and asking questions; though in practice it exerted as much influence on policy as most other parliaments. The Emperor's authority was in fact exercised by the Chancellor who, in the absence of a ministerial system, was personally responsible for all governmental policy; but colonial affairs were for the most part left to the Colonial Minister and the *Kolonialamt*.

From this point German practice was conventional. The *Kolonialamt* combined German administrative efficiency with principles which reflected the emerging European conscience on colonial matters. It rationalized colonial administration, adopted practices from other empires, and trained a corps of professional administrators. Its new professionalism led to the disbandment of the *Kolonialrat*, a nominated council of amateur experts which was set up in 1890 to advise the Foreign Office on colonial questions. The Colonial Office could not, however, altogether avoid external pressures. The Social Democrats, and, for a short time, the Centre Party, criticized waste and alleged abuses in the Reichstag. The Colonial Society and its Economic Committee could not be ignored, since they exerted considerable public influence particularly through their journal, the *Kolonialzeitung*. The office had to stand between such metropolitan pressure groups and the colonies, ensuring that demands for fiscal economy, or for economic policies favouring private interests, did not, as they had done before 1906, produce bad administration and abuse of indigenous peoples.

In this it was largely successful. Colonial administration was simple but had reached a high standard by 1914. Governors had autocratic executive and legislative powers, and were advised by small councils of German officials and other residents. Administration was bureaucratic and efficient, but not militaristic. The civilian police force which was part of the colonial administration was more important than the armed forces, which were directly controlled by the German Department of the Marine. For example, in 1914 Kamerun had about 1,200 native police under thirty officers, and 1,550 African soldiers under 185 officers. For so large a territory this was a small military force and could not have been the basis of government.

German principles on citizenship and law in the colonies were conventional. Since the colonies were all protectorates, only German officials and settlers were subjects of the Emperor and these had German law and courts. Africans and others remained protected persons and had their own courts. These were run by chiefs under European supervision and applied customary law, but Africans could appeal from them to the governor or to the *Oberrichter* who ran the senior European court. Punishments imposed on Africans were severe but normal in Africa. Apart from occasional brutalities during the initial period, German rule has been well described as 'very strict, at times harsh, but always just'.[10]

Native administration was a new problem for Germans. Before 1906 they paid little attention to its moral implications, making vast land grants to concessionary companies, requisitioning forced labour and taking no trouble to preserve traditional native authorities. But they learnt fast and were ready to adopt methods evolved by others. For the most part their later methods were 'direct'. They employed Africans and other chiefs widely, but as officials rather than as hereditary 'authorities' in their own right. They were taught German (for practical rather than assimilationist reasons) and had to wear German uniforms. But in parts of Kamerun and Ruanda, where conditions resembled those of Northern Nigeria, the Germans adopted a policy of loose supervision of indigenous rulers, appointed residents to supervise rather than rule, and interfered as little as possible.

Other aspects of German native policy were in line with the better contemporary standards. The sale of firearms to non-Europeans was first controlled, then prohibited. Liquor imports were restricted everywhere and banned in East Africa and the Pacific islands. Native taxation, mostly head or hut taxes, was not excessive, designed as much to produce revenue as to force Africans to work. Officially there was no forced labour; but the governments used tax-defaulters and criminals on public works, and officials encouraged chiefs to enrol contract workers for European plantations. On some plantations in Kamerun the death rate of these labourers was at one time high; but the government took its responsibilities seriously, and later provided supervision and medical services as good as those in most other African colonies. Land policy also improved after the indiscriminate alienations of the first decade. From 1896 waste lands were normally declared Crown property and were leased out to Europeans for periods of 25 years and on strict conditions. Africans were prevented from alienating land for more than fifteen-year periods. Injustice was sometimes done: the decision to remove Africans from the town of Douala in Kamerun after 1911 to prevent them alienating land to private European interests was unwise and provoked resistance. Yet, given contemporary assumptions that European plantations were necessary for economic development, the policy of native reserves and government leases was evidence of good intentions.

By 1914 the German colonial empire had outgrown the mistakes made in the early period: the case for depriving her of her colonies was false. Yet the evidence also suggests that Germany was deprived of nothing but her status as a colonial power. She had obtained no measurable economic or fiscal advantage from her colonies before 1914, and the powers who took them over fared no better.

All German colonies except Togoland and Samoa relied on subsidies from the metropolis to balance their budgets. By 1914 these totalled over £50,000,000; if concealed subsidies on shipping, naval defence and low-interest loans are included, the accumulated cost to the German taxpayer may have amounted to £100,000,000.[11] These costs were not offset by compensating economic advantages. The total gross value of Germany's trade with her colonies from 1894 to 1913, quite apart from the proportion which constituted metropolitan profit, was less than the amount Germany spent on her colonies. Colonial markets were of small importance to her. The absolute volume of colonial trade with Germany increased from 61,494,000 marks (£3,007,000) in 1904 to 286,172,000 (£14,000,000) in 1913: but they remained only about 0·5 per cent of Germany's total overseas trade. Moreover, despite preferential devices, Germany's share of this trade declined from an average of 35·2 per cent in 1894–1903 to 26·6 per cent in 1904–13.[12] The colonies did not make Germany independent of foreign sources for any raw material or foodstuff. In 1910 they provided 0·25 per cent of her cotton; 2·12 per cent of her oils and fats; and no higher proportion of any commodity than 13·62 per cent of her rubber imports.[13] Even in terms of capital investment they did little to solve what Lenin later alleged to be the desperate need of German banking trusts for new outlets. By 1913 Germany had invested some 505,000,000 marks (£24,694,000) in her colonies, which was about the same as Germans invested in the Rand gold-fields in the 1890s.[14] Even so, much of this colonial investment was extracted only by guaranteed interest rates and official pressure on bankers; and Germans showed a very marked preference for investment in Europe rather than overseas.

The record was clear: the German colonial empire was an economic failure. Yet this fact had remarkably little impact on colonial enthusiasts, who claimed that if the present colonies produced few advantages, Germany should acquire others, such as the Congo or Portuguese colonies in Central Africa. They also fell back on the strategic argument that Germany must not depend for vital raw materials on potentially hostile foreign states, and predicted that at some future time Germany might really need monopolistic outlets for her capital. Such arguments were still being put forward in the 1930s. They were unrealistic. Germany had lost her 'place in the sun' and certain vested interests in the metropolis had suffered. The German nation was relieved of the cost and inconvenience of an unremunerative colonial empire; and in the age of decolonization, her advice and capital were welcomed by the ex-colonies precisely because, for half a century, she had ceased to be a 'colonialist' power.

16

Myths and Realities of the Modern Colonial Empires

It is impossible in a single chapter to pull together the immense diversities of the modern empires, or to analyse all the myths which surround them. Yet an attempt must be made to recapitulate those main features which distinguished the modern empires from the old; to emphasize contrasts and similarities between different modern empires; and to dissect the dominant myth of modern imperialism – the belief that tropical empires were 'exploited' to provide wealth for their masters.

Contrasts Between the Old and Modern Empires

There were, perhaps, five features which made the modern empires obviously different from their predecessors. The first European colonies were in America and were all 'settlement' colonies of varying types – 'pure', 'mixed' or 'plantation'. The modern empires were mainly in Africa, Asia and the Pacific, and were for the most part colonies of 'occupation'. There were, of course, exceptions. The British preserved the earlier tradition in their 'pure' and 'mixed' settlement colonies in Australasia and North America, and in South, Central and East Africa. Algeria became a 'mixed' colony; Russian Central Asia and Siberia were ultimately 'mixed' or settlement colonies; Portugal began to transform Angola and Mozambique into 'mixed' colonies at the end of the colonial period; and the United States took over colonies of settlement in the Caribbean and the Pacific. But these were exotic: in the modern period empire meant primarily European rule over peoples rather than colonization in its true sense.

A second contrast lay in the geographical extent of the new empires and the thoroughness with which they were occupied. In 1800 much of America was still not under effective European occupation after three centuries of activity there: during the later nineteenth and early twentieth centuries Europeans claimed whole continents and sub-continents and then imposed full government within a few decades. By the 1930s colonies and ex-colonies covered 84·6 per cent of the land surface of the globe: parts of Arabia, Persia, Afghanistan, Mongolia, Tibet, China, Siam and Japan were the only states which had never been under formal European government.

This points to the third fundamental contrast. The earlier empires were in no sense inevitable, for Europe had no power advantage over many civilized and well-organized non-European states. The modern empires, however, probably were inevitable. At some point between 1700 and the mid-nineteenth century the balance of power between the western nations and the rest of the world shifted decisively. The west became absolutely stronger as a result of industrial mechanization, improved military techniques and equipment, modern communications, sophisticated finance, scientific medicine and surplus capital. The trend was shown by the British conquest of India, the decline of Ottoman power in the Balkans and Mediterranean, the growth of a favourable trade balance with the advanced economies of the east, the spread of Christian missions, and the universal infiltration of European adventurers and traders. European power remained overwhelming until others adopted the skills which generated it: nothing could have prevented her from dominating the rest of the world. The only question was the particular form this predominance would take. 'Informal empire' – political or economic – was for long its main expression; but, for reasons already considered, 'informal empire' ultimately grew into 'formal empire' almost everywhere. This was not invariably a matter of choice, for Europe did not need new formal empires. Her power was such that she could not escape them.

Two other special features of the modern empires were, paradoxically, their greater political centralization and relative economic freedom. Distance defied the attempts of some of the older imperial powers to govern colonies from the centre: improved communications gave moderns at least the chance to create integrated political systems. Yet empires ceased to be closed economic systems. Economic nationalism never died out, but it was severely modified in the mid-nineteenth century and never regained its full force. British colonies were open to ships and goods of other countries by 1830; the Dutch threw open their colonial trades after 1815; the French, Spaniards and Portuguese followed suit in and after the 1860s. Protectionism soon revived: by 1900 most continental countries and the United States were protecting their home and colonial markets and subsidizing shipping. Yet none completely excluded foreign ships or goods; in most empires monopolistic devices failed even to give the metropolis the larger share of its colonies' trade. Even the intensified 'neo-mercantilism' of the 1930s did not do this. The concept of the *pacte colonial* survived, but it was never again entirely exclusive.

Similarities and Contrasts Between the Modern Empires

There is a much cherished myth that the character of modern colonies differed widely according to which European state owned them: that some empires were good, others bad; that some powers fostered independence in their tropical dependencies, others tried to prevent it. Such distinctions flattered national vanities, and were underlined by contrasts in style reflecting divergent European traditions and colonial situations. Yet fundamentally such distinctions were unimportant. The striking feature of the modern empires was similarity of character and common experience.

There were, of course, obvious contrasts. In its size, variety and continuity with the past the British empire was unique. It was also the only empire with important settlement colonies, which have to be excluded when comparing the British with other empires. All others were either quite new or were virtually reconstituted in the nineteenth century after losing the bulk of their previous holdings. Most were small, geographically concentrated and uniformly tropical. There were contrasts in theory and practice reflecting diverse metropolitan traditions. Britain and Russia made no distinction between full subjects of the Crown and the rest (except, of course, in protectorates); all others distinguished citizens from subjects. Constitutional relationships between colonies and metropolis varied both in fact and theory. France, Portugal, Russia and the United States aimed to incorporate dependencies within themselves, though only Russia entirely succeeded in doing so. The rest treated colonies as distinct political organisms.

These and other contrasts were, however, eclipsed by resemblances which developed in course of time. This was not surprising: uniformity was imposed by common problems. Settlement colonies in America highlighted contrasts in European civilization: tropical empires emphasized its common traditions. American colonists preserved and even exaggerated the diverse political, religious, and cultural traditions they took with them: the difficulty of controlling huge tropical colonies without an intermediate creole population was so great that nice distinctions faded into insignificance. Certainly this was how it seemed in retrospect to the one-time colonial subjects. In the mythology of new states in Africa and Asia 'colonialism' was a unity.

Common problems, shared moral standards and international criticism of the scandals of the early period after partition bred ever more similar methods of colonial administration during the later nineteenth and early twentieth centuries.

Despite conflicting theories on colonial autonomy or incorporation with the metropolis, effective power was generally concentrated in the centre. Despite constitutional distinctions, it was held by executive departments rather than representative legislatures. This was inevitable. Colonial problems were too complex and too peripheral to domestic politics to be dealt with by parliamentary amateurs, and they aroused public interest only when international rivalry stimulated jingoism or when scandals outraged the humanitarian conscience. Tropical empires were a professional concern and were wisely left to permanent officials in the colonial offices.

By 1914 Russia and the United States, both significantly

believing in full incorporation of colonies with the metropolis, were the only colonial powers in which there was no colonial office. In all other empires the colonial office or ministry was the dominant influence on policy and government – so many 'Mr Mother Countries', in the words once applied by Charles Buller to the British Under-Secretary in the Colonial Office, James Stephen. Their files constituted a collective memory and an accumulating conscience. Their unprecedented efficiency – itself the product of modern European bureaucracy – made it possible to supervise world-empires from a single building. Their professional concern for the welfare of their charges was the source of most benefits Europe gave her colonies. They struggled with reluctant parliaments and treasuries for funds. They built up expert advisory committees on medicine, agriculture, communications, industry, etc. They trained colonial administrators and injected them with their own sense of moral purpose. Increasingly they gave dependencies the benevolent paternalism which other metropolitan departments were applying to European societies in the era of modern collectivism.

Equally characteristic of modern imperialism was the professional character of colonial administrators. The European placemen and creole subordinates who had served for the settlement colonies of the *ancien régime* disappeared: in their place were career civil servants forming *élite* corps; trained, reasonably well paid, uncorruptible. Names differed; but the character of the men who administered colonies, provinces, districts, and subdistricts was remarkably uniform. By the 1920s the professional administrator of most colonies embodied the traditions built up in British India since the 1790s, and was probably the highest product of European imperialism – the alien ruler who associated himself so closely with his subjects that he was prepared to defend them against his own compatriots if he thought they were acting contrary to the interests of his charges. The colonial administrator must not be romanticized. He sometimes acted for specifically European interests; for example, by recruiting native labour for plantations or mines. Absolute power did not breed corruption, but it often generated excessive paternalism, and the belief that only the alien administrator could give non-Europeans honest progressive government. He was also perhaps the main beneficiary of his own work, for service in the colonies became a desirable career for members of the European professional classes whose opportunities at home were restricted. Yet, on balance, the European official was an honourable feature of European rule over tropical dependencies, and the main obstacle to abuse of imperial power. The myth that he was a domineering agent of exploiting imperialism is entirely false.

Political forms in the colonies were also remarkably similar. A few dependencies had representative governments in differing degrees: the British settlement colonies and ultimately India and Ceylon; the United States dependencies; Dutch Indonesia. These were exceptional. Most colonies were governed autocratically, irrespective of the constitutional traditions of their masters. There were, of course, differences of degree: the British and Dutch gave their dependencies legislative and fiscal autonomy and emphasized the legislative functions of colonial councils. But the typical tropical government consisted of a governor (or governor-general), a nominated advisory council consisting mostly of officials, and administrative departments whose absolute authority was restricted only by metropolitan supervision. Non-Europeans had virtually no share in their own government at the higher levels, though indigenous notables were sometimes made members of the councils. Theoretical contrasts between colonies, protectorates and mandates made little difference to such patterns: only protected states retained the form, if not the substance, of rule by indigenous authorities. Given the facts of tropical colonization this concentration of power in alien hands was probably inevitable: it certainly did not preclude honest government. Its weakness was that it was not necessarily rooted in public support and therefore lacked the self-confidence to institute major changes. In fact, the common defect of all alien rule was its cautious conservatism. Far from trying to transform non-Europeans into something else, it tended to embalm their indigenous social and economic systems, insulating them from the pressures of the contemporary world.

'Native administration' was the basis of all modern colonial government. Most tropical colonies went through four phases of development; and again the time-scale was similar for most imperial systems. The first phase was commonly the worst. Conquest brought disease, seizure of land, forced labour, depopulation and incompetent administration by men without training or experience. Had these persisted European rule would have been an unmitigated disaster. It was redeemed by the later phases. The second began perhaps a generation after occupation: in the 1790s in India; after 1820 in Ceylon; from the 1870s in Algeria; after about 1906 in most new products of the partition. Its common denominator was humanitarian concern for the interests of subject peoples, which was expressed in the concept of 'trusteeship'. In the 1900s trusteeship was adulterated with disreputable theories of race, derived from 'neo-Darwinism', which assumed non-Europeans to be inherently inferior and fitted by nature only to be subject to the superior races. Fortunately this Aristotelian strand of thought proved less hardy than the other. By the 1930s it had been replaced by universalist assumptions characteristic of eighteenth-century enlightenment. All men were potentially equal and the less 'advanced' should be helped to reach the higher levels. This made trusteeship evolutionary: only the time-scale of evolution to self-government and the form it should take still remained in doubt.

Trusteeship expressed itself in many concrete forms. Growing emphasis on international action to define standards of conduct was shown first in the principles laid down by the international conferences of 1884–5 (Berlin), 1890 (Brussels) and 1906 (Algeciras), and then in the mandate system set up by the League of Nations in 1919. More generally it gradually made the practice of different powers conform to common moral standards. Even Portugal, who was outside the main stream of European consciousness for most of this period, was affected by it. Rationalization of methods of native administration resulted. There was an obvious conceptual difference between the ideal of 'Indirect Rule' as applied in several British colonies, in the Congo and elsewhere, and the more common practice of 'direct rule'. The first aimed to preserve indigenous forms intact, the latter to provide good government through any convenient agency. But the contrast was theoretical rather than fundamental. The reality was that all colonial governments relied on native intermediaries and preserved many indigenous institutions and laws. All native administration became more intense in course of time: so that the real contrast was between this eventually close European supervision and the loose control characteristic of 'frontier' systems in the early years of occupation. 'Direct' and 'indirect' systems alike generated a class of educated '*évolués*', who could not be fitted into traditional or paternalistic structures and eventually formed the nucleus of nationalist parties.

Trusteeship in its earlier phase was negative and conservative: it did little to 'improve' the dependencies. The third phase of European rule preserved its moral principles but reflected a new enthusiasm to develop 'neglected estates'. Motives were mixed, ranging from moral concern with the low living standards of many dependencies to self-interested anxiety to make them more useful to their owners. Revived protectionism and economic nationalism in the 1890s stimulated the '*mise en valeur*': the world slump of the 1930s brought even the free-trading British and Dutch into line with the rest. Tariff systems were tightened to ensure not only markets for European manufactures but also outlets for colonial products. Grants-in-aid and non-commercial investments were stepped up. By 1939 most states were giving economic aid to their colonies, subsidizing educational and welfare services, organizing economic life. The Second World War, which made colonial foodstuffs and raw materials even more important and inured Europeans to high taxation and state collectivism, further intensified these trends. Thus the last phase of European empire was also the most constructive. Moreover it proved habit-forming. The common bequest of all colonial empires to the post-colonial era was the belief that what were now euphuistically called 'developing' countries were entitled to foreign subsidies to compensate them for the alleged indignity of long periods of servitude.

Decolonization also was common to almost all empires and ran to a similar timetable. Nationalism was a growing force in most dependencies before 1939, though its importance varied immensely from one to another. The Second World War affected all colonies and shook the roots of empire. The powers reacted with extraordinary uniformity. In 1945 none thought of dismantling their empires in the near future, but most dropped their previous assumptions that empire would last indefinitely and began to prepare for the ultimate transfer of power. To gain time they made minor concessions to colonial politicians, injecting representative elements into colonial councils, admitting non-Europeans to the higher levels of the bureaucracy, intensifying educational, medical and technical services. Only the Portuguese remained out of step. But in the end all found that these half measures would not serve: full independence had to be conceded before the powers wanted to give it or thought their dependencies ready.

By 1965 the empires were again united in dissolution, but their relics varied. Russia and the United States had been uniquely successful in evading decolonization by incorporating colonies into their own territories. Portugal was still trying to do this in Africa and had succeeded with her Atlantic islands. France had done the same with her smaller *anciennes colonies*, but retained only unilateral treaties with some of her African and other ex-colonies. Holland had no surviving link with Indonesia, and Belgium had only economic interests in the Congo. The British Commonwealth seemed at first sight to represent the most successful attempt to transmute empire into a satisfactory substitute, but this was misleading. The Commonwealth had no necessary functions or common obligations. It was a club whose members shared a common experience as dependencies and saw the advantages of future co-operation in certain fields.

The Myth of Economic Exploitation

The most commonly held and dangerous myth connected with the modern empires is that they were great machines deliberately constructed by Europe to exploit dependent peoples by extracting economic and fiscal profit from them. Its corollary is that the new states had a moral claim to be compensated for losses suffered in the past by being helped to become advanced industrial economics. None denied that it was desirable for wealthy industrial states to help those with primitive economies: but to base their claim to assistance on the premise that they were exploited in the past was wrong. The myth of imperial profit-making is false.

To start with, the modern empires were not artificially constructed economic machines. The second expansion of Europe was a complex historical process in which political, social and emotional forces in Europe and on the periphery were more influential than calculated imperialism. Individual colonies might serve an economic purpose; collectively no empire had any definable function, economic or otherwise. Empires represented only a particular phase in the ever-changing relationship of Europe with the rest of the world: analogies with industrial systems or investment in real estate were simply misleading.

Yet, though the colonial empires were undoubtedly functionless in origin, this is not to say that they did not later provide an economic return, a 'profit', to their owners. Certainly many colonial enthusiasts in Europe alleged that they could and did. Were they right?

To answer this question requires a careful analysis of its meaning. It is, in fact, highly theoretical. An industrial company exists to produce profits: colonies were human societies belonging to a different order of things. It is really as meaningless to ask whether a colony such as Nigeria was 'profitable' to Britain as to ask whether Wales or England was. In each case some form of 'advantage' was obvious. But this was not necessarily economic; and if it was it cannot necessarily be called 'profit' and need not result from 'exploitation'. In short, such concepts reflect a perverted form of thinking about colonies which derived from the 'mercantile' theories of the first empires. The fact that they were commonly held does not make them true. The task of the historian is to analyse the various forms of 'profit' Europe may have gained from her colonies; to compare these with countervailing disadvantages; and to decide whether on balance empire gave economic advantages which Europe would not otherwise have obtained.

The crux of the matter is to define what empire meant in economic terms. A colony differed from an independent state only in that it was governed by an alien power: colonial status was primarily a political phenomenon. This immediately limits the field of inquiry, for it excludes all those influences exerted by Europe which fell short of full political control: 'economic imperialism' and 'informal empire', for example. If empire generated 'profit' this must be directly attributable to alien rule. The question can therefore be redefined: what economic advantages did Europe extract from her colonies which she could not have gained from other countries, however similar in other ways?

There were at least six obvious ways in which this might be done. The first was simply to loot an occupied country of its treasures. This was very rare in the modern empires. Few new colonies possessed hoarded wealth on the scale of Mexico, Peru or India in the past: there was little that could profitably be seized from African or Polynesian chiefs. Moreover, although 'pacifying' armies were often barbarous in their methods, they were normally under direct metropolitan control and conquest was quickly followed by civilized methods of government. The rape of Bengal in the 1760s was not repeated after 1815.

A more sophisticated way of extracting profit before 1815 was to transfer colonial revenues to the metropolitan treasury. This also became very rare. From 1831 to 1877 the Dutch transferred Indonesian surpluses through the 'Culture System'; the British East India Company and other chartered companies sometimes paid dividends out of colonial taxation; but no normal colonial government ever did so. Some demanded contributions to defence costs; the French confused things by integrating the accounts of some colonies with their own. But most colonies were left to use their own revenues and were more likely to receive subsidies than to be robbed of surpluses.

A third possible source of imperial advantage was to transfer money or goods from colony to metropolis as interest on loans, payment for services rendered, the pensions and savings of colonial officials and the profits made by business firms. Much has been made of this 'drain', particularly by Indian historians; but the Indian case is misleading. The greater part – interest charges, profits of alien enterprises, etc. – would have been equally due from independent states which borrowed in the

British capital market or in which British firms operated. The net 'drain' was therefore the cost of services, such as the Indian army, which Britain controlled and which India might not otherwise have chosen to pay for, and the transferred salaries of alien officials. The damage to India was not the absolute cost but the loss of currency and international exchange by a country short of both.

A fourth possible form of exploitation was the imposition of 'unfair' terms of trade on a colony. This had been the basic device of the 'mercantile' empires, and, in its pre-nineteenth-century form, may well have provided artificially high profit levels for metropolitan merchants and producers. But no modern empire operated a comparable system of monopoly. By the 1860s the old controls had been dismantled. Although tariff preferences, shipping subsidies, navigation acts and import quotas were soon disinterred, no country ever entirely closed colonial ports to foreign competition. Even the proportion of colonial trade which fell to the parent states was unimpressive. Britain's share of her empire's trade fell from an average of 49 per cent in the decade after 1854 to 36 per cent in 1929–33:[1] thereafter, even revived protection only increased it slightly. France kept a larger share, always more than half, of the trade of her colonies; even so, the proportion declined with time.[2] Most other empires had a similar experience: only the United States and Russia, which entirely enclosed their colonies within domestic tariff systems, really had a commercial monopoly; and this probably benefited the dependencies as much as the metropolis. Although modern protectionism harmed the interests of colonial subjects as much as it did metropolitan consumers, it was at least reasonably impartial and the losses of colonial consumers were compensated by guaranteed and preferential markets in Europe. It is therefore unlikely that 'neo-mercantilism' produced substantial net 'profits' for metropolitan countries.

By a curious paradox, however, it has been argued that during their era of free trade the British 'exploited' colonies by making it impossible for them to protect their own industries against her exports, so holding back their industrial progress. This did not apply to the settlement colonies, which were allowed their own protectionist policies from 1859, but may have been true of others. India was again the test case, since she was the only British dependency in the nineteenth century with the evident capacity to develop large-scale mechanized industry. There is no doubt that free trade had serious consequences for her. In the early nineteenth century free import of British cottons destroyed Indian hand-loom weaving on a commercial scale: thereafter the British ban on protective tariffs held back mechanized cotton production and kept the market open for Lancashire. Indian cottons were not protected until about 1926, and textile imports from Britain then dropped significantly. India consumed £40,729,000 out of total British manufactured textile exports of £195,805,000 in 1913, but only £11,373,000 in 1934.[3] To some extent enforced free trade may have had similar effects on other nascent Indian industries and on the economic growth of other British dependencies.

Yet it is impossible to be certain that these disadvantages were specifically the result of British imperial authority, for other and totally independent states were also forced, during the nineteenth century, to reduce or abolish import duties in the interests of British exports. China, for example, was restricted by treaty after 1842 to a maximum tariff of 5 per cent on all imports. An 'open door' might, in fact, have been imposed on any weak state by European powers: an independent India might have been as unable as China was to protect her own industries against foreign demands for freedom of access. Thus the 'open door' was a typical product of Europe's general preponderance. Formal empire was one way of imposing it, but by no means the only way; and the benefits resulting from free commercial access to non-European states cannot be regarded as an exclusively imperial 'profit'.

The most commonly alleged form of imperial profiteering was to 'exploit' the natural endowments of dependencies – oil, minerals, natural rubber, ivory, etc. If these were extracted without giving compensating advantages, an ex-colony might hypothetically find itself robbed of assets which might otherwise have financed the creation of a modern industrial economy. A simple model would be the use of petroleum deposits by a company wholly owned and run by citizens of an imperial state. If no colonial labour was employed, no taxes were levied for local use, and the oil was exhausted before independence, the new state might be said to have been looted.

Examples of 'exploitation' on this scale are, however, difficult to find. Extractive industries were never entirely insulated from their environment. All had to use local labour. They paid wages lower than they paid to Europeans but vastly higher than those normal in subsistence economies. All had to build modern communications and other amenities which benefited the colony as a whole. Some part of company profits were always spent locally, lubricating the colonial economy. Most overseas companies had to pay taxes to the colonial government. Thus no extractive industry failed to provide some advantages to the dependency in which it operated. The question is whether these were enough: whether an independent state could have gained more.

The question was pragmatic rather than moral. The value of natural endowments was for the most part created by demand elsewhere: in most cases only alien capital and skills could give them commercial value. What tax was due to the indigenous owners of the soil? The only useful yardstick was what happened in comparable independent countries; and evidence provided by states such as Persia and the Latin American republics suggests that this would have been small simply because their bargaining power also was small. Independence enabled ex-colonies to impose stricter terms on foreign companies, but these were matched by the higher demands also made by previously independent states after 1945. If neither was able to undertake such complex economic operations on its own account, its demands were limited by the fact that Europeans might cease to operate altogether. In short the same principle applied as had always operated in the deserts of the Middle East and the Sudan: caravans passing through could be mulcted only to a certain point, beyond which they would use alternative routes.

It is impossible, therefore, to measure the 'profit' Europe gained from 'exploiting' the natural resources of her dependencies because they were formal colonies. By mid-twentieth-century standards Europeans showed a cavalier disregard for the interests of other societies, taking what was profitable and putting back only what was necessary. Yet this had little to do with political empire and was not limited to it. One-sided use of natural resources reflected an imbalance of power between the west and the non-industrialized areas of the world; and while this lasted no non-European society had sufficient bargaining power to impose fully equitable terms.

The last and most sophisticated way in which empires have been alleged to give economic profit was through the higher return Europeans could obtain by investing capital in colonies than they could get at home. This theory dated back at least to Adam Smith and the classical economists, who were concerned mainly with the advantages of applying capital to fertile land in settlement colonies rather than to marginal land in Europe. In its most influential form, however, the theory was based on the Marxist principle of 'surplus value', and turned on the greater profitability of using capital in tropical lands where labour was cheaper than in industrialized Europe. Lenin, for example, argued in 1916 that the growth of industrial monopoly and 'finance-capitalism' in western states created 'an enormous "superabundance of capital"'.[4] This could not profitably be invested at home without raising wage levels, and therefore reducing profits, simply because the labour supply could not be expanded. The rest of the world lacked capital but had ample labour and raw materials. European capital could generate a higher surplus value there than at home, and this enabled metropolitan capital to go on accumulating. If it could not go abroad, capital would stagnate and capitalism would crack. Lenin predicted that in course of time the non-industrial world would be entirely absorbed by European 'imperialists' (finance-capitalists), and that this would lead to wars for imperial redivision which would destroy capitalist society and usher in the socialist revolution.

Shorn of its ideological trimmings, Lenin's theory simply asserted that the combination of cheap labour, political power to make it work at subsistence wages, and commercial monopoly to exclude foreign rivals, generated excess profits for European empires. The desire for these advantages led to tropical colonization. Was he right?

He was wrong on one point at least, for, as has already been seen, it is impossible to explain the expansion of European empires after 1815 in terms of economic need: there simply was no correlation between the time-scale of European 'finance-capitalism' and imperial expansion, nor between colonies and areas of greatest investment. Yet, once empires existed, the question must be faced: did they provide higher profits for European capital than could have been obtained in Europe or in independent foreign states?

This is the most difficult of all questions to answer. A straight comparison between dividend rates on European and colonial investments is impossible since European rates were necessarily raised by the very possibility of investment overseas. The only useful comparison is between rates actually obtained in Europe and those gained in colonies and in foreign states.

After about 1880 the European public could make three main types of investment at home and overseas: government bonds with fixed interest rates; fixed interest debentures in privately owned companies operating public utilities such as railways, docks or power supplies; and risk stocks – equities – in private companies whose dividends depended on profits made. The first two were the most important. In 1913 known British overseas investments, including those outside the empire, divided in the ratio of 30 per cent government bonds, 46 per cent private transport and utility companies, and 24 per cent all other stocks. By 1934 the proportions had changed to 44, 30 and 26 per cent.[5]

The interest rates on government stocks are easiest to determine. The vital fact is that the margin between those issued by European and colonial governments (or on their behalf) was small, usually only about 0·5 per cent. The domestic rate of interest in France was fairly constant, around 3·0 per cent from the 1880s to 1914, and was normally about 3·5 per cent on colonial bonds.[6] British loans were much the largest and followed the same pattern. In 1905–9, for example, average interest on home loans (including yield on redemption) was 3·61 per cent. On colonial government stocks it was 3·94 per cent and on foreign loans 4·97 per cent.[7] Thus colonial governments, far from paying more because they were under metropolitan control, paid much less than foreign states because they were thought more safe by investors.

Privately owned public utility companies reflected the same influences. Colonial investments gave a slightly higher return than those at home, but markedly less than foreign ones. In 1907–8, for example, the average return on British domestic railway debentures was about 3·5 per cent. On Indian railway stock it was 3·87 per cent; on British colonial railways 4·0 per cent; on American railways 4·5 per cent and on other foreign railways 4·7 per cent.[8] French investors could obtain no more than 5 per cent on debentures in any private utility company operating in their overseas territories before 1914.[9]

Colonies, therefore, were not forced to give outrageous interest rates on public or semi-public gilt-edged investments: if they were 'exploited' in this way it must have been through the profits of risk capital engaged in other ventures. The test is to compare average profits of industrial and commercial firms operating within Europe with those in the colonies and in foreign states. If political power generated excessive profits, companies in the colonies should have given markedly larger dividends than those in Europe or elsewhere. Unfortunately it is quite impossible to answer this question with any precision, for there is inadequate evidence on company profits over a long enough time period to give a true picture: only tentative conclusions can be reached.

Investment in speculative ventures overseas was certainly very attractive to a minority of European investors; but this was partly because the domestic alternatives were particularly unattractive. European stock markets were not organized before 1914 to allow the small investor to take shares in companies operating at home. Few equity shares were available to the public because European firms normally obtained new capital from private funds, banks or their own profits rather than by offering shares for public subscription. Hence overseas companies producing gold, tin, rubber, etc., offered almost the only chance of getting large dividends and capital growth; the alternatives were low-yield fixed interest debentures. It is clear also that some colonial companies provided spectacular returns to those early investors who bought shares at their face value. For example the *Compagnie Française de l'Afrique Occidentale* never paid less than 20 per cent on its nominal capital from 1912 to 1919; British Malacca Rubber Plantations Ltd. paid dividends ranging from 10 to 75 per cent in the same years.[10] In 1907–8 British capital invested in diamonds and other precious stones paid an average interest of 30·5 per cent.[11] These were the rewards which attracted investors to this type of venture.

But they were also exceptional. There was no guarantee that a colonial enterprise would produce high profits simply because it was in a colony. Many investors lost all their money; others got no return for a decade or more while their companies overcame the vast initial problems of tropical enterprises. The British South Africa Company, for instance, paid no dividend from 1889 to 1923. Even established concerns normally paid moderate dividends. The annual yield of capital invested in the Witwatersrand gold mining companies between 1902 and 1932 varied from 4·08 per cent (in 1902) to a maximum of 11·82 per cent (in 1924) but was normally about 8 or 9 per cent.[12] In 1913 the average dividend on nineteen French companies operating entirely in French colonies was only 4·6 per cent.[13] Moreover, investors who bought stocks once these overseas companies were established had to pay more if good profits were being distributed: they could seldom get the same return as those who bought at the beginning.

Yet, even if it is conceded that some colonial investments gave a higher return on capital than equity shares within Europe, the vital question remains. Was this because imperial power created specially favourable conditions, or simply because normal economic factors – such as increasing demand for certain industrial raw materials and the products of tropical agriculture – specially favoured overseas ventures? Was there any difference between the profitability of companies in formal colonies and independent non-European states? The answer is almost certainly that formal empire had little relevance; and for this there were two good reasons.

First, the advantages which Lenin thought European capital engaged in the colonies received from imperial political power were in fact of little significance. Labour was certainly cheap by European standards: otherwise many of these enterprises would have been unprofitable. But low wages were not created by political power: they reflected the social environment of a subsistence economy. In the period before about 1906 many colonial governments provided forced or semi-forced labour; but this was also a period of generally low company profits. Thereafter colonial governments tended to impose restrictions on labour contracts and conditions of work, both tending to raise labour costs. Europeans could have 'exploited' native labour more effectively if they had not been policed by imperial administrations sensitive to humanitarian public opinion at home, and they often did so in independent Latin America and the Middle East. Nor did empire provide a degree of commercial monopoly sufficient to enable capitalists to sell at monopolistic prices at home or in the colonies. European investors showed no marked preference for their own colonies, and often got higher returns by operating in foreign empires. Conversely, the really artificial prices were those set by agreement between companies of different nationalities, especially the oil companies, which transcended imperial systems. Thus, while colonial governments often provided a convenient framework of political security within which private companies could work satisfactorily, formal empire was in no sense necessary for profitable European activity overseas.

Second, the relative profitability of investment in Europe and in tropical dependencies was determined by many complex factors and varied immensely from time to time. Changing economic and political conditions within Europe sometimes encouraged investment at home, sometimes overseas. Another important influence was the relative demand for the products of the advanced economics and those of primary producing countries, in which a large proportion of 'colonial' investment was made. When the terms of trade favoured primary producers, investment in tropical colonies was obviously more profitable than when the terms favoured manufacturing states. During the half century before 1914 European demand for minerals, tropical vegetable oils and food increased considerably, and the terms of trade normally favoured primary producers. This enabled the more fortunate European companies producing such goods to make spectacular profits. Between 1914 and 1939, however, the terms of trade normally favoured industrial producers, with the result that the relative advantage of investing in primary-producing countries was less. After 1939 the war and post-war demand for primary products again favoured the overseas investor, though by the later 1950s his advantage was declining. Such trends cannot confidently be translated into statistics, but some indication of their importance can be gained from estimates of the relative percentage rate of profit gained from investment in industrial concerns operating in Britian and in British companies operating overseas between 1953 and 1961. In 1953 British industrialists made an average net profit of 12·5 per cent on their capital (ordinary capital plus capital and revenue reserves), as against 21·5 per cent from overseas companies. In 1961 British industrials were yielding 12·4 per cent but overseas companies only 13·7 per cent. In the same years the terms of trade, taking 1937–8 as 100, had moved in Britain's favour from 119 to 103.[14]

Such figures are far too limited to prove anything; but they do suggest, in conjunction with other evidence, that the profitability of investment in primary-producing non-European economics, many of which were colonies, depended more on international economic factors than on the special advantages which Lenin thought colonies provided for their masters. By comparison the political status of non-industrialized countries was of little importance, and empire could not of itself generate super-profit for European capital.

It is, in fact, impossible to state whether or not colonies were more profitable for European investors than their own countries or foreign states: only generalizations are safe. Some colonial areas offered high profits because of their natural endowments, but they would have been equally advantageous as independent states. If Europe benefited economically from other parts of the world by 'exploiting' them, it was because of her immense military and economic preponderance. Empire in the formal sense was merely one form in which this was expressed, and had no colonial empires been created in the nineteenth century Europe would still have taken whatever economic assets she needed and dictated the terms on which she did so. By 1964 formal empire was practically over: yet still the advanced western economies were able to dictate to the 'developing' countries, and western capital was even more essential to their development. The balance of advantage may at all times have been unequal, but this was the result of more being added to those that already had the advantage.

One relevant consideration remains. Even if the expansion of Europe brought economic advantage to investors, traders and exporters, these were private interests: it does not follow that European states as a whole benefited correspondingly. Adam Smith had insisted in 1776 that the private profit generated by imperial monopoly was outweighed by the ancillary cost of empire to the state. This may have been equally true of the modern empires. The advantages the states of Europe obtained from political empire were often non-economic: the use of colonial armies as a support for their international power; strategic bases and ports; prestige at international gatherings; employment opportunities for their subjects. These were difficult to quantify in financial terms; but the costs of empire were tangible, and might outweigh advantages. Military occupation, defence against foreign attack, subsidies for colonial budgets, provision of special services, loans on charitable terms, grants-in-aid, all constituted a heavy burden on the imperial taxpayer. They have to be added to private losses resulting from bad speculative investments; the greatly reduced value of capital invested in fixed-interest government stock and company debentures after the two great post-1914 inflations; and the artificially high prices paid by the metropolitan consumer as a result of imperial preferences. In the imperial balance sheet such public and private losses have to be set against the advantages of empire.

In fact, no meaningful balance sheet can be constructed, even in economic terms. One or two small or short-lived empires almost certainly cost their owners more than they repaid. Certainly the German and Italian empires did so, because their colonies lacked natural resources, and because they were in any case destroyed before high initial expenditure could be written off against long-term advantages. All other empires were too complex for such definite verdicts to be made. Most colonies were 'unprofitable' during the period of initial conquest and while later internal rebellions lasted. But there were few such expenses between about 1920 and 1939; and apart from obvious metropolitan expenditure (grants-in-aid, payment for services in particular colonies, etc.) the cost of colonies depends on what proportion of total imperial expenditure (on defence, for example) is debited to them. Hence no one can determine whether the accounts of empire ultimately closed with a favourable cash balance.

This is unimportant, for the value of the colonial empires was not to be measured in money. Colonies were seldom deliberately acquired to produce wealth, and they were retained irrespective of their 'profitability'. Empire in the modern period was the product of European power: its reward was power or the sense of power. The end of empire did not mean economic loss to the one-time imperial states: on the contrary, it meant that the economic advantage of operating in other parts of the world was no longer offset by the cost and inconvenience of political responsibilities. Only the minority of private investors and others, whose assets or business concerns were hampered, destroyed, or taken over without proper compensation by the new states, actually lost through decolonization. The west retained its economic preponderance: some even held that the margin of wealth between advanced and 'developing' countries widened as empire ended. If Europe in fact derived her wealth from her colonies, their loss made remarkably little difference to her.

Yet the west undoubtedly suffered from the end of empire, for Europe and America lost some part of their political power and self-assurance. The world no longer consisted of colonies unable to complicate international politics: the United Nations provided a forum in which the new states could challenge overwhelming power by appealing to alleged moral standards and the principle of one state one vote. The powers were no longer free to use their military power to support their interests: the

Suez crisis of 1956–7 marked the end of 'informal empire' in its nineteenth-century form. The world was no longer ringed by the western bases and colonial armies which had enabled it to impose its will on all continents. Europeans had lost the freedom of movement and economic activity which empire had given them. They were now dependent on a multiplicity of small and often chauvinistic states who needed western enterprise but also resented it and complicated its operations. But above all the end of empire deprived the west of status. The countries of Europe were no poorer than they had been before, but they were infinitely smaller. They had been the centres of vast empires: now they were petty states preoccupied with parochial problems. Dominion had gone and with it the grandeur which was one of its main rewards.

17

Epilogue: Decolonization and After, 1945–81

Nothing in the history of the modern colonial empires was more remarkable than the speed with which they disappeared. In 1939 they were at their peak: by 1981 they had practically ceased to exist. This was the more surprising because none of the classical explanations seemed to apply. When the original American colonies demanded independence they had had from one and a half to three centuries in which to evolve as mature societies, conscious of their separate identity. Most colonies in Africa, Asia and the Pacific which achieved independence after 1945 were annexed only in the last decades of the nineteenth century, and few looked like proto-nation states in 1939. Nor were the great imperial powers deprived of their colonies by victorious enemies, as Germany was in 1919. Italy lost some of her colonies during and after the Second World War, and Japan lost all her possessions. But Britain, France, the United States, Belgium, and Holland were victors in 1945, and Spain and Portugal had been neutrals. Most significant of all, the end of empire cannot be explained in terms of the decadence of the imperial powers. Europe and America were relatively richer and more powerful in the mid-twentieth century than ever before, and decolonization was not evidence of decline in the west. Why, then, did it take place?

It is impossible as yet to give a satisfactory answer, for the events are too recent and have not been fully studied. Moreover no one explanation fits all cases, for decolonization had roots as various as the colonial territories. It is possible only to indicate factors which appear to have been generally influential, and which at the same time throw most light on the character of European colonialism in its last phase.

The disintegration of an empire always has two components – a demand by the subject people for independence and the inability or unwillingness of the imperial power to resist it. Which of these was more important in the period after 1945?

There is no doubt that colonial demands for independence were in many places very strong: the difficulty is to discover their roots. They were certainly not the same in the modern tropical dependencies as they had been in the old settlement colonies of America and Australasia, for these had a natural affinity with their parent states derived from common race, language, religion, and culture. Though habitually disobedient, European settlers were also instinctively loyal. The greed, incompetence or arrogance of the metropolis might strain this loyalty; in course of time awareness that colonial interests were diverging from those of the parent state led to demands for greater devolution of authority within the imperial system. But colonies were likely to demand full independence only if such grievances were not remedied, or if some extraordinary strain, such as isolation from Europe during the Napoleonic wars, was placed on the imperial relationship. Conversely, if an imperial power admitted the reasonableness of colonial demands, it was often possible to avoid total separation. Thus the British self-governing colonies of the nineteenth century became Dominions – sovereign states, yet closely linked to Britain and each other in the Commonwealth. Alternatively, France, Portugal, Spain and the United States were able fully to incorporate some at least of their colonies into their metropolitan constitutional systems, evading the problem of colonial independence altogether. In short, the 'nationalism' of a settler colony was not necessarily incompatible with empire. Association implied no indignity or tyranny: in the mid-twentieth century Canada was no less a nation than the United States because part of the Commonwealth and still subject in certain respects to the British parliament.

Little of this applied to the non-European tropical dependencies which formed the bulk of the modern empires. Unless they had substantial settler minorities they had no necessary community of interest with their masters. Centuries of alien rule might naturalize certain European institutions, implant Christianity, influence habits of mind; but only rarely did they transmute subjects into quasi-Europeans. Tropical empire was based on power. It might be beneficial; it certainly depended for its continuance on at least tacit approval and support from the majority of the subject people. But it could never take colonial loyalty for granted, for it remained alien and its roots were shallow.

It should therefore have caused Europe no surprise that the tropical dependencies ultimately became conscious of having little in common with their masters and demanded independence as nation states. Yet colonial nationalism did in fact surprise the imperial powers in the twentieth century. They were familiar with nationalism in Europe; but they associated it only with relatively small and ethnically homogeneous countries like Italy, Greece, the Balkan states, Poland and Czechoslovakia, and they regarded it as a specifically European phenomenon. Few colonies had any natural unity: most were artifacts created by European statesmen or colonial administrators, without common histories, religions, languages or cultures. For these reasons, and also because they were reluctant to recognize their existence, European states for long minimized the importance of nationalist movements in their colonies. The British had to admit that nationalism was a significant force in India and Ceylon by the 1920s, but in most other places they and other European powers did not take it seriously until after 1945. Thereafter they were surprised by the speed of developments only because they had previously turned blind eyes to what was clearly evident.

Colonial nationalism undoubtedly existed as a growing protest against alien rule; but what were its roots? There are three broad alternative explanations. It may have existed continuously from the moment of occupation; it may have been artificially injected by the infusion of European ideas and practices; or it may have been the product of fundamental changes in colonial society during the period of occupation.

Evidence can be found to support each interpretation. In many places nationalism, in the sense of hostility to alien rule, certainly existed from the beginning, and was expressed in strong initial resistance to effective occupation by Europeans and later in major rebellions. Such resistance was common wherever there were advanced non-Christian religions and non-European cultures – in Islamic North and West Africa, in India, Indo-China and China; but it occurred also in 'pagan' Africa, usually where indigenous states were strong – in Dahomey, Ashanti, Zululand and Matabeleland, or where religious leaders stirred up resistance over an area transcending tribal boundaries, as in the Maji-Maji rebellion in German East Africa. In some colonies this initial hostility survived crushing military defeat, erupting into major rebellions and possibly providing a nucleus for later nationalist movements. But elsewhere initial defeat seemed entirely to eradicate it; and this makes it impossible to generalize. All that seems certain is that resentment against European rule was most enduring in societies with advanced religions and cultures, because there the destruction of indigenous political authorities and institutions did not destroy the main focus of common interest. Yet even where it survived, such indigenous nationalism was never strong enough to unseat colonial rulers so long as it was expressed in traditional forms. The Indian Mutiny of 1857 demonstrated conclusively that hereditary *élites*, once subordinated to alien rule, could not provide the spearhead of successful rebellion, and other colonial dependencies had the same experience. If, therefore, colonial nationalism was as old as colonial occupation, in the modern period it could be effective only by adopting totally new forms of expression.

There is a strong case, also, for seeing the roots of nationalism in the impact of alien ideas and practices which, by infecting dependencies with European ideals of liberty and equality, made them resent subordination. There is no doubt that the easiest dependency to rule was one whose hereditary rulers became willing collaborators, acting as middlemen between their subjects and the alien power. One advantage of indirect rule was that it preserved such hierarchical systems and thus obstructed the growth of liberal and democratic concepts among the masses. Conversely the need for every imperial power to train an indigenous *élite* to serve in the administration was a solvent of stability, for few Europeans could envisage advanced education other than in their own language and using their own concepts; so that the educated *élite* were necessarily imbued with European ideas. Some they rejected; but those they adopted were often incompatible with alien rule: for example, equality before the law in colonies with different legal systems for Europeans and others; the principle of parliamentary elections, where there was no representative legislature; and the right of national self-determination. Once such ideas were fairly grafted they invariably stimulated nationalist movements, normally led by the minority of *evolués* – indigenous peoples who had left their own traditional social groups but found themselves excluded from the preserves of the white man. Personal ambition and idealism combined to give urgency to their demands; although they were seldom able to persuade an area as vast as Nigeria or India that it was a united nation, they found a substitute in the argument that subject peoples were at least united in common subjection and in racial difference from their masters. On this basis they were able to create mass parties in most colonies which were pledged first to greater self-government and ultimately to independence.

Yet, in many ways, this is an unsatisfactory explanation of the strength of colonial nationalism, at least in countries like India which pioneered the demand for independence. Because they were seldom traditional leaders and because their political concepts were alien, many colonial politicians found it difficult to arouse general support: where they could do so effectively a further explanation may be necessary. It is, in fact, possible that modern nationalism became powerful because fundamental changes had taken place in certain dependencies since they were first occupied, destroying the conditions which had made alien rule practicable. European occupation eventually affected most aspects of colonial life. Large-scale manufactures and mining produced urban agglomerations and therefore a new rootless proletariat. Changes in the class structure created a new balance of interests, often unfavourable to indigenous agents of imperial rule. Growing populations often led to land-hunger and resentment. Better communications broke down the isolation of tribal communities. Religious revivals strengthened awareness of the difference between Europeans and subjects. In short, social changes of these and other kinds may, in many if not most places, have generated increasing resentment at many aspects of alien rule, not necessarily because it was alien, but because the imperial power was associated with conditions which the masses now wanted to change. Ultimately it was shrugged off as part of a rejected *ancien régime*.

None of these explanations is completely or generally satisfactory. It is seldom possible to trace continuous hostility to alien rule throughout the colonial period. Few colonies acquired in the later nineteenth century had undergone fundamental social changes by 1939; most seemed all too static. In the years after 1950 many colonial politicians were clearly copying other nationalist leaders and adopting their ideas rather than creating their own or expressing deep-seated national desires. Yet, where two or more of these influences coincided, as they did in India, Indonesia, Indo-China and parts of Islamic Africa, strong movements for independence grew first and became most powerful. India, with a large class of men educated in European principles, with strong religious and cultural traditions and social changes reflecting a century and a half of British rule, played the same role as pioneer and pace-setter for the modern tropical empires as the United States did for the first American colonies and Canada for the nineteenth-century British settlement colonies. India might succeed where other weaker dependencies could not: but the concessions she extracted before 1939 and the independence she gained in 1947 were proof that colonial nationalism was a force which could no longer be ignored.

Colonial demands for self-government or full independence were a challenge to Europe: but it is wrong to assume that the imperial powers were necessarily unable to meet and reject the challenge. Empire would be destroyed only if the forces of nationalism proved too strong to resist, or if the imperial powers changed their attitudes and refused to struggle. Was decolonization the result of Europe's inability to maintain its power or of her declining will to do so?

It is unlikely that any European state could indefinitely have controlled its larger dependencies, once hostility became general, unless it had the support of a strong settler community, as in Algeria, Kenya, Rhodesia and South Africa. But the question is largely academic: no dependency was ever entirely hostile; no European state ever employed all its resources in repressing a colony. The important question was how much a dependency was worth to the metropolis, and so what effort it was prepared to make to retain it. In fact, Europe emancipated most of her colonies long before she was forced to do so; and this can be explained only by considering the purposes for which colonies were occupied and held and the changing moral climate of the west after about 1930.

The essential feature of many tropical colonies was that full occupation and government were an unwelcome concomitant of strictly limited interests – strategic, diplomatic, commercial or moral. Process of time often made even these original functions irrelevant: for example, Britain no longer had a substantial interest in East Africa once there was no German or French threat to her power in the Indian Ocean or in Egypt. Sometimes, of course, new functions replaced the old: some colonies which were acquired for strategic purposes blossomed into producers of oil, minerals or tropical raw materials. But even these did not necessarily make full imperial control essential, for a stable successor state might provide an effective political framework for economic activity, and decolonization would relieve the metropolis of administrative burdens.

It was therefore by no means certain that, in the last resort, European states would resist nationalist demands for self-government: if they considered the question rationally they might even encourage them. At the same time concessions were likely to be made slowly. The habit of power, the assumption that Europeans could supply better government than their subjects, concern for minority interests, fear that colonies could not maintain the complex political and economic systems created by the west; all tended to breed distrust of nationalist demands and encouraged delaying action. Yet, by 1939 co-operation in government was far advanced in India and Ceylon; it was developing, though more slowly, in Indonesia, and concessions were being made in other places whose nationalist movements were still embryonic. The British were the most ready to admit that a dependency was entitled to self-government once it had proved its fitness, for the evolution of the Dominions since the 1840s provided a model for constitutional advance: others were slower to accept evidence of political capacity in their dependencies and slower still to foster it. In any case Europe still felt confident that it could control the timetable of transferring power. Even to liberals there seemed to be an infinity of time and a multitude of intermediate stages before colonies were likely to become autonomous.

Why, then, did the empires fall like a pack of cards after 1945? The explanation lies in two closely related influences. The first was the Second World War, which had an effect on many tropical colonies comparable with that of the Napoleonic wars on the Spanish and Portuguese colonies in America. From 1940 to 1945 France, Belgium and Holland were cut off from their dependencies: coincidentally Japan occupied all European possessions in the east to the borders of India and northern New Guinea. Had these been settler colonies they would have looked forward to reunion with their parent states: since they were not, many nationalists welcomed the Japanese as liberators; and even when reaction against them developed it was focussed on the desire for full independence after Japan was defeated rather than a return to empire. When allied forces reoccupied these dependencies in 1945 France and Holland found it impossible to reconstitute full colonial rule: even in Burma the British found the desire for independence so strong that they conceded it in 1948. Thus the Japanese occupation finally destroyed the already weakened foundations of European power in South-East Asia.

Other parts of the colonial world were less catastrophically affected by the war, for even in French and Belgian territories colonial government continued in isolation from the metropolis.

Yet everywhere the war changed the climate of opinion. In India Congress opposed co-operation with Britain and extracted a firm promise of independence once the war was over. Ceylon also was promised internal self-government. Allied defeats and then the Anglo-American occupation stimulated nationalists throughout Islamic North Africa; and in tropical Africa greatly increased contacts with the outside world and knowledge of European defeats encouraged criticism of colonial régimes. Thus, while Europe retained political control over all dependencies outside South-East Asia in 1945 and could still decide whether or not to make concessions, the task was now considerably harder. The question was whether the imperial powers had sufficient determination to face the moral and physical cost of fighting a rearguard action against colonial nationalists.

The second and more important consequence of the war was that it brought about a fundamental change in European attitudes to empire and weakened the will to rule. In the 1930s believers in empire were already on the defensive against denunciations of 'imperialism' by Marxists and the left; they reacted by liberalizing administrative practices and taking a stand on the doctrine of trusteeship. But empire still seemed morally justifiable, provided its methods conformed to advancing standards. The war changed this self-confidence. Italian and Japanese conquests before 1939 had seemed immoral; German imperialism within Europe aroused horror. Wartime idealism, typified by United States interpretation of the Atlantic Charter, and recognition that many colonies were contributing to the allied war effort generated criticism of colonial régimes and readiness to make major changes after the war. The rise to world dominance of the United States and Russia – the two professedly anti-colonial powers, the creation of the United Nations as a forum for international opinion on colonial matters and the active investigations undertaken by its Trusteeship Council (replacing the far less critical Mandates Commission of the League) combined to put all imperial powers on the defensive.

For these and other reasons the attitude of Europe to its tropical colonies changed rapidly after 1945. There was no sudden determination to liberate them; but it began to be admitted that most would ultimately have to be given self-government. The question was how complete this would be and how soon it would come. The problem was largely confined to Africa, the West Indies, Malaya and the Pacific islands, for the British were committed to full independence for India, Ceylon and Burma, and neither France nor Holland succeeded in re-imposing full control over their eastern dependencies. Caribbean colonies were certain to be given political concessions because of their relative sophistication; Tunisia and Morocco as protected states were clearly destined for full self-government; but it seemed very unlikely that the tropical colonies in Africa, the Indian Ocean or the Pacific would gain independence or even full autonomy in the foreseeable future. In most of them nationalist parties were weak and few possessed sufficient men of political or administrative experience to run government on western lines. European policy in the decade after 1945 was therefore to concede power rapidly in the more advanced dependencies, but to prepare the rest for self-government during a long period of apprenticeship. Had this timetable been maintained few if any colonies in tropical Africa or the Pacific would have achieved more than self-government under restraint, such as the British settlement colonies had before 1914, by the middle 1960s.

In fact this timetable was torn up: during the 1950s the retreat from empire changed from a measured crawl to an uncontrolled gallop. Dogmatism is impossible, but it seems likely that the reason lay in two interacting developments. On the one hand an increasing number in Britain, France and other western countries (Portugal and Spain only excepted) gradually adopted the view that 'colonialism' was morally undesirable and should be ended as soon as possible. They even rejected the traditional claim of white minorities in 'mixed' colonies to predominate by virtue of superior capacity. On the other hand the rapid growth of mass nationalist parties in many colonies made colonial government an ever-increasing nuisance to the powers. Liberals were appalled at the measures taken to suppress sedition, and even those who believed that a long period of political apprenticeship was necessary in the interests of the colonial peoples themselves began to think that the price of retaining power in the interim was becoming too high. Moreover decolonization was a cumulative process: the liberation of one territory stimulated demands in others and at the same time often made it pointless for the imperial powers to hold them. Thus the independence of India in 1947 and the evacuation of the Suez Canal military base in 1956 automatically destroyed most of the interest Britain had previously had both in East Africa and South-East Asia. Empires had to some extent formed interlocking systems: when some parts were removed many others lost their imperial functions.

These were the roots of decolonization after 1945. It is not always possible to give a precise date at which a colonial territory became 'independent' because there were many intermediate steps between full subjection and total sovereignty. In the following chronological survey the criterion used is the acquisition of full internal self-government by a dependency coupled with freedom to sever any remaining links with the metropolis – as in foreign relations and defence – at its own choice.

The twenty years after 1945 divide into two parts. Before 1950 Europe released only those dependencies which had been on the verge of independence in 1939 or were able to demand it as a direct result of the Second World War. During the second phase, which began in about 1956, the majority of the remaining dependencies were released, although in 1945 most of these had seemed unlikely to be fitted for independence within a generation or more. During the first period most of the new states were in the Islamic Middle East or in the east; thereafter the majority were in Africa.

For four years after 1945 the speed of decolonization was breathtaking. In 1946 the Philippines became a sovereign state and Jordan and Syria ceased to be British or French mandates. In 1947 India and Pakistan became independent as members of the Commonwealth. Ceylon followed their example in 1948; but Burma, who became independent in the same year, did not accept membership and Israel, throwing off the British mandate, was not offered it. In 1949 the Netherlands recognized the sovereign independence of Indonesia, but continued until 1956 to hope for close political relations with her. In 1949 France conceded sovereignty to Laos, Cambodia and Vietnam (Annam and Tongking); but these remained within the French Union until France finally lost power in Indo-China in 1954.

Apart from the liberation of Libya in 1951, which had been under British and French military control since its conquest from Italy during the war, there now followed a pause. Europe was not yet convinced that empire was morally objectionable and the problems of multi-racial societies in Algeria, Central Africa and Kenya complicated matters. Most powers therefore tried to temper nationalist demands with judicious concessions. The second phase began tentatively in 1956, when Morocco and Tunisia denounced their relationships with France and left the Union. In the same year Britain evacuated the Egyptian Sudan, and in 1957 Malaya became a sovereign state within the Commonwealth, though Singapore, North Borneo and Sarawak did not join it until 1963 as part of the new Federation of Malaysia. None of these concessions was really surprising, since all were Islamic states which had retained varying degrees of autonomy as French or British protectorates. The crucial event which marked the beginning of the last phase of decolonization and showed that Europe's will to rule was cracking was the independence of the Gold Coast – renamed Ghana – in 1957. This was the first 'pagan' dependency to become entirely free: a tropical African colony which lacked natural unity and had possessed no sort of autonomy in 1945. It owed its primacy partly to its economic wealth but even more to the political skill of Kwame Nkrumah, leader of the main nationalist party, who made it intolerable for Britain to retain power. His appointment as prime minister in 1951 was an epoch-making event, for it stimulated nationalist movements throughout Africa; and Ghana's independence in 1957 pointed to general decolonization. The next major step was taken by France, who abolished the 1946 Union in 1958 and gave all dependencies the option of full independence or sovereignty within the new French Community. French Guinea alone opted for the first and became independent in 1958. The remainder achieved independence in 1960 when the Community was dissolved.

1960 proved the most important year in the period of decolonization, for the greater part of the French empire then became independent. The federations of West and Equatorial Africa split up into a multiplicity of sovereign states, though many retained special links with France and each other: Ivory Coast, Dahomey, Upper Volta, Senegal, Mauritania, Niger, Mali, Gabon, Central African Republic and Chad. Togo and Cameroun, both trust territories, also became independent, the latter including the area previously administered by Britain. Madagascar became independent as the Malagasy Republic. In 1960 also Britain liberated Nigeria; British and Italian Somaliland were fused in the Somali Republic; and the Belgian Congo became independent. Thereafter the 'wind of change' continued to blow strongly. In 1961 Britain ended her control over Cyprus, Sierra Leone, Tanganyika and Kuwait; in 1962 she freed Jamaica, Trinidad and Tobago (following the collapse of the non-independent West Indian Federation set up in 1957), and Uganda. In the same year France ended her long war in Algeria and granted full independence. In 1963 Britain liberated Zanzibar and Kenya: significantly Kenya became an African state in which the once influential British settler community was merely a tolerated minority. The same rejection of the claims of Europeans to rule African majorities was shown by the dissolution of the Federation of Rhodesia and Nyasaland at the end of 1963, and this was followed by independence for Nyasaland (Malawi) and Northern Rhodesia (Zambia) in 1964. Rhodesia remained a British dependency, and was not likely to be given independence until her constitution satisfied the African majority that they would ultimately gain political power. In 1964 also Britain made Malta independent. Since this was against the will of many Maltese it showed that the British were now anxious to wind up the remnants of their empire as quickly as possible.

1965 proved a pivotal point in the history of decolonization, the end of the first and main stage, during which the major imperial states which were democracies had accepted and acted on the principle that the colonies were entitled to independence once they showed clear evidence that they wanted and might be able to sustain it. For Britain, France, the Netherlands and the

United States it remained only to tidy up the loose ends of empire.

But for Spain and Portugal decolonization still lay in the future. In those highly conservative societies with authoritarian régimes the ideological influences which had made the democracies susceptible to the claims of colonial nationalists had made little impact. Portugal, in particular, was still talking in 1965 of suppressing rebel movements and completing the assimilation of Portugese Africa with the metropolis. Ten years later both Iberian states had lost their African possessions. In part this transformation was caused by the rising economic and political cost to Portugal of suppressing revolutionary movements, particularly in Guinea-Bissau and in Mozambique, where the Marxist-dominated Frelimo party had a firm grip on the northern region. But it was inconceivable that Salazar's Portugal could have been compelled to evacuate Angola, whose economic potential was considerable, the nationalist forces weak and divided and the white settler population considerable. In the event it was revolution at home rather than in the colonies that destroyed the Portuguese empire. The military coup in Lisbon on 25 April 1974 resulted in government by a left-wing military junta which quickly accepted General Antónia de Spínola's recent assertion that there was no possibility of permanent military victory in Portuguese Africa. So, much as the Labour party's victory in Britain in 1945 had led to the quick evacuation of India and General de Gaulle's coming to power in France in 1958 to the dissolution of the French Union, political change in Portugal was primarily responsible for the end of her overseas empire.

The process of decolonization after 1965 can now be summarized. For Britain, the question of what to do about the many smaller colonial dependencies had been foreseen long before but still no clear or generally applicable solution had been found. Between 1956 and 1967 there was support in London for creating a new status, lying between that of colony and sovereign state, to which the name 'Associated State' was given. Such ex-colonies would have full internal autonomy but would still be possessions of the British Crown. Their defence and foreign policy would be a British responsibility and they would not be full members of the Commonwealth, so keeping down the numbers attending Prime Ministers Conferences. In 1967 the smaller members of the defunct West Indian Federation were given this status; but the idea was discredited by the early 1970s on two counts: it did not give Britain immunity against critics of colonialism, notably the UN Committee of Twenty-four; and Britain might still find herself involved in an island's domestic affairs, as in the case of Anguilla, which, though part of the St. Kitts–Nevis–Anguilla Associated State, immediately rejected rule from St. Kitts and had to be given special British administrators. As a result it was decided that all the remaining colonies must make a straight choice between remaining full colonies with internal autonomy and being granted full sovereignty.

By 1981 almost all the remaining colonies had chosen sovereignty. The chronology of the transfer of power was as follows: in 1965 The Gambia and the Maldive Islands; in 1966 British Guiana (Guyana), Bechuanaland (Botswana), Basutoland (Lesotho) and Barbados; in 1967 Aden Colony and Protectorate (the Peoples Republic of Yemen); in 1968 Nauru, Mauritius and Swaziland; in 1970 Tonga and Fiji; in 1973 the Bahamas; in 1974 Grenada (one of the Associated States of 1967, followed into full independence by Dominica in 1978, St. Lucia and St. Vincent in 1979, and Antigua in 1981, leaving St. Kitts–Nevis as the sole remaining example of the genre); in 1976 the Seychelles; in 1978 the Ellice Islands (Tuvala), now separated from the Gilbert Islands, and the Solomon Islands; in 1979 the Gilbert Islands (Kirabati). Finally, in 1980, two of the dependencies which had always caused problems – the New Hebrides and Southern Rhodesia – were disposed of. The former, under a very unsatisfactory condominium with France since 1906, was eventually, and after internal disagreement had seemed likely to hold matters up, made independent in July and became Vanuatu. Meantime in March the British government, considerably helped by pressure by other African states on the belligerents in the Rhodesian civil war, was able to establish at least notional imperial authority there for a few weeks in order to hold a general election and go through the motions of transferring power legitimately to the victorious Robert Mugabe and his Zanu party. Since Rhodesia had appeared to be an insoluble imperial problem for a decade and a half, its independence as Zimbabwe marks the final success of decolonization in the British colonial empire.

Thereafter Britain was left with only one colony of any significance, Hong Kong, whose potential evolution to independence was blocked by China's claim to ultimate sovereignty. The other remaining territories were very small in size, population and importance; and, although it was no longer wise to say of even the smallest rock that it could not be liberated because it would not be viable as a sovereign state, it did seem improbable that Britain could ever rid herself entirely of all these places. In the Caribbean Bermuda seemed likely to become independent sooner or later and British Honduras (Belize) was given independence in 1981, despite territorial claims by neighbouring Guatemala. The rest seemed destined to remain dependencies: Anguilla, Ascension, British Ocean Territories (uninhabited), the British Virgin Islands, Cayman Island, Montserrat, Pitcairn, St. Helena, Tristan da Cunha, Turks and Caicos Islands, the Falkland Islands (claimed by Argentina) and Gibraltar (at issue between Britain and Spain).

Other western imperial states had reached the end of their colonial eras before then. For France there was little change after 1960. The incorporation of one-time colonies, by their own choice, with the metropolis as Overseas Departments proved durable; and in 1976 the small islands off Newfoundland, St. Pierre et Miquelon, were added to the list. Between 1975 and 1977 they received an average of $3240 per capita in subsidies from the metropolis, the highest figure recorded by the UN. Mayotte, one of the Comoro Islands off Madagascar, which, with a predominantly Catholic population, preferred not to stay with the rest of the group when it became independent in 1976, was made a *collectivité particulière* and was expected to become an Overseas Department in the early 1980s. Of the remaining Overseas Territories, New Caledonia and Polynesia were given greater autonomy in 1976 and 1977 respectively and seemed likely eventually to become Overseas Departments. But two dependencies decided to go the other way. In 1976 the Comoro Islands became independent, following a referendum in 1974. In 1977 French Somaliland also became independent and adopted the name Djibouti. Thus by 1981 the French overseas empire had almost completed the transition mapped out for it in 1960.

The Netherlands ceased to be an imperial power in 1975. The Netherlands Antilles were fully incorporated into the Kingdom of the Netherlands; but Surinam became an independent republic in November 1975, after fierce disagreement internally between creoles and East Indians, on the understanding that its inhabitants could opt for Dutch or Suriname (as it was now spelt) citizenship. By then Spain also had wound up her empire. The Canary and Balearic Islands remained incorporated as part of the metropolis. Rio Muni and Fernando Po joined to form the independent republic of Equatorial Guinea in 1968. Ifni was ceded to Morocco in 1969; and in 1975 Spain agreed with Morocco and Mauritania that the Spanish Sahara should be divided between them. Spain withdrew after partition in 1976; but Mauritania then withdrew in favour of Morocco, leaving her to struggle with the Polisario nationalists who, with Algerian support, continued to fight for independence.

Thus by about 1970 Portugal was the only western state which still wanted to retain its overseas possessions. By 1976 she had only one, the tiny island of Macao off Canton, together with the Azores and Madeira Islands, long incorporated into the metropolis. Perhaps only Belgium had undertaken decolonization as abruptly; and there are analogies between the consequential chaos in Zaire and Angola. The Portuguese revolution of 1974 resulted in the repeal of that part of the 1933 constitution which had forbidden the surrender of any overseas possession; and between October 1974 and November 1975 Guinea-Bissau, Mozambique, Cape Verde, São Tomé and Príncipe and Angola, in that order, were given full independence. By coincidence Portugal also lost East Timor, in the Indonesian archipelago, within the next year. The Indonesian army occupied the colony in December 1975 on the grounds of endemic civil war there and formally annexed it to the Indonesian Republic in July 1976.

By the early 1980s decolonization by the west European states had resulted in a paradoxical situation in geopolitics. The two greatest powers, America and Russia, which had long denounced imperialism as practised by other states and had done much to ensure that these gave up their possessions after 1945, were now the only surviving imperial powers.

In terms of formal possessions, America gave up less than any other western power. Porto Rico remained a Commonwealth under her control and the Virgin Islands were still colonies in all but name, administered by the Department of the Interior from 1970. In the Pacific, Guam and Samoa remained 'unincorporated territories', even though New Zealand had liberated her part of the Samoan group. The ex-Japanese Trust Territories (Truk, Ponape, the Marshall Islands, Palau, the Marianas and Yap) were still under American rule. For their part the Russians had continued to assimilate their pre-1914 Asian dependencies and those eastern European territories taken in 1945, while confidently asserting that a socialist state could not be imperialist.

Far more significant in each case was the extent of informal empire. By the 1980s the Americans were no longer the hegemonic world power they had been in the decade after 1945. They had met military and political disaster in Vietnam between 1960 and 1973; they had failed to prevent the deposition of the Shah of Iran; they could no longer regard the Pacific, the Mediterranean and the Persian Gulf as American lakes; and western Europe had, with American help, re-emerged as a world power. The Russians, also, had lost ground. Their control over eastern Europe was less unconditional. China had rejected Russian influence and had become perhaps her most serious enemy. Yet, as the one-time colonial empires of Europe became past history and their owners declined into the ruck of middle-rank powers, the reality of the new world system was that these two superpowers could largely determine the course of world development. The consequences of decolonization by others depended largely on how these powers treated the multitude of small or very small states into which the colonial empires had disintegrated.

By the 1980s it was beginning to be possible for historians to sort out the consequences of decolonization, particularly for those dependencies which had been liberated first, in the two decades after 1945. Some of the most important of these effects can be summarized under four heads: the new international system; ideological effects; political developments in the new states; and the economic consequences.

On the face of it, decolonization fundamentally changed the international system. Before 1945 the world had been dominated by a small number of imperial states who, between them, ruled or controlled virtually all Africa, the Middle East, South and South-east Asia, and the Pacific. In 1939 the League of Nations had only 57 members; in 1981 the United Nations had 153. This was the most important formal change in modern world politics, implying a dramatic diffusion of political power and the demotion of one-time first-rank states, much of whose importance derived from their imperial possessions. Britain, for example, was forced to give up her role as a power east of Suez in the 1960s, mainly because the loss of India meant that Britain would have had to bear the full and intolerable cost. Like France, she became a regional, not a world power.

The obverse effect was the creation of a multitude of new, mostly weak, but commonly self-assertive 'third-world' states, whose only power lay in collective bargaining through the UN and regional bodies such as the Organization of African Unity or in producers' cartels, such as OPEC. The resulting pattern of international relations can be seen in two ways. On the one hand there were a number of endemic local conflicts as ex-colonies struggled to reverse unacceptable aspects of their inheritance, such as boundaries. On the other hand the third world was divided into two main blocs, each consisting of a super-power and clients who were prepared to show deference and perform services in return for military and economic assistance, but were unable to cause much damage to international peace because of the restraining hand of the master. Of course, not all the new states committed themselves to regional or international alliances: many claimed to be 'non-aligned' and 93 were members of the non-aligned movement, holding regular conferences. Yet in practice very few of them could afford not to become part of the new patron–client system, which provided not only investment funds and military hardware, but also some protection against local rivals. Thus, for all the protestations made by Nehru about Indian non-alignment, India, in conflict with Pakistan and then China, found it expedient to have very close relations with Russia, while Pakistan, inevitably, joined the American camp. Very few new states proved able and willing, like Burma, to stand out of the new international power and subsidy system.

But, if decolonization could not provide the total independence the new states hoped for, it did have an incalculable impact on how they saw themselves and how they were seen by others. Frantz Fanon, the psychiatrist from Martinique who became a prophet of colonial liberation in the 1950s, described colonialism in his book *Les Damnés de la Terre* (published in 1961) as 'a systematic negation of the other person and a furious determination to deny the other person all attributes of humanity . . .'[1] That was the reaction of a third-world intellectual and it would be wrong to think that any large proportion of the population of the colonies was conscious of such cultural and intellectual subordination. Yet colonialism did undoubtedly inculcate feelings of inferiority in dependent peoples by denying the validity of their own values and by setting up alien substitutes. Behind demands for political independence there was thus a common hope that freedom would permit the full flowering of indigenous culture and personality, exemplified in the French colonial concept of négritude, first coined by Aimé Césaire, a Martinique poet, in 1939, and taken up and publicized after 1945 by Léopold Senghor of Senegal and others. Similar concepts had been voiced by Hindu revivalists in India in the previous century and by nationalists in other colonies. Political independence would free men from their sense of inferiority and give them pride in their own indigenous culture.

Several decades after decolonization it was clear that much of this idealism was misplaced: the clock could not be put back. In 1972 the Pan-Africanist, Ezekiel Mphahlele, confessed that 'I don't think that négritude is necessary .... It romanticizes the past, it is a yearning for the past, and a past which had gone, which had long gone.'[2] In most new states it became plain that independence alone could not create or recreate that intellectual and moral climate which the idealistic nationalists had hoped for. Yet the difference was fundamental, even if its full effects lay in the future. To be an Indian, Tanzanian or Algerian in the 1980s was to be a citizen of one's own country, able to stand as a free person in a world of free men, in control of one's own destiny.

The primary function of decolonization was, of course, to replace alien government by rulers whose legitimacy derived from the support of their own people. In any system of values it is assumed that self-rule is better than alien rule because more responsible and more responsive. There was, however, the danger that these new states, which had been created by imperial powers for their own convenience, had little natural cohesion and almost no experience in the techniques of government, might find it difficult to sustain elementary levels of competence, let alone improve things; in which case decolonization might result in political disorder, social friction and economic decline. The record of many of the new states which grew from one-time colonies in Latin America during the nineteenth century was extremely unpromising. How does the record of the new states of the later twentieth century appear by the early 1980s?

It is impossible to generalize over so varied an experience; but one can, perhaps, divide the new states into three broad categories with imprecise boundaries: the successful few, which were able to maintain stable and, in some cases, liberal political systems along the lines projected when power was transferred; at the other extreme those which experienced major disasters, such as civil war and regional secession; and the majority which, while avoiding such traumas, suffered from dictatorial power, generally incompetent and corrupt administration and, in many cases, chronic instability reflected in repeated political coups. It is impossible here to fit all the new states into these categories but examples have been chosen from each of them to underline factors likely to affect the fortunes of post-colonial societies.

Pride of place among the politically successful must go to India, the largest liberal democracy in the world, the first major dependency to be liberated after 1945. Once the trauma of partition in 1947 was over, and despite gloomy forecasts of further disintegration, India preserved its unity, its parliamentary constitution and the rule of law. There was only one period, from June 1975 to March 1977, when liberalism seemed in danger, during the emergency declared by Indira Gandhi; and in 1976 the odds seemed to be that India would become yet another one-party pseudo-democracy. Yet in 1977 free elections took place, Mrs Gandhi was overwhelmingly defeated and a new government installed. Her reward came in January 1980 when the Janata coalition, cobbled together to defeat her in 1977, had fallen apart and her Congress (I) party won a victory as resounding as its previous defeat.

Among other new states with impressive records of stability, coupled with some degree of liberalism, were Senegal, Ceylon (Sri Lanka), Ivory Coast, Kenya and Malaya. Senegal presents some interesting paradoxes, some of which it shared with India. Nominally democratic, it was in fact ruled continuously by Senghor's *Union Progressiste Sénégalise*, which was the only legal political party until 1976. In both countries stability depended heavily on continuity provided by one man or family and a dominant political party but was bolstered by long-established colonial institutions and a sophisticated, European-oriented élite. Both régimes professed to be socialist, yet both tolerated capitalism, relying heavily on foreign direct investment and official aid. Senegal, however, maintained much closer links with her one-time metropolis, and was not ashamed to use the CFA franc as the national currency.

The stability of states of this type was highlighted by the disasters experienced by some others. The cause of their instability might lie in the nature of the colonial state and its unresolved problems or in the character of a successor régime.

In either case, the new state seemed destined to go through a period of turmoil before it could achieve stability.

French Indo-China was the ex-colonial state which suffered most and longest. From 1945 to 1954 France attempted to compel North Vietnam, which had achieved *de facto* independence under Ho Chi Minh and the communist Vietminh when the Japanese surrendered, to form part of a French-dominated Indo-Chinese Federation. The Paris agreements which ended the war in 1954 specified that general elections were to take place throughout Vietnam by 1956 to decide its future. These were never held and North Vietnam used the Viet Cong to undermine the anti-communist régime in the south. The United States, invoking its rights and obligations as a member of the Geneva Conference of 1954, increasingly supported the Saigon régime. Indo-China suffered immense damage until the Americans withdrew in 1973 and Saigon was defeated in 1975. Thereafter Vietnam became a unitary communist state, rigorously totalitarian but apparently efficient in its attempt to rebuild after two decades of destruction.

Undoubtedly the worst post-colonial experience was that of Cambodia, renamed Kampuchea in 1975. As a component of Indo-China, it reverted to being an independent kingdom in 1955. It was, however, unable to avoid being drawn into the Vietnam war and suffered heavily from both sides. In 1970 the monarchy was overthrown and a republic set up. In the early 1970s a complex civil war between the governing Khmer Republic and the communist Khmer Rouge, supported respectively by America and North Vietnam, further devastated the country and ended with a Rouge victory in 1975. There followed one of the most appalling episodes in modern history. Apparently adopting principles defined in a doctoral thesis completed in Paris in 1959 by Khieu Samphon, president from 1967, the government aimed at complete self-sufficiency and detachment from the international capitalist economy. The immensely swollen population of the capital, Phnom Penh, was forcibly evacuated to the countryside to work on agriculture. The régime ruthlessly killed opponents and suspect supporters: estimates of those killed between 1975 and 1979 range from

500,000 to two million, of a total population of some eight million. Eventually Vietnam, one-time supporter of Khmer Rouge, invaded Kampuchea in December 1979 and set up a new communist government.

Vietnam, Cambodia and also Laos suffered so greatly in the aftermath of decolonization for two main reasons. First, French rule had never resolved the inherent tensions between the component parts of the federation and had further exacerbated them after 1945. After independence these divisions had to be resolved before a stable political system could be established. Second, South-east Asia proved to be a cockpit in which part of the struggle between Russian and Chinese communism and American capitalism was fought out after 1945. This second factor made the area exceptional; but many other ex-colonies faced comparable internal tensions inherited from the colonial situation. Nigeria was one of these. It was regarded with pride by the British when they withdrew: a federation of three regions in which ethnic and religious differences had been rendered harmless by colonial political and social engineering, a liberal democracy well able to sustain independence in 1960. For about six years such optimism seemed justified. But then the underlying tensions of the post-colonial situation erupted. The first of a series of military coups took place in January 1960 when a group of Ibo army officers killed the federal prime minister, a northerner, many other leading politicians and most non-Ibo senior army officers. In April a counter coup by northerners killed many Ibos. The army took control, abolished the constitution and, in 1967, created a new federation of twelve states. The Ibo-dominated eastern region, led by General Ojukwu, challenged the new structure and, as the independent state of Biafra, attempted to secede. Civil war lasted until 1970, ending with the destruction of Biafra and continued army rule. But in 1977/8 a constitutional commission prepared plans for a new democratic federal system based on nineteen states, which came into operation in October 1979.

Other states experienced dangerous secessionist movements which threatened their very existence. Pakistan lost its eastern province, which became Bangladesh in December 1971 after nine months of bitter war. The Belgian Congo came near to disintegration immediately after independence in 1960 and was saved only by large-scale UN intervention. Such events were bound to have a serious effect on the development of these countries. The majority of new states had avoided disruption by the early 1980s; yet the political record of many was almost equally depressing. The common denominator of virtually all the ex-colonies was that they moved from democracy towards one-party rule or dictatorship; from the rule of law to arbitrary power; and from comparative efficiency and honesty in administration to incompetence and corruption.

The slide from democracy was almost universal and commonly rapid. Until 1981 The Gambia cherished the reputation of being the only post-colonial African democracy which had not suffered a political coup; in that year it lost this record, although the coup failed. Normally the elaborate western-style constitutional and legal systems hammered out at pre-independence conferences were jettisoned, usually within months. In many states soldiers took over, claiming to represent the real interests of the nation better than the politicians. Long-lasting civilian régimes commonly restricted politics to a single party, abolished or emasculated parliament, expanded and filled the bureaucracy with party supporters, imprisoned opponents or executed them. Such methods help to explain the political longevity of Sekou Touré, the Marxist dictator of Guinée, Julius Nyerere of Tanzania, Kenneth Kaunda of Zambia and Hastings Banda of Malawi. All were foundation rulers of their countries who had been able to harness the power of the colonial state to their own purposes before opponents had learned the tricks of the trade.

These and others survived into the early 1980s: yet their security was misleading. Many charismatic and apparently impregnable founders of new nation states suddenly and unpredictably lost power in these decades. Three examples demonstrate the occupational hazards they faced. President Sukarno, who had helped to create the Indonesian Republic in 1945, seemed to have an unchallengeable position; yet in 1965 the army reacted to an attempted communist (PKI) coup, took power, and reduced Sukarno to a figure-head until his death in 1967. Equally surprising was the fate of Kwame Nkrumah of Ghana. For long revered both in Africa and overseas as the prototype educated, non-traditional African leader, who believed in democracy as well as socialism, ruler of the first sub-Saharan colony to achieve independence (in 1957), he soon made Ghana a one-party state ruled by himself and sycdophantic supporters. By 1967 the economy faced calamity and a disastrous drop in cocoa prices led to his being brought down by the army; after which Ghana alternated between civilian and military rule, sliding steadily down the hierarchy of third-world countries in terms both of wealth and influence. Finally, Milton Obote of Uganda. At independence in 1962 he was widely admired as a moderate democratic socialist. Yet in 1964 he suspended the quasi-federal constitution, used military force to destroy the Buganda assembly, and in 1969 established one-party rule. In January 1971, while he was returning from the Singapore Commonwealth Prime Ministers Conference, he was unseated in a military coup led by his own strong man, General Idi Amin. Uganda then began a decade of military dictatorship which caused perhaps 100,000 deaths and the partial destruction of its political and economic life before Amin was removed by invading Tanzanian forces. Obote could then return to power after a general election, once again pledged to democracy.

The evidence, therefore, suggests that the short-term political consequence of decolonization in most new states was the destruction of democracy followed by some form of dictatorship; and that even dictatorship was unlikely to provide stability. How does one explain these tendencies? Three factors seem to have been commonly, though not invariably, responsible: limited preparation for independence; inherent weakness in the claim of the new states to general obedience; and a decline in the quality of the public service, resulting in bad government.

Very few of the colonies were given adequate training in self-government. In the 1940s experts in most imperial capitals held that it would take several decades before the majority of colonies could be prepared for independence; yet from about 1957 the British, French and Belgians became so concerned to avoid the growing problems caused by colonial nationalists that they discarded all the conditions previously set for decolonization. Thus, whereas India had some sixty years experience of elective self-government of some sort by 1947, including ministerial responsibility in the provinces from the 1920s, Ghanaian politicians had only seven years of fully representative government and five of cabinet government before independence day in 1957. By later standards even that was a generous preparation. In Tanganyika Nyerere did not found the first real political party, TANU, until 1954; the first elections to the previously nominative legislative council were in 1958; the first cabinet was formed in May 1961; and independence followed in December. Yet in 1959 the British Colonial Office had not expected Tanganyika to have full internal self-government, let alone independence, before 1969 at the earliest. It was hardly surprising that democracy had shallow roots in such new states.

Of greater practical concern to these states was the maintenance of unity and order; and this was made very difficult by their limited claim to have legitimate authority over all the territorial, ethnic and other groups within the arbitrary boundaries of the colonial state. Legitimacy had seemed no problem to nationalist leaders in the heady days of the struggle against the alien power because any 'nationalist' party seemed legitimate compared with imperialism. But once that external focus of unity was removed, the claim of any leader or party to general support became suspect. Why, for example, should an Ibo obey a Hausa prime minister of Nigeria for whose party he had not voted and with whom he had no demonstrable interests in common? Why should the Nigeria constructed by the British exist at all? Thus perhaps the most difficult single task facing the governments of new states was the creation of a genuine sense of common interest which was co-extensive with the territory of the nation state and which entitled the ruler to demand obedience. In its extreme form the lack of such a sense might result in wars of regional secession; more commonly it produced sectional struggles for power and chronic bad government.

Bad government was also in most countries the result of a rapid decline in the quality of the public service, to the point at which the state could no longer fulfil its basic functions. This surprised many because to a nationalist leader it must have seemed that the colonial state apparatus was omnipotent and indestructible. He could control it as well as the Europeans, so that post-independence government would present no problem. This was to misunderstand realities. Colonial governments in their mature form were the joint product of a long period of administrative development in Europe and of shorter periods of adaptation to the needs of a particular dependency, artefacts which depended on constant attention to standards for their efficiency. They were not native to African and Asian societies; and although most new states inherited a nucleus of indigenous officials, trained by and up to the standards of the expatriate administrators who were leaving, the chances of the new men maintaining the old standards were slight. Because they were not expatriates, they were subject to intense local pressures and were often conscious that their jobs depended on pleasing important party members. Appointments usually became part of the political spoils system, and qualifications were diluted. Once the reputation for honesty and efficiency laboriously built up by the colonial state had been destroyed, faith in the government of the new state was likely to wither. Discontent resulting from obviously corrupt administration would intensify political instability; the much enlarged army would intervene to eliminate corruption, eject 'selfish' politicians, and rule on its own account. But, since the military faced the same problems as its civilian predecessors, the cycle might continue indefinitely.

To record this depressing tendency is not to blame nationalist leaders for demanding independence or the imperialists for decolonizing when they did. It would have required extraordinary prescience by the nationalists to foresee the problems they were laying up for themselves by insisting on early independence, and impossible determination on the part of the metropolitan governments to resist what, by the 1950s, seemed the tide of history. Only a despotic state, such as Portugal before 1974, could have ignored the general conviction that colonialism was immoral. It is more realistic to say that, because modern colonialism, in contrast with white settlement colonization, was originally seen as a static system of control, imposed on an unstable periphery in the interests of the West, there was no logical time or way to end it. In retrospect it is easy to say that the metropolitan states should have withdrawn according to a timetable drawn up long in advance with colonial leaders. But no colonial power ever thought in such terms and no colonial politician could have afforded to admit the value of a slow, phased imperial withdrawal, for that would have been to accept that alien rule conferred benefits. There are only two examples of decolonization being decently delayed – India and Ceylon; and it is arguable that the partition of India was the price paid for too long a period of dialogue during which fanatics and vested interests were able to muster their forces and oppose the transfer of power to a united India.

There remains the question of wealth. If, as many critics of colonialism argued, alien rule exploited the colonies and prevented them from growing rich, did political independence enable them to narrow or eliminate the gap between them and the metropolitan countries? There were certainly many in the 1950s and 1960s who believed that this would happen, for three main reasons. First, colonies would no longer be forced to accept economic regulations intended to benefit the metropolis or its citizens in the colonies. Second, it was assumed that the new states would adopt enlightened policies geared to growth. Finally, national governments might be able to tap reserves of capital and human energy not available to alien rulers. By adopting a 'socialist' approach, as most nationalists proposed to do, they could match the then highly rated Soviet industrial achievements of the Stalin era, reducing dependence on manufactured imports and correcting the imbalance of their 'lop-sided' colonial economies.

Such optimism was not entirely misplaced. The two decades after 1950 were a period of unprecedented growth for the world economy as a whole and most of the less developed countries (LDCs) made substantial advances. The table below shows changes in the index of per capita incomes at constant prices, and also in the per capita domestic product at current prices, in 1960, 1970 and 1976 for a number of developed and less developed countries. These statistics, taken from the *United Nations Statistical Year Book*,[3] have very wide margins of error and cannot be taken literally; but they suggest two broad and to some extent contradictory trends.

First, the index (1975=100) rose for all the LDCs in this table for which data is available between 1960 and 1970, though for four of them it dropped between 1970 and 1976. In current prices, average per capita domestic production for all LDCs with market economies rose by a factor of 1·6 between 1960 and 1970 and by 2·4 between 1960 and 1976. Since population growth in the LDCs was considerable, rising at an annual rate of 2·7 per cent in Africa and 2·2 per cent in Asia between 1965 and 1977, this was a considerable achievement. Decolonization seemed to have resulted in an absolute increase in the wealth of the third world.

On the other hand, the table shows that, in relative terms, the LDCs as a whole were not catching up on the developed countries. A few of them did outstandingly well and joined the rich men's club: Japan, Singapore, Hong Kong (still a colony) and Taiwan, which is not included in the UN statistics. Ivory Coast also had an outstanding record. But these were the exceptions. The average per capita domestic product of all LDCs in 1976 was only $331, compared with $5900 for the developed countries with market economies; and a number of recently independent countries were far below the average. In Asia, Burma's GDP was $112, that of India $141, Indonesia $267, Pakistan $200, Sri Lanka $229; in Africa, Uganda $266, Tanzania $177 and Kenya $247. Even oil-rich Nigeria had only $399. Meantime, the absolute gap in GDP between rich and poor countries had widened from an average of $1350 to some $5569. In so far as they are reliable, these figures suggest that independence by itself had limited economic consequences.

The economic growth of the period 1960–75 was, however, unprecedented and it was partly made possible by the equally unprecedented flow of resources from the developed to the less developed countries. Much of this flow consisted of official 'aid' which was largely a post-war phenomenon, though its origins can be traced back to the British Colonial Development Act of

The Economic Performance of Selected Developed and Less Developed States, 1960–76

State	1960		1970		1976	
	A	B	A	B	A	B
Australia	68	1600	93	2900	103	7200
Belgium	55	1200	84	2600	99	6900
France	54	1300	86	2800	104	6600
Germany (W)	65	1300	92	3000	106	7200
Japan	33	458	84	1900	105	5000
Portugal	53	300	88	700	103	1600
UK	76	1400	94	2200	102	3900
USA	72	2800	93	4800	105	7900
Burma	—	61	100	80	102	112
Ghana	93	198	95	257	—	498*
Guyana	83	304	93	382	104	562
Hong Kong	—	348	84	778	116	2100
India	83	73	97	100	99	141
Indonesia	75	73	78	77	104	267
Ivory Coast	—	179	—	347	102	929
Jamaica	—	398	106	916	92	1683*
Kenya	—	84	96	143	102	247
Malaysia	—	278	83	333	107	781*
Nigeria	60	79	78	143	—	399*
Pakistan	66	81	94	175	98	200
Senegal	—	173	—	197	—	331*
Sierra Leone	—	—	102	147	99	214
Singapore	43	432	69	916	106	2600
South Africa	65	421	90	774	99	1300
Zimbabwe	—	219	87	285	95	537
Sri Lanka	—	142	89	177	103	229
Uganda	99	60	117	135	96	266*
Tanzania	—	53	93	97	103	177
Zaire	—	—	98	88	96	148*
Zambia	—	183	96	418	99	523
All Developed Market Economies	—	1490	—	2970	—	5900
All Less Developed Market Economies	—	140	—	230	—	331

Columns A: Index of per capita product at constant prices: 1975=100
Columns B: Estimates of per capita gross domestic product in purchasers' values: US$
Source: *UN Statistical Year Book, 1978* (New York, 1979); tables 184 and 192
Note: *indicates 1975 figure,

1929 and comparable French policies in the 1930s. By 1975–7 the annual average of official aid from the developed market economies to the LDCs was $13,593,500,000, or $7·04 a head, though the contribution varied immensely between different recipients: in Africa it ranged from under $0·90 for Nigeria to $293·60 a head for Djibouti. For the more favoured recipients, however, this official aid, coupled with smaller amounts of direct private foreign investment, considerably increased the ability of the new states to invest in modernization. For example, during the First and Second Five Year Indian Plans, for the years 1950/1–1960/1, the official total for new investment in public and private sectors was Rs 10,110 crores. External official assistance actually used (more was authorized) was Rs 1631 crores. From 1948 to 1961 foreign private business investment increased by about Rs 324·5 crores. Unreliable as such figures necessarily are, they suggest that the overseas contribution to Indian investment may have been as high as 19 per cent in that critical period.[4]

It is, however, difficult to be certain how relatively important overseas aid was in generating the real growth achieved by LDCs; nor whether those rates of growth could be sustained after the initial burst. Much foreign aid was used to pay for 'technical assistance', that is largely the salaries of expatriates. More money was used to cover recurrent government expenditure than for investment. A great deal was wasted through incompetence or corruption in the recipient states. By the 1970s the real value of aid was tending to decline as the donor states felt the impact of higher oil prices and recession. By that time, also, many new states had completed the first and easiest stage of industrialization which had the most dramatic impact on GDP figures, building factories to manufacture consumer goods previously imported and protecting non-competitive local products with high tariffs or import controls. Once the home market for such goods had become saturated further industrialization became far more difficult, since it depended on growth in other sectors of the domestic economy or on entering highly competitive export markets. By the 1970s, and still more in the 1980s, the rate of development in many, though not all, ex-colonies was slowing up or even becoming negative; and the world recession, low commodity prices and the growing cost of servicing past borrowing combined to destroy much of the optimism of the 1950s and 1960s.

One result of this downturn was to increase the influence of so-called 'dependency' theories which, starting with hypotheses specifically relating to Latin America, were broadened to account for surviving or widening disparities between rich and poor countries everywhere. Such theories took various forms; but their common denominator was the proposition that decolonization could not, by itself, end the dependence of the ex-colonies, the 'periphery', on the European and North American 'core'. That dependence had been created during the colonial period, when the economic and social systems of the colonies had been fundamentally restructured to satisfy the needs of the imperial powers. Old handcraft industries were destroyed to create a market for imported manufactures and obstacles placed in the way of new modern factory industries. Forms of primary production were established to maximize production of commodity exports rather than food for local consumption. Foreign companies were enabled to establish a firm grasp on the indigenous economy. A stratum of indigenous collaborators was created which had a vested interest in alliance with the imperialists. In these ways a colony was positively 'underdeveloped', in the sense that it was deprived of its original potential for true growth. Decolonization made little difference since the imperial states transferred local control to their trusted indigenous allies, the 'compradors', who paraded their nationalism but in fact felt primary loyalty to their overseas paymasters. Hence, after a short burst of post-decolonization investment, the ex-colony found itself becalmed, held immobile by poverty, indebtedness and the disloyalty of its own ruling élite. Only total revolution, involving a change from capitalism to socialism and withdrawal from the international economy, could enable such a state to break out of 'underdevelopment' and achieve 'real growth'.

There is obviously some evidence in the post-independence record of many new states to support the general proposition that decolonization did not necessarily, or even commonly, lead to genuine independence and economic development. The momentum of development in the two decades after 1950 does not, in many cases, appear to have been sustained; often it lost momentum once the easy foothills of industrialization had been climbed. Many successor régimes undoubtedly do consist of selfish élites which are as remote from the mass of their own people as the officials of any colonial régime; and they are often far more brutal in the means they use to gain and sustain power. Yet this does not mean that decolonization cannot lead to good government and affluence; nor that the Marxist prescription of revolution and isolation would necessarily be more successful. A number of ex-colonies have been strikingly successful in their use of western economic and political systems. Conversely, although comparable statistics are not available, it is not clear that countries such as Cuba and Guinea-Bissau, which have followed the Stalinist model of political and economic development, have performed any better; while the post-1975 Kampuchean experiment had such horrific consequences that even the Vietnamese found it impossible to accept them.

It would, therefore, be unwise to suggest any firm conclusion on the past or future consequences of decolonization. If early hopes were too optimistic, current pessimism may be exaggerated. The transition from colonial status was bound to be traumatic; and by the time-scale of modern European history one would expect it to take many more decades for states as artificial as most of these to resolve their social and political problems. In the 1980s it was still too soon to discard the possibility that some at least of the one-time colonies would become prosperous and well-governed nations.

Notes

Chapter 1

1 Smith, A., *The Wealth of Nations*. ed. E. Cannan, New York, 1937, Book IV, ch. vii, part 3, p. 590.

Chapter 2

1 Pares, R., 'The economic factors in the history of the Empire'. *Economic History Review*, vol. VII (1937), p. 120.
2 Madariaga, S. De, *The Fall of the Spanish American Empire*. London, 1947, p. 69.
3 Haring, C. H., *The Spanish Empire in America*. New York, 1947, p. 305.
4 —— p. 342.
5 Lannoy, C. De and Linden, H. V., *Histoire de l'Expansion coloniale des Peuples Européens: Portugal et Espagne*. Brussels, 1907, pp. 226–36.

Chapter 3

1 Moreau De Saint-Méry, M. L. E., *Lois et Constitutions des Colonies françoises* (sic) *de l'Amérique sous le vent*. Paris, n.d. vol. I, p. 714.
2 —— IV, pp. 339–40.
3 Girault, A., *Principes de Colonisation et de Législation coloniale*. 5th ed. Paris, 1927, vol. I, p. 219.
4 Saintoyant, J. *La Colonisation française sous l'Ancien Régime*. Paris, 1929, vol. II, p. 432.
5 Turgot, A.-R.-J., '*Mémoire au Roi sur la guerre d'Amérique*', in L. Deschamps, *Histoire de la Question coloniale en France*. Paris, 1891, p. 314.

6 Deschamps, L., *op. cit.*, p. 316.
7 Lannoy, C. De and Linden, H. V., *Histoire de l'Expansion coloniale des Peuples Européens. Néerlande et Danemark*. Brussels, 1911, pp. 353–4.

Chapter 4

1 Schumpeter, E. B., *English Overseas Trade Statistics, 1697–1808* Oxford, 1960, p. 18.
2 —— p. 18.
3 Jensen, M. (ed.), *American Colonial Documents to 1776*. London, 1955, p. 392.
4 Miller, J. C., *Origins of the American Revolution*. Stanford, 2nd rev. ed., 1959, p. 53.
5 Harper, L. A., 'The Effect of the Navigation Acts on the Thirteen Colonies', in R. B. Morris (ed.), *The Era of the American Revolution*. New York, 1939, p. 37.
6 Quoted Jensen, M., *op. cit.*, p. 807.
7 Cobbett, W. (ed.), *Cobbett's Parliamentary History of England*. 36 vols. London, 1806–20, vol. XVII, cols. 1236–7.

Chapter 5

1 Haring, C. H., *op. cit.*, p. 305.
2 Harper, L. A., *loc. cit.*, pp. 32 and 37.
3 Smith, A., *op. cit.*, p. 581.
4 Tucker, J., *The True Interest of Great Britain set forth in regard to the Colonies*, 1774. R. L. Schuyler (ed.), *Josiah Tucker, a selection from his ... writings*. New York, 1931, p. 365.
5 Haring, C. H., *op. cit.*, p. 305.

Chapter 6

1 *Parliamentary History*, vol. XVII, col. 1241.
2 Saintoyant, J., *op. cit.*, II, pp. 333–4.

Chapter 8

1 Lannoy, C. De and Linden, H. V., *Histoire de l'Expansion coloniale des Peuples Européens. Néerlande et Danemark*. p. 344, *et seq.*
2 —— pp. 356–7.

3 *Cambridge History of India*, vol. V, *British India, 1497–1858*. Cambridge, 1929, pp. 96 and 109.
4 —— p. 108; Schumpeter, E., *op. cit.*, p. 18.
5 —— vol. V, p. 102.
6 Weber, H., *La Compagnie francaise des Indes*. Paris, 1904, pp. 492–500.
7 —— p. 394.

Chapter 9

1 Clark, G., *The Balance Sheets of Imperialism*. New York, 1936, pp. 5–6.

Chapter 10

1 Taylor, A. J. P., *Germany's First Bid for Colonies, 1884–1885*. London, 1938, p. 6.
2 Fuller, T., *The Church History of Britain* (*1655*), 3 vols. London, 1837, vol. II, p. 275.
3 Remer, C. F., *Foreign Investments in China*. New York, 1933, p. 73, table 6.

Chapter 11

1 Clark, G., *op. cit.*, p. 23.
2 Madden, A. F., *Imperial Constitutional Documents, 1765–1952*. Oxford, 1953, p. 5.
3 Keith, A. B., *Selected Speeches and Documents on British Colonial Policy, 1763–1917*. London, 1953, part one, p. 139.
4 —— pp. 174–5.
5 Bennett, G., *The Concept of Empire*. London, 1953, p. 282.
6 Keith, A. B., *Speeches and Documents on the British Dominions, 1918–31*. London, 1948, p. 161.
7 —— p. 164.
8 —— p. 305.

Chapter 12

1 Stokes, E., *The English Utilitarians and India*. Oxford, 1959, p. 45.
2 —— p. 46.
3 —— p. 284.

4 Anstey, V., *The Economic Development of India*. 4th ed. London, 1952, pp. 628–33 for the statistics from which these proportions were calculated.

5 Hicks, U. K., *British Public Finances, 1880–1952*. London, 1954, p. 14.

6 Knowles, L. C. A., *The Economic Development of the British Overseas Empire*. London, 1928, p. 386 for this and later percentages.

7 *Cambridge History of India*, vol. VI. *The Indian Empire, 1858–1918*. Cambridge, 1932, p. 505.

8 Keith, A. B., *Speeches and Documents on Indian Policy, 1750–1921*. London, 1922, vol. II, p. 133.

9 McPhee, A., *The Economic Revolution in British West Africa*. London, 1926, p. 313.

Chapter 13

1 Clark, G., *op. cit.*, p. 23.

2 Leroy-Beaulieu, P. *De la Colonisation chez les Peuples modernes*, 6th ed. Paris, 1908, vol. II, p. 540. In the 1st ed. (1874) Leroy-Beaulieu called them simply '*colonies de commerce*', '*colonies agricoles*' and '*colonies de plantations*', (p. 534).

3 Roberts, S. H., *History of French Colonial Policy, 1870–1925*. 2 vols. London, 1929, vol. I, p. 44.

4 Southworth, C., *The French Colonial Venture*. London, 1931, p. 61 and tables III and IV.

5 Roberts, S. H., *op. cit.*, vol. I, p. 67.

6 Southworth, C., *op. cit.*, p. 50 and tables I and II.

7 Brunschwig, H., *La Colonisation française*. Paris, 1949, p. 184.

8 Roberts, S. H., *op. cit.*, vol. I, p. 113.

Chapter 14

1 Vandenbosch, A., *The Dutch East Indies*, 3rd ed. Berkeley and Los Angeles, 1944, p. 253.

2 Vlekke, B. H. M., *Nusantara*. Cambridge, Mass., 1943, p. 273.

3 Furnivall, J. S., *Netherlands India*, 2nd ed. Cambridge, 1944, p. 338.

4 —— *Colonial Policy and Practice*. Cambridge, 1948, p. 255.

5 —— *Netherlands India*, p. 336.

6 Pierce, R. A., *Russian Central Asia, 1867–1917*. Berkeley and Los Angeles, 1960, p. 137.

7 —— pp. 218–19.
8 Pratt, J. W., *America's Colonial Experiment*. New York, 1950, pp. 243–4.

Chapter 15

1 Duffy, J., *Portuguese Africa*. Cambridge, Mass., 1959, p. 1.
2 —— p. 295.
3 Clark, G., *op. cit.*, p. 23.
4 Wauters, A. J., *Histoire politique du Congo Belge*. Brussels, 1911, quoted: Naval Intelligence Division: *The Belgian Congo*. London, 1944, pp. 206–7.
5 Frankel, S. H., *Capital Investment in Africa*. London, 1938, pp. 292–5.
6 —— pp. 158–9.
7 Martelli, G., *Leopold to Lumumba*. London, 1962, p. 215.
8 —— p. 215.
9 Henderson, W. O., *Studies in German Colonial History*. London, 1962, p. 5.
10 Rudin, H. R., *Germans in the Cameroons, 1884–1914*. London, 1938, p. 419.
11 Henderson, W. O., *op. cit.*, pp. 33–4.
12 Clark, G., *op. cit.*, p. 11.
13 Henderson, W. O., *op. cit.*, p. 134.
14 —— p. 58; Townsend, M. E., *The Rise and Fall of Germany's Colonial Empire*. New York, 1930, p. 263.

Chapter 16

1 Clark, G., *op. cit.*, p. 78.
2 Southworth, C., *op. cit.*, p. 62.
3 Schlote, W., *British Overseas Trade*. Oxford, 1952, pp. 154 and 172.
4 Lenin, V. I., *Imperialism, the Highest Stage of Capitalism (1916)*. Moscow, 1947, pp. 76–7.
5 Brown, M. B., *After Imperialism*. London, 1963, p. 153.
6 Southworth, C., *op. cit.*, table V.
7 Cairncross, A. K., *Home and Foreign Investment, 1870–1913*. Cambridge, 1953, p. 227.
8 Paish, G., 'Great Britain's Capital Investments in Other Lands' in *Journal of the Royal Statistical Society*, LXXII (1909), p. 475.

9 Southworth, C., *op. cit.*, pp. 108–9.
10 —— Appendix, table 7.
11 Paish, G., *loc. cit.*, p. 475.
12 Frankel, S. H., *op. cit.*, table 15, pp. 96–7.
13 Southworth, C., *op. cit.*, p. 110.
14 Brown, M. B., *op. cit.*, pp. 248 and 389.

Chapter 17

1 Quoted Fetter, B. (ed.), *Colonial Rule in Africa*. Madison, 1979, p. 206.
2 Quoted Austin, D., *Politics in Africa*. Manchester, 1978, p. 153.
3 *United Nations Statistical Year Book, 1978*. New York, 1979.
4 From Bhagwati, J. N. and Desai, P., *India: Planning for Industrialization. Industrialization and Trade Policies since 1951*. London, 1970, tables 9.2, 10.2 and 11.1.

Bibliography

Chapter 1

Since the period before 1700 is outside that covered by this book, no bibliography of European expansion during the previous two centuries is provided. The following books provide an introduction to the first expansion of Europe and contain good bibliographies.

Elliott, J. H., *The Old World and the New, 1492–1650*. Cambridge, 1970.

Parry, J. H., *The Age of Reconnaissance*. London, 1963.

—— *Trade and Dominion*. London, 1971.

Scammell, G. V., *The World Encompassed: the First European Maritime Empires*. London, 1981.

Chapter 2

THE SPANISH EMPIRE

Bakewell, P. J., *Silver Mining and Society in Colonial Mexico*. Cambridge, 1971.

Brading, D. A., *Miners and Merchants in Bourbon Mexico, 1763–1810*. Cambridge, 1971.

Burkholder, M. A. and Chandler, D. S., *From Impotence to Authority: the Spanish Crown and the American Audiencias, 1687–1808*. Columbia, Miss., 1977.

Farriss, N. M., *Crown and Clergy in Colonial Mexico, 1759–1821*. London, 1968.

Gongora, M., *Studies in the Colonial History of Spanish America*. Cambridge, 1975.

Lang, J., *Conquest and Commerce: Spain and England in the Americas*. New York, 1975.

THE COLONIAL EMPIRES

Lynch, J., *Spanish Colonial Administration, 1782–1810*. London, 1958.

—— *Spain and America, 1598–1700*. Oxford, 1969.

Macleod, M. J., *Spanish Central America: a Socio-economic History, 1520–1720*. Berkeley, 1973.

Parry, J. H., *The Spanish Theory of Empire in the Sixteenth Century*. Cambridge, 1940.

—— *The Sale of Public Office in the Spanish Indies under the Hapsburgs*. Berkeley, 1953.

—— *The Spanish Seaborne Empire*. London, 1966.

Walker, G. J., *Spanish Politics and Imperial Trade, 1700–1789*. London, 1979.

THE PORTUGUESE EMPIRE IN AMERICA

Alden, D. (ed.), *Colonial Roots of Modern Brazil*. Berkeley, 1973.

Boxer, C. R., *The Golden Age of Brazil, 1695–1750*. Berkeley, 1962.

—— *Race Relations in the Portuguese Colonial Empire*. Oxford, 1963.

—— *The Portuguese Seaborne Empire, 1415–1825*. New York, 1969.

Freyre, G., *The Masters and the Slaves*. 2nd edn, New York, 1956.

Furtado, C., *The Economic Growth of Brazil*. Berkeley, 1963.

Livermore, H. V., *A History of Portugal*. Cambridge, 1947.

—— (ed.), *Portugal and Brazil*. Oxford, 1953.

Maxwell, K. R., *Conflicts and Conspiracies: Brazil and Portugal, 1750–1808*. Cambridge, 1973.

Prado, C. Jr., *The Colonial Background of Modern Brazil*. Berkeley, 1973.

Chapter 3

THE FRENCH COLONIES IN AMERICA

Banbuck, C. A., *Histoire politique, économique et sociale de la Martinique sous l'Ancien Régime*. Paris, 1935.

Butel, P., *Les Négociants bordelais: l'Europe et les Iles au XVIII*[e] *siècle*. Paris, 1974.

Chailley-Bert, J., *Les Compagnies de Colonisation sous l'Ancien Régime*. Paris, 1898.

Deschamps, H., *Les Méthodes et les Doctrines coloniales de la France*. Paris, 1953.

Duchêne, A., *La Politique coloniale de la France*. Paris, 1928.

—— *Histoire des Finances coloniales de la France*. Paris, 1938.

Eccles, W. J., *France in America*. New York, 1972.

Hanotaux, G. and Martineau, A., *Histoire des Colonies françaises*. 6 vols, Paris, 1929–33.

Saintoyant, J., *La Colonisation française sous l'Ancien Régime*. 2 vols, Paris, 1929.

Stanley, G. F. C., *New France: the Last Phase, 1744–1760*. Toronto, 1968.

Tarrade, J., *Le Commerce colonial de la France à la fin de l'Ancien Régime*. Paris, 1972.

Yacomo, X., *Histoire de la Colonisation française*. Paris, 1963.

THE DUTCH COLONIES IN AMERICA

Boxer, C. R., *The Dutch Seaborne Empire*. London, 1965.

Clementi, C., *A Constitutional History of British Guiana*. London, 1937.

Lannoy, C. de and Linden, H. V., *Histoire de l'Expansion coloniale des Peuples européens: Néerlande et Danemark*. Brussels, 1911.

Chapter 4

THE BRITISH EMPIRE, 1700–1815

Andrews, C. M., *The Colonial Period of American History*. 4 vols, New Haven, 1934–8.

Armytage, F., *The Free Port System in the British West Indies*. London, 1953.

Bonomi, P. U., *A Factious People: Politics and Society in Colonial New York*. New York, 1971.

Boorstin, D. J., *The Americans: the Colonial Experience*. New York, 1958.

Bushman, R. L., *From Puritan to Yankee: Character and the Social Order in Connecticut, 1690–1765*. Cambridge, Mass., 1967.

Cambridge History of the British Empire.
Vol. I. *The Old Empire*. Cambridge, 1929.
Vol. II. *The Growth of the New Empire, 1783–1870*. Cambridge, 1940.

Clarke, C. M. H., *A History of Australia*. Vol. I, Melbourne, 1962.

Craig, G. M., *Upper Canada, 1784–1841*. London, 1963.

Creighton, D. G., *The Commercial Empire of the St Lawrence, 1760–1850*. Toronto, 1937.

—— *Dominion of the North*. 2nd edn, London, 1958.

Davies, R., *The Rise of the Atlantic Economies*. London, 1973.

THE COLONIAL EMPIRES

Gipson, L. H., *The British Empire before the American Revolution.* 13 vols, New York, 1936–67.

Greenberg, M., *British Trade and the Opening of China, 1800–1842.* Cambridge, 1951.

Greene, J. P., *The Quest for Power: the Lower House of Assembly in the Southern Royal Colonies.* Chapel Hill, 1963.

Harlow, V. T., *The Founding of the Second British Empire.* 2 vols, London, 1952, 1964.

Harper, L. A., *The English Navigation Laws.* New York, 1939.

Innis, H. A., *The Fur Trade of Canada.* Toronto, 1927.

Knorr, K. E., *British Colonial Theories, 1570–1850.* Toronto, 1944.

MacNutt, W. S., *The Atlantic Provinces, 1712–1857.* Toronto, 1965.

Manning, H. T., *The Revolt of French Canada, 1800–1835.* London 1962.

Mills, L. A., *Ceylon under British Rule, 1795–1932.* London, 1933.

Nash, G. B., *The Urban Crucible: Social Change, Political Consciousness and the Origins of the American Revolution.* Cambridge, Mass., 1979.

Neatby, H., *Quebec: the Revolutionary Age, 1760–1791.* Toronto, 1966.

Pares, R., *Merchants and Planters.* London, 1960.

—— *War and Trade in the West Indies.* Oxford, 1936.

Parry, J. H. and Sherlock, P. M., *A Short History of the West Indies.* London, 1956.

Ragatz, L. J., *The Fall of the Planter Class in the British Caribbean, 1763–1833.* New York, 1928.

Schumpeter, E. B., *English Overseas Trade Statistics, 1697–1808.* Oxford, 1960.

Schuyler, R. L., *Parliament and the British Empire.* New York, 1929.

—— *The Fall of the Old Colonial System, 1770–1870.* New York, 1945.

Simmons, R. G., *The American Colonies: from Settlement to Independence.* London, 1976.

Steeg, C. V., *The Formative Years, 1607–1763.* New York, 1964.

Walton, G. M. and Shepherd, J. F., *The Economic Rise of Early America.* Cambridge, 1979.

Chapter 6

THE REVOLT OF THE BRITISH COLONIES

Bailyn, B., *The Ideological Origins of the American Revolution.* Cambridge, Mass., 1967.

Bemis, S. F., *The Diplomacy of the American Revolution*. New York, 1935.

Christie, I. R., *Crisis of Empire: Great Britain and the American Colonies, 1754–1783*. London, 1966; 2nd edn, 1974.

Donoughue, B., *British Politics and the American Revolution*. London, 1964.

Gipson, L. H., *The Coming of the Revolution, 1763–1775*. New York, 1954.

Mackesy, P., *The War for America, 1775–83*. London, 1964.

Miller, J. C., *Origins of the American Revolution*. 2nd rev. edn, Stanford, 1959.

Morgan, E. S. and H. M., *The Stamp Act Crisis*. Chapel Hill, 1953; 2nd rev. edn, 1963.

Nelson, W. H., *The American Tory*. Oxford, 1961.

Pole, J. R., *The Decision for American Independence*. London, 1977.

Sosin, J. M., *Whitehall and the Wilderness*. Lincoln, Neb., 1961.

Thomas, D. G., *British Politics and the Stamp Act Crisis, 1763–67*. Oxford, 1975.

THE REVOLT OF SPANISH AMERICA

Clissold, S., *Bernado O'Higgins and the Independence of Chile*. London, 1969.

Halpérin-Donghi, T., *Politics, Economics and Society in Argentina in the Revolutionary Period*. Cambridge, 1975.

Humphreys, R. A., *Liberation in South America, 1806–27*. London, 1952.

—— and Lynch, J. (eds), *The Origins of the Latin American Revolutions, 1808–26*. New York, 1965.

Kaufman, W. W., *British Policy and the Independence of Latin America, 1804–28*. New Haven, 1951.

Lynch, J., *The Spanish American Revolutions, 1808–26*. London, 1973.

Masur, G., *Simon Bolivar*. Albuquerque, 1948.

Whitaker, A. P., *The United States and the Independence of Latin America, 1800–30*. Baltimore, 1941.

Chapter 7

EUROPEANS IN AFRICA BEFORE 1815

Ajayi, J. F. A. and Crowder, M. (eds), *History of West Africa*. Vol. I, London, 1971.

Cambridge History of Africa. Vol. IV, Cambridge, 1977.
Cohen, W. B., *The French Encounter with Africans*. Bloomington, Indiana, 1980.
Coupland, R., *The British Anti-Slavery Movement*. London, 1933.
Curtin, P. D., *The Atlantic Slave Trade*. Madison, 1969.
Davies, K. G., *The Royal African Company*. London, 1957.
Duffy, J. E., *Portuguese Africa*. Cambridge, Mass., 1959.
Fyfe, C., *A History of Sierra Leone*. London, 1962.
Martin, E. C., *The British West African Settlements, 1750–1821*. London, 1927.
Oliver, R. and Fage, J. D., *A Short History of Africa*. Harmondsworth, 1962.
Wilson, M. and Thompson, L. (eds), *The Oxford History of South Africa*. Vol. I, Oxford, 1969.

Chapter 8

EUROPEANS IN THE EAST BEFORE 1815

Boxer, C. R., *The Dutch Seaborne Empire*. London, 1965.
Bromley, J. S. and Kossmann, E. H. (eds), *Britain and the Netherlands in Europe and Asia*. London, 1968.
Cambridge History of India. Vol. V. *British India, 1497–1858*. Cambridge, 1929.
Chaudhuri, K. N., *The Trading World of Asia and the English East India Company, 1660–1760*. Cambridge, 1978.
Danvers, F. C., *History of the Portuguese in India*. 2 vols, London, 1894.
Das Gupta, A., *Malabar in Asian Trade, 1740–1800*. Cambridge, 1967.
Dodwell, H., *Dupleix and Clive*. London, 1920.
Furber, H., *John Company at Work*. Harvard, 1951.
Glamman, K., *Dutch Asiatic Trade, 1620–1740*. The Hague, 1958.
Hall, D. G. E., *A History of South-East Asia*. 2nd edn, London, 1964.
Hunter, Sir W. W., *History of British India*. 2 vols, London, 1899–1900.
Marshall, P. J., *Problems of Empire: Britain and India, 1757–1813*. London, 1968.
—— *East India Fortunes: the British in Bengal in the Eighteenth Century*. London, 1976.
Martineau, A., *Dupleix et l'Inde français*. 3 vols, Paris, 1920–7.

Philips, C. H., *The East India Company, 1784–1834*. Manchester, 1940.

—— *India*. London, 1949.

Spear, T. G. P., *A History of India*. 2 vols, 2nd edn, London, 1970.

Sutherland, L. S., *The East India Company in Eighteenth-Century Politics*. Oxford, 1952.

Vlekke, B. H. M., *Nusantara: a History of the East Indian Archipelago*. Cambridge, Mass., 1944.

Weber, H., *La Compagnie française des Indes*. Paris, 1904.

Chapters 9 and 10

EUROPEAN EXPANSION, 1815–1939

Andrew, C. M., *Théophile Delcassé and the Making of the Entente Cordiale*. London, 1968.

—— and Kanya-Forstner, A. S., *France Overseas: the First World War and the Climax of French Imperial Expansion*. London, 1981.

Beloff, M., Renouvin, P., Schnabel, F., and Valsecchi, F. (eds), *L'Europe du XIXe et du XXe siècle (1870–1914)*. 2 vols, Milan, 1959–62.

Cady, J. F., *The Roots of French Imperialism in Eastern Asia*. New York, 1954.

New Cambridge Modern History. Vols X–XII, Cambridge, 1960–2.

Faivre, J.-P., *L'Expansion française dans le Pacifique, 1800–1842*. Paris, 1953.

Fieldhouse, D. K., *Economics and Empire, 1830–1914*. London, 1973.

Gann, L. H. and Duignan, P. (eds), *Colonialism in Africa, 1870–1960*. Vol I, *The History and Politics of Colonialism, 1870–1914*. Cambridge, 1969.

Gifford, P. and Louis, W. R. (eds), *Britain and Germany in Africa*. New Haven, 1967.

—— *France and Britain in Africa*. New Haven, 1971.

Gilliard, D., *The Struggle for Asia, 1828–1914*. London, 1977.

Hargreaves, J. D., *Prelude to the Partition of West Africa*. London, 1963.

Hobson, J. A., *Imperialism: a Study*. London, 1902.

Kanya-Forstner, A. S., *The Conquest of the Western Sudan: a Study in French Military Imperialism*. Cambridge, 1969.

Koebner, R. and Schmidt, H. • D., *Imperialism, 1840–1960*. Cambridge, 1964.

Koskinen, A. A., *Missionary Influence as a Political Factor in the Pacific Islands*. Helsinki, 1953.

Langer, W. L., *European Alliances and Alignments, 1871–1890*. 2nd edn, New York, 1950.

—— *The Diplomacy of Imperialism, 1890–1902*. 2nd edn, New York, 1951.

Le May, G. H., *British Supremacy in South Africa, 1899–1907*. London, 1965.

Lenin, V. I., *Imperialism, the Highest Stage of Capitalism*. 1916; Moscow, 1947.

Lowe, C. J., *The Reluctant Imperialists. British Foreign Policy, 1878–1902*. 2 vols, London, 1967.

Marais, J. S., *The Fall of Kruger's Republic*. Oxford, 1961.

Miège, J.-L., *Expansion européenne et Décolonisation de 1870 à nos Jours*. Paris, 1973.

Moon, P. T., *Imperialism and World Politics*. New York, 1927.

Morrell, W. P., *Britain in the Pacific Islands*. Oxford, 1960.

Oliver, R. and Mathew, G. (eds), *History of East Africa*. Vol. I, Oxford, 1963.

Pierce, R. A., *Russian Central Asia, 1867–1917*. Berkeley, 1960.

Platt, D. C. M., *Finance, Trade and Politics in British Foreign Policy, 1815–1914*. Oxford, 1968.

Porter, A. N., *The Origins of the South African War, 1895–99*. Manchester, 1980.

Robinson, R., Gallagher, J., with Denny, A., *Africa and the Victorians*. 1961; 2nd rev. edn, 1982.

Schreuder, D. M., *The Scramble for Southern Africa, 1877–95*. Cambridge, 1980.

Thornton, A. P., *The Imperial Idea and its Enemies*. London, 1959.

Townsend, M. E., *Origins of Modern German Colonialism, 1871–1885*. New York, 1921.

Woolf, L. S., *Empire and Commerce in Africa*. London, 1920.

Chapter 11

BRITISH IMPERIAL GOVERNMENT

Cell, J. W., *British Colonial Administration in the Mid-Nineteenth Century: the Policy-Making Process*. New Haven, 1970.

Garner, J., *The Commonwealth Office, 1925–68*. London, 1978.

Howell, P. A., *The Judicial Committee of the Privy Council, 1833–76*. Cambridge, 1980.

Jeffries, Sir C. J., *The Colonial Office*. London, 1956.

Jenkyns, H., *British Rule and Jurisdiction Beyond the Seas*. Oxford, 1902.

Murray, D. J., *The West Indies and the Development of Colonial Government, 1801–1834*. Oxford, 1965.

Seton, Sir M. C. C., *The India Office*. London, 1926.

Swinfen, D. B., *Imperial Control of Colonial Legislation, 1813–65*. Oxford, 1970.

Wight, M., *The Development of the Legislative Council 1606–1945*. London, 1946.

Young, D. M., *The Colonial Office in the Early Nineteenth Century*. London, 1961.

THE SETTLEMENT COLONIES AND RESPONSIBLE GOVERNMENT, 1815–1914

Bassett, J., *Sir Harry Atkinson, 1831–1892*. Auckland, 1975.

Brady, A., *Democracy in the Dominions*. Toronto, 1947.

Cambridge History of the British Empire.

Vol. II, *The Growth of the New Empire, 1783–1870*. Cambridge, 1940.

Vol. III, *The Empire–Commonwealth, 1870–1919*. Cambridge, 1959.

Vol. VI, *Canada and Newfoundland*. Cambridge, 1930.

Vol. VII, Part 1, *Australia*; Part 2, *New Zealand*. Cambridge, 1933.

Vol. VIII, *South Africa, Rhodesia and the High Commission Territories*. 2nd edn, Cambridge, 1963.

Canadian Centenary Series.

Careless, J. M. S., *The Union of the Canadas, 1841–1857*. Toronto, 1967.

Morton, W. L., *The Critical Years: the Union of British North America 1857–1873*. Toronto, 1963.

Waite, P. B., *Canada, 1874–1896*. Toronto, 1971.

Craig Brown, R. and Cook, R., *Canada, 1896–1921*. Toronto, 1974.

Clarke, C. M. H., *A History of Australia*. Vols I–IV, Melbourne, 1962–78.

Crawford, R. M., *Australia*. London, 1952.

Davenport, T. R. H., *South Africa: a Modern History*. 2nd edn, London, 1978.

Eddy, J. J., *Britain and the Australian Colonies, 1818–31*. Oxford, 1969.

Fitzpatrick, B., *The British Empire in Australia: an Economic History, 1834–1939*. Melbourne, 1941.

Gollan, R. A., *Radical and Working Class Politics: a Study of Eastern Australia, 1850–1910*. Melbourne, 1960.

Hyam, R. and Martin, G., *Reappraisals in British Imperial History*. London, 1975.

Inglis, K. S., *The Australian Colonists: An Exploration of Social History, 1788–1870*. Melbourne, 1974.

Keith, A. B., *Responsible Government in the Dominions*. 3 vols, Oxford, 1912; 2nd edn, 2 vols, Oxford, 1928.

Kiewiet, C. W. de, *British Colonial Policy and the South African Republics, 1848–72*. London, 1929.

—— *The Imperial Factor in South Africa*. Cambridge, 1937.

—— *A History of South Africa, Social and Economic*. Oxford, 1941.

Loveday, P. and Martin, A. W., *Parliament, Factions and Parties: the First Thirty Years of Responsible Government in New South Wales, 1856–1889*. Melbourne, 1966.

Mansergh, N., *The Commonwealth Experience*. London, 1969.

McLintock, A. H., *Crown Colony Government in New Zealand*. Wellington, 1958.

Melbourne, A. C. V., *Early Constitutional Development in Australia: New South Wales, 1788–1856*. 2nd edn, Brisbane, 1963.

Morrell, W. P., *British Colonial Policy in the Age of Peel and Russell*. Oxford, 1930.

—— *British Colonial Policy in the Mid-Victorian Age*. Oxford, 1969.

Oliver, W. H., *The Story of New Zealand*. London, 1960.

—— and Williams, B. R. (eds), *The Oxford History of New Zealand*. Oxford, 1981.

Rutherford, J., *Sir George Grey*. London, 1961.

Serle, G., *The Golden Age: a History of the Colony of Victoria, 1851–61*. Melbourne, 1963.

—— *The Rush to be Rich: a History of the Colony of Victoria, 1883–89*. Melbourne, 1971.

Shaw, A. G. L., *Convicts and the Colonies*. London, 1966.

Sinclair, K., *A History of New Zealand*. Harmondsworth, 1959.

—— *The Origins of the Maori Wars*. 2nd edn, Wellington, 1961.

Thompson, L. M., *The Unification of South Africa, 1902–10*. Oxford, 1960.

Ward, J. M., *Colonial Self-Government: the British Experience, 1759–1856*. Cambridge, 1976.

Wilson, M. and Thompson, L. (eds), *The Oxford History of South Africa*. Vol. II, Oxford, 1971.

IMPERIAL FEDERATION AND THE COMMONWEALTH

Bennett, G. (ed), *The Concept of Empire*. 2nd edn, London, 1962.

Bodelsen, C. A., *Studies in Mid-Victorian Imperialism*. 2nd edn, London, 1960.

Dawson, R. M., *The Development of Dominion Status, 1900–1936*. Oxford, 1937.

Drummond, I. M., *British Economic Policy and the Empire, 1919–39*. London, 1972.

Gordon, D. C., *The Dominion Partnership in Imperial Defence, 1870–1914*. Baltimore, 1965.

Hancock, Sir W. K., *Survey of British Commonwealth Affairs*. 2 vols (in 3 parts) London, 1937–42.

Holland, R. F., *Britain and the Commonwealth Alliance, 1918–39*. London, 1980.

Mansergh, N., *Survey of British Commonwealth Affairs*. 2 vols, London, 1952, 1958.

Marshall, G., *Parliamentary Sovereignty and the Commonwealth*. Oxford, 1957.

McIntyre, W. D., *The Commonwealth of Nations: Origins and Impact, 1869–1971*. Minneapolis, 1977.

Miller, J. D. B., *The Commonwealth in the World*. London, 1958.

—— *Survey of Commonwealth Affairs: Problems of Expansion and Attrition, 1953–69*. London, 1974.

Tyler, J. E., *The Struggle for Imperial Unity, 1868–95*. London, 1938.

Wheare, K. C., *The Statute of Westminster and Dominion Status*. 5th edn, Oxford, 1953.

—— *The Constitutional Structure of the Commonwealth*. Oxford, 1960.

Wigley, P. G., *Canada and the Transition to Commonwealth: British–Canadian Relations, 1917–26*. Cambridge, 1977.

Chapter 12

INDIA, 1815–1947

Anstey, V., *The Economic Development of India*. 4th edn, London, 1952.

Bagchi, A. K., *Private Investment in India, 1900–1939*. Cambridge, 1972.

Blunt, E., *The Indian Civil Service*. London, 1937.

Brown, J., *Gandhi's Rise to Power in Indian Politics, 1915–22*. Cambridge, 1972.

Brown, J., *Gandhi and Civil Disobedience*. Cambridge, 1977.

Cambridge History of India. Vol. VI, *The Indian Empire, 1858–1918*. Cambridge, 1932.

Chandra, B., *The Rise and Growth of Economic Nationalism in India*. New Delhi, 1966.

Dutt, R. C., The *Economic History of India in the Victorian Age*. London, 1904.

Gallagher, J. A., Johnson, G. and Seal, A. (eds), *Locality, Province and Nation: Essays in Indian Politics, 1870–1940*. Cambridge, 1973.

Gopal, S., *The Viceroyalty of Lord Ripon, 1880–1884*. London, 1953.

—— *British Policy in India, 1858–1905*. Cambridge, 1965.

—— *Jawaharlal Nehru: a Biography*. Vol. I, 1889–1947. London, 1975.

Hardy, P., *The Muslims of British India*. Cambridge, 1972.

Low, D. A. (ed.), *Congress and the Raj*. London, 1978.

Masselos, J., *Nationalism in the Indian Sub-continent: an Introductory History*. Melbourne, 1972.

Misra, B. B., *The Indian Middle Classes*. London, 1961.

Moore, R. J., *The Crisis of Indian Unity, 1917–40*. Oxford, 1974.

Panikkar, K. M., *The Foundations of New India*. London, 1963.

Philips, C. H., *The Evolution of India and Pakistan, 1858–1947: Select Documents*. London, 1962.

Ray, R. K., *Industrialization in India: Growth and Conflict in the Private Sector, 1914–47*. New Delhi, 1979.

Sayeed, K. B., *Pakistan: the Formative Phase*. London, 1960; 2nd edn, 1968.

Seal, A., *The Emergence of Indian Nationalism*. Cambridge, 1968.

Stokes, E., *The English Utilitarians and India*. Oxford, 1959.

Tomlinson, B. R., *The Political Economy of the Raj, 1914–47*. Cambridge, 1979.

Wolpert, S. A., *Tilak and Gokhale: Revolution and Reform in the Making of Modern India*. Berkeley, 1962.

THE BRITISH DEPENDENT EMPIRE AFTER 1815

African Territories

Ajayi, J. F. and Crowder, M., *History of West Africa*. Vol. II, London, 1974.

Austen, R. A., *North-west Tanzania under German and British Rule, 1889–1939*. New Haven, 1968.

Bennett, G., *Kenya: a Political History*. London, 1963.

Cambridge History of Africa. Vol. V, Flint, J. E. (ed.), *c. 1790–c. 1870*. Cambridge, 1976.

Chidzero, B. T., *Tanganyika and International Trusteeship*. London, 1961.

Crowder, M., *West Africa under Colonial Rule*. London, 1968.

Fyfe, C., *A History of Sierra Leone*. London, 1962.

Gann, L. H., *The Birth of a Plural Society*. Manchester, 1958.

—— *A History of Northern Rhodesia*. London, 1964.

—— and Duignan, P., *Colonialism in Africa*.

Vol. II, *The History and Politics of Colonialism, 1914–60*. Cambridge, 1970.

Vol. IV, *The Economics of Colonialism*. Cambridge, 1975.

Vol. V, *A Bibliographical Guide to Colonialism in Sub-Saharan Africa*. Cambridge, 1973.

Genoud, R., *Nationalism and Economic Development in Ghana*. London, 1969.

Gray, J. M., *A History of The Gambia*. Cambridge, 1940.

Hailey, Lord, *An African Survey*. 2nd rev. edn, London, 1957.

Hall, H. D., *Mandates, Dependencies and Trusteeship*. London, 1948.

Hall, R., *Zambia, 1890–1964: the Colonial Period*. London, 1977.

Hanna, A. J., *The Story of the Rhodesias and Nyasaland*. London, 1960.

Hetherington, P., *British Paternalism and Africa, 1920–40*. London, 1978.

Huxley, E., *White Man's Country*. 2 vols, London, 1935.

Iliffe, J., *A Modern History of Tanganyika*. Cambridge, 1979.

Ingham, K., *The Making of Modern Uganda*. London, 1958.

—— *A History of East Africa*. London, 1962.

Leys, C. T., *European Politics in Southern Rhodesia*. Oxford, 1959.

Low, D. A. and Pratt, R. C., *Buganda and British Overrule, 1900–55*. London, 1960.

Low, D. A., *Buganda: a Modern History*. London, 1971.

Mair, L. P., *Native Policies in Africa*. London, 1936.

Mason, P., *The Birth of a Dilemma: the Conquest and Settlement of Rhodesia*. London, 1958.

Nicolson, I. F., *The Administration of Nigeria, 1900–60: Men, Methods and Myths*. Oxford, 1969.

Oliver, R. A., *The Missionary Factor in East Africa*. London, 1952.

—— and Fage, J. D., *A Short History of Africa*. London, 1962.

—— *et al.* (eds), *History of East Africa*. 3 vols, Oxford, 1963–76.

Perham, Dame Margery, *Native Administration in Nigeria*. Oxford, 1937.

—— *Lugard*. 2 vols, London, 1956, 1960.

Roberts, A., *A History of Zambia*. London, 1977.

Smith, M. G., *Government in Zazzau, 1800–1950*. London, 1960.

Zwannenberg, R. M. A., *An Economic History of Kenya and Uganda, 1800–1970*. London, 1975.

The British West Indies

Burns, A. C., *History of the British West Indies*. London, 1954.

Curtin, P. D., *Two Jamaicas: the Role of Ideas in a Tropical Colony*. Cambridge, Mass., 1955.

Knight, F. W., *The Caribbean: the Genesis of a Fragmented Nationalism*. New York, 1978.

Levy, C., *Emancipation, Sugar and Federalism: Barbados and the West Indies, 1833–76*. Gainesville, Florida, 1980.

Lewis, G. F., *The Growth of the Modern West Indies*. London, 1968.

Olivier, Lord, *Jamaica: the Blessed Island*. London, 1936.

Parry, J. H. and Sherlock, P. M., *A Short History of the West Indies*. London, 1956.

Will, H. A., *Constitutional Change in the British West Indies, 1880–1903*. Oxford, 1970.

Williams, E., *Capitalism and Slavery*. Chapel Hill, 1944.

Pacific Territories

Belshaw, C. S., *Island Administration in the South West Pacific*. London, 1950.

Brookes, J. I., *International Rivalry in the Pacific Islands, 1800–75*. Berkeley, 1941.

Kennedy, P. M., *The Samoan Tangle: a Study in Anglo-German-American Relations*. Dublin, 1974.

Legge, J. D., *Australian Colonial Policy*. Sydney, 1956.

—— *Britain in Fiji*, 1858–80. London, 1958.

Morrell, W. P., *Britain in the Pacific Islands*. Oxford, 1960.

Ross, A., *New Zealand Aspirations in the Pacific*. Oxford, 1964.

Scarr, D., *Fragments of Empire: a History of the Western Pacific High Commission, 1877–1914*. Canberra, 1967.

Thompson, R. C., *Australian Imperialism in the Pacific*. Melbourne, 1980.

South-East Asia and Ceylon

Bailey, S. D., *Ceylon*. London, 1952.

Cady, J. F., *A History of Modern Burma*. Ithaca, 1958.

Cowan, C. D., *Nineteenth Century Malaya*. London, 1967.

Emerson, R., *Malaysia: a Study in Direct and Indirect Rule*. New York, 1937.

Hall, D. G. E., *Burma*. London, 1950.

Heussler, R., *British Rule in Malaya: the Malayan Civil Service and its Predecessors, 1867–1942*. Oxford, 1981.

Ingrams, W. H., *Hong Kong*. London, 1952.

Mendis, G. C., *Ceylon under the British*. Colombo, 1944; 3rd edn, 1952.

Mills, L. A., *British Rule in Eastern Asia*. London, 1942.

Sadka, E., *The Protected Malay States, 1874–95*. Kuala Lumpur, 1968.

Sidhu, J. G., *Administration in the Federated Malay States, 1896–1920*. Hong Kong, 1981.

Tregonning, K. G., *Under Chartered Company Rule: North Borneo, 1881–1946*. Singapore, 1958.

Chapter 13

THE FRENCH EMPIRE SINCE 1830

Ageron, C. R., *Les Algériens musulmans et la France, 1871–1919*. 2 vols, Paris, 1968.

—— *France coloniale ou parti coloniale?* Paris, 1978.

Andrew, C. M. and Kanya-Forstner, A. S., *France Overseas: the First World War and the Climax of French Imperial Expansion*. London, 1981.

Amin, S., *Le développement du Capitalisme en Côte d'Ivoire*. Paris, 1967.

—— *L'Afrique de l'Ouest bloquée: l'Economie politique de la Colonisation, 1880–1970*. Paris, 1971.

—— and Coquery-Vidrovitch, C., *Histoire économique du Congo, 1880–1968*. Paris, 1969.

Bouvier, J. and Girault, R., *L'imperialisme français d'avant 1914*. Paris, 1976.

Brunschwig, H., *French Colonialism, 1871–1914: Myths and Realities*. London, 1966.

Cohen, W. B., *Rulers of Empire: the French Colonial Service in Africa*. Stanford, 1971.

Crowder, M., *Senegal: a Study of French Assimilation Policy.* London, 1967.

Deschamps, H., *Histoire de Madagascar.* Paris, 1960.

Duiker, W. J., *The Rise of Nationalism in Vietnam, 1900–41.* Ithaca, 1976.

Ganiage, J., *L'expansion coloniale de la France sous la Troisième République.* Paris, 1968.

Girardet, R., *L'idée coloniale en France de 1871–1942.* Paris, 1972.

Gonidec, P.-F., *Droit d'Outre-Mer.* 2 vols, Paris, 1959.

Hargreaves, J. D. (ed.), *France and West Africa.* London, 1969.

Julien, Ch.-A., *Les Technicians de la Colonisation.* Paris, 1945.

Le Vine, V. T., *The Cameroons from Mandate to Independence.* Berkeley, 1964.

Masson, A., *Histoire de l'Indochine.* Paris, 1950.

Michel, M., *Le concours de l'AOF à la France pendant la Première Guerre Mondiale.* Paris, forthcoming.

Peterec, R. J., *Dakar and West African Economic Development.* New York, 1967.

Sarraut, A., *La Mise en Valeur des Colonies françaises.* Paris, 1923.

Southworth, C., *The French Colonial Venture.* London, 1931.

Suret-Canale, J., *French Colonialism in Tropical Africa.* New York, 1971.

Tourneau, R. Le, *Evolution de l'Afrique du Nord musulmane, 1920–61.* Paris, 1961.

Chapter 14

THE DUTCH EMPIRE AFTER 1815

Arx, A. van, *L'évolution politique en Indonésie de 1900 à 1942.* Paris, 1949.

Boeke, J. H., *The Evolution of the Netherlands Indian Economy.* New York, 1946.

Dahm, B., *History of Indonesia in the Twentieth Century.* London, 1971.

Furnivall, J. S., *Netherlands India.* 2nd edn, Cambridge, 1944.

—— *Colonial Policy and Practice.* Cambridge, 1948.

Kat Angelino, A. D. A. de, *Colonial Policy.* 2 vols, The Hague, 1931.

Palmier, L. H., *Indonesia and the Dutch.* London, 1962.

Ricklefs, M., *A History of Modern Indonesia.* London, 1980.

RUSSIAN COLONIES

Dallin, D. J., *The Rise of Russia in Asia*. London, 1971.

Kolarz W., *Russia and her Colonies*. London, 1952.

Pierce, R. A., *Russian Central Asia, 1867–1917*. Berkeley, 1960.

Stahl, K. M., *British and Soviet Colonial Systems*. London, 1951.

THE UNITED STATES EMPIRE

Blanshard, P., *Democracy and Empire in the Caribbean*. New York, 1947.

Campbell, A. E. (ed.), *Expansion and Imperialism*. New York, 1970.

Coulter, J. W., *The Pacific Dependencies of the United States*. New York, 1957.

Day, A. G. and Kuykendall, R. S., *Hawaii: a History from Polynesian Kingdom to American Commonwealth*. New York, 1948.

Friend, T., *Between Two Empires: the Ordeal of the Philippines, 1929–46*. London, 1965.

LaFeber, W. *The New Empire: an Interpretation of American Expansion, 1860–98*. Ithaca, 1963.

May, E. R., *Imperial Democracy: the Emergence of America as a Great Power*. New York, 1961.

—— *American Imperialism*. New York, 1968.

May, G. A., *Social Engineering in the Philippines: American Colonial Policy, 1900–13*. Westport, 1980.

Perkins, D., *The United States and the Caribbean*. London, 1947.

Pratt, J. W., *Expansionists of 1898*. Baltimore, 1936.

—— *America's Colonial Experiment*. New York, 1950.

Stevens, S. K., *American Expansion in Hawaii, 1842–98*. Harrisburg, 1945.

Tansill, C. C., *The Purchase of the Danish West Indies*. Baltimore, 1932.

Thompson, L. M., *Guam and its People*. 3rd rev. edn, Princeton, 1947.

Tugwell, R. G., *The Stricken Land: the Story of Puerto Rico*. Garden City, 1947.

Wiens, J. J., *Pacific Island Bastions of the United States*. Princeton, 1962.

Winks, R. W., 'Imperialism' in C. Vann Woodward (ed.), *The Comparative Approach to American History*. New York, 1968.

Chapter 15

THE PORTUGUESE EMPIRE AFTER 1815

Abshire, D. M. and Samuels, M. A., *Portuguese Africa: a Handbook*. London, 1969.

Axelson, E. V., *Portugal and the Scramble for Africa, 1875–1891*. Johannesburg, 1967.

Bender, G. J., *Angola under the Portuguese: the Myth and the Reality*. London, 1978.

Chilcote, R. H., *Emerging Nationalism in Portuguese Africa: Documents*. Stanford, 1972.

Duffy, J. E., *Portuguese Africa*. 2nd edn, Cambridge, Mass., 1968.

Figueiredo, A. de, *Portugal and its Empire: the Truth*. London, 1961.

Hammond, R. J., *Portugal and Africa, 1815–1910: a Study in Uneconomic Imperialism*. Stanford, 1966.

Marcum, J., *The Angolan Revolution*. Vol. I, *Anatomy of a Revolution, 1950–62*. Cambridge, Mass., 1969.

Warhurst, P. R., *Anglo-Portuguese Relations in Southern Central Africa, 1890–1900*. London, 1962.

Wheeler, D. I., *Angola*. New York, 1971.

THE BELGIAN EMPIRE

Anstey, R., *King Leopold's Legacy: the Congo under Belgian Rule, 1908–1960*. London, 1966.

Ascherson, N., *The King Incorporated: Leopold II and the Age of Trusts*. London, 1963.

Brausch, G., *Belgian Administration in the Congo*. London, 1961.

Cornevin, R., *Histoire du Congo, Léopoldville-Kinshasa*. 2nd edn, Paris, 1966.

Emerson, B., *Leopold II of the Belgians: King of Colonialism*. London, 1979.

Fetter, B., *The Creation of Elisabethville, 1910–40*. Stanford, 1976.

Franck, L., *Le Congo Belge*. 2 vols, Brussels, 1928.

Gann, L. H. and Duignan, P., *The Rulers of Belgian Africa, 1884–1914*. Princeton, 1979.

Hostelet, G., *L'Oeuvre civilisatrice de la Belgique au Congo de 1885–1945*. Brussels, 1954.

Joye, P. and Lewin, R., *Les Trusts au Congo*. Brussels, 1961.

Katzenellenbogen, S. E., *Railways and the Copper Mines of Katanga*. Oxford, 1973.

Lacroix, J.-L., *Industrialisation au Congo*. Paris, 1966.

Morel, E. D., *History of the Congo Reform Movement*. Completed by Louis, W. R. and Stengers, J. Oxford, 1968.

Slade, R. M., *English-speaking Missions in the Congo Independent State, 1878–1908*. Brussels, 1959.

—— *King Leopold's Congo*. London, 1962.

Stengers, J., *Combien le Congo a-t-il coûté à la Belgique?* Brussels, 1957.

—— *Belgique et Congo: l'Elaboration de la Charte coloniale*. Brussels, 1963.

Willequet, J., *Le Congo belge et la Weltpolitik, 1894–1914*. Brussels, 1962.

THE GERMAN EMPIRE

Bley, H., *South-West Africa under German Rule, 1894–1914*. Eng. tr. Evanston, 1971.

Brunschwig, H., *L'expansion allemande outre-mer du XVe siècle à nos jours*. Paris, 1957.

Büttner, K., *Die Anfange der deutschen Kolonialpolitik in Ostafrika*. Berlin, 1959.

Esterhuyse, J. H., *South West Africa, 1880–94*. Cape Town, 1968.

Gann, L. H. and Duignan, P., *The Rulers of German Africa, 1884–1914*. Stanford, 1979.

Gifford, P. and Louis, W. R., *Britain and Germany in Africa*. New Haven, 1967.

Hallgarten, G. W. F., *Imperialismus vor 1914*. 2 vols, rev. edn, Munich, 1963.

Hausen, K., *Deutsche Kolonialherrschaft in Afrika*. Zurich, 1970.

Henderson, W. O., *Studies in German Colonial History*. London, 1962.

Iliffe, J., *Tanganyika under German Rule, 1905–1912*. Cambridge, 1969.

Louis, W. R., *Ruanda-Urundi, 1884–1919*. Oxford, 1963.

Moses, J. A. and Kennedy, P. M. (eds), *Germany in the Pacific and Far East, 1870–1914*. St. Lucia, 1977.

Müller, F. F., *Deutschland-Zanzibar-Ostafrika, 1884–90*. Berlin, 1959.

Rudin, H. R., *Germans in the Cameroons, 1884–1914*. London, 1938.

Smith, W. D., *The German Colonial Empire*. Chapel Hill, 1978.

Stern, F., *Gold and Iron: Bismarck, Bleichröder and the Building of the German Empire*. London, 1980.

Stoecker, H. (ed.), *Kamerun unter deutscher Kolonialherrshaft*. 2 vols, Berlin, 1960.

Taylor, A. J. P., *Germany's First Bid for Colonies, 1884–85*. London, 1938.

Tetzlaff, R., *Koloniale Entwicklung und Ausbeutung: Wirschafts-und Sozialgeschichte Deutsch-Ostafrikas, 1885–1914*. Berlin, 1970.

Wehler, H.-U., *Bismarck und der Imperialismus*. Cologne, 1969.

Chapter 16

MYTHS AND REALITIES OF THE MODERN COLONIAL EMPIRES: THE ECONOMICS OF EMPIRE

Bauer, P. T., *West African Trade*. Cambridge, 1954.

Cain, P. J., *Economic Foundations of British Overseas Expansion, 1815–1914*. London, 1980.

Cairncross, A. K., *Home and Foreign Investment, 1870–1913*. Cambridge, 1953.

Clark, G., *The Balance Sheets of Imperialism*. New York, 1936.

Dewey, C. and Hopkins, A. G. (eds), *The Imperial Impact: Studies in the Economic History of Africa and India*. London, 1978.

Feis, H., *Europe the World's Banker, 1870–1914*. New York, 1961.

Fieldhouse, D. K., *Colonialism*. London, 1981.

Frankel, S. H., *Capital Investment in Africa*. London, 1938.

Gann, L. H. and Duignan, P., *Colonialism in Africa*. Vol. IV, *The Economics of Colonialism*. Cambridge, 1975.

Hall, A. R. (ed.), *The Export of Capital from Britain, 1870–1914*. London, 1969.

Hancock, Sir W. K., *Survey of British Commonwealth Affairs*. Vol. II, *Problems of Economic Policy, 1918–39*. 2 parts, London, 1940–2.

Hopkins, A. G., *An Economic History of West Africa*. London, 1973.

Imlah, A. H., *Economic Elements in the Pax Britannica*. Cambridge, Mass., 1958.

Kilby, P., *Industrialization in an Open Economy: Nigeria, 1945–66*. Cambridge, 1969.

Knowles, L. C. A., *The Economic Development of the British Overseas Empire*. 3 vols, London, 1924–36.

Kubicek, R. V., *Economic Imperialism in Theory and Practice: the Case of South African Gold Mining Finance, 1886–1914*. Durham, N.C., 1979.

Latham, A. J. H., *The International Economy and the Underdeveloped World, 1865–1914*. London, 1978.

McPhee, A. *The Economic Revolution in British West Africa*. London, 1926.

Meier, G. M., *International Trade and Development*. New York, 1963.

Meyer, F. V., *Britain's Colonies in World Trade*. London, 1948.

Morgan, D. J., *The Official History of Colonial Development*. 5 vols, London, 1980.

Munro, J. F., *Africa and the International Economy, 1800–1960*. London, 1976.

Owen, R. and Sutcliffe, R. (eds), *Studies in the Theory of Imperialism*. London, 1972.

Platt, D. C. M. (ed.), *Business Imperialism, 1840–1930*. Oxford, 1977.

Rippy, J. F., *British Investments in Latin America, 1822–1949*. Minneapolis, 1959.

Saul, S. B., *Studies in British Overseas Trade, 1870–1914*. Liverpool, 1960.

Schlote, W., *British Overseas Trade from 1700 to the 1930s*. Oxford, 1952.

Stahl, K. M., *The Metropolitan Organization of British Colonial Trade*. London, 1951.

Chapter 17

DECOLONIZATION AND AFTER, 1945–81

General Studies

Albertini, R. von, *Decolonization. The Administration and Future of the Colonies, 1916–60*. New York, 1971.

Betts, R. F. (ed.), *The Ideology of Blackness*. Lexington, 1971.

Emerson, R., *From Empire to Nationhood*. Cambridge, Mass., 1960.

Grimal, H., *Decolonization: the British, French, Dutch and Belgian Empires, 1919–63*. 1965: English edn, London, 1978.

Kirkman, W. P., *Unscrambling an Empire: a Critique of British Colonial Policy, 1956–66*. London, 1966.

Lee, J. M., *Colonial Development and Good Government, 1939–64*. Oxford, 1967.

Little, I., Scitovsky, T. and Scott, M., *Industry and Trade in Some Developing Countries: a Comparative Study*. London, 1970.

Marshall, D.B., *The French Colonial Myth and Constitution Making in the Fourth French Republic*. New Haven, 1973.

May, B., *The Third World Calamity*. London, 1981.

Morgan, D. J., *The Official History of Colonial Development*. Vol. V, *Guidance Towards Self-Government in British Colonies, 1941–1971*. London, 1980.

Morris-Jones, W. H. (ed.), *Decolonization and After: the British and French Experience*. London, 1978.

Nwabueze, B. O., *Constitutionalism in the Emergent States*. London, 1973.

Sorum, P. C., *Intellectuals and Decolonization in France*. Chapel Hill, 1977.

Yacomo, X., *Les Etapes de la décolonisation française*. Paris, 1971.

Africa

Austin, D., *Politics in Ghana, 1946–60*. London, 1964.

—— *Politics in Africa*. Manchester, 1978.

—— and Luckham, R., *Politicians and Soldiers in Ghana, 1966–72*. London, 1978.

Davidson, B., *In the Eye of the Storm: Angola's People*. London, 1972.

Dunn, J., *West African States: Failure and Promise*. Cambridge, 1979.

First, R., *Power in Africa*. New York, 1970.

Gertzel, C., *The Politics of Independent Kenya*. London, 1970.

Gutteridge, W. F., *Military Régimes in Africa*. London, 1975.

Hargreaves, J. D., *The End of Colonial Rule in West Africa: Essays in Contemporary History*. London, 1979.

Hodgkin, T. L., *Nationalism in Colonial Africa*. London, 1956.

—— *African Political Parties*. London, 1961.

Horne, A., *A Savage War of Peace: Algeria, 1954–62*. London, 1977.

Hoskyns, C., *The Congo since Independence*. London, 1967.

Hyden, G., *Beyond Ujama in Tanzania: Underdevelopment and an Uncaptured Peasantry*. London, 1980.

Iliffe, J., *A Modern History of Tanganyika*. Cambridge, 1979.

King, J. R., *Stabilization Policy in an African Setting: Kenya, 1963–73*. London, 1978.

Kirk-Greene, A. H., *Crisis and Conflict in Nigeria*. London, 1971.

—— and Rimmer, D., *Nigeria since 1970: a Political and Economic Outline*. London, 1981.

Leys, C., *Underdevelopment in Kenya*. London, 1975.

Maitland-Jones, J. F., *Politics in ex-British Africa*. London, 1973.

Panter-Brick, K. (ed.), *Soldiers and Oil: the Political Transformation of Nigeria*. London, 1978.

Pratt, C., *The Critical Phase in Tanzania, 1945–68*. Nairobi, 1980.

Rotberg, R. I., and Mazrui, A. A., *Protest and Power in Black Africa*. New York, 1970.

Smith, T., *The French Stake in Algeria, 1945–62*. Ithaca, 1978.

Tordoff, W. (ed.), *Politics in Zambia*. Manchester, 1974.

Williams, D. T., *Malawi: the Politics of Despair*. Ithaca, 1978.

Asia and the Pacific

Buchanan, I., *Singapore in South-east Asia: an Economic and Political Appraisal*. London, 1972.

Choudhury, G. W., *Constitutional Development in Pakistan*. London, 1969.

Dommen, A. J., *Conflict in Laos: the Politics of Neutrality*. London, 1971.

Emmerson, D. K., *Indonesia's Elite*. Ithaca, 1976.

Farmer, B. H., *Ceylon: a Divided Nation*. London, 1967.

Feith, H., *The Decline of Constitutional Democracy in Indonesia*. Ithaca, 1968.

Feldman, H., *The End and the Beginning: Pakistan, 1969–71*. New Delhi, 1975.

Fryer, D. W., *Emerging South-east Asia: a Study in Growth and Stagnation*. London, 1970.

Jacobs, N., *Modernization without Development: Thailand as an Asian Case Study*. New York, 1971.

Jha, P. S., *India: a Political Economy of Stagnation*. Bombay, 1980.

Jupp, J., *Sri Lanka: Third World Democracy*. London, 1978.

Legge, J. D., *Sukarno*. London, 1972.

Lim, D., *Economic Growth and Development in West Malaysia, 1947–70*. Kuala Lumpur, 1973.

Maung, M., *Burma and Pakistan: a Comparative Study in Development*. New York, 1971.

McAlister, J. *Vietnam: the Origins of Revolution*. New York, 1969.

Menon, V. P., *The Transfer of Power in India*. Princeton, 1957.

Morris-Jones, W. H., *The Government and Politics of India*. London, 1971.

Osborne, M. E., *Politics and Power in Cambodia: the Sihanouk Years*. Melbourne, 1973.

Palmer, I., *The Indonesian Economy since 1966*. London, 1978.

Pandey, B. N., *South and South-east Asia, 1945–79: Problems and Policies*. London, 1980.

THE COLONIAL EMPIRES

Pluvier, J., *South-east Asia from Colonialism to Independence*. Kuala Lumpur, 1974.

Shalom, S. R., *The United States and the Philippines: a Study of Neocolonialism*. 1981.

Sicat, G. P., *Economic Policy and Philippines Development*. Quezon City, 1972.

Skinner, G. W. and Kirsch, T., *Change and Resistance in Thai Society*. Ithaca, 1975.

Weinstein, F. B., *Indonesian Foreign Policy and the Dilemma of Dependence: from Sukarno to Soeharto*. Ithaca, 1976.

Woodside, A. B., *Community and Revolution in Modern Vietnam*. Boston, 1976.

Zasloff, J., *Communism in Indo-China*. Lexington, 1975.

Index